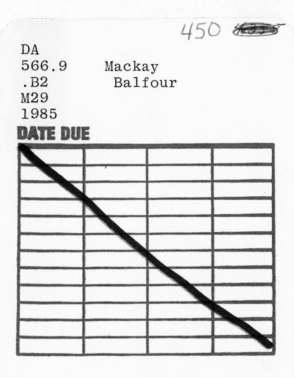

BALFOUR

Balfour and Joseph Chamberlain, *c.* 1902
National Portrait Gallery

BALFOUR

INTELLECTUAL
STATESMAN

RUDDOCK F. MACKAY

Oxford   New York

OXFORD UNIVERSITY PRESS

1985

Oxford University Press, Walton Street, Oxford OX2 6DP

London New York Toronto
Delhi Bombay Calcutta Madras Karachi
Kuala Lumpur Singapore Hong Kong Tokyo
Nairobi Dar es Salaam Cape Town
Melbourne Auckland

and associated companies in
Beirut Berlin Ibadan Mexico City Nicosia

Oxford is a trade mark of Oxford University Press

British Library Cataloguing in Publication Data
Mackay, Ruddock F.
Balfour: intellectual statesman
1. Balfour, Arthur James Balfour, Earl of
2. Prime ministers—Great Britain—Biography
I. Title
941.082'092'4   DA566.9.B2
ISBN 0-19-212245-2

Library of Congress Cataloging in Publication Data
Mackay, Ruddock F.
Balfour, intellectual statesman.
Bibliography: p.
Includes index.
1. Balfour, Arthur James Balfour, 1st Earl of,
1848–1930. 2. Great Britain—Politics and government—
1837–1901. 3. Great Britain—Politics and government—
1901–1936. 4. Great Britain—Foreign relations—1837–
1901. 5 Great Britain—Foreign relations—1901–1936.
6. Prime ministers—Great Britain—Biography.   I. Title.
DA566.9.B2M29 1985   941.082'092'4 [B]   84–16484
ISBN 0-19-212245-2

Set by Getset(BTS)Ltd.
Printed in Great Britain by
Butler & Tanner Ltd.
London and Frome

Preface

BEFORE research for this book began in 1975, there were already three biographies of Balfour in existence and a fourth was published before the actual writing of this book had begun. At the outset, the publisher had suggested that brevity was desirable, and a target of some 350 pages of text might be in order. I agreed whole-heartedly with this suggestion. I wanted to contribute to a surer understanding of Balfour by concentrating on documentary materials which, despite their probable importance, seemed not to have been exhaustively investigated. These materials were certainly of considerable significance, and it seemed prudent at that stage to avoid a lengthy rehearsal of what had already been published on Balfour's life and work—except where new evidence had been found or when there were other reasons for reinterpretation.

As far as Balfour's term as Chief Secretary for Ireland (1887–1891) was concerned, an excellent book had already been written out of the available materials, namely *Coercion and Conciliation in Ireland* by L. P. Curtis, Jr. Then there were areas, such as Balfour's opinions on foreign policy at certain dates, especially before 1902, where the documentary material was thin and did not encourage the allocation of scarce space to mere speculation as to his influence.

It had also to be borne in mind that, especially before 1914, Balfour was deeply sceptical as to the beneficial effects of any legislation whatever and that he was not, by nature, an initiator of reform. Very often his influence on policies for which he was not ministerially responsible tended to be critical and negative. In these cases, his opinions may well have tended to escape specific record. He never kept a diary and was generally devoid of autobiographical interest. (His *Chapters of Autobiography* were occasioned mainly by an ominous reduction in his inherited fortune.)

A further limit on information about his various roles, even when he was a minister, was his lifelong disinclination to hold a pen. This explains the notable scarcity of minutes handwritten by Balfour. As Stephen Roskill has remarked, such minutes are not very easy to read when they do occur; but, with much practice, they can mostly be accurately deciphered.

Nevertheless, the Balfour Papers at the British Library do constitute a great collection of major historical value thanks to the fact that, in the course of official business and other substantial correspondence, Balfour dictated his letters and copies were kept. This material and, to a lesser extent, the papers remaining at Whittingehame, have been persistently—if not quite comprehensively—quarried by various investigators. What remained to be scrutinized was the extensive body of evidence at the Public Record Office relating to defence policy from 1902 onwards to the end of Balfour's career, education policy, especially in 1901–2, and foreign affairs from 1902 onwards. With material gleaned from other sources, these documents yielded a more precise knowledge of the main areas of· Balfour's work as a statesman. It has long seemed to me that an evaluation of Balfour should depend on further such elucidation of the useful work he did for his country and of the spirit in which he did it.

Otherwise, in a biography, it was naturally important to explain once more how Balfour, given his reluctance to lead, ever became Prime Minister and, more generally, to chart his development as an individual.

In the final chapter, an attempt is made to provide a balanced Overview and Estimate.

R. F. M.

Acknowledgements

I WISH to thank the Court of the University of St. Andrews for its support through its Research and Travel Funds and all those who made documentary materials available to me. In the latter respect, I am most grateful to Lord Balfour; also to Lord Rayleigh and the Hon. Guy Strutt, Lord Salisbury (and Mr. R.H. Harcourt Williams), and the staffs of all the relevant libraries and centres of research, including: Birmingham University Library (and Dr. D.S. Benedikz), the Bodleian Library, the British Library, Churchill College Archives Centre, the House of Lords Record Office, the National Library of Scotland, the Public Record Office, the National Maritime Museum, and St. Andrews University Library. Likewise, with regard to copyright permissions, I wish to thank the Keeper of Public Records (Crown copyright); also Birmingham University, the British Library, Lord Esher, Lord Lansdowne, Mr. Robin Malcolm, Lord Salisbury, Lord Selborne, and the Master, Fellows, and Scholars of Churchill College, Cambridge; also Lady Wilson (quotations from Sir Duncan Wilson's life of Gilbert Murray).

Finally, I wish to record the learned advice of Mr. Alan Sykes and the invaluable assistance which I received in a number of ways from Mr. John Bates. I am also very conscious of the guidance and help given me in connection with this, and two previous books, by Mr. Peter Sutcliffe of Oxford University Press; and I likewise remember Miss Irene Kurtz in this regard. Mrs. Nancy Wood gave timely assistance with the typing. My wife—as ever—provided constant and indispensable background support.

R. F. M.

Contents

Abbreviations

A.C.P.	Austen Chamberlain Papers, Birmingham University Library
A.−F.P.	Arnold Forster Papers, B.L.
B.	Balfour
B.E.F.	British Expeditionary Force
B.L.	British Library
B.L.P.	Bonar Law Papers, House of Lords Record Office
Bodl.	Bodleian Library
B.P.	Balfour Papers, British Library
Cab.	Cabinet
C.I.G.S.	Chief of the Imperial General Staff
D.N.B.	*Dictionary of National Biography*
Ed.	Education Dept. Papers, Public Record Office
E.P.	Esher Papers
F.O.	Foreign Office
H.R.P.	*A Diary of the Home Rule Parliament 1892−1895* by Henry Lucy
J.C.P.	Joseph Chamberlain Papers, Birmingham University Library
L.C.C.	London County Council
L.E.A.	Local Education Authority
mins.	minutes
n.d.	no date
N.M.M.	National Maritime Museum
P.	Papers or printed
P.D., 4th, 41/1369	*Parliamentary Debates*, 4th series, volume 41, column 1369
R.F.C.	Royal Flying Corps
R.N.A.S.	Royal Naval Air Service
S.P.	*A Diary of the Salisbury Parliament 1886−1892* by Henry Lucy
U.P.	*A Diary of the Unionist Parliament 1895−1900* by Henry Lucy
WHI	Whittingehame MSS (Balfour P.)

1
Pondering and Playing
1848–1874

IF signs of promise were not entirely absent from Arthur James Balfour's early years, they made little impact on his contemporaries. But the potential for statesmanship was there, and for its ultimate development it was important that his uncle was Lord Robert Cecil, who became the third Marquess of Salisbury in 1868 and Prime Minister in 1885, and that his mother was Lady Blanche, very much a Cecil, not only by birth but also by dint of her lively intellect and marked individual character.

Arthur Balfour was born at Whittingehame in East Lothian on 25 July 1848. He was the eldest son of Lady Blanche, the wife of James Maitland Balfour (1820–1856). The latter had inherited, by way of property, not only Whittingehame but also Strathconan in Ross-shire, together with a considerable fortune. Like his father before him, James Maitland Balfour was an MP, representing a local constituency as a Conservative from 1841 to 1847.

Since her marriage in 1843, Lady Blanche had had two daughters. First came Nora (Eleanor Mildred) for whom Arthur was to feel special affection and who would marry Henry Sidgwick, Arthur's tutor in philosophy at Cambridge. She would become a leader in women's education and the Principal of Newnham College; and, as Mrs Sidgwick, she should receive honorary doctorates from four universities. Then came Evelyn who, in 1871, would marry another friend of Arthur's at Cambridge, John William Strutt. He would in 1873 become the third Baron Rayleigh; and in 1904 he would receive a Nobel prize for physics, a signal achievement for an English aristocrat. After Arthur's birth in 1848 came that of Cecil in 1849. Alice followed in 1850, Frank (Francis Maitland) a year later, Gerald in 1853, and Eustace in 1854. Cecil died in Australia in 1881 as the result of an accident. Alice never married. She would watch over Arthur's households at Whittingehame and in London; and she would outlive him by six years. Frank would lose his life on Mont Blanc in 1882. A brilliant biologist, he died at 31 when already Professor of Animal Morphology at Cambridge. Gerald would become a Fellow of Trinity College, Cambridge, and a

University Lecturer in Greek before embarking on a political career which brought him cabinet rank from 1895 to 1905. In 1887 he married the delightful Lady Elizabeth Lytton, a future suffragist, usually known as Lady Betty, and on Arthur's death in 1930 he became the second Earl of Balfour. Finally there was Eustace who would become an architect and a territorial soldier. In 1879 he married Lady Frances Campbell, a daughter of the Duke of Argyll who seceded from Gladstone in 1881. Frances was something of a stormy petrel at times. Although she, like Lady Betty, would live with her children at Whittingehame for up to six months of most years from the 1880s, she retained a strong vein of her father's original Liberalism; and her independence of mind would extend to her publishing in 1925 a laudatory *Memoir of Lord Balfour of Burleigh*, a free trader pushed out of office by her brother-in-law Arthur in 1903. Like Lady Betty, she became an active campaigner for women's suffrage.[1] Eustace and Lady Frances would have two sons and three daughters—the eldest of these being afterwards known as Mrs Blanche Dugdale and as Arthur Balfour's biographer.[2]

James Maitland Balfour died of tuberculosis in 1856 at the age of 36. Lady Blanche gave way, at first, to violent grief and was prostrate for some weeks. She then re-established an unshakeable control over her emotions and devoted herself to the care and education of her children. A similar emotional pattern would appear in Arthur's life. It was certainly not a case of emotions being absent; but it was the extent to which they were subordinated to reasoning that was remarkable. Lady Blanche paid great attention to maintaining a regime of fresh air and good food for her none too robust brood, and she surely deserves some credit for their subsequent longevity—where accidents did not supervene. All the boys grew to stand at least six feet tall. Although Arthur, during his school days, was classed as unfit to take part in outdoor games, he would play them with passionate enjoyment from his time at Cambridge (1866–1869) till he was a sprightly 79. A chair-bound Asquith four years his junior would have the mixed pleasure of watching Arthur in action on the tennis court at Whittingehame as late as 1927.

In his never-completed memoirs, composed late in life, Arthur recalled how his mother 'encouraged every nascent taste, and a taste for science among others'. She was also 'a woman of profound religious convictions' and it was 'in an atmosphere saturated with these convictions' that her children were brought up. Sectarian differences between Presbyterians and

[1] Lady Frances Balfour, *Ne Obliviscaris*, London, 1930, 2 vols., ii, 148–74.
[2] Her *Arthur James Balfour*, London, 1936, 2 vols., remains an indispensable source.

Anglicans were 'quietly ignored' and Arthur remained a lifelong communicant in both churches. By the later 1860s he had become preoccupied with a matter which was discussed a great deal at home, namely the 'conflict between a religious view of the universe and a naturalistic view'. Lady Blanche, according to Arthur's later recollections,

was never tempted to discourage scientific study; she never treated it as dangerous to the higher life; she never took refuge in bad science when good science appeared to raise awkward problems. On the other hand, she never surrendered her own convictions as to the inestimable value of her central religious beliefs. This point of view, if I rightly represent it, may have lacked theoretic finish; but it appealed to me in 1866, and after more than sixty years' reflection, it appeals to me still. [3]

A surviving fragment of a letter written by Lady Blanche after Disraeli had passed the Second Reform Act of 1867—a radical breach with Conservative tradition which had occasioned her brother Robert's resignation from the Cabinet—gives an impression both of her vitality and of her deeply Conservative colour:

. . . in all that long series of dishonesty and double dealing and truckling to the powers that be, I see nothing approaching the disgracefulness of our present session. Many individuals, each seeking his own interests, did secretly act against their opinions and eat their words—but for a whole party to do it openly, systematically, to lick the feet of King Mob and thank him for his kicks, all for the sake of place without power, remained for the Conservatives of 1867.

Yet having thus hotly condemned the party, she remarks with cool Balfourian detachment: 'As to the move itself it is an experiment which may or may not turn out well.' The 'mechanics' in the trade unions may, she suggests, react to attainment of the franchise by 'elevating their principles'. 'If not', she concludes (foreshadowing Arthur in January 1906), 'we are actually in a revolution without knowing it.' [4]

In 1870 Lady Blanche became seriously ill of a heart complaint. By 1872, she was dead.

Meanwhile, Arthur had come of age in 1869 and had inherited the estates. In 1870 he acquired a house at 4 Carlton Gardens, conveniently close to the Houses of Parliament, as it proved. From his mother he had received encouragement of his natural interest in science and religion. As to attitudes, her strong emphasis on duty had left its mark, as will be seen at various stages of Balfour's political career. It may be added that his relations with his mother had not lacked humour and fun. Their flavour is

---

[3] Balfour, *Chapters of Autobiography*, London, 1930, pp. 16–19.
[4] WHI/147.

caught by Lady Blanche's account of an educational session when Arthur was not yet six: 'Last night proverbs as usual. Arthur the questioner. He put himself astride on my lap and gave his question ''Can you tell me why I love you so much?'' ' [5]

Arthur did not particularly distinguish himself during his time at school. Having derived no great benefit from Latin tutors at home, he was sent in 1859 down to Hoddesdon in Hertfordshire where his schoolmaster, the Revd. C. J. Chittenden, found him singularly lacking in 'vital energy'; but he noted a boy's remark that Arthur was 'always pondering'. Chittenden was flexible in his teaching methods, not forcing the reluctant Balfour to take part in the games but encouraging his natural interests. He found that Arthur was quick to take in 'the purport of a number of connected facts' and to spot 'any apparent inconsistency between them'. His 'interest in anything which he learnt varied in proportion as it gave room for reducing chaos to order'. [6]

These attributes might eventually serve Balfour well in the upper reaches of political life, but they gained him small credit at Eton where he went in 1861. The high proportion of his time consecrated to Latin and Greek proved as unrewarding to him as to his teachers. He impressed his housemaster of 1864–1866 with an essay on English constitutional history; [7] but in later life he could recall only one truly memorable event at Eton—one moment of 'magic'—and that was a conversation with his Uncle Robert. Arthur remembered the visit as taking place when his uncle was Viscount Cranborne, which places the event in 1865–6. The future Lord Salisbury doubtless felt very sorry for Arthur having to endure Eton, the more brutal aspects of which filled him with a lifelong revulsion. But what impressed Arthur about the visit was the way in which his uncle 'spoke as a man speaks to a man, and not as a man speaks to a boy'. Salisbury would later conform to convention by sending his own sons James, William, Robert, Edward and Hugh (all born between 1861–1869) to Eton. On arrival they would be staggered by the immaturity of their coevals, having previously been educated—and addressed like ambassadors—by their remarkable father at Hatfield. [8] Their cousin, Arthur Balfour, resembled them in tending to intellectual clannishness. But he seems to have coasted imperturbably through Eton, despite suffering from short sight. He was

---

[5] WHI/157, extract copied from a letter to Miss Emily G. Faithfull, probably of May 1857.
[6] WHI/195. Chittenden's reminiscences of B. as a schoolboy are substantially reproduced in Dugdale, i, 21–3.
[7] WHI/195, notes by the Revd F. J. Thackeray, Dec. 1901.
[8] Kenneth Rose, *The Later Cecils*, London, 1975, pp. 54–7, etc.

denied the remedy available in the form of spectacles by a social convention which insisted that boys should brace up and forget their myopia! Not till he went to Cambridge in 1866 was he granted relief and a new fulness of life.

A letter of December 1864 to his eldest sister Nora, bent on self-education, is worth quoting, partly for its early date and partly for a hint of the indomitable, sometimes teasing, spirit lying quietly beneath it:

My dear Nora,
I shall attempt to the best of my poor abilities to answer your questions . . . The periods to be read in trials are (i) From the death of Elizabeth (1603) to the death of Charles I. (ii) Roman Hist. to the end of the 1st Punic War. (iii) Greek from the death of Philip of Macedon to the conquest by the Romans . . . As for the books to be read, you must judge for yourself but I rely on a small list for selection:

(i) English Hist. Clarendon's Hist. of Rebell. (2 vols). Hallam's Constitutional Hist. (1 vol). Hume (1 vol). Popular Hist. of England. Macaulay's essay 'John Hampden'; Guizot's Essay on the Revolution. Some of Milton's controversial works; Carlyle's Edition of Cromwell's letters; Lord Nugent's Memorials of John Hampden; also various novels. But seriously I should advise you to read the period in some Short History such as the Student's Hume; and then study Hallam and bits of Clarendon . . . [9]

I leave [the magazine] to anyone that wants it—for my part I never got farther than the advertisements . . . I am exceedingly glad Eustace is looking his old self again. But I am at a loss to conceive why it should be his 'old' self—would you mind writing and answering the question? . . .

Your affectionate
Arthur James Balfour [10]

At Cambridge (1866–1869) he still presented that appearance of indolence which remained a lifelong characteristic. But, equipped at last with spectacles, he was able to throw himself into the sporting pleasures which, together with music and conversation, were to be his most constant joys. The chief sporting attraction, as far as he was concerned, was court tennis—to be replaced in due course by golf and lawn tennis. Looking back, he commented: 'the amount of time I spent, or wasted, in playing tennis myself, or, when this was impossible, in watching it played by others, verged (I admit) on the scandalous.' [11] He made lasting friendships through the tennis, for instance with George, eldest son of the great Charles Darwin, who became Professor of Astronomy at Cambridge.

---

[9] Hinting at his future contempt for newspapers, he says that he does not want the *Cornhill Magazine* back.
[10] WHI/195.
[11] *Autobiography*, p. 16.

However, Cambridge meant a good deal more than play to Balfour. His mother had somehow discovered the opportunity, later abolished, of Arthur's going up to Trinity College as a Fellow-Commoner. This anomaly conferred on Balfour the 'incalculable advantage' of dining at the high table where he made close friends of such as Henry Sidgwick, the philosopher, and John Strutt, the physicist—respectively ten and six years his senior. This, and his intense curiosity about the philosophical basis of scientific knowledge, led him to read Moral Sciences under Sidgwick. The question arises: why did Balfour not finish with better than a Second Class in his final Tripos examination in 1869? An undergraduate friend wrote to his sister, Alice, in 1893:

I suppose it will not be new to you to tell you that your brother was considered in those days very indolent, as indolent in fact as clever. He constantly lay in bed—as for all I know he does still—most of the morning. He was not reputed to be a great reader, but to have a wonderful capacity for picking the brains of other people. [12]

To those acquainted with Balfour's habits in later life this account comes, indeed, as no surprise. But in so far as there are many indications from his Cambridge days of that persistent mental activity so characteristic of him in high ministerial office, it still remains rather astonishing that Balfour did not achieve First Class Honours in a philosophical Tripos—even granting the time spent on the tennis court, the lack of sustained reading, and the distraction consequent upon his own 'speculative efforts'. For these efforts were devoted to the groundwork of his own first book, *A Defence of Philosophic Doubt*. Even if he thought at the material time, and later, that the Tripos, though crucial to his hopes of becoming a Fellow of Trinity, 'was but an unimportant episode' in his 'philosophic activities', this surely suggests just the stuff of which a First in philosophy might be made! Apparently Sidgwick gave Balfour to understand that it was quantity rather than quality that was lacking in his examination answers. [13] This strongly suggests an explanation of Balfour's result in addition to what has commonly been said. This is simply that, throughout his life, he hated the physical processes involved in writing with a pen and found legibility painfully difficult to achieve. [14]

Between 1869 and 1873, Balfour seems to have lacked a settled aim in

[12] WHI/195, The Hon. Hugh Elliott (3rd son of the 3rd Earl of Minto and a Liberal MP, 1885; Liberal Unionist 1886–9) to Alice Balfour, 13 Sept. 1893.

[13] *Autobiography*, pp. 50–63.

[14] See, for example, the Downing Street 'Memories' of F. S. Parry in WHI/81, p. 7: Balfour 'had a profound distaste for the mechanical labour of writing . . . dictating everything except his signature to his confidential shorthand-writer'. However, it was due to this habit of

life. Then he passed through an emotional experience which left an indelible mark upon him. It came about through his friendship at Cambridge with Spencer Lyttleton. Through him, Balfour became closely acquainted with the Lyttleton and Gladstone families. The Hon. George William Spencer Lyttleton (to give him his full name) was a year older than Balfour. He was the fourth son of the fourth Baron Lyttleton. Lord Lyttleton was a fine scholar and an F.R.S. who had married Mary, a daughter of Sir Stephen Glynne, Bt. Her sister Catherine Glynne had married William Ewert Gladstone. It was a joyous double wedding, in 1839. The resultant cousinhood numbered seven Gladstones and twelve Lyttletons. In the summer of 1870, Spencer Lyttleton took Balfour to Hagley Hall, his home in Worcestershire. There he met the Lyttleton brothers who were accomplished sportsmen—among them Neville, who in 1904 would become the first Chief of a British General Staff, and Alfred, who would enter Balfour's Cabinet in 1903. Mary Gladstone and Lavinia Lyttleton were also there and became Balfour's lifelong friends; but it was the tall, vivacious May Lyttleton who moved his heart. During the 1870s, Balfour came, through his languid charm and wit, to play a leading role in a coterie deriving from Hagley and Hawarden, and extending to other great country houses. By the 1880s the intellectually and aesthetically oriented group known jocularly as 'the Souls' had grown out of that coterie. But before that stage was reached, Balfour suffered a blow which seems to have hardened him until the emergence of what Mary Gladstone (by then Mrs Drew) described as 'the younger generation' of Balfours—the nieces of the admiring 'Greek Chorus'—brought 'a softer, happier atmosphere into his life' before the Great War. [15] This event was the death of May Lyttleton.

By January 1875, Balfour had decided that he wished to marry her but, through a mixture of shyness and sexual fastidiousness, he failed to get beyond hinting at a prospective proposal of marriage. May, having then recovered from a deep infatuation for one Rutherford Graham who had died suddenly, seems to have been quite receptive to Balfour. As has been said, he was a leading light with the coterie and, subsequently, he exercised great charm over women throughout his life. However, the question of his marriage to May Lyttleton was never brought to a head because she

dictation that B. built up so complete a collection of all his more important out-letters from the 1880s forward to 1929, thus greatly enhancing the B.P. as a historical source.

[15] WHI/80, 'Mr. Balfour' by Mary Drew, Sept. 1917 (a typescript copy for Alice Balfour, 69 pp.), p. 64. In the same file there is a copy of a substantial letter from Nora (Mrs Sidgwick) to Alice Balfour of 6 Sept. 1918. She approves Mary's 'general picture' of 'the early days', of which use has been made in this chapter, but she appends a shrewd critique of other parts of Mary's assessment.

contracted typhoid fever. Ten weeks later, on 21 March, she died at the age
of 24. Balfour attended the funeral service at Hagley and in various ways
exposed his passionate distress to Edward and Lavinia Lyttleton. Thereaf-
ter he restored and reinforced his habitual control over his emotions and
some of the spontaneous gaiety which (according to Mary Gladstone) was to
the fore in 1870–1874, went out of his life for ever. [16]

Balfour never married. It is probable that even his long friendship with
Mary Wyndham, later Countess of Wemyss, involved no direct physical
relationship. He evidently experienced no urgent sexual drive. Indeed,
Professor L. P. Curtis has written: 'At Cambridge his collection of blue
china and fondness of repose had won him the title of "Pretty Fanny"'; and
he notes that, after entering the House of Commons, Balfour attracted from
'seemingly more virile members' a string of soubriquets such as ' "Clara" ',
"Niminy-piminy", "Tiger Lily", "Daddy Long Legs", and "lisping
Hawthorn Bird" '! [17] However, indications of homosexuality are entirely
lacking, whereas signs of heterosexual interest are not.

Yet all the physiological possibilities attributed to Balfour are not
covered by such generalizations. A. J. P. Taylor's life of Beaverbrook
includes the index-entry 'Balfour, A. J., amateur philosopher . . . a
hermaphrodite'. The corresponding text reveals that, having been put in his
place by Balfour when Minister of Information in 1918, Beaverbrook
'could only retaliate later in life by saying: "Balfour was a hermaphrodite.
No one ever saw him naked." '. Mr Taylor responded to this assertion by
asking Beaverbrook 'whether it was usual to see cabinet ministers naked'. [18]
Setting aside all other occasions when Balfour may have been seen naked, it
was precisely because he was a cabinet minister of high rank that he was, at
least once, interviewed while wearing no clothes. In 1931 Sir Sydney
Parry, who had been Private Secretary to the First Lord of the Treasury
from 1897 to 1902, sent to Alice Balfour his 'Memories of No. 10 Downing
Street' appertaining to those five years. He recalls that, during the Boer
War, 'a very pressing despatch' was sent across from the War Office early
in the day, before Balfour had come downstairs.

I ran up with it, heard him splashing in his bathroom, and knocked at the door: 'Lord
Lansdowne wants an immediate reply. Shall I come back in twenty minutes?' 'Is it

[16] The May Lyttleton episode has been extensively covered by previous biographers. See
especially Dugdale, ii, 31–5; Kenneth Young, *Arthur James Balfour*, London, 1963,
pp. 29–37; Max Egremont, *Balfour*, London, 1980, pp. 30–8.

[17] L. P. Curtis, Jr., *Coercion and Conciliation in Ireland 1880–1892*, Princeton, 1963,
p. 175.

[18] Taylor, *Beaverbrook*, London (Penguin), 1972, pp. 209–10 and n.

very urgent?' 'Yes.' 'Bring it in, then. If you don't mind, I don't.' So I slipped in and read it aloud, while A.J., in native majesty like Milton's Adam, towelled himself and dictated his reply simultaneously. [19]

So, all in all, it seems fair to conclude that Balfour was not a herma-phrodite. As he was sometimes heard to observe to pessimists, 'This is a singularly ill-contrived world, but not so ill-contrived as that.'

[19] WHI/81, Parry, 'Memories', pp. 19–20.

2

Whittingehame and Hatfield; Philosophy and Religion

1874–1885

UNDERSTANDING Balfour's outlook, and thus his political career, is assisted by a closer look at his family life at Whittingehame. Three women have left records which illuminate various parts of the period 1880 to 1911. The major source, Lady Frances Balfour's memoirs, has already been mentioned. It provides substantial information about the earlier years. Beatrice Webb, on the other hand, has left brief but perceptive accounts written between 1906 and 1910.[1] The third source is provided by Mary Drew in the unpublished memoir of Balfour to which reference has already been made.[2] Compiled during the Great War, it focuses on the Balfour family circle, sometimes seen on a visit to Cambridge or at Carlton Gardens in London. It agrees fairly well with Lady Frances's account of the early 1880s.

It will remain for a later chapter to chart the breakdown of Balfour's leadership of the Conservative and Unionist party in 1911. But some significance may doubtless be attached to assertions that, from the time of his succession as Prime Minister in 1902, a cliquish atmosphere became more apparent at cabinet meetings than had been the case under Salisbury who maintained the traditional formalities. J. S. Sandars, who was Balfour's political private secretary from 1892 to 1905, and acted as his confidential aide till 1911, wrote as follows to J. L. Garvin some two years after Balfour's death in 1930:

> Balfour was slow in confidential relations. Pleasant enough in society of many types, and engaging in his easy manner and appearance of interest, he admitted but few to that political confidence which he extended to such friends as Lansdowne, Lyttleton and his own near relatives.[3]

[1] Webb, *Our Partnership*, London, 1948.
[2] WHI/80.
[3] J.C.P. 18/16/30. See also Webb, p. 359 (her diary for 1 Oct. 1906) for the cliquy atmosphere at cabinet meetings.

In similar vein, Lady Frances Balfour wrote of her brother-in-law as Prime Minister:

> What was wrong with him as a leader was, that he did not seek out the dissenting Minister, and find out what was at the root of the objection. He gave the impression of not caring, or not realising, or of not making up his mind, and so his Cabinet left him, few of them with a grievance against himself, for their affections were deeply engaged.[4]

Lady Frances's account of life at Whittingehame in the 1880s sheds light on the origins of this exclusive tendency and also on the impression sometimes given by Balfour that (in Beatrice Webb's words) he regarded 'politics as only part of a somewhat amusing game'.[5] Lady Frances, after marrying Eustace Balfour in 1879, found at Whittingehame an intellectual family group more dissociated from its neighbours than any she had seen. Balfour reigned unquestioned. The soubriquet 'Prince Arthur' could not have been more apt. At that stage 'the isolation of Whittingehame, so entirely grateful to the Balfours', struck Lady Frances as 'dreary, and very lonely'. She missed the 'comradeship', extending through the local people even to hordes of sightseers, which marked life at Inverary. 'The Balfours at this period', she wrote retrospectively, 'were as inclusive and exclusive as it was possible to be.' News of the approach of anyone, whether 'gentle or simple', was received 'with complete horror'.

Should 'carriage company' be reported in the offing while the Balfours were

> engaged out of doors in playing croquet or lawn tennis, they would run with great dignity, and equal agility within the sheltering arms of a lime tree which at that time, swept its covering boughs over these inhospitable inmates. There they imagined that they were invisible, from their covert they would emerge when the danger of seeing a neighbour was over, and highly amused at the success of their stratagem.
>
> Wide was their reputation for their inhospitable hermit ways. If any of their neighbours asked them out to dinner, it was treated as a matter of despairing boredom. If no excuse could be raised, they went on the desperate enterprise with gloomy forebodings, and they returned as speedily as might be . . .
>
> On my honeymoon Eustace took me a round of visits to see old retainers and friends, on the estate. To me it was an extraordinarily stiff affair . . .

However, she thought that this dourness was quite characteristic of the Lowland, as distinct from the Highland, Scot; and later in her memoirs she indicates that the Balfours' relations with their neighbours eased with the

---

[4] Lady Frances Balfour, ii, 368.
[5] Webb, p. 359.

passing of time. Meanwhile, after Balfour's striking success as Chief Secretary for Ireland, the family circle was frequently penetrated by politicians.

Visitors came and went at their own proposing, always received with groans, as disturbing to the large family circle, but very often enhancing its attractions. Sometimes an outsider would complain that Arthur was too much the centre of the family life and thought. That all conversation was directed to make him talk, and that no one was considered worth listening to when he spoke. Nor were they . . . Not that he did not want to hear everything the youngest might say: one of his great gifts was that of being an appreciative listener. His form of conversation was always debating. Leading the talk on with illuminating comment, and then showing the deductions to be drawn. If himself cornered for a moment, he would dexterously leap over the fence, and be away in the open country. How maddening it used to be when the conscientious dull guest would 'entertain us with small talk' while the best of general talk was going on, and everyone straining to hear . . . though often going deeply into science or philosophy, he would always pull it up before it got heavy, and turn it into byways in which all could join.[6]

Mary Drew's recollections of the Balfours in Cambridge and elsewhere in 1880 supplement Lady Frances's account.

The party used to dine every week with each other by turns in [Frank's and Gerald's] Trinity rooms, or the Sidgwick or Rayleigh houses. Arguments between the brothers were frequent and, whatever the subject, always most interesting to watch and hear. On one occasion A. J. B. was up against Gerald and Frank, no mean antagonists, on some point scientific and religious. Flushed and eager, the veins stand out on their foreheads—was it possible such sharp antagonism should not lead to serious dissension? But no. What was certainly most surprising and most remarkable was the extraordinary good temper kept alongside of the very hardest hitting and contradiction.[7]

A case has been made by Sir Robert Ensor and others for regarding Balfour mainly as an administrative statesman; but the view, apparently held by Balfour himself up to 1911, that he was pre-eminently a debater,[8] is certainly illuminated by these reminiscences of Lady Frances and Mary Drew. It was as a debater that, by the early 1880s, he was beginning to stake a claim to ministerial office. His debating flair was much to the fore in the Commons from 1887 to 1905; and even after his party's electoral disaster in January 1906 and the derision with which he was received on his return to a much more radical House, he had reasserted his debating stature before the

[6] Lady Frances Balfour, i, 307–8; ii, 284–5.
[7] WHI/80, pp. 43–4.
[8] See B.'s statement of 30 Sept. 1911 in B.P. 49767, ff. 295–6.

end of the session. His political career grew largely out of the extempore skills exercised and developed over many years within his family group.

Lady Frances stresses the primacy awarded to intelligence, especially in the guise of clarity and logic, in the life of the Balfour family. For example, when Alice Balfour returned home from Dunbar railway station with the news that she had been involved in one of the accidents then common on the east coast line, she was keenly interrogated about her actions during the incident. Once it had been confirmed that she had behaved logically, all interest in the affair instantly terminated. In general, conversation was steered firmly away from mundane recitals and 'shop', and directed towards clarification of concepts and arguments of an intellectual nature. Show of emotion was eschewed. Stupidity was 'the one unforgivable sin'.

On one occasion, the discovery of an empty canoe suggested the possibility that Frank Balfour had drowned. Lady Frances experienced 'considerable agitation' on this account, but she 'noted with astonishment the cool calculation of the family that the probabilities were all in favour of his being safe. And so it turned out.' At such times, she would conclude that 'they were the most extraordinary people that she had yet met.'[9]

If due weight is given to what may be termed the Whittingehame factor, together with Balfour's inherited qualities, it comes as no surprise to read Sir Frederick Ponsonby's comment, apropos the Boer War, that 'Balfour always imagined that had fate decreed that he should be a soldier he would have been a great tactician. All that was necessary was to apply the principles of logic and you pulverised the enemy.'[10] The propensity for rapid apprehension and the application of logic did indeed mark Balfour's approach to all the problems of government.

The question now imposes itself: how was it that a man whose most serious interest was in the intellectual respectability of religion, who seemed congenitally indolent, whose only unambiguous love was for golf and other games (including politics, but largely excluding personal ambition from that sphere), who during his subsequent political career was criticized for indecision, was nevertheless able to react to the challenge of Ireland in 1887 with consistent firmness, with conspicuous courage, and a notable absence of vacillation? His comparative youth at the time provides some part of the answer. More important, however, was his relationship with his uncle, the Prime Minister.

It has already been seen that, after the death of his father in 1856, Balfour was mainly brought up by his mother. However, until Balfour attained the

---

[9] Lady Frances Balfour, i, 313–14.
[10] Ponsonby, *Recollections of Three Reigns*, London, 1951, pp. 74–5.

age of 21 in July 1868, his uncle Lord Robert Cecil was a trustee of the Whittingehame estate and he came up as a visitor from time to time. Lord Salisbury (as Cecil had become by April 1868) was only eighteen years older than his nephew. The impression left on Balfour by his uncle's visit to Eton has already been mentioned. Alike as they were in their aversion to letter-writing, it is not surprising that Balfour's earlier visits to Hatfield after 1868, when Salisbury and his family took up residence there, are scarcely documented. In Balfour's papers, the earliest of his uncle's letters consist of two brief but affectionate communications of 1872. The second of these letters to 'My dear Arthur' bears out the saying that Balfour was always Salisbury's favourite nephew. Salisbury writes: 'I wish you had been here to talk to your poor "Fitz" who is much bored: and far too aged to join in the gaieties of the rest who are most of them sexagenarians.' He adds: 'You did not carry off a vol. of "Nature" from my room did you?'[11]

Besides informally educating his seven children by dint of endless argument and sharp attention to definitions, Salisbury spent many hours in the laboratory beneath his study—a habit emulated by Balfour. In 1886 the uncle was elected a Fellow of the Royal Society as was the nephew but two years later. The quoted letter of 1872 is an early pointer to their common interest in science. Politics, however, provided the main substance of the incessant conversational exchanges at Hatfield. In style, if not in subject matter, these conversations resembled those at Whittingehame. Both families delighted in such intellectual activities and rejoiced in their self-sufficiency. At Hatfield, however, religious speculation, especially with regard to Anglican tenets, was persistently discouraged by Salisbury. The balance and stability of his powerful mind depended on unquestioning belief. He took the attitude that the Anglican faith, like Christianity in general, was not basically a rational matter. It seems that his sons James (later the fourth Marquess of Salisbury), William (who became Bishop of Exeter), Robert (subsequently Viscount Cecil of Chelwood), Edward (whose remarkable widow, Violet, would marry Lord Milner), and Hugh (later Baron Quickswood), despite their highly intellectual upbringing, themselves never seriously questioned the validity of the Anglican creed. Indeed, they could even be accounted fanatical Anglicans, as their cousin Arthur would be reminded when the education issue came to a head before and during 1902.[12]

---

[11]   B.P. 49688, ff. 4–5, Salisbury to B. from Hatfield House, 20 Dec. 1872. The journal *Nature* dates from 1870.

[12]   See Rose, pp. 27–8, etc., and Viscountess Milner, *My Picture Gallery 1886–1901*, London, 1951, pp. 78–82.

Balfour, for his part, was preoccupied with the question of belief essentially from a philosophical standpoint. Could the intellectual respectability of Christianity be established by rational processes? Darwinism had raised what many people took to be a mortal challenge to Christian belief. Balfour, when taken home by his Cambridge friend George Darwin in 1869 or thereabouts, was charmed by the venerable Charles Darwin. But by then Balfour had decided to combat the threat posed to religious belief by showing that the intellectual basis of science was equally open to doubt. [13] The dispassionate tone of his latter-day references to his philosophic project understates its central importance in his life. His typically cool, rather self-deprecating, account should be read in the light of his lifelong 'dread' of emotion. [14] This dread is firmly contained beneath his habit of referring to his own opinions and feelings in a fastidiously diffident way. Potentially ungovernable emotions lie neutralized within an idiom of graceful understatement. Thus in a Gifford Lecture published in 1915 he flatly observes: 'My business was with the groundwork of living beliefs; in particular with the goodness of that scientific knowledge whose recent development had so profoundly moved mankind.' [15]

More revealing are his remarks to his niece Blanche Dugdale, made in the later 1920s:

I took *Defence of Philosophic Doubt* very seriously. I thought I was making a contribution to religious thought of an original kind, and whatever may be its merits it *was* the solid background of twenty years of my life. In my youth it was my great safeguard against the *feeling* of frivolity. This is much more important now—biographically—than the book itself. [16]

In other words he felt at the time that, if he could not demonstrate that religious beliefs could be held as confidently as the beliefs underpinning science, life would be meaningless for him, nothing but a cosmic joke. The evolution of his *Defence of Philosophic Doubt*, published in 1879, had proceeded far enough by about 1877 to give Balfour sufficient self-assurance not only to accept life, but to turn more seriously to politics. He had entered Parliament in 1874. But right through the 1880s, and even beyond, it seems that Balfour still ascribed a higher level of importance to his continuing philosophical reflections than to politics. For instance, he returned with relief and enthusiasm to work on his second philosophical

[13] *Autobiography*, pp. 37–8, 63.
[14] See Algernon Cecil on B. in the *D.N.B.* and also Mary Drew's 'Mr. Balfour', p. 6, in WHI/80.
[15] *Theism and Humanism*, London, 1915, p. 138.
[16] Dugdale, i, 49.

book after the fall of the second Salisbury Government in 1892. Entitled *The Foundations of Belief*, it developed in a more positive and popular form the findings of the first book. When published in 1895, it received much more praise and attention than had the *Defence* because Balfour had, since 1887, achieved political celebrity. But the following passage is worth requoting for its strong feeling about the consequences of abandoning religion for a naturalistic philosophy:

> We survey the past and see that its history is of blood and tears, of helpless blundering, of wild revolt, of stupid acquiescence, of empty aspirations. We sound the future, and learn that after a period, long compared with the individual life, but short indeed compared with the divisions of time open to our investigation, the energies of our system will decay, the glory of the sun will be dimmed and the earth, tideless and inert, will no longer tolerate the race which has for a moment disturbed its solitude. Man will go down into the pit, and all his thoughts will perish . . . Imperishable monuments and immortal deeds, death itself, and love stronger than death, will be as though they had never been. Nor will anything that *is* be better or be worse for all that the labour, genius, devotion and suffering of man have striven through countless generations to effect. [17]

In a manner casual when compared with his approach to philosophy, Balfour absorbed—or found himself in ready agreement with—many of his Uncle Robert's political views. His mother's influence had certainly been no bar to such a meeting of minds.

Basic from Salisbury's viewpoint in the 1870s was the need to resist radicalism, especially that represented by Gladstone, and to guard against redistributory socialism in any form. On the other hand, Salisbury equalled Gladstone in his dislike of collectivism. Balfour, born and bred a Tory, found no difficulty in accepting these tenets. However, in what they came to see as a desperate situation, both uncle and nephew were prepared to make an exception of Ireland. It was characteristic of Balfour to be marginally more flexible than his uncle around the edges of principles held in common between them. Again, while his uncle often held his views with a passionate commitment which commanded widespread respect, Balfour fundamentally lacked enthusiasm in politics, as his sister Nora would accurately remark. [18] While Salisbury, in politics, was driven by fear, Balfour was more of an observer from afar and accounted himself an optimist.

---

[17]   *The Foundations of Belief*, London, 8th edn., 1901, pp. 33–4.
[18]   WHI/80, Mrs Sidgwick to Alice Balfour, 6 Sept. 1918: 'Notes on Mary Drew's Paper on A.J.B.', pp. 7 and 9.

However, when it came to Ireland and the Empire, Balfour seems to have identified thoroughly enough with his uncle's basic views. With characteristic intensity, Salisbury wrote in 1872: 'Ireland must be kept, like India, at all hazards, by persuasion if possible, if not by force.'[19] Balfour's social acquaintance—and opponent on Irish policy—Wilfred Blunt, afterwards wrote about the outlook of imperialists like the Irish Secretary of 1887. According to Blunt, they

> were obliged to look elsewhere than to theology for a moral sanction in their dealings with subject peoples, and this was found by men of Balfour's scientific temperament in the evolutionist creed of man, which in the sixties and seventies imposed itself on the thought of the day as a development of Darwin's 'Origin of Species'. This represented the world of life no longer as an ordered harmony, but as in its essence a struggle for existence . . . The rule of survival of the fittest was seized on eagerly by our imperialist politicians . . . This line of reasoning . . . was in 1887 confined to a very few political thinkers, perhaps only to the family group of which Balfour was presently to become the accepted leader. In both Balfours, Gerald no less than Arthur—and both in succession filled the office of Irish Chief Secretary—it had the effect of giving characters naturally kind and just a certain amount of political insensibility, hardening at times into ferocity.[20]

The striking affinity of view between uncle and nephew can be discerned elsewhere. In 1865 Salisbury had written in the *Quarterly Review*, 'The question is whether England shall be governed by property and intelligence, or by numbers.' On this issue hung 'hopes of freedom and order, and civilisation'. Speaking at Newcastle in October 1881, he indicated how the aberrations of a popular electorate might be judiciously checked by the House of Lords. It was the proper function of the Lords, he said, to reflect 'the permanent and enduring wishes of the nation as opposed to the casual impulse which some passing victory at the polls may in some circumstances have given to the decisions of the other House'. Balfour would use similar language after the catastrophic defeat of the Unionists in January 1906, and his subsequent handling of the House of Lords—'Mr. Balfour's poodle' in the words of Lloyd George—would resemble the Salisburian tactics of 1880–1885 and 1892–1895. Even in the more technical sphere of the tariff question, Balfour would adopt a line of policy which had appealed to his uncle. In the early 1880s Salisbury reacted to the Fair Trade agitation by favouring at least the threat of tariff retaliation by Britain. Moreover, while adhering basically to free trade, Salisbury was by 1884 corresponding sympathetically with fair traders on the subject of preferential tariffs on

[19]   Robert Taylor, *Lord Salisbury*, London, 1975, p. 40.
[20]   Wilfred Scawen Blunt, *The Land War in Ireland*, London, 1912, p. 298.

trade between Britain and her colonies. [21] Promotion of international free trade by use of 'retaliation', combined with sympathy for Chamberlain's schemes for imperial preference, was to characterize Balfour's response to the Tariff Reform crisis of 1903. It will also be seen that, in Balfour's hands, both 'retaliation' and the 'poodle' policy were to prove unfortunate answers to the problems facing him as a party leader.

Finally, the affinities subsisting between uncle and nephew were expressed in the value which they both placed upon individual freedom. As a champion of individual freedom Salisbury opposed recourse to conscription during the South African War. With equal aversion to the idea of war but a much greater natural bent for its conduct, Balfour was the only leading Conservative in Asquith's coalition of 1915 to oppose conscription. Some three years after Salisbury's death in 1903, Beatrice Webb recorded an exchange with Balfour which further defines the latter's view both of government and of the inviolability of the individual conscience:

> 'Have you [she inquired] ever wished to bring about another state of affairs to what at present exists?' . . . 'I am a Conservative,' he rejoined quietly, 'I wish to maintain existing institutions.' Then, presently, he added: 'There are some things about which I have been keen: take for instance the clause in the Scotch Free Church Bill enabling the established Church of Scotland to change its formulas—freeing it from the dead hand—I worked very hard to secure that.' I sympathised and we dropped the subject. [22]

Salisbury's political impetus and Balfour's political tenacity were nourished by a common inherited sense of patriotic duty. It was, above all, the challenge of war that put this sense of duty to the test. Although Salisbury hated war, had been grievously bereaved, and was increasingly burdened by age and ill health, he stuck to his post as Prime Minister till the end of the South African War, thus providing an element of reassurance to a disenchanted country. Balfour, for his part, was particularly whole-hearted and tenacious in administrative roles during periods of national emergency, notably during the Boer War and again from 1915 until the end of the peacemaking process. But the classic example of such Balfourian activity was his reaction to the challenge of the Irish Secretaryship. Lasting through the four years 1887–1891, it was seen by Balfour as a dire emergency. At stake were law and order within the United Kingdom and the claim of property-and-intelligence to rule within its boundaries. Moreover, at a time when the Raj began to be threatened by the foundation of the Indian

[21]   Peter Marsh, *The Discipline of Popular Government*, Sussex (Harvester), 1978, p. 28.
[22]   Webb (diary, 2 July 1906), pp. 345–6.

National Congress (1885), Balfour saw no reason to question his uncle's view of the Irish crisis as a test of Britain's imperial power.

However, before passing on to Balfour's Irish phase, it is necessary to look more closely at his political career from 1874 to 1885.

3

Political Beginnings

1874–1885

BY the early 1870s Balfour had come to the conclusion that, in addition to philosophy, music, society, family duties, conversation, reading, and games, he needed an occupation, and it occurred to him that the rather serious game of politics might suit him well. But at first no opening presented itself. Then, in 1873, 'suddenly the situation changed.' As Balfour afterwards recalled: 'I was lunching, I remember, with Lady Salisbury in Arlington Street, when my uncle, with whom I had never seriously discussed either my political opinions or my political future, tentatively approached the question of the representation of Hertford.'[1] Seeing that the borough of Hertford was subject to Salisbury's influence, Balfour's adoption in July 1873 as the Conservative candidate was less than a remarkable achievement. But interest resides in the speechifying at the local Conservative Association dinner held in the Hertford Corn Exchange on 17 October in that same year.

On proposing a toast, Salisbury said that he could vouch for Balfour as son of a Conservative member of Parliament 'who stood by the Conservative Party in the darkest hour of its trial' and who had himself given pledges that he would 'ever be true to the banner' of that party. In so far as Balfour's father had been an MP only from 1841 to 1847, Salisbury was clearly aiming his 'darkest hour' allusion at Peel's abolition of the Corn Laws and the subsequent debilitating split in the party. Therefore Balfour's determination as Conservative leader after 1902 that he must on no account follow Peel's example and split his party may be traced back to a public pledge, explicitly reinforced by his uncle on Balfour's first acceptance as a candidate. Balfour, responding to the toast, then proceeded to spell out the virtual identity between his own political views and those of his uncle:

> I can only say before I sit down that if there are any here present who have been seduced by the name of Liberalism, but have mistrusted its promises and are still doubtful which party they shall give their adhesion to, I would ask them to cast their

---

[1] *Autobiography*, pp. 85–6.

eyes back upon the legislation of the last 5 years, and consider how in that time by one measure individual liberty has been threatened; how by another measure private property has been violated. I would ask them to remember that these are not accidents, but are of the very essence of the party to whom change, violent change, not that sober steady change which is necessary to the permanence of all human institutions, but that change which excites the passions and furnishes a cry, is the very bread the party feeds on, the very air it breathes. I would ask them to consider the fate of Ireland, and then see in the fate of her Church and land, foreshadowed in no uncertain outline, the fate that that party pre-destinates for our own.[2]

Balfour later remembered the acuteness of his 'preliminary sufferings' before making his early political speeches, including this first one at Hertford.[3] Here, as subsequently in Parliament, he forced himself to learn to speak from skeletal notes amounting to nothing more than a few headings. While he was gradually to become more fluent, his hesitations, as he groped for the *mot juste*, continued to mark his speeches. Even in the 1880s his discriminating sister-in-law Lady Frances was irritated by these 'uninspiring' hesitations and yearned for more 'conviction and fire'.[4] But eventually Balfour's extempore oratorical invention was to delight a generation of parliamentary *cognoscenti*.

Having been duly elected to the Disraelian Parliament of 1874–1880, Balfour had still by the end of 1875 made no contribution to its deliberations. However, in response to Lady Salisbury's declared opinion that the session of 1876 should not be permitted to close 'without overt signs of Parliamentary activity' on his part, Balfour delivered a maiden speech on Indian currency during the dinner hour when attendance was restricted to a few members likewise intent on saying something for the record.[5] This speech, in Committee on the East India Revenue Accounts, referred to the problems caused by the fall in the value of silver (which was the standard of value in India). Balfour described India's relationship with Britain as being 'that of a country paying tribute to another'. However, he 'believed the ultimate form which the tribute took was not silver or gold currency, but goods'. He therefore deprecated any precipitate move to solve the problem on a purely monetary basis.[6]

[2] WHI/60. Notes for B.'s use when writing his *Autobiography*—headed '1873' and including extracts from the *Hertford Mercury*. B. is there described as 'Captain Balfour' by virtue of his service with the Lothian and Berwickshire Yeomanry. In 1928 he told Mrs Dugdale that the whips continued till 1880 to address messages to 'Captain Balfour'; but he deprecated the inclusion in his memoirs of such 'a touch of pure farce'. (Dugdale, ii, 392–3.)
[3] *Autobiography*, p. 89.
[4] Lady Frances Balfour, i, 377.
[5] *Autobiography*, pp. 91–5.
[6] *P.D.*, 3rd, 231/1033–4, 10 Aug. 1876.

Notwithstanding Balfour's deprecatory references in his *Autobiography* to this maiden speech, his choice of subject is significant. Indian silver currency was not merely a safe topic for a diffident speaker: it was an area in which Balfour was closely, and indeed persistently, interested. His grasp of currency problems was acknowledged in 1886 when he was appointed a member of the Royal Commission on Gold and Silver, under Lord Herschell; and his 'extraordinary aptitude' for intricate discussion soon won the regard of his expert fellow member, Sir Thomas Farrer (later Lord Farrer of Abinger).[7] For light on Balfour's potential as a statesman, what is here significant is not that he looked to bimetallism to rescue the western world from a trade-constricting shortage of gold, nor that he came to see bimetallism as the answer to India's problems in particular. It is rather the tenacity with which he continued to pursue this complicated subject well into the nineties—beyond the point when, in fact, the production of gold in South Africa had risen to meet the need. The fascination that such a subject could hold for Balfour provides an important clue to understanding his oft-criticized handling of the Tariff Reform problem. If he was a man who could act decisively over Ireland, why did he seem incapable of giving an effective lead when faced with Chamberlain's challenge to free trade? Why did he persist after 1903 with his own unexciting compromise solution of tariff retaliation? At least part of the answer is that this was, for him, more than a compromise. It was, like bimetallism, a policy which he had examined over a period of years and found appropriate to the complex circumstances of the time. In such cases, Balfour could not easily accept that what seemed logical to him would not in the end prove self-evident, and thus a sound basis for political tactics as well. Unlike, for example, Lloyd George, he was fundamentally an intellectual rather than an instinctive politician, trusting to his own analytical processes rather than looking outwards to the drift of other people's opinions; and he would ultimately, as a politician, pay the price. Yet, in an even longer run, he would remain established near the top in politics because he could by 1916 perceive, more clearly than Asquith, the reasons for Lloyd George's effectiveness as a politician; and because he could likewise understand, by 1924, that Baldwin's instinctive qualities as a political leader outweighed his intellectual limitations.

It remains to add that India itself continued to be a major focus of Balfour's attention throughout his political career. In a final letter to

[7] WHI/65, Farrer to B., 11 Dec. 1886 and 5 Mar. 1887—marked 'Keep' and carrying the P.S.: 'May I express my admiration of your examination of Gibbs. I wish we had more witnesses who could answer your questions.'

Baldwin of late 1929, India is still for Balfour 'the greatest of all subjects'. [8]

But it was Balfour's concern for the position of religious minorities that was first to gain him a degree of recognition. The particular issue involved was the Nonconformist grievance over burial in Anglican churchyards. Not infrequently, until Gladstone settled the matter in 1880, there was no alternative to interment in the parish churchyard; yet the parson might insist on using a form of service obnoxious to the family of the deceased. Balfour's tenacity in a matter of personal conviction—which in this instance conflicted with Salisbury's view—is borne out by what is apt to be overlooked, namely that Balfour introduced two private bills to amend the burial laws, not just one. Salisbury's expectation of failure[9] did not deter his nephew. On 15 April 1878 he was given leave to introduce a Burial Law Amendment Bill. It had four sponsors but did not progress beyond its first reading.[10] Balfour's latter-day memory of 1878 was avowedly hazy and tends to obscure the sequence of events. After Salisbury went to the Foreign Office in March 1878 to deal with the Near Eastern crisis, he appointed Balfour his private secretary and took him to the Congress of Berlin in the summer—and from that time onwards Balfour became versed in the details of foreign policy. But after such experiences as conversing with Bismarck, Balfour again took up the burials question, moving in the Commons on 6 December 1878 'that leave be given to bring in a Bill to amend the Burial Laws'. On this occasion the Bill had three sponsors, and it was read a first time despite Beresford-Hope's intimation of his total opposition to the measure.

Alexander Beresford-Hope was not only a keen high-churchman. He was Balfour's uncle-by-marriage and, before 1880, the two always sat together on the Conservative front bench below the gangway. According to a leading lobby-correspondent, the older man's encouraging chuckles were a 'delightfully touching' accompaniment to most of Balfour's speeches in the Commons—especially during Balfour's association in the early 1880s with the lively Fourth Party, when Hope sat a few feet further away, above the gangway. [11] But the 'fond smile' with which Balfour was wont to greet his kinsman in the House may have been less evident when, on the second reading of Balfour's Bill on 19 February 1879, Beresford-Hope virtually talked it out. [12]

[8] Dugdale, ii, 404; B. to Baldwin, 8 Nov. 1929.
[9] B.P. 49688, ff. 9–10, Salisbury to B., 19 Mar. 1878.
[10] *P.D.*, 3rd, 239/1358–9.
[11] Henry Lucy, *A Diary of Two Parliaments*, London, 1886, ii, 85.
[12] *P.D.*, 3rd, 243/1447–99. B.'s *Autobiography*, pp. 117–20, conflates the two bills.

The standard account of Balfour's parliamentary apprenticeship is to the effect that he was first noticed by the lobbyists as an adherent of the Fourth Party, Churchill's opposition ginger group, in 1880; that he made a momentary impact on the House by attributing 'infamy' to Gladstone over the 'Kilmainham Treaty' with Parnell in 1882; but that, as Henry Lucy records: 'Up to the day when all the world wondered to hear that Mr. Balfour had been appointed Chief Secretary for Ireland, he was a person of no consequence. His rising evoked no interest in the House.'[13]

This perspective is indeed largely accurate. It was only on the rare occasions when he shook off his rather picturesque boredom that his exceptional powers of argument could be glimpsed. Yet these powers did in fact make some impression by 1879. The *Annual Register* of that year not only describes Balfour as 'a rising member of the Conservative party' but goes so far as to allocate more than a whole page to his second Burials Bill. On 19 February 1879, according to the *Register*, there was an 'animated' debate on the second reading and the commentary implies respect for Balfour's solution by comparison with other proposals then being canvassed.

The principle of Mr. Balfour's compromise was to throw open the churchyards to all persons not members of the Church of England with certain restrictions. One restriction had reference to the nature of the Burial service; it need not be performed by the clergyman of the Established Church, but it must be of 'a solemn and Christian character', agreeable to the usages of the religious society to which the deceased belonged. Another class of restrictions safeguarded the rights of the Church; the privilege was not to be conceded when there was a public cemetery within three miles of the churchyard, nor when the churchyard had been acquired by gift or contribution within the last fifty years.

The *Register* also notes the favourable reception given to Balfour's proposal by Nonconformist opinion. The Liberation Society hoped that MPs would vote for the second reading. But this alone was enough to convince Beresford-Hope—a veteran of die-hard opposition to the abolition of Church Rates—of the need to wreck Balfour's compromise, even though it fell short of the conclusive measure passed by Gladstone in 1880. He found no difficulty in harping at pulverizing length on questions raised by Balfour's restrictive clauses. However, as far as he was concerned, the conclusive defect in the Bill derived from the support it had received from the Liberation Society. 'Our contention is', he declared, 'that his Bill not only surrenders absolutely everything that is asked for by the other side, but

[13] Henry W. Lucy, *The Salisbury Parliament*, London, 1892, p. 425.

surrenders that one thing also, which the French King is said to have boasted that he preserved—our honour—in the vain struggle.'[14] Soon after Beresford-Hope had at last reached his conclusion, time duly ran out.

Balfour's lack of any definite aspiration for office is well established. When roused over a religious or Irish question he could, for the moment, make an impression; but his languorous manner and apparent cult of amateurism certainly tended to diminish him as a politician. From about 1878 until he went to the Irish Office in 1887, his one persistent aim as an MP was evidently to improve his effectiveness as a debater, as an end in itself. Nevertheless, his experience as Salisbury's private secretary from March 1878 undoubtedly quickened his interest in foreign and imperial matters—and also in the competition of parties. Moreover, there can be no doubt that for Balfour politics derived some of its growing fascination from its resemblance to a game. He gradually strengthened his skills as a debater to such a point that they enabled him to juggle the conflicting elements in the Unionist party, and thus retain power, for more than two years after 1903—an astonishing, if ultimately disastrous, parliamentary feat. But his book *The Foundations of Belief* (first published in 1895) clarifies the perspective in which he regarded politics in those earlier years. Continuity and stability were important, but party cries were not. It was the conservatism represented by the Conservative Party that mattered rather than the party itself. His rejection of Lloyd George's coalition proposal of 1910, but his support of the wartime coalitions of Asquith and Lloyd George, may be seen in this light; so may his neglect of the party machine when Prime Minister. He was, by inclination, a true conservative; but, unlike Salisbury, he could not as leader bring himself to quell his aversion to 'wire-pulling'.

But these attitudes were combined with a boundless curiosity. While this curiosity was often directed to the world of ideas, his intimacy with his uncle stimulated his interest in India and the Near East. Fortified by his first-hand experience at the Congress of Berlin, he countered the criticisms levelled at government policy by Lord Hartington (official opposition leader in the Commons *pro tempore*) during a debate of 1 August 1878. Turning to the main bone of contention, the Anglo-Turkish Convention binding Britain to defend Turkey against Russian attack, he even adopted a high ministerial line:

The noble Lord the Leader of the Opposition, the hon. Member for Birmingham [Joseph Chamberlain], and other speakers, had loudly, but he hoped hastily,

[14] *Annual Register*, 1779, pp. 35–6; *P.D.*, 3rd, 243/1454.

announced their conviction that in a few years England would not consider herself bound by this Treaty. Whether they did that in the interests of that public morality which they supposed the present Government had lowered he did not know. But he thought better of them than they apparently did of themselves. He did not believe that any English Government would at any time think itself absolved at its own free will from a Treaty entered into by Constitutional means . . . Russia, knowing that we had a consistent policy, would not run counter to it . . . [15]

As Prime Minister, Balfour would successfully base his handling of Russia on the last-quoted principle.

The Disraeli Government was fundamentally most concerned, in its Russian policies, with the defence of India. Salisbury, as Secretary for India (1874−1878), had tried to restrain what he came to see as the 'gaudy and theatrical ambition' of the Viceroy, Lord Lytton. The latter was for his part greatly alarmed by the threat of a Russian advance towards Herat in Eastern Afghanistan. Not only did this menace Persia. It bade fair to bring the Russians on to the traditional route for the invasion of India. When the Amir of Afghanistan refused to allow British agents to go to his northern frontier to observe the Russians, Lytton on his own responsibility pre-cipitated an Afghan war in late July 1878. By December, the House of Commons was debating a government resolution to charge the expense of the Afghan expedition to the Indian revenues. The subject was, of course, grist to Gladstone's anti-imperialist mill: 'My opinion is a very simple one. I consider that this war is an unjust, a guilty, an unreasonable, and an impolitic war—one of mischief to the fame of England—one of mischief to the future of India.' Those who made the war, he said, were the ones who should pay for it—not the people of India. [16]

When the debate continued on the following day, Balfour disputed Gladstone's argument that a charge upon the Indian revenues would be illegal. But it is where he goes on to answer Fawcett's phrases about 'a great Imperial undertaking' and 'an Imperial war' that those who, a century later, have seen Russia actually invade Afghanistan may read his speech with special interest. Balfour said that 'imperialism', a term which was not yet in common currency and which had not previously been used in the debate, had been irresponsibly denigrated by the Opposition. It meant, he declared, that the British

recognized themselves as parts of a great Empire spread over the world which had great responsibilities and duties; and, further, that this was not a burden to be

[15] *P.D.*, 3rd, 242/943−7.
[16] *P.D.*, 3rd, 243/904, 16 Dec. 1878.

grumbled at and thrown off at the first opportunity, but one that had great privileges which no English Government would have the courage to throw off, whatever its members might say when they were not in power. There could be no doubt that the immediate occasion of the war was an insult offered to England; but the more profound cause of the war was the necessity which every Indian Government felt, and must feel, of keeping Afghanistan in such a position that it should not be a menace, but a cause of safety to India. That feeling lay at the root of all our Indian policy.

Not only, he argued, should the Indian Government be prepared to meet the cost of the present operations.

Were we to leave India tomorrow, our successors would at once find that Afghanistan was not a place which could be left to become the centre of intrigue and of military operations against that country. That was the case before we went to India; it was the case now, and it would be the case after we left there. Even if England had not been the possessor of India, the Russian movement in that direction would have to be made sooner or later. [17]

As will in due course appear, Balfour was concerned with the Afghan question during his first months as Prime Minister and was able to draw on a store of knowledge when composing a classic paper on the subject for the Cabinet—an immediate forerunner of an unrivalled series of memoranda for the burgeoning Committee of Imperial Defence.

It was the victory of the Liberals, surprising to both sides, in the General Election of April 1880 that aroused the competitive attributes camouflaged beneath Balfour's languid exterior. Already, by 8 April, Lord Beaconsfield at 10 Downing Street was confiding to Balfour, for Salisbury's information, his intention of resigning ahead of certain defeat in the new House of Commons. On the 10th Salisbury was replying to his nephew in terms which Balfour would echo after his own electoral catastrophe of January 1906. Salisbury wrote: 'The hurricane that has swept us away is so strange and new a phenomenon that we shall not for some time understand its meaning.' The 'enthusiasm' for Gladstone might turn out to be purely ephemeral, or it might (he continued) be 'the beginning of a serious war of classes'. Gladstone, according to the Marquess, was doing his best 'to give it the latter meaning'. [18]

The extent to which Balfour himself was becoming engrossed in the party game is suggested by a letter of 21 April which he wrote to Blackwood, the

[17] Ibid., 243/996–8, 17 Dec. 1878.
[18] *Autobiography*, pp. 122–32.

Edinburgh publisher (who had published a speech by Balfour in that city on
12 December 1879):

Dear Mr. Blackwood,
  I think it would be advisable to have a reprint of Gladstone's recent speeches,
which if not complete would at all events contain all the utterances which *we* shall
find it most convenient to remember and which *he* will find it easiest to forget . . .
  My idea is that we should publish it at a price which will prevent it having a very
wide circulation among the poorer classes (when it might do harm) but which would
not prevent anybody at all interested in contemporary politics among the well-to-do
classes from obtaining it.

Yours truly
Arthur James Balfour [19]

Nothing seems to have come of this initiative. However, the ensuing
Gladstone parliament of 1880–1885 was marked by the meteoric rise of
Lord Randolph Churchill as an independent critic not only of the government front bench but of his own leader in the Commons, the sedate former
Peelite, Sir Stafford Northcote. Northcote tended to defer to Gladstone as
his political mentor, having been his private secretary and electoral helper
between 1842 and 1853. This situation was to stimulate Balfour's political
development.

As far as domestic politics were concerned, this parliament of
1880–1885 was dominated by two issues. At the outset, there was the rise
of the Irish National Party led by Charles Stewart Parnell (who, incidentally, was only two years older than Balfour). This brought the issue of Irish
Home Rule to the forefront of British politics. Secondly, there was the
question of equalizing the rural with the urban vote in the wake of the 1867
Reform Act. The Conservatives realized that Gladstone was likely to
attempt this equalization; and Salisbury, for his part, wished to ensure that
it would be associated with a redistribution of seats favourable to the
Conservatives. His successful use of the House of Lords to achieve this aim
would constitute an object lesson for Balfour. However, this second issue
did not come to the fore till after Parnell had, by 1882, become the
uncrowned king of Ireland and established a *modus vivendi* with the
Liberals.

After Parliament met in the spring of 1880, Randolph Churchill moved
swiftly into aggressive action as a self-appointed opposition spokesman. He
soon became linked with two older Conservatives of independent tendency,

---

[19]   National Library of Scotland, Blackwood P., 4401.

John Eldon Gorst and Sir Henry Drummond Wolff. Balfour's latter-day note on Gorst is accurate:

The oldest Parliamentarian among us, Sir John Gorst as he afterwards became, was a good mathematician, a good lawyer, and an experienced organizer. In this last capacity, so I always understood, he had before my time done work for the Party, which (as I suspect) had, in his opinion, been inadequately recognized. He was an acute and ready debater, of more force than charm . . . He was often unanswerable, but not so often persuasive. [20]

In years, Wolff was senior by quite a margin to Gorst. (Wolff was born in 1830; Gorst in 1838.) Wolff had first entered Parliament only in 1880 from a Foreign Office background. In contrast to Gorst, he was an easy and widely acceptable mixer 'with a great aptitude'—as Balfour remarks—'for amusing and being amused'. Wolff could also be seen as the originator of the group of three *frondeurs* who were soon to be known as the 'Fourth Party'. It was he who led the protests against the free-thinking Charles Bradlaugh taking the parliamentary oath. He was quickly joined by Lord Randolph and Gorst. It was, as Henry Lucy records in his parliamentary diary, 'a great tribute' to the vibrant spirit of Lord Randolph (who, at 31, was seven months younger than Balfour) that, by August 1880, he had taken over the leadership of the group and, despite the maturity of his confederates, surrounded it 'with a halo of youth'. [21] On the evening of the 6th the approach of dinner had denuded the opposition front bench below the gangway. It was suddenly occupied by the dauntless three who proceeded to halt business in its tracks by sustaining a fusillade of objections.

Balfour soon after this episode aligned himself with the group; but he was always more of an associate than a member of the Fourth Party. He was motivated partly by genuine sympathy with the wish for a more lively opposition to the Government and partly by his constant desire to improve his debating skills, as an end in itself rather than through ambition for ministerial office. (This latter assertion receives ample confirmation from his subsequent career taken as a whole.) Lucy first deemed Balfour worthy of notice in the group's attempt to censure the Government for slow progress with serious business. He thought that the device of putting up the languid Balfour to move the resolution had, by its piquancy, saved the Fourth Party from becoming something of a bore. He added that Balfour was

one of the most interesting young men in the House. He is not a good speaker, but he

---

[20] *Autobiography*, p. 135.
[21] Lucy, *Diary of Two Parliaments*, ii, 76 (6 Aug. 1980).

is endowed with the rich gift of conveying the impression that presently he will be a
successful Parliamentary debater, and that in the meantime it is well that he should
practise . . . He is not without a desire to say hard things of the adversary opposite,
and sometimes yields to the temptation. But it is ever done with such sweet and
gentle grace, and is smoothed over by such earnest protestations of innocent
intention, that the adversary rather likes it than otherwise. [22]

As Balfour remarked to Mrs Dugdale in 1928, his connection with
the Fourth Party was fundamentally altered by Beaconsfield's death on
19 April 1881. This not only meant the end of an epoch in Conservative party
history. From Balfour's viewpoint, his uncle's speedy confirmation as
leader of the Conservative peers also marked him out as a prospective
Prime Minister at the next change of government. In so far as Lord
Randolph was working to replace Northcote as Conservative leader in the
Commons, he could only be seen as a rival to Salisbury for leadership of the
party as a whole. Balfour was never in doubt about which aspirant would
receive his support. His loyalty, and his confidences about Churchill's
tactics and likely intentions, were always at Salisbury's disposal.

During 1883–4, Randolph Churchill attempted to extend his hold over
the party by achieving control of the National Union—the party organization. As Balfour relates, he himself 'became partially separated' from
the Fourth Party 'at the opening of the National Union dispute'; and Gorst,
for his part, broke away through characteristic dislike of Churchill's
sensible agreement with Salisbury that the Chairman of the National Union
(i.e. Churchill) must not encroach on the party leadership. Balfour also
argues plausibly that Randolph had, by 1884, achieved a special place in
the party, not on account of the tiresome dispute over the role of the
National Union, but through his 'brilliant Parliamentary and platform
performances' at that very time. [23]

But as far as Balfour himself was concerned, he made little impact on the
House of Commons before Gladstone's resignation in June 1885. In the
eyes of most members, he remained a dilettante of no particular consequence. Only for a moment, in May 1882, was there a revelation of his
passionate commitment on an issue. Significantly, in the light of his
subsequent career, it was an Irish matter. Under what became known as the
Kilmainham Treaty, Parnell had been released from prison on the understanding that the Government would drop coercion and ease the position of
those tenants who, because of rent arrears, were unable to take advantage of
the Land Act of 1881—otherwise a concession of fundamental importance

[22] Ibid., pp. 84–5 (20 Aug. 1880).
[23] *Autobiography*, pp. 133–73.

from the viewpoint of the Irish tenantry. The Government, for its part, understood that Parnell, on his release from Kilmainham, would cool down the Irish agitation against the Land Act. A recent biographer of Gladstone comments that the contention that there had been no treaty was 'a piece of Gladstonian casuistry, for there had definitely been a bargain', but that it was 'not a bargain to be ashamed of' and did not justify 'the fierce party passion which subsequently represented it as a deal with traitors'. [24] Revelation on 15 May of some of the details led to further questioning of Gladstone in the House of Commons on the 16th; and Balfour moved the adjournment of the House so that the Government might better explain its conduct and the Opposition have a fuller opportunity to criticize it. He went so far as to declare that the deal, in so far as its details had been revealed, stood alone in its 'infamy'.

Gladstone, who in private life had looked on Balfour as a close friend of his family, was stung into a heated reply and called for withdrawal of an unworthy and unsustainable charge. But Balfour did not retract.

By the time that Salisbury, in June 1885, was asked by the Queen to form a caretaker government, the 'infamy' incident had long since passed into a general oblivion. But the new Prime Minister and Conservative leader was not unaware of his nephew's mettle in matters appertaining to British sovereignty, law, and order.

[24]   E. J. Feuchtwanger, *Gladstone*, London, 1975, pp. 209–10.

4

A Fighter Revealed

1885–1891

BALFOUR had drawn even closer to his uncle Robert when the latter asserted his primacy in the party over Randolph Churchill before 1885; but he certainly did not ask the Prime Minister, in 1887, to confront him with the supreme challenge of an increasingly lawless Ireland. Nor did the Irish Nationalists in the House of Commons, by then a formidable disciplined force, see his appointment as more than a laughable gesture. If Churchill's Fourth Party had made a parliamentary mark before 1885, it had betrayed little dependence on Balfour's languid and unpredictable adherence. Yet various reasons, beyond those indicated above, can be discerned for Salisbury's choice.

Firstly, by January 1885 Balfour had drafted a 'little book' entitled 'Land Reform'. With Henry George in mind, it was designed to provide useful hints for anyone proposing to the electorate the reform or continuance of the existing system of land ownership in Great Britain. Only the third and final part of this work was printed—apparently intended for a periodical not traced by the present writer. Bearing the title 'Land, Land Reformers, and the Nation', it attracted comment from Eustace Balfour: 'A.J. read us his paper on Henry George written for the Conference in London. Very good.'[1] A citation of some of the opening paragraph, with its remarkably modern ring, provides some indication of the quality of the whole argument (which ends with an assertion of the relative altruism of the average landowner compared with his industrial counterpart):

One of the most conspicuous peculiarities of contemporary political speculation is the degree to which it concerns itself with the social condition, as opposed to the strictly political constitution, of the community . . . In the West, where, under whatever variety of external form, the supremacy of democracy is thought to be assured, discussions on the distributions of power are slowly being replaced by discussions on the distributions of wealth. It is not merely in the socialistic and semi-socialistic speculations, with which all in this room are more or less familiar,

[1] WHI/231, Jan. 1885.

that this tendency is displayed. It is manifested also in the increased sensitiveness which is felt in regard to the hardships which, under the seemingly inevitable operation of existing social arrangements, fall to the lot of large sections of the community . . . We no longer acquiesce with resignation in their existence, as though, like pain, decrepitude, and death, they were part of an inevitable order of things . . . and whether we have a panacea in our pockets or not, whether we believe a panacea to be possible or not, we are no longer serenely content to preach charity to those who do not suffer from want and resignation to those who do.

Having thus demonstrated the range and flexibility of his mind, Balfour affords more glimpses of his capacity to provide for a constructive policy, should this be required. Referring to Henry George, he continues:

With no new progress in science or the arts, with no elaborate reconstruction of the social mechanism, by legislation not more complicated than that which is required to put another penny on the income-tax, we are gravely assured that the darkest stain on our social system may be immediately wiped away . . . As will readily be believed I am no socialist; but to compare the work of such men as Mr. George with that of such men, for instance, as Karl Marx, either in respect of its intellectual force, its consistency, its command of reasoning in general, or of economic reasoning in particular, seems to me absurd. But Marx deals chiefly with capital, the school of which I am speaking deals entirely with land. Marx is but little read in this country, Mr. George has been read a great deal; on both these grounds, therefore, it is with the least interesting and, as I conjecture, the least important theory, that I must to-day chiefly concern myself.[2]

As far as Ireland was concerned, the main source for Marx's views—his correspondence with Engels—was not published in English till much later. With all such sources at his command Nicholas Mansergh has remarked on the shared 'miscalculation' of Marx and Balfour that the Irish Question derived from the land problem rather than from genuine nationalism—the inference drawn by Balfour being that land purchase and economic amelioration could solve the conundrum.[3] Even if he lacked knowledge of Marx's specific views on Ireland, it is still of some significance that already in 1885 Balfour held in such high regard the Marxian works then available to him. As for Salisbury, while he was unlikely to pay intellectual tribute to Marx, he could have no doubt about Balfour's capacity to supply Ireland with the economic first aid which he was coming to see as necessary.

[2] B.P. 49894–7, 'Land Reform', comprising 3 small exercise books and a print of 'Land, Land Reformers, and the Nation'. The date 17 Jan. 1885 may be found on p. 72 of the 3rd exercise book.
[3] Mansergh, *The Irish Question 1840–1921*, London, 3rd edn., 1975, p. 123.

Again, Salisbury appreciated Balfour's help in defeating Randolph Churchill's bid to control the Conservative party machine;[4] and by 16 June 1885 Balfour was acting for his uncle in negotiating the conditions under which Salisbury would head the caretaker administration of 24 June 1885 to 28 January 1886.[5] In June 1885 Balfour was also closely involved in the process of ministerial selection, though he does not seem to have been considered for a cabinet appointment himself. Salisbury wrote to him on the 26th:

My dear Arthur,
I entirely forgot to ask you tonight who I was to make Scotch Law Officers. Is Macdonald to be Lord Advocate—and who is to be Solicitor General?

Yours ever aff[y]
Salisbury[6]

Balfour became President of the Local Government Board (without a seat in the Cabinet) and he did a fair amount of work, between September and January, on preparing a County Councils bill—a forerunner of the important Act of 1888.[7] A letter written at the end of the caretaker government shows that Balfour had already enlisted that regard which he would receive from official staff throughout his long ministerial career. Sir John Lambert hoped (28 January 1886) that he would be able 'at no distant date' to complete 'that portion of the work' on the 'County Government Bill' assigned to him by Balfour. He wrote: 'I shall always retain a most grateful remembrance of your kindness and consideration.'[8]

On returning to office in July 1886, after the failure of Gladstone's first Home Rule Bill, Salisbury appointed Balfour as Secretary at the newly established Scottish Office. Through his cousin 'Jim' (Lord Cranborne) Balfour learned that his uncle thought of the post as one that could shortly be given cabinet rank.[9] Certainly Balfour's firm handling of the Scottish Land League—modelled on the formidable Irish Land League—allowed Salis-

---

[4] B.P. 49688, ff. 61–74, Salisbury to B. from 3 Apr. 1883 to 1 May 1884; *Autobiography*, pp. 156–72.

[5] WHI/64, B. to Gladstone, 16 June 1885 (draft on paper headed 4 Carlton Gardens).

[6] WHI/64, Salisbury to B., 26 June 1885. Enclosed is a provisional list of ministers, in Salisbury's hand, including 'I. O. Randolph' and 'L. G. B. Balfour'.

[7] WHI/35, 13 sheets in B.'s hand, including 'Resolutions' adopted by a committee consisting of Hicks Beach, Churchill, and B., 23 Oct. 1885. See also WHI/64, Francis Radcliffe to B., 30 Sept. 1885 and B.P. 49688, ff. 82–6, 12 Jan. 1886: B.'s proposal of compulsory purchase of land for allotments rejected by Salisbury.

[8] WHI/65.

[9] Dugdale, i, 108–9, Cranborne to B., 30 July 1886. However, the evidence of this letter alone suffices to cast doubt on the received interpretation (Ibid., pp. 88–9 and 107–8) that Salisbury 'thought rather poorly' of B.'s efforts at the Local Government Board. B.'s set-back

bury to tell the Cabinet on 17 November, without much fear of a charge of nepotism, that Balfour was to join that body.[10] Balfour's comment was very characteristic: 'I like it, but I am provoked with myself for not liking it more.'[11]

Meanwhile Salisbury's declared intention of bringing a period of firm government to Ireland was running into trouble. In October the Plan of Campaign renewed in subtler guise the war of attrition between Irish tenants and their landlords. By the device of demanding an abatement of rent and, on the landlord's refusal, paying him the rent minus the abatement—which latter sum went into a trust fund—the tenants gave their actions an appearance of legality. Having quarrelled over Irish local government with Sir Michael Hicks Beach (the Irish Secretary), Lord Randolph Churchill—disastrously for his own career—soon afterwards resigned his post as Chancellor of the Exchequer on another issue. The jubilant Irish Nationalists came back to Westminster in late January scenting governmental weakness; and they greeted proposals to strengthen the criminal law against the Plan of Campaign with seventeen nights of obstruction. Then, early in March, the often formidable Hicks Beach, afflicted with eye troubles, also had to resign. The Government seemed to be crumbling. Salisbury reiterated his view that the whole future of the Empire was at stake in the Irish struggle. On hearing that Balfour was to succeed him as Chief Secretary for Ireland, Hicks Beach feared that he too would collapse under the strain of what had become a fearsome office. However, on 5 March 1887 the physician Sir William Jenner pronounced the thirty-nine-year-old Balfour 'a sound man' and 'a first class life'.[12]

In 1898 Henry Lucy was favoured with a 'monologue' from an unnamed but 'eminent publicist' on the various contenders for leadership of their parties. From that chronological perspective, the speaker summarized in masterly fashion the 'romance' of Balfour's rise from parliamentary obscurity to his handling of his Irish challenge. Balfour, he said, was first noticed, but only just, 'as a sort of fragile ornamentation' of the Fourth Party, otherwise consisting of Churchill, John Gorst, and Drummond Wolff. 'They suffered him, liked him, but could very well do without him.' Omitting reference to Balfour's parliamentary performance as head of the Local Government Board, he continued:

over the Medical Relief Disqualification Removal Bill (to the meaning of which the word 'Removal' is, by the way, indispensable) could not have loomed large in his uncle's mind.
[10] B.P. 49688, ff. 129–31, Salisbury to B., 17 Nov. 1886; and see Dugdale, i, 107–18.
[11] WHI/65, B. to Lady Frances Balfour (copy), 17 Nov. 1886.
[12] Curtis, pp. 147–52, 161–71; WHI/66, Jenner to B., 5 Mar. 1887.

In his first Ministerial office as Secretary for Scotland, Balfour did not stir the pulses of the House. His chance came when illness drove Hicks Beach from the Irish Office, and a belated Premier was peremptorily called upon to find a successor. From the very first, Arthur Balfour set his back against the wall and let it be seen that if the Irish members wanted fight, here was a man who would give them plenty. From the time he went to the Irish Office up to the present day, he has, with occasional lapses due to physical lassitude and exhausted patience, steadily pressed forward. On the death of W. H. Smith [in 1891] he was the inevitable Leader of the House of Commons, and took his seat on the Treasury bench, with Randolph Churchill finally out of the running, John Gorst in subordinate office under him, Drummond Wolff comfortably shelved in Ambassadorial quarters. Thus shall the last be first, and the first last. [13]

However, Balfour was called upon to save the Union not only in Parliament but also, by dint of statesmanship, in Ireland. This aspect of his double-sided achievement has been so substantially covered by Professor Curtis that little more than a summary is needed here.

When Balfour was questioned, soon after taking up his office in March 1887, why he thought he would succeed where his predecessors as Chief Secretary had failed, he observed that Cromwell had miscarried in his day through relying on repression alone. While he (Balfour) would be 'as relentless as Cromwell in enforcing obedience to the law', he would be 'as radical as any reformer in redressing grievances', especially with regard to the land. [14] Captain Lord Charles Beresford, a popular naval hero and then an MP on the Board of Admiralty, is remembered as author of the appellation 'the Souls' for Balfour's aesthetically orientated country-house clique—at its zenith in 1887. Tickled by the incongruity of Balfour's Cromwellian stance, he hailed the Chief Secretary thus:

Dear Bloody Minded Cromwell,
    You are a 'Hare-ah' who is only happy when you are up to your knees in blood and whisky and you have only been known to smile when you see your victims writhing upon the gibbets . . . [15]

Balfour did not quite live up to 'Charlie's' colourful prognostication; but he did acquire the soubriquet of 'Bloody Balfour' and soon emptied his Irish opponents of any zest for hilarity at his expense. Deeming the Irish land campaigners and their British sympathizers as little better than rebels, he introduced a Criminal Law Amendment Bill in the Commons on 28 March

[13] Lucy, *Later Peeps at Parliament*, London, 1905, pp. 127–32.
[14] Bernard Alderson, *Arthur James Balfour: the Man and his Work*, London, 1903, p. 71.
[15] B.P. 49713, ff. 1–3, Beresford to B., 15 Apr. 1887.

and as soon as, by means of a strengthened closure rule, it had become law on 18 July, he set out for Dublin Castle to superintend its administration.[16]

Together with the Crimes Bill, Balfour had inherited from his predecessor a Land Bill. As with his later measures in education and the co-ordination of defence, he had come only reluctantly to accept the necessity of a constructive programme in Ireland.[17] In so far as he had acted as an intermediary between Salisbury and Joseph Chamberlain when the latter was breaking with the Liberal Party over Home Rule, and had established friendly relations with the great radical, the question arises: how far was it Chamberlain who persuaded Balfour to adopt constructive policies in Ireland? At bottom, the crucial influence on Balfour was always his uncle. Balfour shared Salisbury's conviction that the rift between Catholic and Protestant in Ireland was such that reconciliation could only be achieved within the framework of the United Kingdom; also that a bipartisan approach was probably needed for such a solution, but that this had been rendered unlikely by Gladstone's Home Rule pledge of 1886. Like Salisbury, he saw Home Rule as a doom-laden, politically unstable halfway house. It was a threat to the security of the United Kingdom and also to the fragile basis of imperial rule, especially in India. Therefore the best hope of a Unionist solution lay in measures designed to whittle away the sources of support for Home Rule in Ireland itself. While Balfour readily agreed with his uncle on restoration of respect for the law as a first priority, Salisbury had already approved conciliatory measures when in office in 1885—including Ashbourne's Land Purchase Act. Salisbury asserted, in a famous speech of May 1886, that it made good economic sense to encourage mass emigration from congested areas of Ireland to parts of the Empire where labour was needed.[18] Equally, however, he saw the need for more immediate action to reduce Irish grievances against bad landlords and, beyond that, to assist market forces to bring greater prosperity to Ireland. In all this, as well as in trying to preserve as much as possible of the landlords' position, Balfour acted according to his uncle's ideas rather than Chamberlain's. But in the interests of preserving the Unionist alliance he consulted Chamberlain a good deal and benefited from his advice on administrative detail, especially in 1887–8.[19]

On 31 March 1887, some hours before the Land Bill's introduction in the Lords, and some three months before it reached the Commons, Balfour sent

[16] Curtis, pp. 179–83.
[17] Hatfield House MSS, 3M/Class E, B. to Salisbury, 15 June 1886.
[18] Robert Taylor, pp. 104–5 and 117–21.
[19] Curtis, pp. 334–5, 358.

Chamberlain a lucid commentary on the divisive subject of judicial rents.
Here, Balfour and Salisbury aimed, unavailingly as it proved, to maintain
the post-1881 level of rents, despite the subsequent depression. In a
covering note Balfour hurriedly wrote: 'Can we meet anywhere after 2.30
and before the H of Lords assembles? My memo only relates to the broad
outlines of the scheme, the details and phraseology of which could be
modified to meet yr wishes.'[20] Indeed, the subject of the land inevitably put
a special strain on the alliance between the Conservatives and the Chamberlainite radicals. However, after Balfour and Salisbury had—to the dismay
of many Conservatives—conceded the need for revision of rents in line
with the fall in prices, the Bill at length became law on 18 August.[21]

Balfour had the necessary youth and toughness to triumph in the sphere of
the Crimes Act. He wasted little time in getting together a team of officials
and assistants on whom he could rely; and so consistent was he in the
backing which he gave them that the depleted morale of the whole law-
enforcing service was much invigorated. Key figures were Sir Joseph West
Ridgeway as Permanent Under-Secretary, Peter ('the Packer'—of juries)
O'Brien as a leading law officer (Irish Solicitor-General in 1887, Attorney-
General in 1888, and Lord Chief Justice in 1889–1914), and Edward
Carson as chief prosecutor. As Balfour remarked long afterwards to Mrs
Dugdale: 'I made Carson, and Carson made me.'[22] The youthful George
Wyndham, a member of Balfour's intimate circle for many years, acted as
Balfour's private secretary and made himself useful as his public relations
man until he himself became an MP in 1889.[23]

It was necessary not only to quell disorder, agrarian outrages, and
agitation but to defeat the subtler methods of the Plan of Campaign. From
1888, Balfour concentrated on a number of 'test estates'. This entailed
encouraging the landlords to combine in their turn to use the law and thus
defeat the Plan. By 1889, Balfour was beginning to win on this front as
well. Before he gave up his post in 1891, respect for the law had been
restored.[24]

On the conciliatory front, Balfour had meanwhile passed a Land Purchase Act in 1888 which in effect doubled the financial contribution of

[20] J.C.P. 5/5/1, B. to Chamberlain, 31 Mar. 1887. Although this is placed first in the file of
letters from B. to Chamberlain, there is one of earlier date at 5/5/4—of 25 Feb. 1887, from the
Scottish Office.
[21] Curtis, pp. 333–43.
[22] Dugdale, i, 147.
[23] For more about the officials and assistants see Curtis, pp. 186–98.
[24] Ibid., pp. 237–69.

government represented by the Ashbourne Act of 1885. At the same time Balfour was drafting bills for railway construction; and, when Railway Acts had been passed in 1889 and 1890, light railways were built in the poor and congested areas of the west and south. These railways did bring inland markets within the reach of fishermen; but they mainly amounted—as expected—to a fairly expensive way of providing paid work and thus relief.[25]

In 1891 Balfour passed what was intended to be a major Land Purchase Act which would go far towards creating a stable situation where both landowners and peasant proprietors would have a stake in the status quo. However, the measure was not very successful, partly because tenants were bewildered by its complexity and partly because landowners placed little faith on the future value of the land stock in which they would be paid.[26] Coupled with the Land Purchase Act was the establishment of a Congested Districts Board which provided a variety of palliatives and educative initiatives in parts of the west and south. Guided by ideas formulated by Chamberlain in 1888, the Board purchased and developed estates, and gave encouragement to scientific farming, fishing, spinning, and weaving, and helped to develop communications. In line with Salisbury's and Balfour's basic convictions, migration was assisted.[27]

These measures may have done no more than lubricate a general economic improvement due to natural causes, but nothing like them had been attempted by any previous British government, let alone a Conservative one. Although they agreed in dismissing panaceas and were motivated primarily by what they deemed a pressing political necessity, Salisbury and Balfour had certainly done something for Ireland. Neither had many illusions about the economic value of what had been done; but Balfour was here, as in the future, sustained by a degree of optimism which contrasted with his uncle's deep-rooted pessimism.

[25] Ibid., pp. 349–50, 365–7.
[26] Ibid., pp. 350–5.
[27] Ibid., pp. 355–62.

5

Leading in the Commons

1891−1902

WHEN Lady Frances Balfour came to write her memoirs in the late 1920s, she was firm in her opinion that her brother-in-law Arthur had always lacked political ambition. She held that the term implies 'one who will advance himself over others'; also that it 'is a word often used of one who feels his own power, while other men do not see it as clearly.' Further, she pungently observed: 'I think I should say about statesmen, that if they are not ambitious, they will not succeed.' Her account of Balfour's rise to a leading role in the Conservative Party is as follows:

> Arthur's opportunities were all made for him. He did not work or push or pull himself into the Irish Secretaryship. Once there, he proved what was in him because the situation demanded it. His next position was incidental on the first; had another [candidate] been obvious, he would not have intrigued to take his place . . . He was not the success as Leader that he had been as Irish Secretary, it needed qualities more commonplace than he possessed, but ambition had nothing to do with his life. What I should say of him and his family is this, they liked to excel and were slow to see when they had failed to do so. [1]

In so far as Lady Frances deems Balfour a failure as a leader, she clearly has an arguable case. Yet, during the period 1891 to 1902, when Salisbury remains the party leader and Balfour leads the Conservatives in the House of Commons, the latter's parliamentary performance does not consistently support her contention. However, on the fundamental point of Balfour's lack of ambition, she is surely correct. This absence of personal ambition is one important explanation of his acceptability, after 1911, as a ministerial colleague to such as Bonar Law, Asquith, Lloyd George, and Baldwin, when his own exceptional distinction might have marked him out as a potential rival. The same characteristic cannot be dissociated from his resignation as Unionist leader in 1911.

Must it, then, also be inferred that Balfour could not commit himself whole-heartedly to a cause? Indeed not. In a private conversation of July

---

[1] Lady Frances Balfour, i, 199.

1916, he confirmed that defence of the Union against the Home Rule threat had been the central purpose of his political life.[2] The continuance of this threat into the 1890s goes far to account for his acceptance of what was, for him, a tiresome burden—namely the leadership in the Commons. It will be seen that having accepted this role, however uncongenial, he felt it his duty not to permit himself to fail. As the Duke of Devonshire (the Lord Hartington of Ch. 2 above) accurately observed at the time of Balfour's selection, 'his only fault, if fault it can be called, is a sort of indolence and a strong contempt for popularity—but his sense of duty is strong enough to overcome all this.'[3]

From 1887 to 1891, Balfour had handled the Irish Nationalists in the Commons partly by speed and skill of riposte, partly by an air of unshakeable detachment. Indeed his acute sense of boredom with repetitive speechifying was entirely genuine. Thus his use, as Irish Secretary, of deflating tactics merely indulged a natural inclination. However, towards the end of his term in that office, he measured up better to the requirements of a Leader of the House by paying more attention to the parliamentary questions of the Irish and to his duties in the House.[4] But underneath, the impatience remained, as shown by a letter of 1890 written to Lady Elcho (formerly Mary Wyndham):

> I am not looking forward to North Berwick [and golf] quite so much as usual, partly because the people I want will not be there, partly because the people I do *not* want will. Among the latter class I emphatically rank . . . a Manchester M.P., whom you have the happiness not to know. He is a man with very large scientific and historical attainments, considerable political knowledge, and every qualification for being, at all events, an interesting companion. But he ruins everything by an intolerable mania for telling stories . . . usually old and always dull, with which he pursues his flying friends and which he pours in an unceasing stream into any ear that comes handy . . . I know with a certain prescience, that he will render life intolerable at N.B. . . . The Speaker [Arthur Peel] will be there . . . as I much like him and his daughter, I should not object to this, were it not that he reminds me too forcibly of the H. of Commons . . .[5]

Likewise, after becoming First Lord of the Treasury and Leader of the House in October 1891, he continued to complain about the tedium of Irish speeches and Commons routine—in which he was, of course, now expected

---

[2] Bodl., MS Eng. Hist., Sandars P., C.769, f. 181.
[3] Devonshire to Akers-Douglas, 14 Oct. 1891, cited in Peter Gordon, *The Victorian School Manager*, London, 1974, p. 207.
[4] *S.P.*, p. 425
[5] WHI/67, 22 Aug. 1890—a copy.

to play a central part. On 15 March 1892 he compensated for his imprison-
ment on the government front bench by writing to Lady Elcho:

> I am listening with one ear to the dreary rhetoric of one Pongo McNeil who is
> denouncing me for various offences committed when I was Chief Secretary. I have
> written as much as I can of my letter to the Queen; what better can I do than indite a
> short letter to you?
> I have little to say. Politics have been going on much as usual. I am being violently
> abused for quite a new set of crimes. It used to be bloodthirsty tyranny; it is now a
> variety of smaller offences for which doubtless I shall be more leniently punished in
> another world, but which appear to produce quite as much stir in the present one![6]

An impression of this 'new set of crimes' had been recorded elsewhere,
for example in Henry Lucy's parliamentary comment of 26 February 1892:

> For not quite three weeks [since the meeting of Parliament] has Mr. Balfour held
> the office of Leader of the House of Commons, and already he is aweary. The light
> is fading from his eye, the ready smile from his lips; his temper is growing short,
> and his face grey. It seemed bad enough whilst he was Chief Secretary with back to
> the wall fighting, often singlehanded, the then United Irish Party. Two conditions
> then existent are absent now, which sadly vary the situation. Then he was on the
> war-path, might deal blow for blow, meet concentrated attack by a brilliant foray
> into the enemy's country. Also he had behind him an enthusiastically admiring host
> of backers . . . every parrying stroke or skilful thrust was watched with keen delight
> and hailed with rousing cheers.
>   It is altogether different with the Leader of the House. Almost the last quality
> needed in him is that he should be a fighting man. This is illustrated in the case of
> Mr. W. H. Smith . . . [He] instinctively recognised that the Leader of the House of
> Commons is something more than the chief of a political party. Gentlemen grouped
> on the right hand of the Speaker are his particular flock; but the gentlemen opposite
> also form a component part of the House, and he is Leader of the House . . . when
> proposing or discussing business arrangements, or the provisions of a measure, he
> habitually ignored the existence of his own side, addressing himself exclusively
> with painstaking courtesy and subtly winning deference to gentlemen opposite.
>   This habit, natural to a kindly, peaceable, unaggressive nature, worked wonders
> upon the Opposition . . . For the despatch of business, dependent as it is upon the
> equable temperament of the House, Mr. Smith as Leader was worth more to the
> Conservative Party than an addition of twenty votes on any one of their recorded
> majorities.
>   It is impossible to conceive two men more antipathetic than Mr. W. H. Smith and
> Mr. Arthur Balfour. Where in given circumstances one succeeded, the other might
> be counted on as sure to fail.

[6] WHI/68.

Thus the House, 'grown accustomed to Mr. Smith's gentle sway', was 'startled into an attitude of censoriousness' by the magnitude of the change. Moreover, the attacks of the Irish on Balfour did not decrease on account of his promotion. What did evaporate was the counter-cheering of the members seated behind him. Their former enthusiasm for him was 'chilled' by the manner in which he performed his new role.[7]

Indeed, after a lapse of two years, Lucy was to remark:

There was a time early in his new career when Mr. Balfour shared the doubts of his best friends as to whether he was exactly fitted for the post to which the dilemma of his party had called him. Its trammels irritated him, and, above all, the duty of remaining in his place hour after hour through dull nights bored him. He came late, went away early, and when there were signs of restlessness among his following he intimated that, if they did not like it, he would gladly leave them.[8]

Balfour certainly had no qualms, after the General Election of July 1892, at the prospect of losing office. When Parliament met in August, Kate Courtney (sister of Beatrice Webb and wife of the uncompromising Liberal Unionist MP Leonard Courtney) noticed 'Mr. Balfour beaming like a boy about to have a long-deferred holiday';[9] and it was more generally observed that Balfour had been 'in the merriest humour since the fall of his Government was decreed at the poll'.[10]

Had Balfour not improved as leader of his party in the Commons, he could hardly have been seen as his uncle's prospective successor. On the party's eventual return to power, he might have been offered a departmental post. The party was not overloaded with ministerial talent. In that event, he might have made a further useful, if essentially subordinate, contribution in a departmental capacity, rather as he was to do, though with more renown, after May 1915. More probably, he might have retired from politics altogether, and devoted his time to conversation, house parties, music, golf, tennis, and some further writing on philosophy. This, however, was not the outcome.

Certainly, Balfour found it more congenial to lead the Opposition in the Commons than to lead the House. This was especially so in a parliament which Gladstone consecrated to the passing of Home Rule for Ireland. Meanwhile however, a possible, if still somewhat alien, rival for the leadership of the anti-government forces in the House was making himself felt. This was Joseph Chamberlain. In the parliament of 1886 to 1892, he

---

[7] *S.P.*, pp. 455–9 (26 Feb. 1892).
[8] *H.R.P.*, p. 348 (20 Apr. 1894).
[9] G. P. Gooch, *The Life of Lord Courtney*, London, 1920, p. 296.
[10] *H.R.P.*, p. 12 (9 Aug. 1892).

had, despite his vehement opposition to Home Rule, continued to occupy a seat on the Liberal front bench in Gladstone's immediate vicinity. Indeed, this proximity had caused Gladstone—for instance in 1892—to turn his back on the Speaker in order to administer vigorous verbal castigation to the redoubtable opponent seated on his immediate left, while 'good Conservatives on the benches opposite rolled about in their seats with uncontrollable laughter'. Meantime Balfour, as Leader of the House and Chamberlain's ally, sat with bent head and tried to conceal 'a certain twitching at the corners of his mouth'. [11] At the beginning of the 'Home Rule Parliament' of 1892 to 1895, Chamberlain moved from Gladstone's immediate scrutiny to a seat on the Liberal front bench below the gangway. Thus he and his personal followers did not formally associate themselves with the main body of Unionists until 1895.

As one would expect, Balfour made a good showing, at least at times, during the progress of the Home Rule Bill through the Commons in 1893. This was especially so when he spoke against the Bill on its second reading in April. Lucy's account of the evening of 22 April shows how Balfour, who rarely excelled at set speeches, reacted brilliantly in a parliamentary fracas, with the Union at stake:

> Like Mr. Gladstone, Mr. Balfour greatly profited by the circumscribed space [of time] within which he was obliged to talk. It was a quarter past ten when he rose, and it had been made known to him through the usual channels that Mr. Gladstone was disposed to speak about eleven. In any case it was desirable, in view of the hospital of invalids and convalescents gathered for the great division that the end should not be postponed beyond half past twelve. Thus there was no time for exordium or excursion into ancient history. Any hitting to be accomplished was to be done by blows delivered straight from the shoulder. The condition exactly suited Mr. Balfour's disposition and habits . . .
> The scene was one calculated to draw forth the fullest powers of a capable man. The House was filled on every bench. From the side gallery facing him two unbroken lines of members looked down eagerly attentive. The Prince of Wales sat over the clock, a closely packed peerage on the left, and a gallery crowded with distinguished strangers on the right. Behind the . . . Prince rose tier on tier the strangers who had the good fortune to obtain admission. They had been in their places all the evening; had slept awhile, soothed by Sir Henry James's monotone . . . Now the Leader of the Opposition was up business had begun, and the erewhile jaded mass of humanity piled up to the topmost range of the gallery visibly brightened.
> Mr. Balfour had accumulated voluminous notes, and from time to time referred to them. But it was obvious that he discarded whole sheets, the course of his speech

[11]   *S.P.*, p. 482.

being, in truth, frequently marked out for him by interruption from his old adversaries below the gangway, where though Ministries come and go the Irish camp remains. These he answered with brilliant effect, not once losing command of himself or his audience, cheers and counter-cheers ringing with sharp rattle as one or the other of the well-matched adversaries made a palpable hit.

Gladstone, in reply, rose to his usual high level of argument and eloquence, denying that the Conservatives had found the key to the government of Ireland. Shortly after midnight, 'he finished almost as fresh as he had commenced, and when the Speaker put the question involving the rejection of Sir Michael Hicks Beach's hostile amendment, his shout of "No!" rose in full-chested note above the roar of his followers.'

As Gladstone returned to the House after the division 'with head erect and springy step', his supporters 'with one accord sprang to their feet, waved their hats, and frantically cheered'. As they stood acclaiming the result, the Chamberlainites beside them remained stubbornly in their seats. The second reading had been carried by 347 to 304. It was a crowning triumph for the venerable Gladstone. Yet it was also a pyrrhic victory for him, for the Liberal Party, and for the Irish Nationalists. The Bill faced massive rejection by the Lords, secure in the general support of British opinion. It remained for Balfour, on the formation of a Unionist government in 1895, to oversee the continuation of Balfourian policies in Ireland. [12]

But Balfour's spirited showing in this principal debate on the Home Rule Bill did not mark his firm establishment as a leader. For instance in May 1893, while the Bill was being gradually forced through committee by diligent use of the closure, Chamberlain—though still not formally allied with the Conservatives—was beginning to overshadow Balfour.

Anyone [noted Lucy] who closely watches the course of events in Committee knows that the real Leader of the Opposition, the life and soul of obstruction, is Mr. Chamberlain. It is he that sets the battle in array . . . The rank and file are already tired of a business that interferes with their social arrangements . . . The House of Lords, they say, is sure to throw out the Bill. Why should they toil . . .?

Mr. Balfour shows by his languid manner and his hurried speech that he is sick of the whole business. But needs must when Mr. Chamberlain drives. He sits there in constant attendance, relentless, implacable, resolved at any cost to baulk Mr. Gladstone's desire . . . [13]

As long as the Committee stage lasted, 'Conservatives observed with chagrin, not always successfully hidden, that their titular leader was

---

[12] *H.R.P.*, pp. 111–14 (22 Apr. 1893).
[13] Ibid., p. 143 (20 May 1893).

disposed to play second fiddle' to one whom they admired as a potent ally, but did not love. Yet when in August the Bill at last reached the report stage, the House was treated to a display of Balfour's capacity for effortless predominance. On another subject, too, at about this time he produced 'a masterpiece of effective attack masked under light raillery'; and again, thrusting at Gladstone's 'proposal on the question of single-member constituencies, he comported himself in a manner that delighted his supporters'. [14]

By December 1893, the diarist is describing a Balfour more amiable and familiar than the openly bored but spasmodically active fighting man who has figured in his accounts:

The House of Commons has through the week been deprived of the presence of Mr. Arthur Balfour, and the Opposition have been the poorer for lack of his counsel. The occasion, which all regret, is useful in showing how large is the place the still young Leader fills in the historic assembly. If only he were there to be gazed upon, it would be something gained. His graceful presence, bright looks, pleasant voice and ready smile, are something to be thankful for amid the arid pleasures of the Parish Councils Bill . . . Mr. Balfour is, according to the almanack, four years older than Mr. Asquith. In manner the Home Secretary is at least forty years older than the Leader of the Opposition . . . His humour, even in lightest moments, is perhaps a little grm . . . Mr. Arthur Balfour, on the contrary, ever bubbles over with lighthearted humour, a sunny nature breaking through all the clouds that cares of State may bring. This natural gift is one of inestimable value to a Leader in the House of Commons. [15]

While Balfour could not equal Gladstone's double-sided excellence in the delivery of set speeches and also in debate, he rose to the challenge presented by the retirement from the House of Commons of the Grand Old Man himself. Debating on the Address in March 1894, Balfour 'charmed the crowded House' in lamenting 'the withdrawal from the scene of the great example of all that was most splendid and most vivid in its proceedings'. [16] A week later, Lucy was able to record:

Mr. Arthur Balfour has now finally settled in the saddle of Leader of the Opposition, and rides well. There was a time when it seemed as if he were loath to stay, finding the drudgery of leadership uncongenial. He came late, went away early, and when he took part in debate displayed an air of aloofness and indifference

[14] Ibid., p. 213 (11 Aug. 1893).
[15] Ibid., pp. 284–5 (1 Dec. 1893).
[16] Ibid., pp. 317–18 (12 March 1894).

that was very curious. That is all changed now. He sticks to his post, and is always on the alert for conducting operations against the enemy.[17]

Already since the opening of the session Balfour had delivered three successful speeches, starting with the one on Gladstone. The third had found him placed in an awkward position by a motion of the ailing Randolph Churchill aimed at Rosebery. Balfour could not support the motion and yet he 'would not throw over a friend. He managed to dance among the eggs with a vigorous grace that delighted the House.'[18]

During Balfour's earlier days of half-heartedness as a leader, Joseph Chamberlain was not the only rival in the wings. Randolph Churchill had then reappeared in the House, apparently restored to good health, and 'wistful eyes were turned towards him' as 'good Conservatives thought of what might have been'. By 1894, Churchill's malady had taken decisive toll. Balfour, however, was far from deriving secret satisfaction from the elimination of a possible rival—the erstwhile meteor of the Fourth Party and the favourite of the Strangers' Gallery. As he had confided a few years earlier to Lady Elcho, he found it 'very painful' when his friends made 'fools of themselves' in Parliament;[19] and when, on 20 April 1894, Churchill delivered one of his last and barely comprehensible speeches, Balfour offered a spectacle relevant to any assessment of his capacity for feeling:

Since the day when Job sat himself down amid the dust of the land of Uz and covered his head with ashes the world has not seen so anguished a figure as Mr. Arthur Balfour presented to the view of the House of Commons tonight whilst Lord Randolph Churchill was championing the claims of the Duke of Coburg. With head bent to the level of his knees, both hands tightly clasped around the back of his neck, he sat abashed, abased, as if desirous of shutting out all sights and sounds. This extraordinary evidence of physical and mental suffering presented to the gaze of a perplexed Gallery certainly could not have arisen from considerations of his own unworthiness, or of any untoward event following upon his personal action. Also like Job, Mr. Balfour is 'a man perfect and upright, one that fears God and eschews evil.'

But constrained to witness Churchill's plight, Balfour could scarcely fail to remember how for five years his former leader, 'with a numerically insignificant party, had daily striven with the greatest Parliamentarian of the age, at the head of an overwhelming majority'; how, 'distrusted by his

[17] Ibid., p. 327 (20 Mar. 1894).
[18] Ibid., p. 327 (19 March 1894).
[19] WHI/69, 14 Mar. 1893.

own leaders', Churchill had 'pegged away till the stately structure of Mr. Gladstone's second Administration, riddled through and through, toppled into the dust'. Lord Randolph had reached (wrote Lucy) 'the highest pinnacle to which sheer merit can lift a man'; and Balfour had been content to act as a humble 'supernumerary'. Although Churchill had, in 1892, seemed fit and well on his return to the House, he had noticeably refrained from attacking Balfour and making a bid for the leadership. Whatever his actual thoughts may have been on that sad occasion, Balfour's suffering on Churchill's account was manifest. As Lucy noted in December, after Lord Randolph's death, 'those who were present' on 20 April would 'never forget the scene.' [20]

On Gladstone's retirement, the brilliant but erratic and unpredictable Earl of Rosebery had become Prime Minister. Against a background of dissension within the Liberal Party, not least on the policy of Home Rule, the Government fell in June 1895 on a vote of censure aimed at insufficiency of cordite for the Army; or, rather, the Cabinet jumped at the opportunity to resign.

For a third time, Lord Salisbury took office. Balfour again became First Lord of the Treasury and Leader of the House of Commons. Salisbury assumed that, after the ensuing General Election, he would have to depend for a majority on the Liberal Unionists. Devonshire, having refused the Foreign Office, Salisbury's normal preserve, accepted the post of Lord President of the Council. But the key Liberal Unionist to satisfy was obviously Chamberlain. He astonished Balfour and the Prime Minister by opting for the Colonial Office. The implications of this arrangement will be noted in due course. Meantime, it remains to chart Balfour's further progress as Leader of the House, for on this depended the whole of his subsequent career.

Ian Malcolm (who later married the daughter of Lillie Langtry and was thus the father of Mary Malcolm, the television newsreader of the 1950s, and who himself assisted Balfour in secretarial roles between 1917 and 1919) entered Parliament as a Conservative in 1895 and has left an account of Balfour's performance in the later 1890s. Like Randolph Churchill at his zenith, Balfour was able to 'show the field good sport'; and indeed, from 1895 to 1900, 'sport was frequent and good'. Admittedly, the Opposition were weak, now that Gladstone had passed from the scene. 'Sir William Harcourt was too unwieldy and of too uncertain a temper to be really formidable; Mr. John Morley, with the stern grey banner of the doctrinaire,

---

[20] *H.R.P.*, pp. 347–9 (20 Apr. 1894), 418 ('Christmas Eve', 1894); Lucy, *Peeps at Parliament*, London, 1903, p. 65.

could count on but little support; Sir Charles Dilke, a man of encyclopaedic knowledge, was too omniscient to be popular.' Lloyd George had not fully emerged. Yet, according to Malcolm, even Harcourt, Morley, Fowler, and Grey, were more effective in prepared statement than Balfour. On such occasions, Balfour's delivery was halting and tiresome—even to the speaker himself. He showed every sign of inadequate preparation, inaccurately substituting thousands for millions, and generally demonstrating statistical incompetence. When his errors were pointed out, he would calmly respond that they did not affect his argument. But then he would totally redeem himself by 'the grace and lightning rapidity of his thrust and parry in debate', or by his skill in suddenly changing 'the whole disposition of his argument' and travelling across 'a quite unexpected line of country, knowing that the enemy guns had been carefully trained and manned to meet a more usual avenue of attack'.[21]

This sketch is corroborated by Lucy. But what emerges from the latter's day-by-day commentary is that, having successfully adjusted to the role of an opposition leader, Balfour had to undergo yet another course in self-discipline, now that he had been duly reinstated as Leader of the whole House. After reaching the stage, by December 1894, of having 'the Premiership in certain view',[22] in less than a year after the meeting of the 1895 parliament Balfour was once again reckoned to be 'a failure as Leader of the House of Commons'. This fall in repute was partly due to unimpressive handling of an education bill which was the Government's principal measure of the session but had to be dropped after much expenditure of parliamentary time. Of this, more will be said in the next chapter. Again in the case of an Irish land bill, 'curiously analogous tactics were observed', in that Balfour seemed abruptly to change tack during the committee stage to the confusion of his followers and the irritation of the House in general. There was an impression of muddle, due to lack of thorough preparation of the bills. At a deeper level, as in 1892, the explanation lay in Balfour's personal characteristics:

This is certainly not due to lack of capacity for the high position. The secret of his failure Mr. Balfour with characteristic fearlessness wears on his sleeve. He has every quality of genius save the one which high authority has extolled as being genius itself. He has not the disposition to take pains . . . It was, probably no punishment for Mr. Smith to sit hour after hour, through night after night of a long Session, listening to the heavy monotonous flow of talk, only here and there glistening with the sheen of fancy, or rippled by a stroke of humour. To a man of

[21] Sir Ian Malcolm, *Lord Balfour: a Memory*, London, 1930, pp. 22–4.
[22] *H.R.P.*, p. 418 ('Christmas Eve', 1894).

Mr. Balfour's intellectual impatience and keenly cultured taste such an experience must be torture. Yet, if the House of Commons is to be successfully led, it must be endured . . .

As in 1892, Balfour could not endure the tedium of question time. He stayed out of the chamber until the questions specifically addressed to him were reached.

That [commented the diarist] would be well enough in the case of any other Minister concerned only for the business of his own department. But the question hour, touching on all subjects under the sun, is a microcosm of the sitting . . . The offence of absence at this particular stage might be condoned were Mr. Balfour accustomed to remain on the Treasury Bench when at length he reached it. But after Charles Lamb's manner at the India Office, he makes up for coming late by going away early . . . Of late, more especially in connection with the Irish Land Bill, Mr. Balfour has seemed to recognise this truth. His attendance on the dull procedure of an ordinary sitting has been almost heroic in its constancy. Every other quality that goes to make a successful Leader he possesses in the highest form. Only is needed the long-suffering patience that enables a quick-witted man to sit through eight hours' average talk in the House of Commons.[23]

It is the story of the next few years that, however painfully and reluctantly, Balfour adjusted himself to his role.[24] Joseph Chamberlain, in official coalition with the Conservatives after 1895—though a separate Liberal Unionist organization persisted till 1911—always looked, at least superficially, like a possible rival for the succession to Salisbury. But in fact, most Conservatives placed great value on Balfour precisely because he stood between 'Joe' and the leadership of the conjoint parties. In this blocking role, Sir Michael Hicks Beach was regarded as a useful reserve, in case Balfour dropped out of the picture.[25]

As far as the management of the House of Commons was concerned, Balfour succeeded in reforming the rules for dealing with Supply. Jack Sandars, Balfour's political private secretary from 1892, considered in retrospect that this was a 'great reform' for which Balfour had received inadequate recognition. Under the previous system, the Opposition had been able to spend much time discussing minor aspects of the Finance Bill, thus shutting out other prospective government measures, and prolonging the parliamentary session till as late as the end of September. Moreover, important provisions of the Finance Bill itself were often not discussed at all. Sandars wrote that, dull as the subject was, Balfour 'set to work to

---

[23]   *U.P.*, pp. 100–4 (31 July 1896).
[24]   Ibid., p. 352 (4 May 1900).
[25]   Lucy, *Later Peeps*, pp. 127–33 (Feb. 1898).

master it' and that he convinced the House of the 'propriety of his reform, ultimately overcoming the first resistance of old pundits like Harcourt and Fowler'. Where votes had not been passed by August, the closure would operate. Sir Reginald Palgrave, for long the Chief Clerk of the House, told Sandars of 'his profound admiration' of Balfour's explanatory speech, 'not only in respect of detail, but also the interest with which he had clothed an unattractive subject'. At the material time, the improvement in the efficiency of Parliament was appreciated by Henry Lucy. By February 1900 he was noting that, three years after the reform:

Mr. Arthur Balfour is, with lessening vehemence, accused of burking debate because he strictly limits to something over a score the number of nights allotted to discussion in the Committee of Supply. Everyone who pays close attention to the business of the House knows that since that rule was established, with its condition of giving one night a week to Committee from the beginning of the Session, Supply is more fully and intelligently discussed than at any period within the memory of the oldest member. [26]

Landmarks in Balfour's advance were provided by his formal speeches on the death of Gladstone in 1898 and on the demise of Queen Victoria in January 1901. These occasions did not suit Balfour's normal parliamentary style, but he negotiated them with credit. Of the speech on Gladstone, the diarist observes: 'Death is, after all, so monotonous that eulogists must repeat themselves'; yet

Mr. Balfour succeeded in imparting some felicitous new turns into his monody. Particularly beautiful was the passage wherein he lamented the hopelessness of attempts to reconstruct from ordinary records living likenesses of Mr. Gladstone's greatest parliamentary triumphs.
'The words, indeed,' he said, 'are there, lying side by side with the words of lesser men, in an equality as of death. But the spirit, the fire, the inspiration are gone. He who alone could revive them has now, alas, been taken away.' [27]

Insight into Balfour's mode of preparation for such ceremonious events is available for his speech on the death of Queen Victoria. This comes from Sydney Parry who was Balfour's second official private secretary from 1897 to 1904. It should doubtless be explained that, as First Lord of the Treasury, Balfour was entitled to nominate one private secretary from outside the civil service. Jack Sandars—'ablest and most devoted of public servants, and the most delightful of colleagues' who lived 'solely and wholly for our chief', according to Parry—had left the civil service in 1892

[26]   Sandars P., C.771, ff. 326–7; Lucy, *Later Peeps*, pp. 24–5, 161–2, 317–18.
[27]   *U.P.*, p. 225 (20 May 1898).

and had served Balfour as a secretary when he was in opposition. He resumed work as Balfour's nominated private secretary in 1895. After Balfour resigned as Prime Minister in 1905, Sandars continued to act as a sort of chief-of-staff until 1911 and remained in touch on a friendly basis for a further four years. Parry, on the other hand, spent his working life as a civil servant and 'dealt with departmental matters', while Sandars was concerned with 'the more distinctively political work'. This is Parry's note on Balfour's oration of 25 January 1901:

To him [the Queen's] death came as a personal blow, and the thought of having to move the necessary Address in the House of Commons lay heavy on his mind. After the manner of private secretaries I had hunted up the materials for his speech, and produced a list of epoch-making changes and discoveries that had marked that long reign. But he gave it back to me. 'No,' he said. 'That won't do. I want to speak of her personality, and you can't help me there.' When the House met, he delivered one of the most charming and touching funeral orations on record . . . No one who heard that speech could have thought him hard or unemotional. Such occasions were, however, quite exceptional, and in the ordinary ebb and flow of office life the dominant feature was A.J.'s serenity and quiet strength . . . He never fussed or wasted time, never hesitated to take responsibility, and never troubled about attacks in the House or the press . . . I seldom saw him consult a newspaper, and then never for mere relaxation. He had an invaluable power (acquired, I think, rather than innate) of deliberately clearing his mind of worries . . .[28]

In his full account of the proceedings, Lucy thought that Balfour's speech on the Queen 'came off' better than Salisbury's in the Lords. On the opposition side of the Lords, nobody 'expected Lord Kimberley to shine, hence there was no disappointment' at his pedestrian effort.

In the House of Commons Mr. Balfour struck a loftier note . . . He was profoundly moved. It seemed at first he would have difficulty in finding words . . . They came in slow sequence, the very hesitancy adding to the effect. His speech had the simplicity of Lord Kimberley's, but of quite another kind. In exquisite sentences he pictured the end [to which he had been personally summoned].
'She passed away with her children and her children's children to the third generation around her, beloved and cherished of all. She passed away without, I well believe, a single enemy in the world. Even those who loved not England loved

[28] WHI/81, 'Memories', pp. 22–4. There is an interesting note about Parry, written by Sandars to B. on 5 Jan. 1904 to recommend him (successfully) for a high post with the Board of Customs. 'Parry would like it, but he is far too modest to ask. You know my very high regard for his energy and abilities . . . May I add that he has very strong claims on you? He succeeded here to most hopeless chaos. He spent laborious months in getting the place in order.' (B.P. 49762, ff. 3–4). Parry's predecessor was Bernard Mallet (K.C.B., 1916), author of that enduring stand-by *British Budgets* (1887–1933).

her. She passed away not only knowing that she was, I had almost said, worshipped and reverenced by all her subjects, but that their feelings towards her had grown in depth and intensity with every year she was spared to rule over us.'[29]

In sum, despite his natural aversion to important aspects of his role, Balfour became by 1902 a considerable success as Leader of the House of Commons. By dint of a particular parliamentary effort, lasting for seven months and spanning the end of Salisbury's premiership and his own succession, Balfour saw the major Education Bill—of which more in the next chapter—through to its final division in the Commons. Already, on 14 July 1902, when he had for the first time entered the chamber as Prime Minister, he had been embarrassed by 'a ringing cheer from the Ministerial side'. Yet so much was doubtless to be expected. But soon after came an unconventional interruption from Campbell-Bannerman, Leader of the Opposition since 1899, who warmly congratulated Balfour on the honour done him.

The absence of premeditation, the informality, amounting to a breach of order, added considerably to the effect created. The demonstration was primarily due to the personal popularity of Lord Salisbury's successor. Undoubtedly it gained access of warmth from consideration of the fact that once again the First Minister of the Crown is seated in the House of Commons.[30]

Balfour may be said to have reached the zenith of his parliamentary career on 3 December 1902 when the final vote had been taken on the Education Bill which had met prolonged opposition. Lucy's assessment was as follows:

The spontaneous cheer that at midnight greeted Mr. Balfour as he returned from the division lobby after the last division on the Education Bill testifies to one patent result of the long and dreary fight. It has established the Premier's personal supremacy, and seated him firmly in the saddle as Leader of the House. Close attendance on this measure through a period of seven months is a big price to pay by a man of Mr. Balfour's temperament. The sacrifice has gained a priceless prize. To those long acquainted with his mercurial temperament, his constitutional aversion to drudgery round details, his management of the Education Bill has been a marvel. Only those who have actually suffered know what it is to sit hour after hour in Committee, keeping a more or less firm grasp on the position as it develops itself. For the man personally in charge of the bill, bound to follow the utterances of the most inconsiderable member, liable to be called upon at any moment to take an important decision, or make a speech on a critical issue, the strain has been superlatively great.

[29] Lucy, *Balfourian Parliament*, London, 1906, pp. 24–5 (25 Jan. 1901).
[30] Ibid., pp. 188–9 (14 July 1902).

Mr. Balfour has borne it with a courage, a good humour and a never-failing courtesy that have strengthened his hold on the confidence, esteem, almost affection of the House, tightening through the last few years. That this feeling is not confined to the Ministerial ranks was shown tonight, members below the gangway on the Opposition side, who have been foremost and fiercest in the long fight, heartily joining in the personal tribute. [31]

Such then, from a parliamentary viewpoint, was the manner in which Balfour advanced to the premiership. It now remains to re-examine the years 1891 to 1902 for signs of his development, after his Irish achievements, in the role of constructive statesman.

[31]   Ibid., p. 210 (3 Dec. 1902).

6

Constructive Statesman?

1891–1902

BALFOUR has quite often been credited with constructive instincts as a politician. However, it has been seen that, as Irish Secretary, he produced a constructive programme only in response to a great political emergency. So, before any attempt is made to assess his constructive intention and achievement in the years 1891 to 1902, it will be useful to identify some of the main problems facing Britain at that time and to consider, however briefly, the remedies (if any) which seem in historical perspective to have been required.

The most important long-term problem demanding the attention of British statesmen was that of industrial efficiency. On this depended the country's ability to deal with most of the other problems of the day. No less did Britain's future throughout the twentieth century depend on it. Industrial efficiency was, of course, relative to that of other countries. In the naval sphere, the mounting challenge from nations industrializing later than Britain had already made itself felt. Politicians could hardly escape knowing that in 1884 and again in 1889 the Exchequer had been compelled to find money to maintain British naval strength against the challenges of France and Russia. In 1896 an alarm was raised, this time in the commercial sphere, by E. E. Williams in his book *Made in Germany*. Before 1900, the Germans had manifestly surpassed the British in several fields, not only in sheer production but also in techniques. This was true of metal and mining technology; also, crucially, of electrical engineering which was a great and growing industry. In chemicals, the position was similar. The relatively few British chemists then existing had, in many cases, sought their training in Germany for lack of equivalent facilities in British schools or universities.[1]

Widespread interest in the possibility of social reform—centring on housing, destitution, low wages, pensions, working hours—also dated

---

[1] See, for example, Peter Mathias, *The First Industrial Nation*, Oxford, 1969, pp. 421–6. This statement seems, in the early 1980s, even more dramatically relevant to current ills than it did when published.

from the mid-1880s. Its impact has been registered in excerpts from Balfour's paper of 1885 on land reform. (See p.32 above.) Again, it is clear that this second problem area could have been more effectively managed if the basic problem of relative industrial efficiency had been successfully tackled at the same time, or, indeed, tackled first.

By way of remedies, one possible course of government action was familiar to British statesmen. From 1858 onwards, Parliament had passed legislation to permit British colonies of white settlement to impose tariffs on imported goods. These colonies had at first used such tariffs simply to raise revenue; but the key to Britain's problem of the 1890s was signposted by the colonies' more recent imposition of tariffs to protect their infant industries. As will be seen below, British statesmen, by no means excluding Balfour, would, after the Boer War, become embroiled in the controversies arising from Joseph Chamberlain's schemes for 'Tariff Reform'. However, the fostering kind of tariff—shielding new rather than dying industries—which conferred benefit on other countries, received no particular attention in Britain. [2]

Quite apart, however, from the question of Britain's possible adoption of a tariff scheme, there was an obvious remedy to hand which might have eased the fundamental industrial problem. This lay in recognizing that education had an indispensable modernizing role, and in substituting an appropriate system of state education for the existing provision which was utterly inadequate in extent and chaotic in its organizational structure. As educationists had often remarked, much more attention to technical and commercial education was urgently required. However, while it was widely appreciated in the 1890s that British provision was insufficient compared with that of Germany and many other countries, the subject was a hot potato politically. From the beginning of state elementary education in 1870, sectarianism had obscured the cardinal issue of industrial efficiency. Anglicans were allied with the Conservative Party and Nonconformists provided a vital element of electoral support for the Liberals. The Liberal Unionists, not least the Chamberlains, often depended on Nonconformists to retain their parliamentary seats. Once the Unionist coalition had been formed in 1895, it was a ticklish matter to persuade the Chamberlainites to agree to increased financial provision, especially by way of local rates, to lift standards in the often inferior Anglican schools, which catered for about half the children in English and Welsh elementary schools. The Anglicans, on the other hand, would not accept absorption into the existing

[2] See, for instance, Peter Cain in Alan O'Day (ed.), *The Edwardian Age 1900–14*, London, 1979, p. 49, etc.

undenominational system run by the School Boards. As for the Liberal Party, it could accept no other solution.

On secondary education there was something of a consensus, buttressed by the finding of royal commissions, that a state system should be brought into being. But retrospectively it seems that a most damaging anti-industrial attitude was gaining ground in the upper reaches of society. In the last analysis, it was this tendency which determined the form assumed by the emergent national system of education and, through much of the twentieth century, steered too much of the country's highest talent away from industrial management and technology.[3]

A further range of problems was represented by foreign and imperial affairs. As already implied, the British colonies of white settlement were becoming more protectionist at a time when British industry was having greater difficulty in selling its wares abroad. Since the 1880s, the major powers of continental Europe had both erected tariff protection against imports (from which the British suffered) and extended such protection to their colonial empires. Thus the market available to British exporters, who were in any case suffering from falling relative efficiency, was noticeably restricted. Obsolescence of plant in older industries like iron and steel, shipbuilding, and some of the textile industry underlay some of the growing competitive weakness. But if new domestic industries had been rising to take the place of the old, then the question of imperial co-operation and control would have seemed less crucial. On the side of defence against possible foreign aggressors—notably France and Russia in the 1890s—improved industrial and commercial efficiency would yet again have provided the best long-term answer. But if no effective action was taken in this area, foreign and imperial difficulties were bound to become increasingly unmanageable by British statecraft.

It goes without saying that, placed against such a scheme of retrospective assessment, all British statesmen of the period under consideration must be deemed to have failed! But the greatness of a statesman is relative. If Balfour failed, was his failure more or less comprehensive than that of other politicians of the day?

In the 1890s, there were not many politicians in the ministerial category who believed that they should be making far-reaching constructive plans for Britain's future. Joseph Chamberlain was the greatest exception. He had already proposed a programme of social reform in 1884–5. However, even

---

[3] See Martin J. Wiener, *English Culture and the Decline of the Industrial Spirit 1850–1980*, Cambridge, 1981.

if it had been adopted, it would have done little to reduce such blots on the social landscape as bad housing and destitution. In any case, as far as the Liberals were concerned, Gladstone never modified his passionate opposition to 'construction' and his party remained possibly more doctrinaire in its dislike of government intervention than the Conservatives. Certainly, in the Irish sphere, at least, the Conservatives continued to intervene with improved productivity as one of their objectives. But Salisbury remained thoroughly pessimistic about the likelihood of such action doing much to improve the lot of man; and Balfour, though more optimistic, regarded radical action as a gamble to be taken only *in extremis*. Balfour continued, much as in the '80s, to pay frequent visits to Hatfield and Arlington Street where politics were endlessly discussed;[4] and the 'undivided counsel that nephew and uncle had from the earliest years' persisted.[5] There survives in Balfour's hand a draft of an essay or speech, date-stamped 18 November 1891 and labelled 10 Downing Street, which echoes Salisbury's philosophy of government:

> . . . If the business of such a government [based on public opinion] was to deal with the essential framework of society as an engineer deals with the wood and iron out of which he constructs a bridge, it would be as idiotic to govern by household suffrage as to make the Forth Bridge by household suffrage. Indeed it would be much more idiotic, because as we have seen sociology is far more difficult than engineering . . . We habitually talk as if a self-governing or free community was one which manages its own affairs, or by any possibility could manage them. It manages only a narrow fringe of its affairs, and that in the main by delegation. In healthy societies it is only the thinnest surface layer of law and custom, belief and sentiment, which is subjected to destructive treatment, or is deliberately made the nucleus of new growth . . .[6]

In the case of Ireland, however, it was still agreed by uncle and nephew that a radical approach was necessary and Balfour was closely associated with the constructive policies followed there until the culminating Land Act of 1903. He continued to see Home Rule as the most obvious threat to Britain's empire and her role in world affairs. But a letter which he wrote from 10 Downing Street to Chamberlain on 27 November 1895 defines his attitude to similar intervention by government in Great Britain:

> It is impossible to doubt that, under existing economic conditions and with the example of Ireland fully in view, the pressure for Government assistance to public

4   Viscountess Milner, p. 81.
5   Lady Frances Balfour, ii, 92. She refers here to 1887, but elsewhere implies continuance.
6   WHI/67.

works in the poorer districts of the country will increase rather than diminish. Though I was the Minister principally responsible for the great expenditure in Ireland, I yet confess to have looked with alarm at any great extension of the system. It has led abroad to some of the worst kinds of parliamentary corruption, and has cast upon foreign exchequers some of the heaviest burdens by which they are overweighted.[7]

Ireland apart, Balfour was already, by the early 1890s, interested in the subject of imperial defence, as will soon be illustrated; and by 1895 he was prepared to take an initiative in Cabinet about the co-ordination of defence policy. Thus far, he may well be seen as much more of a constructive statesman than his predecessor as First Lord of the Treasury, W. H. Smith, who was fully extended by his duties as Leader of the House. But it would be erroneous to infer that, because he was involved in an attempt to pass a major Education Bill in 1896, he had a premeditated plan for greater national efficiency which he saw through to ultimate fulfilment in 1902.

At this point, it will be helpful to look back to a letter written by Balfour to Salisbury in November 1888. This has been construed as evidence of Balfour's sympathy with Chamberlain's constructive plans for mainland Britain.[8] It does indeed show that Balfour was, at that time, prepared to entertain the idea of a fusion of parties and also Chamberlain's emergence as Liberal Unionist Leader in the House of Commons. He wrote the letter to his uncle while in bed with a cold—a recurrent ailment—and it records his thoughts on the uncertain health of W. H. Smith. On the following day, however, he endorsed the letter 'Not sent. A.J.B. 24.11.88'. Still, remembering that uncle and nephew much preferred verbal exchanges to correspondence—and in so far as Balfour rarely, if ever, kept a document for autobiographical purposes—the letter remains a valuable account of his attitude to Chamberlain and his schemes at the time. Also, remembering the constancy of Balfour's political attitudes, the letter may be taken as a useful pointer to his relationship with Chamberlain in the 1890s. He wrote:

My dear Uncle Robert,

My uneasiness about Smith's health which I expressed to you this morning, and which was increased rather than diminished by the few words I had with him after you left my bedroom, induced me to put down the following stray thoughts, [with] most of which however you are probably familiar!

If Smith goes there are so far as I can see only two men on the Bench who can possibly succeed him: Goschen and myself. There are many grave objections to the latter.

[7] J.C.P. 5/5/24, B. to Chamberlain, 27 Nov. 1895.
[8] See, for instance, Marsh. p. 220.

In any case, Balfour continued, Goschen would be fully justified in not wishing to serve under 'one who was not in Parliament when he first became a Cabinet Minister'. Of course Goschen (now Salisbury's Chancellor of the Exchequer but still a leading Liberal Unionist) would have to 'call himself a Conservative and join the Carlton Club'. Objections could be made to Goschen. There was his 'fussiness', which 'drives Smith mad', his fidgeting while on the ministerial bench, and his 'perpetual commentary' on the proceedings. But these, Balfour thought, were 'small matters' compared with his merits;

he is so able, loyal, good tempered and good natured, so obviously honest, and so incapable of intrigue that, faute de mieux, he will I believe do very well both by his colleagues and by the party.

But is nothing better to be had? This brings one at once to the old question of coalition. Shall we gain or not gain by having Hartington as leader and James as (say) Home Sec.?

But this arrangement would raise difficulties over ministerial appointments, and it 'would introduce into the cabinet two counsellors, one of whom always recommends standing still and the other of whom always recommends running away'.

A forward movement under such leaders is always difficult . . . Chamberlain could not and would not join . . . He would probably rapidly drift back to the bosom of the true Radical Church and we shall lose the value of his support. I rate this perhaps more highly than you do. But it does mean the Birmingham seats *certainly*, other doubtful seats in the Midlands *probably*, and one of the most useful speakers and debaters in the House. It is true that he would hardly leave us while Gladstone [and Home Rule] lives; and that after Gladstone dies he would probably leave us anyhow. Nonetheless I am convinced that Joe as leader (though in the second place) of eighty Liberal Unionists, and Joe as the leader of half a dozen radical Unionists would be very different people indeed.

Moreover, as Balfour remarked, Hartington would soon, by succeeding his ailing father as Duke of Devonshire, leave the way open for Chamberlain to lead the Liberal Unionists in the House of Commons. Thus

the fusion of parties might (as Randolph would say) 'influence the popular imagination' and gain votes . . . It would provide us with a leader [Chamberlain] who would certainly command the highest admiration of his followers. And it would save us from the difficulties on which we have more than once nearly made shipwreck [namely a] separate and irresponsible Council of War directing the movements of one wing of the allied force. This difficulty is not likely to diminish. It will become formidable as soon as ambitious legislation is attempted. It may become formidable on the Scotch Local Government Bill; on an Irish University

Bill or an Irish Land Purchase Bill. Some of these *must* be undertaken; all of them we *may* undertake, in the course of the next Session. And therefore it is important I think to keep the policy of coalition at least *in view* [when considering] possible vacancies in the Cabinet . . .[9]

The letter does imply a degree of approval of Chamberlain's ideas. However, in so far as this approval is firmly set in a context of party-political calculation and expediency, there is not the slightest indication that Balfour envisaged a costly social programme, which would certainly annoy the main body of Conservatives. The Education Act of 1891, abolishing most of the fees in elementary schools, probably went further than Balfour had foreseen. It seems to have arisen from Salisbury's decision to pre-empt Liberal wishes to provide 'tax support for all elementary schools, including denominational ones, but strictly on condition that denominational schools be subjected to supervision by elected representatives from the locality'. [10] Although Salisbury's Act saved the Church schools from this fate, at least for a time, it caused ructions among Conservatives because of the implied increase in taxation; [11] and in any case, it could not safeguard the Church schools against the menace of rising standards in the rate-based Board schools.

What light, then, does the letter throw on Balfour's reference to 'ambitious legislation'? It was primarily a matter of further Irish legislation, some of it 'constructive', in the sense (at least) that it would entail a moderate financial burden on central government. Indeed, as Balfour indicates, it was the anti-landlord Chamberlainites who would provide the main opposition in Unionist ranks to the most 'ambitious' item, namely the Land Purchase Act. Only evident political necessity would make Balfour contemplate further social expenditure in mainland Britain.

However, there can be no doubt about Balfour's deepening interest, by the 1890s, in the area of defence policy. His duties as Leader of the House did not distract him from composing a notable minute dated 12 March 1892.

In the background was the Hartington Commission's report of 1890. This arose from an invasion inquiry of 1888—a year of public anxiety about Franco-Russian naval power—which had revealed the absence of satisfactory co-ordination between Army and Navy. The report 'recommended for the overseeing of imperial defence as a whole "the formation of a Naval and Military Council, which should probably be presided over by the Prime

[9] B.P. 49689, ff. 38–41, B. to Salisbury, 23 Nov. 1888, 'Not sent'.
[10] Marsh, p. 170.
[11] Ibid., p. 171.

Minister, and consist of the Parliamentary Heads of the two services and
their principal military advisers''.'[12] It also advised abolition of the old-
fashioned post of Commander-in-Chief and the establishment of a general
staff on modern lines. But Salisbury took no effective action on these
matters till 1895–6, and even then the co-ordinating machinery proved
inadequate and nothing was done to set up a general staff for the Army.

Balfour's minute is notable, first for its lucidity and grasp, qualities to be
found in his better known memoranda of later years, and secondly for the
prophetic touches displayed at that early date. Few cabinet ministers of the
time could have written such a paper on defence problems at all; yet it bears
the usual hallmarks of Balfour's having dictated it.

I return herewith Col. Swain's memorandum of his recent conversation with the
Emperor, [the youthful William II of Germany] and a brief Minute of Lord George
Hamilton thereon. It is quite true, as the First Lord of the Admiralty [Hamilton]
remarks, that the Emperor has somewhat changed his ground . . . But I must confess
my own personal opinion that the dangers of which he now speaks are the [more]
real . . .

We are accustomed to say that our Navy is better than our Army, and in a sense
this is true. We have a Fleet numerically stronger than that of any other Power, and
more efficient than that of any other Power in proportion to its numbers. No similar
propositions, I am afraid, can be made about the Army. It may nevertheless be
doubted whether the Army is not better able to discharge the duties which may be
thrown upon it in consequence of International difficulties than is the Navy.
Practically, only three things are asked of the Army: (1) a sufficient strength at
home for the purposes of National defence; and for the purposes of supplying the
wear and tear of the Army in India; (2) a sufficient Army in India to deal with any
force which the Russians might bring against it; and (3) a sufficient amount of men
and material to enable us to send out a small and well equipped expedition if such
should be rendered necessary by any of our small wars. With all its shortcomings, I
am disposed to think that the Army is equal to these duties. Can a like statement be
made about the Navy?

The Navy has two entirely different sets of duties to perform according to whether
the country is at peace or at war. The Peace functions are partly Police and partly
what may perhaps be described as diplomatic. Whether it is at present well equipped
for carrying out either of these kinds of work economically and efficiently may be
doubted, but this point I do not propose to dwell upon . . . Its functions in time of war
are also, broadly speaking, twofold; namely, (a) to protect our own commerce, and
to destroy that of the enemy by means of cruisers, and (b) to drive the enemy's fleet
off the high seas by means of battle-ships. The last is the most important, for it is the

¹²   Correlli Barnett, *The Collapse of British Power*, London, 1972, p. 335.

essential condition of carrying out the first, and it is also the condition for preserving our foreign possessions from capture, and our shores from invasion.

Thus far, points of interest include Balfour's placing home defence as first priority for the Army, whereas the Stanhope Memorandum of 1888 had placed that duty fourth; and his logical guidelines for the Navy held good till the advent of the submarine at least. Throughout the Great War, indeed, the increasing role of the submarine did not obviate the need to maintain battle-fleet superiority.

Balfour goes on to criticize the Admiralty's lack of clear criteria for comparing British naval strength with that of France and Russia. He wants it to be made clear in tables of comparison whether or not the Admiralty accepts the controversial view that a first-class armoured cruiser is 'a match' for a third-class battleship. He continues:

Without, however, going into these controverted points, (on which a layman cannot express an opinion of any value,) it appears to be admitted that the portion of our Fleet actually in the Mediterranean is inferior to the French Force at Toulon; that, for diplomatic and other reasons, it is a good deal scattered; and that the first operation in the case of war with France would be one of retreat and of concentration at Gibraltar, until the advent of the portion of the Mediterranean Fleet lying in British waters enabled us to meet the enemy on equal terms. Whether this operation could be performed without any risk of the fragments of the Fleet now stationed in the Eastern Mediterranean being attacked and destroyed in detail, I cannot say. Even at best, however, it is evident that we should have temporarily to vacate the Levant; and further, that if we wished to protect the Coast of Italy from attack, our Forces would permanently have to be stationed West of Malta. Nor could we detach any important ships to do duty at Besika Bay or Alexandria. The French Fleet, and the Mediterranean Fleet even when reinforced, are too nearly matched to make any such procedure safe before we had won a naval battle.

Balfour's parenthetical comment on the limited value of lay opinion in such a context will not have escaped the reader's notice. It was, indeed, Winston Churchill's failure to respect this principle which would lead to his replacement at the Admiralty by a sixty-six-year-old Balfour in 1915.

The memorandum terminates with a passage on the prospects of a successful British naval attack on the Dardanelles. Even if the defenders in this case are Turks and Russians, the paragraph deserves to be given virtually in full.

How far then are we in a position to carry out the two objects which the Emperor has in view?—namely, the protection of the Italian Coast from a French raid; and the protection of Constantinople from a Russian *coup de main*. As regards the first, there is nothing that I can see to hinder the French from carrying out the suggested operation during the time that our Fleet is concentrating at Gibraltar. Whether it would be worth their while to do it, and whether their doing it would have the serious consequences upon Italy's Foreign Policy which the Emperor contemplates, may be doubted. Raids of the kind indicated are perfectly useless strategically, and are much better calculated to arouse the indignation of an enemy than to weaken his military strength. But the defence of Constantinople presents, as it appears to me, far more serious difficulties. The Emperor contemplates a Russian descent by sea upon the City with the practical acquiescence of the Sultan, and he suggests that we should prevent it with out fleet. I do not believe that this is possible without dangerously imperilling our Naval superiority. If the Commanders of the forts on either side of the Dardanelles followed the policy of their Sovereign, as is probable, they would fire upon our ships when they attempted to force the entrance. If they hesitated to take so strong a step without direct orders from the Sultan, our ships would be allowed to go through unmolested, but when in the Sea of Marmora would always be subject to the risk of having their retreat cut off, and their communications cut off, should the Commanders of the forts change their minds. It may be asked—what is the use of having a Fleet at all unless you are prepared to risk it for the purpose of carrying out some great policy? The answer is that an engagement with powerful Forts is not one of the risks to which a Fleet should be exposed. In such engagements Fleets scarcely ever come off victorious; indeed, I recollect no case in which such a result has occurred, except the bombardment of Algiers. The conditions of Modern Naval Warfare, which appear to render it necessary to concentrate Naval strength in very few and very costly vessels, make it more than ever necessary not to risk those ships in the unequal struggle between a Fort on land, whose guns are mechanically trained so as to cover the assailing ship; which can hardly be seen; and which cannot be sunk; and a ship which can be destroyed or disabled by one or two well directed shells. It may be said that if the forcing of the passage of the Dardanelles is an operation involving great risks, so also is the attack by sea on Constantinople from the North. This is true; but while the Russians in the latter operation would only risk the destruction of a few thousand men, to which they are probably quite indifferent, we should be risking our Naval superiority, upon which, without exaggeration, our National existence may be said to depend. The proper function for our Fleet is to keep the high seas clear of the Fleet of the enemy. The margin of superiority which should enable us to do this is not large enough at the present time to justify us in throwing it away in an operation of war for which a Fleet is intrinsically unsuited . . . The only effective counter-move that I can see to the Russian advance would be a joint military and Naval expedition to Gallipoli which would take the forts in the rear and give us permanent possession of a position which would render Constantinople untenable. But such an expedition, if it be possible at all, (a point on which I cannot offer an opinion,) would evidently have to be worked out most carefully *beforehand* in all its details, and would necessitate transports etc. being kept in constant readiness at Malta.

A. J. B.

12.3.92[13]

However, between 1892 and 1895 there was little more to show for Balfour's flair for elucidating matters defensive. As already related, his parliamentary travails were considerable. Otherwise, his conservative attitudes were generally to the fore. In the summer election of 1892, Balfour lost votes in his Manchester constituency (where he had first been elected in 1885) by opposing an eight-hour day for miners. But his main effort was devoted to fighting Home Rule. Despite his dislike of the platform, he spoke in Gladstone's own constituency of Midlothian on the eve of the poll along the lines of 'Ulster will fight, and Ulster will be right.' Gladstone's majority dropped by over 3,000 to a mere 690.[14] Otherwise the summer recess was largely taken up with work on his *Foundations of Belief*; and the book was much on his mind till the winter of 1894–5. Indeed, his closeness during 1892 to giving up politics altogether is perhaps implied by his message of 21 November, via Sidgwick, for his sister Eleanor: 'Will you tell Nora that I have accepted the Presidency of the Society for Psychical Research and that I do not care a hang for my political reputation?'[15] As for *The Foundations of Belief*, if the book carried any political message, it was to the effect that reason and human conduct alike depended on authority, tradition, and custom, and that

reasoning is a force most apt to divide and disintegrate; and though division and disintegration may often be the necessary preliminaries of social development, still more necessary are the forces that bind and stiffen, without which there would be no society to develop.[16]

In other words, statesmen should proceed cautiously in such infinitely complex matters as social reform. While they should move with the times, they should beware of panaceas. Such institutions as the Monarchy, the Church, and Parliament should be preserved.[17]

However, by the time that the Conservatives returned to power in June 1895, Balfour had proposals in mind for the better co-ordination of

[13] WHI/68, typescript copy with B.'s holo. amendments. A note on the back says: 'See Salisbury's Correspondence'; but original not found at Hatfield.

[14] Dugdale, i, 209.

[15] B.P. 49882, f. 24.

[16] *Foundations*, p. 242.

[17] See also B.'s 'Fragment on Progress' in *Essays and Addresses*, Edinburgh, 1893, pp. 282–2.

defence. On 16 March 1894 he had, in response to Sir Charles Dilke, committed the Conservatives to take appropriate action when they returned to power.[18] Parliament met briefly in August 1895 and during the next few months Balfour was in close touch with Lord Lansdowne, a Liberal Unionist who had been appointed Secretary for War. Balfour showed concern about the organization of the War Office and the role of the Commander-in-Chief. The Duke of Cambridge had been dislodged from the post by the Rosebery Government but the Unionists, despite the report of the Hartington Commission, failed to abolish this anachronism.[19] However, at a meeting of 24 June 1895, attended by Salisbury (again Prime Minister and Foreign Secretary), Balfour (again designated as First Lord of the Treasury and Leader of the House), and Devonshire and Chamberlain (representing the Liberal Unionists), it was decided that Devonshire would be Lord President—and thus chairman of an advisory defence committee inaugurated by the Rosebery Government—and that Chamberlain would go to the Colonial Office. As a result of this agreement and of Devonshire's high status within the Unionist coalition thereby established, Balfour did not replace the Duke in the role of defence committee chairman, to which (despite his work in 1888–1890) the Duke was unsuited, until Devonshire resigned from Balfour's Cabinet in October 1903. But it was Balfour who, on 24 August 1895, initiated a ministerial exchange of minutes on the subject of the Cabinet's Defence Committee:

1. It is quite certain that on Army Estimates questions will be asked with regard to the position of the President of the Council in his capacity as Chairman of the Committee of Defence. To these questions some answer will have to be forthcoming.

2. The subject has not been discussed as yet by the Cabinet, nor, so far as I know, by any members of the Cabinet; and I throw out the following proposals merely as hints towards the final solution:

    I. The President of the Council is to be the Permanent Chairman of a Committee of the Cabinet.

    II. Of this Committee, the Secretary for War and the First Lord of the Admiralty will be permanent members, assisted, of course, by the experts of both departments.

    III. Such other Members of the Cabinet will take part in the deliberations of the Committee as from time to time may seem desirable, having regard to

---

[18] *P.D.*, 4th, 22/473–4 and 490–5.
[19] B.P. 49727, ff. 22–6, 40, 46–54.

the questions under discussion.

IV. The President of the Council will have no authority to intervene in the departmental work, either of the War Office or of the Admiralty. Nor will he have the right either to send for or to give orders *directly* to the officials of either department.

V. The records of the decisions to which the Defence Committee will come will be kept in duplicate at the War Office and Admiralty.

VI. The functions of the Committee will be to decide all questions of importance connected with Imperial Defence, which involve the co-operation of Army and Navy.

VII. Speaking for myself, I should like to see a very wide interpretation given to this definition. There must be very few strategical plans of any magnitude in which the interests of both Services are not to some extent—though it may be only to a small extent—involved; and all such plans I should like to see passed through the Committee of Defence, and kept in duplicate by both departments. For example, the War Office have, I imagine, elaborate schemes for dealing with invasion. I do not know whether these schemes have ever been communicated to the Admiralty; but, if not, I think they ought to be, and the opinion of the naval experts taken upon certain portions of them. It is impossible really to consider the problem of invasion without taking maritime affairs into account. In the same way, I suppose the Admiralty have worked out strategical schemes for protecting our interests in the Mediterranean and elsewhere in the event of war. Military considerations cannot evidently be wholly excluded in the contrivance of these plans; and I think they should be passed through the Committee of Defence, and kept in duplicate.

VIII. In addition to strategical plans there must be a large number of subjects which such a Committee could, with great advantage to the Public Service, be asked to consider. With the assistance of the Chancellor of the Exchequer, controversies with regard to the Estimates might be there decided; and, with the assistance of the Secretary for Foreign Affairs, controversies with regard to the distribution of ships, where political considerations appear to point in one direction and considerations of naval strategy in another. It is needless to add that such subjects as the ports and coaling stations, whose *raison d'être* is to form a base for the Fleet, but which are, as a matter of fact, garrisoned by the Army; the pattern and character of the guns and ammunition supplied by Woolwich; and other matters involving the interests of both Services, are likely to supply a large sphere of usefulness for the exertions of the proposed Committee.

A. J. B. [20]

[20] Cab.37/40/46, Committee of Defence: Minute by first Lord of Treasury, 24 Aug. 1895.

This proposal comprises many features of the Committee of Imperial Defence finally established by Balfour in December 1902. The most notable deficiency is the absence from the chair of the Prime Minister. However, Balfour recognized Salisbury's incapacity in dealing with defence problems and presumably felt it impolitic to contest the claims of the Duke of Devonshire—the Hartington of the famous Report of 1890. By November 1895, minutes contributed by Salisbury and Devonshire demonstrated inability to appreciate the considerable merits of Balfour's proposal.[21] Some support for his scheme came from Goschen (a Conservative since 1893 and now First Lord of the Admiralty);[22] but the over-all result was a comprehensive bungle. The members of the cabinet Defence Committee were Devonshire (chairman), Balfour, Goschen, Lansdowne, and Hicks Beach (now Chancellor of the Exchequer). However, the fact that the Committee, despite Balfour's above-quoted view, was not attended by either the Commander-in-Chief or the Senior Naval Lord of the Admiralty ensured that its deliberations were so much waste of time. Meetings were held when it occurred to the Duke of Devonshire that a long time had elapsed since the last one; and it hardly comes as a shock to find that Sandars remembered the Committee as an 'absolutely useless body'. Sensitive, perhaps, to the quizzical eye of posterity, it kept no proper records.[23]

Even if Balfour's grasp of the co-ordination problem was impressive, it should be noted that he did not take up a more radical proposal than his own which nevertheless had a future. This was contained in a public letter of early 1894 which advocated a Ministry of Defence. The letter was signed by the Liberal ex-minister Sir Charles Dilke, General Sir George Chesney (a Unionist MP), H. O. Arnold-Forster (a Unionist destined for an unhappy spell at the War Office under Balfour in 1903–5), and Spenser Wilkinson (a writer on military subjects and future Chichele Professor of the History of War at Oxford). Dilke had conducted a preliminary correspondence with Balfour who manifested a close, though critical, interest in the suggestion.[24] But when, in March 1894, Balfour spoke on co-ordination in the Commons, he rejected Dilke's proposal of a Ministry of Defence on the grounds that it would reduce the First Lord of the Admiralty and the Secretary for War to

---

[21] Ibid., minutes by the Prime Minister and the Lord President, dated Oct. and 3 Nov. 1895. See also B.P. 49769, ff. 80–1, Devonshire to B., 11 Nov. 1895.

[22] Ibid., minute by First Lord of Admiralty, 22 Nov.

[23] Sandars P., C.771, f. 328: material supplied by Sandars to Alfred Lyttleton for his article on B. in *The Nineteenth Century and After* (published Dec. 1911).

[24] Roy Jenkins, *Sir Charles Dilke*, London (Fontana), 1968, pp. 398–400.

the status of Under-Secretaries.²⁵ Characteristically, he was sufficiently open to new ideas to give the matter serious consideration. Equally it is illustrative of his conservatism that he would not strike at the institutional root of the inter-service rivalry which, together with the chronic inefficiency of the War Office itself, bedevilled Britain's defensive arrangements. Instead he gravitated with true Balfourian consistency towards the semi-solution provided by his C.I.D. (Committee of Imperial Defence) from 1902 to 1914, and again in the inter-war period. Yet the C.I.D. had to be replaced by experimental machinery for conducting the war of 1914 to 1918 and was found inadequate to deal with the defence problems of the 1930s.

But it is difficult not to admire Balfour's instant recognition that a Ministry of Defence must entail the downgrading of the two historic ministerial posts. In 1940, Winston Churchill became Minister of Defence as well as Prime Minister; and in 1946 Attlee created the first peace-time Ministry of Defence. But both arrangements left the First Lord of the Admiralty, the War Secretary, and the Air Secretary at least nominally intact. It was not until seventeen years later that a Conservative ministry reduced these service ministers to the level of Ministers of State, without cabinet rank. Only after this astonishing lapse of time was it recognized that otherwise departmentalism would unduly hinder the efficient use of limited resources.

Probably nothing short of the establishment after 1895 of a Ministry of Defence could have prevented the humiliation of the Army in the South African War. The War Office of 1895 to 1899 has been fairly depicted as an augean stable. A long-standing feud between senior officers supporting Lord Roberts, on the one hand, and Lord Wolseley, who replaced the Duke of Cambridge as Commander-in-Chief in 1895, was transmitted to South Africa in 1899. More fundamental still, perhaps, were the vested interests entrenched in compartments of the War Office with their time-honoured but stultifying habits and practices. Some improvements were made in 1895 but co-operation between soldiers and civilian officials remained poor, while Lord Wolseley carried on a war of attrition against Lansdowne in an effort to shield his office from the inroads of reform. Certainly, the idea of a Ministry of Defence had little appeal for the leading soldiers. They based their opposition on the plausible argument that the Army would be subordinated to 'Blue Water' theories (to the effect that the Navy could perform

²⁵ *P.D.*, 4th, 22/490–1, 16 Mar. 1894.

all the main duties of home and imperial defence).[26] As will be seen in subsequent chapters, Balfour's C.I.D., for all its usefulness, could not promote a complete and satisfactory reform of the Army before his resignation in December 1905.

Yet a thorough reform of the War Office might have been accomplished after 1895 by direct assault. For at the aforementioned meeting of 24 June 1895 on the distribution of cabinet posts, Chamberlain actually volunteered to take the War Office. At the start Chamberlain duly expressed his wish to go to the Colonial Office, but he said he would accept the War Office if he was needed there. This timely offer apparently met with no articulate response. Both Salisbury and Balfour were amazed at Chamberlain's apparent modesty. Balfour remarked that he could have the Exchequer if he liked, thus showing his ignorance of Chamberlain's current thinking and also his lack of concern about him as a possible rival. So it was the Colonial Office that was energized, not the War Office. Also the stage was set for Chamberlain's bid for preferential tariffs within the Empire, and for the devastating impact of Tariff Reform on Balfour's party leadership.[26a]

Evidently Balfour felt no great urge to reopen the question of national and imperial defence during the later 1890s. Predominant is the fact developed in the previous chapter that he was much tied down by his duties as Leader of the House. Understandably, given his disposition and his non-political interests, he was eager to get away from London to Whittingehame and North Berwick during the second half of each year. Even then, however, his mind was constantly at work on political problems; and neither golf nor house parties stopped him dictating substantial memoranda during odd hours of the day. Although Jack Sandars became rather critical of his old chief after severing relations with him in 1915, he never accused him of laziness—despite all superficial appearances to the contrary. Indeed, from the standpoint of 1911 his opinion was as follows:

> More was devolved upon A. J. B. between 1895 and 1902 than I suppose ever fell to the lot of the second in command. Moreover, Lord Salisbury entrusted him with a great amount of Patronage, which he found irksome, although of course this was unknown to the general public.
>
> In the House of Commons itself, as leader, he assumed responsibilities never attempted by his predecessors . . . Disraeli, Northcote and W. H. Smith . . . none of these ever attempted the detailed preparation, and ultimate management in the House, of Bills of importance.

[26] Marsh, pp. 290–3; Nicholas d'Ombrain, *War Machinery and High Policy 1902–1914*, Oxford, 1973, pp. 2–3; John Gooch, *The Plans of War*, London, 1974, p. 17.
[26] J. L. Garvin and J. Amery, *The Life of Joseph Chamberlain*, iii, 5.

By way of illustration, Sandars went on to cite the case of the London Government Act of 1899. Henry Chaplin ('the Squire') was 'quite unequal' to the difficulties presented by this bill which was 'practically prepared by A.J.B. and the draughtsman'; and the 'grip that A.J.B. acquired of the subject' was 'well shown in the speech in which he introduced the Bill'. He 'carried the House in his account of the reform'. It 'required no small skill' to render uncontroversial a measure which removed the authority of the London County Council from areas which then became Boroughs. [27]

If, then, Balfour's achievements in the reorganization of defence remained potential rather than concrete before the South African War, what of the imperial sphere in a wider sense? Denis Judd shows in his study of *Balfour and the British Empire* that, through his long ministerial career, Balfour wisely 'chose to swim with the course of imperial evolution rather than attempt to create an artificial harmony'. [28] His generally cautious and empirical approach governed his view of Indian and South African questions, but his acceptance of Unionist assumptions—that British predominance must be maintained in such areas—was never in doubt. [29]

But if no clear evidence of constructive intent is to be found in the imperial sphere, what of education? Here, Balfour's reputation as a constructive statesman is particularly well established. Did he not, at great party-political cost, pass the Education Act of 1902? and is not this Act a major landmark in British educational history? The answer to both questions is in the affirmative. In the previous chapter, we have seen Balfour receiving the acclamation of the House of Commons—friend and foe alike—on completion of his sustained parliamentary performance in that regard. It was here, indeed, that he most impressively demonstrated his capacity to lead the Unionist coalition. Few previous Conservative Prime Ministers could have equalled his consistent mastery of so complicated a matter through seven months of debate. The opportunistic Disraeli, for instance, could hardly have performed this particular feat. Peel, no doubt, possessed the necessary attributes, and Gladstone, of course, among ex-Conservatives. But none of this proves Balfour's constructive intent throughout the preliminary period (1895–1902). Understandably, Balfour's progressive motivation has sometimes been simply taken for granted. Denis Judd, for instance, points out an apparent inconsistency in Balfour's attitudes:

[27] Sandars P., C.771, ff. 322–3: material for A. Lyttleton, 1911.

[28] Judd, *Balfour*, London, 1968, p. 17.

[29] See, for example, A. N. Porter, *The Origins of the South African War*, Manchester, 1980.

In South Africa Balfour denied the possibilities of equality between black and white. Nor did he believe that the abyss between the two races could be bridged by the passage of time and educational endeavour. Such pessimism ill-became the ardent advocate of the 1902 Education Act.[30]

But Balfour can hardly be accused of inconsistency on this account, for it will turn out that he was far from seeing himself as 'the ardent advocate' of the Education Act. From 1895 to 1901, there are indeed signs of his usual enlightened interest—and even some useful practical moves—in certain areas of the educational scene. But as far as state schooling in England and Wales are concerned, indications of constructive intent are scarce. However, the matter is of such fundamental importance for an assessment of Balfour as a constructive statesman that the relevant sequence must be closely examined. '

As mentioned above, the Education Act of 1891 did nothing to safeguard the future of the Church schools. By the time of the election campaign of July 1895, they were again hard pressed by the competition of the School Boards. Indeed, numbers of them had gone to the wall and been taken over by the Boards. This competition derived support from the Education Department where George Kekewich was Secretary from 1890. When the Liberals were in power (1892–1895) Kekewich experienced no political opposition to the standard-raising activities—and increasing rate demands—of the School Boards. In so far as central government grants to both types of school were on a similar basis, the Voluntary (denominational) Schools could offer comparable standards only through constant increases in voluntary subscriptions, a discouraging prospect. Therefore there was, to put it mildly, little enthusiasm in Tory circles for Kekewich and his drive for educational improvement.[31] In Salisbury's view, government-supported compulsory education in elementary schools was an expensive duty fecklessly accepted by Disraeli's administration in 1876,[32] and he frequently deplored what he saw as the reckless extravagance of the School Boards. Balfour was usually less eloquent on the subject than his uncle, but it will be seen that he did not basically disagree with him. In view of his close alliance with the Liberal Unionists, with their Nonconformist contingent, Salisbury refrained from mentioning education in his election manifesto of 6 July. Balfour however, as second-in-command, promised in his constituency that something would be done for the Church schools. The

[30] Judd, *Balfour*, p. 19.
[31] Sir George Kekewich, *The Education Department and After*, London, 1920, pp. 110–11.
[32] Marsh, p. 171.

parsons and their flocks worked hard to secure a Conservative victory at the polls. Indeed, second only to Liberal disunity, the Anglican effort was widely credited with a result which, rather ironically, gave the Conservatives an absolute majority in the Commons without absolutely necessitating Liberal Unionist aid; and even opponents of the Government conceded that it had been given a mandate to help the Voluntary Schools. [33]

Balfour therefore, although he had no administrative responsibility for education, felt committed to see that a measure was passed for the relief of the Voluntary Schools. The degree to which the Unionists were seen as the champions of all denominational schools was demonstrated by the strong support given to them by the Roman Catholic Irish, an unusual electoral phenomenon.

Looking ahead to the parliamentary session of 1896, Balfour tried to quicken the preparation of legislation, including the Education Bill. On 12 December he informed Sandars:

I have nothing to correct as regards the order of the Government Bills with which the Government Draughtsmen have got to deal. I cannot understand why the Employers' Liability appears to be in so backward a state . . . This Bill [dear to Chamberlain], and the Educational Bill, are probably the two most important measures of the Session: it is to be regretted that they are also the most backward. [34]

The minister in charge of the Education Bill was Sir John Gorst, formerly of the Fourth Party, now Vice-President of the Council, and as keen as Balfour to save the Voluntary Schools. His bill turned out to be a much bigger affair than Balfour, for one, had expected. Initially, Gorst relied on Michael Sadler and R. L. Morant of the Education Department's Special Inquiries Branch, although by November he was allowing Kekewich to take a full part. [35] The draft bill followed the recommendations of past royal commissions in proposing new local authorities, namely the county and county borough councils working through education committees. These would have a co-ordinating role in both the elementary and secondary fields. In a letter of 21 December to Bernard Mallet, Parry's predecessor as his civil-servant private secretary, Balfour defined his attitude to the draft bill:

I shall be content if we succeed in saving the Voluntary Schools: I shall *not* be content if we fail in this object; and, in my opinion, the whole question should be

---

[33] J. E. B. Munson, 'The Unionist Coalition and Education, 1895–1902', in *Historical Journal*, xx, 3 (1977), p. 614. See also Marsh, p. 250.

[34] Sandars P., C.727.

[35] Munson, p. 616.

looked at from this point of view, and no extraneous provisions should be introduced into it except with the object of smoothing the passage of an effective measure through the House.

Let me add that I am disposed to think that the very large suggestions made by Kekewich and others (with the spirit of which I heartily agree) may, in spite of their magnitude, help, rather than hinder, the progress of the Bill . . . [36]

Balfour presumably felt that a bill which moved towards a coherent national system might appeal to the 'educationists'—execrated by Salisbury, but constituting an articulate cross-party, but mainly Liberal, group. But above all, the new education committees bade fair to devour the School Boards and thus open the way for the Voluntary Schools to qualify for rate aid. Balfour openly subscribed to this view in May 1896. [37]

Gorst—as ever, witty and volatile—piloted the Bill which was passed by an overwhelming majority in May 1896. Balfour, winding up for the Government, stressed the burden that would fall on the ratepayer if the Voluntary Schools foundered. The School Boards would then have to fill the gaps. This would cost about £4,200,000 a year. 'That', he declared, 'is a burden which anyone interested in local taxation must contemplate with something akin to absolute despair.' [38]

However, earlier in the debates, Asquith had laid a basis for the fierce opposition which was to catch the Government off its guard at the committee stage. On 5 May he pointed out that the Bill imposed a perpetual limit on School Boards' expenditure out of the rates—in order, of course, to save the Church schools from having to finance matching expenditure (especially on teachers' salaries).

Why [Asquith asked] are you going to limit, of all forms of expenditure, the expenditure on education? [Cheers.] At a moment when you are spending upon Naval Defence out of the accumulated funds of last year and out of a mortgage of the funds of future years vast sums of money, at a moment when you are dipping into the surplus of this year and next year to provide special relief for the owners and occupiers of agricultural land, that is the moment selected for placing a limit for all time to come on that which should be the most fruitful, and the most beneficent of all forms of expenditure. [Cheers.] [39]

The Government had already, before the committee stage, taken the crucial decision not to use the closure. It was not difficult, therefore, when the clauses of the Bill came up for detailed consideration, to smother the

---

[36] B.P. 49781, ff. 57–8.
[37] *P.D.*, 4th, 40/1244, 12 May 1896.
[38] Ibid., 40/1242, 12 May 1896.
[39] Ibid., 40/480; 583.

measure with amendments. Nonconformist anger was mainly focused on
Clause 27 which tried to solve the question of religious instruction in Board
and Voluntary Schools on a basis of reciprocal provision. [40] On 11 June
Balfour made a sudden concession to one of his own backbenchers, Sir
Albert Rollit, who represented small authorities wishing to retain a stake in
education. Balfour hoped that he might at the same time appeal to some
members of the Opposition and thus change the general atmosphere.
Whereas Gorst had earlier defended his proposed county authorities as by
no means too large, which was correct, Balfour now accepted municipal
authorities with a minimum population of 20,000. [41] This turnabout was
casually announced by Balfour on returning to the House after a breather.
As the Liberal 'educationist' Yoxall soon afterwards remarked, the First
Lord of the Treasury had got up 'in a light, airy, and dégagé fashion' and
thereupon 'entirely threw over the Vice President'. [42] The concession
attracted much criticism from both sides of the House and the Bill remained
firmly bogged down. By 18 June Balfour was brought to the point of
declaring: 'For my part I do not profess to know anything about education; I
am the last person to pose as an authority on that subject.' [43] After a
dispirited party meeting, at which he abortively suggested carrying the Bill
over to a short special session in January, Balfour announced in the
Commons on 22 June that the measure had been abandoned. Not only did
this failure lower his reputation as Leader of the House. The Cabinet's
decision to withdraw the Bill had attracted the Queen's disapproval in a
cipher telegram to Salisbury. She asked the Cabinet not to withdraw the
measure because the resultant discredit would weaken British ability to deal
with foreign governments. [44]

Balfour's quick, logical mind was always vigilant for ways of making
legislation more effective. He was a talented draftsman in his own right: the
case of the L.C.C. Bill has been mentioned and licensing will follow. But as
far as education was concerned, it has to be said that there was, in the
1890s, little rapport between Balfour's genuine interest in scientific and
technical education and his feelings about state elementary schools.
Although he inevitably made some use of the arguments developed by a
generation of 'educationists', he showed little explicit concern for the
failure to develop the potential of four-fifths of the population. Of course,

[40] Munson, pp. 617–18.
[41] *P.D.*, 4th 40/906–7.
[42] Ibid., 915.
[43] Ibid., 41/1369.
[44] Sandars P., C.729.

this was a prevalent attitude, especially in the Conservative Party. As previously indicated, he was almost as strongly opposed to costly state collectivism in all its forms as was his uncle. Yet he was not unaware of the need for industrial modernization. For example, in a speech of 1900 he focused on the need for adequate finance 'to establish the modern laboratory and to equip it with modern appliances'. Men of science, he said, naturally asked private sources

to aid them with that pecuniary assistance which in some other countries—many other countries—is extended to them by the Government but which in this country, rightly or wrongly, by an almost immemorial tradition has been left chiefly to the energy of private enterprise.[45]

Meanwhile the political pledge to the Church schools had to be fulfilled. Balfour himself undertook to prepare a new bill to be presented to Parliament in 1897, and he hankered after rate aid as a final solution. The language of his cabinet memorandum of 8 November 1896 establishes this point. It also echoes his uncle's hostile attitude towards the annoyingly progressive School Boards:

The general objections to rate aid are familiar to the Cabinet, as also is the single strong argument in its favour—the argument, namely, that without rate aid it is difficult, perhaps impossible, in the face of the growing appetite of parents for educational luxuries and the growing expenditure of School Boards to meet, and very often to anticipate, that appetite, for the Voluntary Schools in large towns to hold their own now, or to avoid extinction in the near future.[46]

In the same memorandum he revived an alternative plan which had been 'unanimously rejected' by the Cabinet in 1895:

It provided that, after the maintenance rate per child reached a certain point in any School Board district, any additional maintenance rate must be divided equally among Voluntary Schools and Board Schools alike in proportion to average attendance.

This plan is admirably contrived to effect its main object—that of putting an end to the competition between Board and Voluntary Schools . . .[47]

However, neither this memorandum of 8 November nor its predecessor of 10 October (which was not circulated to the Cabinet) shows that Balfour seriously wished to do more than work for 'the single object of aiding

[45] W. M. Short, *Arthur James Balfour as Philosopher and Thinker*, London, 1912, p. 183.
[46] B.P. 49698, ff. 13–14.
[47] Ibid., f. 15.

Voluntary Schools'.[48] It has been inferred from Garvin's account of an argument in the Cabinet at the beginning of December that Balfour wanted to raise efficiency all round, but that Chamberlain and Salisbury blocked him for fear of Nonconformist objections. The evidence points rather to arguments on the level of political expediency. What kind of bill would both pass the Commons easily and bring adequate relief to Voluntary Schools?[49]

The upshot was that a simple bill, providing a subsidy for Voluntary Schools, passed into law in 1897. Balfour informed the House of Commons that it was still the Government's aim to enact the reforms embodied in the Bill of 1896; but the perversity of the Opposition meant that legislation would have to be 'piecemeal'. So, for the present, five more shillings would be granted per scholar, Voluntary Schools would be exempted from paying rates, and the capitation limit of 17/6d dating from 1876 would be repealed.[50]

During the debates on the Bill, Harcourt did not fail to attack Chamberlain for his inconsistency in supporting a measure to help the Church schools; but the latter 'sprang straight at the throat' of his one-time colleague, overwhelming him with a list of his own past political inconsistencies.[51] But Chamberlain and his group remained vulnerable to any solution of the schools problem which gave universal rate aid without universal popular control at the level of school management. All the signs are that Balfour, for his part, hoped never to be personally involved in another education bill.

Meanwhile he had had some other bad moments in helping his brother, Gerald, to pass the Irish Land Act of 1896. Henry Lucy thought that the tactics here followed were curiously analogous to those which had put paid to the Education Bill of 1896. The Irish landlords had understood that the Government would amend the Bill in their favour at the committee stage. Yet:

No sooner did the House get into Committee than the amendments were withdrawn. After that no one knew what a day might bring forth. It was only an unexpected access of firmness on the part of Mr. Gerald Balfour and the personal support he received from the Leader of the House that succeeded in driving the Bill through the House of Commons.[52]

[48] Ibid., f. 11, etc.
[49] Ibid., ff. 20–3, for Salisbury's memo of 30 Nov. 1896; J.C.P. 5/5/25 for the exchange of 2 Dec. between B. and Chamberlain. See also Garvin, iii, 154.
[50] *P.D.*, 4th, 45/926–8, 1 Feb., and 1314–15, 4 Feb. 1897.
[51] *U.P.*, p. 126.
[52] *U.P.*, pp. 100–1 (31 July 1896).

Gerald Balfour certainly worked hard during his term at the Irish Office (1895–1900), speaking in those years more frequently than any other minister, his brother included. [53] But in Lucy's opinion Gerald lacked, as Irish Secretary, 'the steel-hardiness of his brother' and he was less 'imperturbable' when assailed by the Irish contingent. Fortunately 'the weather' which 'the gentler Gerald' had to face was 'all summer-time compared with the Alpine storms through which the hardier Arthur resolutely pressed his way'. [54] Thus the Land Law (Ireland) Act of 1896 duly took its place in the series of Land Acts leading up to Wyndham's Land Purchase Act of 1903.

Now that the Gladstonian phase of Home Rule was over, Balfour could feel that the policies of Unionism stood a chance of success. On 20 October 1896 he wrote from Whittingehame to his old second-in-command Sir West Ridgeway, now Governor of Ceylon, about Ireland:

> That distressful country is in the most quiescent condition. The divisions among the Nationalists show no signs of healing. The National Convention was a total failure; and crime has reached its lowest limit. The storm caused by the Land Bill is rapidly going down. There never was a more remarkable instance of the power which one able man has of doing infinite mischief. I really believe that if Carson had not 'put his finger in the pie', we should not have had the slightest difficulty with the measure . . . The provoking thing is that the whole row was about nothing at all, and that there is not a single provision in the Act from which I believe the Irish landlords will suffer . . . [55]

In 1898 Balfour again devoted attention to Ireland. The object was to carry a major reform of Irish Local Government; and in the judgement of F. S. L. Lyons, the Bill 'deservedly ranks as one of the most important measures of conciliation passed during the whole period of the Union'. [56] In that context, a sheet of notepaper recording an exchange between Chamberlain and Balfour illuminates the latter's relations with his brother Gerald— and of the brothers with Chamberlain.

> [In Chamberlain's hand:] Who is to bring in the I.L. Govt Bill—*you* or Gerald
> [In Balfour's hand:] I strongly think Gerald ought to do it
> (a) because he is in daily contact with details of Irish local administration and has already drawn up the rough proposals for a bill.
> (b) because I think he was very ill-used over the Irish land bill, and it seems hard that he should be required to do the unpopular work of the Government, and refused the popular work.

[53] *P.D.*, indexes, 1895–1900.
[54] *U.P.*, p. 91.
[55] Sandars P., C.729.
[56] F. S. L. Lyons, *Ireland Since the Famine*, London (Fontana), 1973, p. 323.

(c) I think he will do the *Committee* work very well—I say nothing of 2nd reading.
[This debate took place on 21 March and elicited no comment from Lucy.]
(d) I shall regard myself as associated with him in the conduct of the measure, and shall be there all the time. [57]

The importance of the Irish Local Government Act of 1898 lay not only in the conciliatory effect of instituting an electoral system on the English model, with county councils, and urban and district councils. Valuable political experience was thus provided in an Irish setting in time to lay a basis for parliamentary institutions in an independent Ireland. A further major consequence was that, in most of Ireland, the Catholic majority displaced the ascendancy landlord class in the seats of local power—which explains the resistance of the said class to the measure.

In 1898 Balfour is also to be found playing an active role in the conduct of foreign policy. However, during his first spell at the Foreign Office from March to May, during his uncle's illness, he allowed Chamberlain to take the initiative. On 29 March Chamberlain, on his own responsibility, proposed an Anglo-German alliance at a meeting with Hatzfeldt, the German ambassador. As Grenville remarks, this approach 'embarrassed Hatzfeldt, Bülow and Balfour. Balfour at first treated the Colonial Secretary's effort as something of a joke, ignoring the fact that it made a mockery of ministerial responsibility.' [58] Salisbury, for his part, well understood that the Germans—who were, as it happens, secretly planning to challenge British naval power—were not interested in any alliance that met British needs. What Britain required was an alliance against Russia which had just occupied Port Arthur and was threatening the maintenance of the 'open door' to the Chinese market. Balfour, however, was inclined to support Chamberlain's quest of an alliance to ease Britain's growing difficulties in the foreign and imperial spheres. Secondly, Chamberlain's independent initiative in an area for which Balfour was responsible, set something of a precedent for Chamberlain's independent pronouncements about Tariff Reform in 1903.

In August 1898, Balfour again found himself acting as Foreign Secretary. He brought to a conclusion negotiations which had been going on with Germany about a loan to Portugal, on the security of the Portuguese colonies in Africa. If those colonies ever had to be distributed between the creditors, the details would affect the British position in South Africa.

[57] J.C.P. 5/5/37, n.d.—Jan. 1898?
[58] J. A. S. Grenville, *Lord Salisbury and Foreign Policy*, London, 1964, p. 156.

Balfour settled on terms 'more conciliatory to Germany than either Salisbury's or Chamberlain's.[59] Balfour was to continue to incline towards a (probably unattainable) German alliance right up to the conclusion of the Japanese Alliance in January 1902. In December 1901, he contended that if Britain were dragged by an ally into war with Russia (always the main potential enemy up to 1905), then it would be better if that ally were Germany than Japan. His argument was well worked out in its ramifications.[60] However, in so far as a German alliance on acceptable terms was not on offer, his contribution led nowhere. Yet his disagreement with his uncle on the principle of British 'isolation' possessed a constructive quality. It helped to provide the foundation on which the Japanese Alliance and the French and Russian *ententes* could be built.

Meanwhile, at the Foreign Office in April 1898, Balfour had also been preoccupied with the onset of the Spanish – American War. Even more decidedly than in the case of Germany, Balfour hoped that Britain would find a 'perpetual' ally in the United States; and he was careful to avoid any move that would annoy the latter power, irrespective of the merits of its case.[61]

Quite apart from the question of alliances, the Anglo-German Treaty concluded by Balfour in August 1898 was linked to British policy in South Africa. The Cape was, as ever, of strategic importance and it was an open question whether the whole of South Africa would, in the longer run, be dominated by the British or the Afrikaner element. Since the discovery of gold on the Rand, the Transvaal, the citadel of Afrikanerdom, had become rich; yet Balfour, for one, entertained the dubious belief that the Boers there were actually outnumbered by the *uitlanders*—mainly British—who ran the mines.[62] At the Cape, the Boers were certainly more numerous than those of British stock. In January 1896 the Kaiser William II had angered British opinion by sending a telegram of support to President Kruger when he defeated the Jameson raid, mounted in aid of the *uitlanders*. In August 1898, however, Balfour thought that his Treaty would weaken Germany's link with the Transvaal. Hatzfeldt had admitted to him that the arrangement 'would be a public advertisement to the Transvaal Government that they had nothing more to hope for from Germany'.[63]

[59]   Ibid., p. 193.
[60]   G. W. Monger, *The End of Isolation*, London, 1963, pp. 63–4.
[61]   Grenville, pp. 202–3.
[62]   J.C.P. 5/5/39, B. to Chamberlain, 6 May 1899; and see Porter's comment, p. 205 and n.3.
[63]   J.C.P. 5/5/78, B. to Chamberlain, 18 Aug. 1898.

Having found Chamberlain over-impulsive in the matter of a German alliance, so, in South African matters, Balfour had doubts about the wisdom of his rough handling of the Boers. Chamberlain himself did not want war and Balfour, in May 1899, gave him friendly advice—which was graciously received—not to overplay his hand. Balfour argued that the British had not established 'anything like a *casus belli*' against the Transvaal.

If, for example, we were to suppose some mining town in a South American Republic, occupied principally by foreigners, where the mode of government was similar to that of which we complain at Johannesburg, we might feel ourselves justified in sending friendly representations, but we certainly should not fight. [64]

But Balfour did not oppose the general tendency of Chamberlain's policy. After all, the Unionists were the party of Empire; and, in the colonial field, Chamberlain rode high on a wave of imperialist sentiment.

The Cabinet drifted into the South African War.

During the War, which began in October 1899, the British public was staggered by the news of a series of early defeats. Balfour deputized for the ailing Salisbury during most of December, including 'Black Week'; and in January 1900 he was much criticized for a lack of patriotic ginger in some speeches he made about the course of events. However, some of those closer to the seat of power took a more favourable view of his performance. According to Sandars, Balfour's

courage never failed . . . It was his nerve and promptitude which led to the appointment of Lord Roberts after Buller's terrible failure at Colenso. When things were at their darkest he was never gloomy or despairing. He stuck manfully to Lord Lansdowne and incurred the maximum of odium among the unthinking by his defence of him at a very cold public meeting in his own constituency of Manchester. [65]

Writing privately of the early weeks, Balfour admitted: 'the time of anxiety I have been going through is far greater than anything of which I have had experience, even in the worst periods of our Irish troubles.' [66] But Almeric FitzRoy, the Secretary of the Privy Council, detected no hint of what Balfour was feeling at the most worrying time. On 27 December 1899 he noted:

Council at Windsor. Mr. Balfour, Ritchie [Home Secretary], and myself went down. Certainly anything that brings me into contact with the former is a matter of

[64] J.C.P. 5/5/39, B. to Chamberlain, 6 May 1899.
[65] Sandars P., C.771.
[66] Dugdale, i, 306: B. to an unnamed friend, 24 Jan. 1900.

congratulation. There is a freshness, a serenity, almost a buoyancy about him which is as attractive as it is inspiring.[67]

Sir Sydney Parry's recollections reinforce FitzRoy's contemporary impression:

It was not, I think, until the outbreak of the Boer War that I fully realized the existence of another A. J. of whom I had only heard rumours before. In the early days of the war, when every new despatch from the front was more incoherent and contradictory than the last, when the 'Black Week' in December 1899 brought three catastrophes one on top of another—Magersfontein, Stormberg, Colenso—and when some hearts showed signs of failing for fear, then A.J. was indeed a 'tower of strength which stood foursquare to all the winds that blew'. He never fussed or flurried. He always kept his head. The country has never known what it owed him for the grim determination to hold Ladysmith to the last and the mission of Lord Roberts to retrieve our shaken fortunes.[68] How well I remember the fateful Saturday when the Prime Minister was ill and ungetatable out of town, and a succession of incoming telegrams brought the news of Colenso and an outgoing message summoned Lord Roberts post-haste from Dublin.

The next morning, Balfour went to the War Office soon after breakfast, in response to Lansdowne's phone-call informing him that Roberts was there. Parry continues:

On his return, some three hours later, he looked ten years younger. 'Thank God!' he said: 'I've seen a man, and a man who knows his own mind'; and then he told how Lord Roberts, heartbroken as he was at the news that his only son had fallen at Colenso in a gallant attempt to save the guns, had braced himself up to outline his carefully thought-out plan of campaign; how the question had been raised whether the physical strain of such a campaign would not be too great for a man nearing the seventies; and how Lord Roberts had answered: 'I've avoided evening parties, I go to bed early, I think I ride to hounds as well as I did a dozen years ago'; and then, after a moment's hesitation, 'You see, I've always felt the country might some day have need of me.' One could hear from the catch in A. J.'s voice how keenly the patriotic note had appealed to him.[69]

Balfour always found it difficult to put such feelings on display in public; but other people besides Parry long remembered how Balfour recounted, in various private settings, this interview with the Field Marshal at the War Office.[70]

[67]   Sir Almeric FitzRoy, *Memoirs*, London, 4th edn., 1925, p. 28.
[68]   See also Winston S. Churchill, *Great Contemporaries*, London (Fontana), 1959, p. 210.
[69]   WHI/81, Parry, 'Memories', pp. 14–16.
[70]   See, for instance, Lady Milner, p. 160.

Examination of Balfour's constructive work in the years before his premiership now returns to the cardinal issue of education from 1897 to 1902. Balfour's interest in science and in British universities extended back into his early life. It has been noted that, before the end of Salisbury's second administration, he was already a Fellow of the Royal Society (1888). In December 1887 George, second son of the great Charles Darwin and Plumian Professor of Astronomy and Experimental Philosophy at Cambridge from 1883, had written to Balfour: 'It has occurred to several F.R.S., myself amongst others, that it would be a very good thing if you would join the R.S. You are one of the few political men who really understand what Science is.'[71] Balfour may have seen little value in teaching science below the level of the country's intellectual élite;[72] but his connection with the passing of the University of London Act (1898) was entirely another matter. He had been Chancellor of Edinburgh University since 1891; and as early as 1887 he had discussed the problems of London's fragmented university with Richard Burdon Haldane (who had entered Parliament as a Liberal in 1885 and who shared Balfour's interest in philosophy).[73] In 1897 Haldane approached Balfour with a scheme for the central organization of London's teaching staff which required help from the Government if a plethora of disagreement was to be overcome. This was at a time when government involvement with universities was limited to small grants-in-aid to the various university colleges (a system dating from 1889)—there being, of course, no full-blown unified universities in England and Wales outside Oxford and Cambridge. Balfour agreed to have a bill drawn up, saying that he would be glad to get the 'London University question out of the way'.[74] Gorst introduced the Bill, Haldane made a good speech on the second reading (including a reference to the provision of higher technical education to meet the foreign challenge), and when the committee stage was reached Haldane himself was given charge of the Bill. However, it may be noted that the Act cost the Government very little by way of new grants-in-aid; also that Haldane's political fraternization with Balfour did nothing to enhance his popularity with his own party.[75]

[71] WHI/66.
[72] Eric Eaglesham, 'Planning the Education Bill of 1902', in *British Journal of Educational Studies*, Vol. ix, No.1, Nov. 1960, pp. 23–4.
[73] E. Ashby and M. Anderson, *Portrait of Haldane at Work on Education*, London, 1974, p. 27.
[74] Ibid., p. 36.
[75] Ibid., pp. 47, 75. See also Haldane, *An Autobiography*, London, 1929, pp. 124–7, for the London University Act.

Balfour also approved of Haldane's attempt, in 1898, to solve the question of Irish universities on a basis acceptable to Catholic and Protestant alike; but the proposal was dropped after Balfour privately confessed to Haldane that he could not carry the Cabinet with him. Haldane recalls that Balfour 'made a speech a few weeks afterwards in the north of England in which he declared that if the Unionist Party could not deal with the University question in Ireland it would have failed in a vital part of its mission'.[76] However, Balfour successfully endorsed Haldane's initiative in establishing English provincial universities, teaching and examining internally. To prevent the cheapening of degrees, Haldane proposed that independent external examiners should be appointed. He also stressed that the newly constituted universities should 'organise education from top to toe in their district'.[77]

As regards the grant of charters to Manchester (1903), Liverpool (1903), Leeds (1904), Sheffield (1905), and Bristol (1909), the decisive moment had come with the Cabinet's agreement in August 1902—soon after Balfour became Prime Minister—to set up a Committee of the Privy Council to hear evidence on Haldane's proposals. Balfour himself, despite his prolonged involvement with the Education Bill, sat as a member of the Committee which met from 17 to 19 December and reported in February 1903.[78] Chamberlain, who shared Haldane's views about the modernizing kind of education required, had already secured a charter for Birmingham University in 1900. While not excluding the humanities, the new university was intended to lead the world in knowledge relevant to industry, commerce, and transport.[79] Balfour, for his part, had acceded in May 1902 to Haldane's invitation to serve on a committee to promote the establishment of the Imperial College of Science and Technology. Modelled on the German Charlottenburg, it finally received its charter in 1907.[80]

Of course, it accorded with the political philosophy of Balfour, Haldane, and Chamberlain alike that these new universities depended largely on money raised from private sources. The over-all result was that Britain, even with Imperial College, was poorly provided compared, say, with Germany and her ten technological universities. By comparison with other leading industrialized states, Britain rejected education as an essential modernizing force. Her highest talent either remained undeveloped or was

[76]   Haldane, pp. 128–33.
[77]   Ashby and Anderson, pp. 60–6.
[78]   Ibid., pp. 64–8; Haldane pp. 138–41, 145–6.
[79]   Amery, iv, 214.
[80]   Ashby and Anderson, pp. 50–8.

taught to aspire to 'read' purely academic subjects at Oxford and Cambridge. The economy was expected to succeed without a pro-industrial thrust from society and from an appropriate national system of education. In the long run, of course, it could not.

Meanwhile, as far as schools were concerned, the Government had decided by 1899 to act on the first of the recommendations of the Bryce Commission of 1895: to concentrate executive power in a Board of Education. This replaced an arrangement whereby control was shared between three authorities. The measure was generally recognized as long overdue and Gorst saw it through the Commons without difficulty. Balfour stated on 26 June that the Bill was not regarded as a settlement of the question of secondary education. It was 'only to be taken as an instalment of some further Bill' which would 'place secondary education on a more satisfactory basis'. [81] Up to that time, various private institutions had offered secondary education, and the School Boards had done their best to provide something beyond an education that was strictly elementary. Balfour, however, did not realize when making his statement that a fuse leading to reform had already been lit.

In that month of June what might have been taken as a minor administrative judgement had been made by the auditor of the Local Government Board, T. B. Cockerton. He upheld the objection of various bodies, including the Camden School of Art, that the London School Board's expenditure on instruction in Science and Art was *ultra vires*. This rather innocuous-looking decision set in train a process. This was to end in the abolition of the School Boards and a radical reform of the whole system of state schooling along lines advocated by reformers since the report of the Cross Commission in 1888. However, an appeal delayed the absolute necessity of governmental action till April 1901, when Cockerton in his turn was upheld by the Master of the Rolls.

The Cockerton case had not arisen unbeknown to Sir John Gorst. In so far as he was a keen Churchman, he was in tune with Salisbury and Balfour. But he resented their low opinion of his competence, manifested in and after 1896. Though clever and witty, he was generally felt to be an impossible colleague. Among those who veered, through experience, towards this view was George Kekewich—Permanent Secretary of the Education Department until his impermanence was conveyed to him in 1902, a year that also saw Gorst's removal from the Department. According to Kekewich's memoirs, Gorst delighted in scoring off his superior, the 'dull,

[81]   *P.D.*, 4th, 73/681, 26 June 1899.

silent, and impassive' Lord President of the Council. Indeed, in Kekewich's not unprejudiced view, the Duke was 'a living wet blanket'. 'Puck
was for ever dancing round Jupiter, while administering pinpricks with
perfect impartiality to all who came near him.' Gorst would regale
Kekewich with rehearsals of planned subversive speeches, punctuated with
asides such as 'This will tickle them up' and 'Balfour won't like this bit;
he'll squirm!' [82]

Balfour was to an extent insulated from such shafts by his disinclination
to read the newspapers; but in the House of Commons he could hardly avoid
hearing repetition of treasured excerpts from Gorst's speeches by Liberal
members opposite. For instance on 15 July 1901 Dr MacNamara, an
educationist, enlivened an attack on the Government's education policy by
quoting a speech made by its own Vice-President for Education in December 1897. Speaking at Bristol, Gorst had asked rhetorically why the
Government had not supplied the elementary schools with such benefits as
better teachers and longer schooling. His answer, said MacNamara, was
that

> the members of the Government were selected from a class which was not entirely
> convinced of the necessity or the desirability of higher education for the people.
> They held the opinion, which was sometimes expressed by great professors of the
> Universities in their speeches, that there were certain functions which had to be
> performed in the modern life of civilised communities which were best performed
> by people ignorant and brutish. [83]

It is difficult to imagine that such episodes appealed to the Duke of
Devonshire any more than to Salisbury or Balfour. Indeed, at one point the
Duke had wondered aloud about the possibility of finding other work for
Gorst. Kekewich, then in the Duke's 'good books', suggested that a
moderately attractive governorship might be appropriate, for instance
Trinidad. With slow deliberation, 'not moving a muscle of his face', the
Duke responded: 'I cannot imagine that the Government would offer Sir
John Gorst the governorship of any colony that they wished to *retain!*' [84]
Yet by the end of 1900, the Duke was agreeing with Gorst that a com-
prehensive bill should be mounted to settle the whole question of ele-
mentary and secondary schools. Both Almeric FitzRoy, formerly an H.M.
Inspector of Schools, and Henry Lucy believed that the Duke was absolutely

[82]   Kekewich, pp. 92, 96, 100.
[83]   *P.D.*, 4th, 97/475–6.
[84]   Kekewich, pp. 94–5.

sincere in wishing to improve the system.[85] But Balfour was loathe once more to face the political dangers involved. On 5 January 1901 he wrote to Salisbury:

I go to Chatsworth on Monday, and Devonshire is sure to talk to me at length upon his educational schemes. I confess they alarm me: not because they are defective but because they are too complete. I fear a repetition of our parliamentary experience in '96![86]

At this stage, with Chamberlain's proposals for social reform coming forward as well as the education question, one may ask: What was Balfour's general view of the Government's financial situation and its bearing on proposals involving increased expenditure? On the one hand, he does not seem to have been obsessed, to the extent that Chancellors of the Exchequer were after 1895, by the growth of the national debt and the shortage of revenue. Yet he was better versed in financial and economic matters than most of his cabinet colleagues. As previously mentioned, he had participated in intricate public discussion of bimetallism.[87] From 1895 to 1902 he was kept posted on budgetary difficulties by Hicks Beach and Goschen (ex-Chancellor, and First Lord of the Admiralty, 1895–1900). In January 1896, for example, the latter plied him with suggestions for the re-ordering of naval finance.[88] Balfour certainly accepted the orthodox party view that direct taxation must not be increased, except in case of pressing necessity.

In response to Joseph Chamberlain—and doubtless to forestall the Liberals—the Government passed a Workmen's Compensation Bill in 1897 to cover industrial accidents; but here the financial burden was placed on the employers. When it came to Old Age Pensions, broached by Chamberlain in 1891 and vaguely adumbrated by Salisbury, it proved difficult to find an acceptable answer without increasing taxation, a politically unacceptable solution for a Unionist government. In retrospect, of course, income tax in the late '90s at a standard rate equivalent to 3p in the pound seems less than an agonizing burden. But only one-tenth of the nation's breadwinners were then liable to the tax, and those who had voted Unionist in 1895 obviously expected their party to shield them from any increase on the standard rate of

[85] Munson, pp. 615 and 623; FitzRoy, p. xviii; *U.P.*, p. 283; B.P. 49769, f. 169, Devonshire to B., 25 Sept. 1899.

[86] Hatfield House MSS, 3M/Class E, B. to Salisbury, 5 Jan. 1901. For once, B.'s amended wording was not recorded on the copy—see Short's note on f. 121 in B.P. 49691.

[87] See, for instance, *The Currency Question: Address by the Right Hon. A. J. Balfour*, London, 1893.

[88] Sandars P., C.728.

8d in the pound. It should be remembered that the Liberals also sought government economy and, for some years to come, hoped to compensate for any increase in social expenditure by cutting the cost of defence.

In 1896 a Treasury Committee under Lord Rothschild investigated the feasibility of purely contributory pensions. It predictably reached negative conclusions. But in April 1899 Chamberlain, without, it would seem, the sanction of the Cabinet, indicated in the Commons that the Government would produce a bill.[89] As in the case of foreign policy in 1898, Balfour acquiesced in Chamberlain's insubordination and, on winding up the debate, endorsed his initiative.[90] Consequently, a Select Committee of the House of Commons was set up under the doubtfully competent chairmanship of Henry Chaplin (who was soon to be dropped from the Presidency of the Local Government Board). Significantly, the Committee reported in July 1899 that the revenue for pensions would have to come from a new tariff policy.[91] November saw the printing of cabinet memoranda on pensions by Balfour and Chamberlain. They both advocated a strictly limited contribution from central government, the rest of the money coming from the ratepayer.[92] In December, at the Cabinet's request, Balfour submitted a draft bill entitled 'Pensions and Deserving Poor'.[93] However, what was apt to be called 'Chamberlain's War' halted progress. In a letter to Knollys, Edward VII's private secretary, Balfour summarized his views as of February 1901:

> I ought to have remembered when speaking to the King, and afterwards to you, on the subject of the Aged Poor that there is an overwhelming reason against attempting anything at the present moment—the reason, namely, of *expense*. I am afraid the public have very little notion of the immense additional burdens which must be thrown on the taxpayer in consequence not only of the War, but of the increases in the Army and Navy, which are quite independent of the War. Nor have they probably foreseen the amount of loans and new taxation which will have to be raised to meet this expenditure. It is, I think, hardly possible at such a moment to ask the Chancellor of the Exchequer to find anything more—even for so valuable a domestic reform as that for which the King is so properly anxious . . .[94]

But if this marked the limit of Balfour's association with an innovatory pensions bill, in educational policy the year 1901 proved to be a watershed.

[89]   Garvin, iii, 626.
[90]   Ibid.
[91]   Dennis Judd, *Radical Joe: a Life of Joseph Chamberlain*, London, 1977, p. 241.
[92]   Cab. 37/51/87 is B.'s memo 'Pensions and Poor Law Reform; Preliminary Suggestions for Discussion', dated 15 Nov. 1899.
[93]   Cab. 37/51/95–6, 12 Dec. 1899.
[94]   Sandars P., C.718, B. to Knollys, 9 Feb. 1901.

The Cockerton judgement having been finally upheld in April, the Government was at once compelled to give temporary legality, and thus finance, to the non-elementary education provided by School Boards. On 7 May, however, Gorst, yet again, introduced an abortive bill which attempted to establish the oft-recommended but still controversial paramount local authorities, instead of merely dealing with the immediate crisis. In the view of the Liberal educationist J. H. Yoxall, 'a short Suspensory Bill, affirming that, for a given date, it would be within the power of the school boards to go on maintaining the higher grade schools' would have met with general acceptance. Instead they had been given 'a most disappointing Bill'; and, if Britain enjoyed 'educational chaos at present, it would add to that chaos'.[95]

In June, just before the Cabinet dolefully decided to abandon the Bill, Balfour wrote to the Bishop of Coventry:

The whole question is one of time. I never anticipated dealing with the Education Question this Session: nor should I ever have permitted any Bill even to be introduced had it not been for the Cockerton judgement. It was quite evident, with the war going on in South Africa, with the enormous amount of financial work that had necessarily to be got through in connection with the Budget, etc., a less convenient season for original legislation could not well be imagined. The Cockerton judgement renders it necessary to do something to this end, and the Education Bill was read a first time. It has provoked a degree of opposition which seems to be wholly irrational, and which is only worth consideration because it involves an expenditure of parliamentary time which it may be impossible to find before next year.[96]

In July Gorst did at least get through the Commons the single-clause Education (No.2) Bill so that, for the time being, the School Boards could continue with non-elementary education. Balfour minimized his involvement in the debates, but during the second reading, he replied to a question whether the Government thought that the School Boards should be the authorities to oversee secondary education. His answer was unambiguous: 'we do not think so.' He also referred to the comparisons constantly made with Germany. 'You tell us we are falling behind the Germans in industrial matters because we do not educate our people.' If, he said, Britain was to learn from such countries as France, Germany, and the United States, it was 'incumbent on this House, as soon as may be, to establish that

[95] *P.D.*, 4th, 93/970–1; 1000–2; 7 May 1901.
[96] B.P. 49854, ff. 119–20, B. to the Bishop of Coventry, 25 June 1901.

secondary authority which shall deal with secondary education for all classes of the country'.[97]

In thus appealing to the Opposition, Balfour certainly hoped to lower the level of parliamentary hostility to any major bill introduced in 1902. But he still showed scant enthusiasm for being personally cast in the role of educational reformer. On 25 July he wrote to Devonshire who, as Lord President, still bore the chief ministerial responsibility for education:

My dear Duke,

. . . I have as you know been dragged (much against my will) into questions connected with Education . . . We have to deal with a certain number of School Boards which are sulky, a certain number of Borough Councils which are ambitious, and a certain number of County Councils which are somewhat slow. The two latter are sensitive, and I am afraid that unless we avoid . . . friction . . . we may find ourselves in a position of considerable embarrassment. I know from gossip which, though it be gossip, is I am sure well-founded, that your Permanent Secretary neither loves your policy nor is anxious to further it . . .[98]

On 8 August 1901 a cabinet committee met to draft proposals for a major bill. It consisted of Balfour, Devonshire, and Walter Long, together with Gorst, Kekewich, Robert Laurie Morant, and Sir Courtenay Ilbert (the parliamentary counsel and draftsman). At the early meetings in August, Morant realized that only Balfour could get a comprehensive bill through the Commons; and a substantial memorandum already prepared by him on 1 August shows how, as a politically aware pro-Anglican, he was able to commend himself to Balfour as an adviser. In his 'Conclusion' he summarizes the legislative problems presented by a bill for secondary education alone. Demonstrating political acuity, he adds:

[If] we are tempted to include Elementary Education in the Bill, in order to save for ever the Denominational Schools (which will otherwise be swept away by the next Radical Government) and to raise enthusiasm for our Bill, we must necessarily face the question of removing the existing anti-denominational restrictions upon all rate-aid, of losing the cumulative vote, of raising denominational struggles in the election of local bodies, and above all of deciding on a proper relation between a County and its component areas, and on the proper organisation of Local Authorities, each with clearly defined functions for various types and grades of Schools.[99]

Some notes survive of the first meeting of the cabinet committee on

---

[97]   *P.D.*, 4th, 96/1446–8, 9 July 1901.

[98]   B.P. 49765, ff. 191–2.

[99]   Ed. 24/14/13a. As Eaglesham remarks in 'Planning the Education Bill of 1902', p. 9, no.2, this memo is safely attributable to Morant.

8 August. [100] The questions discussed imply that a comprehensive bill was to be drafted, and indeed Gorst's subsequent draft was on such broad lines. Among the participants Gorst, Balfour, and Kekewich were prominent. In the Bill, as it was actually presented to Parliament, the adoptive clause was of great political significance. This left the new Local Education Authorities free to choose whether or not to take over primary as well as secondary schools. So it is interesting to read at this early stage that 'AJB seemed to approve of suggestion that local option as to abolition of Schl Bds shd be exercised by provl. order'; also that he apparently agreed with Gorst on some kind of rate aid for the Voluntary Schools. But where a borough did take over Board Schools, Balfour wanted Clause 27 of the 1896 Bill to operate. It was this clause that had enraged Nonconformists by breaching the Cowper–Temple Clause of 1870. For under the Cowper–Temple rule, there was to be no denominational religious instruction in a Board School. Even though the Government had, under Clause 27, offered Nonconformists the kind of religious instruction they preferred in Voluntary Schools, reciprocity in Board Schools for those wanting denominational instruction was rejected by Nonconformists.

Balfour was strongly in favour of religious instruction in primary schools; but he also wanted toleration in the matter, rather as he had done over burials in the 1870s. Whenever the subject of elementary schools was discussed, he found it difficult to credit that the Clause 27 solution could not be accepted by all rational men: that is, that where a 'reasonable' number of the parents of *any* kind of school—Voluntary or Board—so desired, religious instruction of the required description should as far as practicable be provided. As he wrote a few months later to an old Trinity College contemporary:

I do not approach the topic in the least as a Member of one particular denomination. Indeed, the divisions among Protestants have, in my judgement, done such incalculable harm to Christianity that I should be reluctant indeed to do anything to embitter them. [101]

If Balfour's view was logical, bigotry on both sides ensured the exclusion of a Clause 27-style solution from the Bill of 1902. It was this aspect of the education issue which Balfour found particularly distasteful.

At the meeting of 8 August, Morant's role was restricted to the supply of information, e.g. 'How much wd 2d [rate] limit raise. RLM has

[100] Ed. 24/16/79f, 'Meeting in 1st Lord's room', 8 Aug. 1901.
[101] B.P. 49854, ff. 313–14, B. to Revd H. Arnold Thomas, 22 April 1902.

figures.'[102] But it is significant that, even then, he was tapped as a source for Chamberlain's views on the Cowper – Temple Clause. Who, then, was the principal author of the Bill which Balfour presented to the House of Commons in March 1902?

About a week after the committee meeting of 8 August, Morant met Balfour at lunch through the good offices of Edward Talbot, Bishop of Rochester, who had married Lavinia Lyttleton and had for long been a close friend of Balfour's. Over coffee, Morant was able to demonstrate his mastery of the education problem and its political aspects.[103] On 17 August the parliamentary session ended and Balfour was soon re-established at Whittingehame. On 14 September Morant wrote: 'You were good enough to say, on the last day of the session, that you would be glad to hear from me if I thought any matters were arising that needed your notice.' Realizing that Balfour already distrusted Kekewich and Ilbert as committed to the Liberal line on education, he felt that some confirmatory remarks would not go amiss. He indicated that 'the poor old Duke' was being hoodwinked by the 'happy collaboration' of Kekewich, Ilbert, and 'young *Acland*' (who had been the Liberal Vice-President for Education from 1892 to 1895). Kekewich was 'most anxious that only Secondary should be touched' and that action on the primary sector should be delayed till a regime 'more favourable to his friends the Schl Boards and N.U.T.' should come into office. 'The Duke, however, does not realize this but "only wonders" how all the "difficulties can ever be met".'[104]

Balfour invited Morant to discuss the whole problem with him at Whittingehame in October. There can be no doubt that, while retaining full independence of judgement, Balfour relied a great deal on Morant after this visit.[105] But by 30 October 1901, Morant was admitting to some previous underestimation of the Duke. With unfeigned astonishment, he informed Balfour that the Duke was preparing a memorandum for the Cabinet 'all by himself'. This would provide the basis for three draft bills; and with regard to elementary education 'the Duke himself gave Ilbert his instructions, at first hand: one drastic', abolishing all School Boards, and 'the other on his own lines of local option'.

In the same letter Morant went on to touch Balfour on a sensitive spot, the memory of his disastrous concession in 1896 to Sir Albert Rollit on authority status for non-county boroughs. In discussion Morant had found

[102]   Ed. 24/16/79 f.
[103]   B. M. Allen, *Life of Sir Robert Morant*, London, 1938, pp. 154–6.
[104]   B.P. 49787, ff. 20–1.
[105]   This is emphasized in Lady Rayleigh's diary entry for 28 Sept. 1902, quoted below.

that Rollit at first 'seemed exceedingly reasonable'; but the latter went on to say that he '*hates* any rate-aid to Denominational Schools' and if it were put in a bill he 'might vote against it'. 'But on the small area difficulty he was still more difficult.' [106]

Indeed, the next day Morant wrote to Wilfred Short (Balfour's long-standing confidential shorthand-writer): 'I am beginning to fear so much the opposition of the Non-County Boroughs to our plan of full County Suzerainty that I am wondering whether it might not be better . . . to attempt some Equalisation of Rates Clause.' [107]

On 1 November Balfour, at Whittingehame, composed one of his comparatively rare letters to Morant in a mood unusually close to despair:

> There are two fundamental difficulties ahead of us in connection with the new Education Bill, through which I utterly fail to see my way. The first is the opposition of the non-County Boroughs. I confess I think Rollit's arguments are, in a Parliamentary sense, unanswerable . . . if non-County Boroughs unite against us, our position will be hopeless. Possibly your suggested solution may offer a loop-hole of escape; but I should like to see it worked out before giving an opinion on it.
>
> The second difficulty is, of course, the future position of Voluntary Schools. As I understand the present situation, those interested in the maintenance of these Schools desire to have all their current expenses connected with secular education paid out of the rates, they in exchange to hand over their existing buildings, and to engage for the future to keep them up, and, where necessary to add to them . . . But I take it that in a *very* large number of cases the buildings are inferior to the Board Schools, and that if the Voluntary School Managers were required to bring them up to that standard, their financial position would hardly be improved by the change.
>
> This points to making any arrangement between the Managers and the Local Authority a voluntary one and a variable one, as was originally proposed. But it is undeniable that such a plan is open to the criticism that it would please nobody very much, and that it will bring the denominational question into local elections.
>
> You will see by this that I am in the lowest possible spirits about the whole question, and am beginning to think it far more insoluble even than the South African problem. [108]

Meanwhile, on Friday, 1 November, Morant was sending the draft bills to Balfour so that he could read them before the Cabinet met on Tuesday the

---

[106] B.P. 49787, ff. 29–30, Morant to B., 30 Oct. 1901. See Cab. 37/59/111 for the Duke's memo of 2 Nov. 1901.

[107] Ibid., f. 31, Morant to Short, 31 Oct. 1901.

[108] Ed. 24/14/26, 'Memorandum to RLM from AJB', a typed copy, n.d., but probably 1 Nov. 1901.

5th. He remarked: 'Ilbert still drafts the things in a highly hostile spirit. He admitted this morning that they could not possibly work as now drafted.' [109]

The following day, 2 November, was a Saturday; but the threat to the comprehensive principle implied by Balfour's above-quoted communication brought an instant response from Morant's Whitehall desk:

> I do earnestly hope (if I may venture to express this to you) that you will not let any definite decision be taken by Tuesday's Cabinet that Elementary Education shall be left out of the Bill. Could not a week or two longer be given, in which you could go more fully into the pros. and cons.?

After rehearsing the fair-deal argument that public maintenance would save the Voluntary Schools while they, for their part, offered a 'substantial' *quid pro quo* in the form of their buildings, he admitted that the 'ultimate difficulty'—the religious issue—was 'forever and everywhere insoluble'. 'But at any rate we should be offering a solution far more nearly complete than (as we now see) was attained in 1870.' [110]

On 5 November 1901 the Cabinet, fearing a split in the Unionist coalition, rejected rate aid for the Voluntary Schools. Indeed, as the Duke's memorandum of the 2nd had indicated, they had hardly dared to discuss the matter hitherto. The Cabinet resorted to voting on more than one issue; but the main outcome was a decision not to confine the Bill to secondary education. [111]

A new cabinet committee was now formed. Balfour again presided. His colleagues were Devonshire, Selborne, Lord James of Hereford, Walter Long, and R. W. Hanbury. Gorst was dropped; and Kekewich and Ilbert were also henceforth excluded. By December Lord Thring had come in as draftsman, while Morant had already superseded Kekewich as the committee's principal adviser. By the following year Morant would be the Education Department's *de facto* Permanent Secretary—an appointment made official in 1903.

Few of the ideas discussed by the relevant cabinet committees and in the Cabinet itself between August 1901 and March 1902 were fresh contributions to educational thought. Virtually all of them were to be found in such compilations as the Bryce Commission's Report of 1895 or in the Bill of 1896. In 1901 the problem confronting the legislators was how to provide a long-term solution while minimizing the consequent damage to the Unionist Party. As to key principles, the Government was virtually committed to

---

[109]   B.P. 49787, f. 34, Morant to B., 1 Nov. 1901.

[110]   Ibid., ff. 35–6, Morant to B., 2 Nov.

[111]   FitzRoy, i, 63; Munson, pp. 625–6.

establish County and County Borough Councils as Local Education Authorities for secondary education and was under pressure from many of its keenest supporters to give rate aid to the Voluntary Schools. If the Cabinet decided to opt for a comprehensive rather than a secondary bill, it would have to decide how far it should go towards abolishing School Boards and in giving rate aid. At what point would the enhanced enthusiasms of supporters be outweighed by the augmented fury of the opposition? It was always crucial to remember that Nonconformist discontent would be shared by Chamberlain's flock. In such circumstances, a major share of the Bill's authorship must clearly be attributed to the two politicians who bore the heat and burden of the day both in the cabinet committee and in the Cabinet, Devonshire and Balfour. The Duke was slow to feel his way forward, but he was steady in his advance. Balfour, on the other hand, grasped complexities and spotted dangers with a lightning speed beyond the Duke's capability. But he lacked Devonshire's sense of purpose. Balfour's sister, Lady Rayleigh, noted at Terling in January 1902:

A. J. B. lunched with us and told us the Cabinet insisted on his conducting the Education bill in the Commons—they would not have Gorst at any price and the worst of it was he (A.) did not believe in Education—and whatever line he took the bill would be torn to pieces, and there was no really satisfactory line to take. [112]

But Balfour's tortured contributions were linked with his crucial underlying assumption, that the Cabinet would not be able to stop short at secondary education alone. [113] He also gravitated towards *limited* rate aid for Voluntary Schools on a *compulsory* basis throughout the country, whereas the Duke gradually moved towards full rate support, coupled with an Adoptive Clause allowing the L.E.A.s (Local Education Authorities) to opt out of the commitment altogether. Balfour, for his part, sought to mitigate ratepayer hostility by leaving some of the maintenance expenses of Voluntary Schools to be met by subscriptions. As subscriptions would in any case cover religious instruction, Nonconformists would have little ground for opposing the Bill. It was one of Balfour's most persistent fears that County and County Borough Councils would refuse to implement the scheme either on a question of religious instruction or on account of the financial and administrative burden involved. [114]

[112] Lady Rayleigh's Diary, 22 Jan. 1902.
[113] See esp. Cab. 37/59/134, B.'s 'Memorandum on the Proposal to Introduce two Bills for Education', 17 Dec. 1901.
[114] B.P. 49769, f. 213, B. to Devonshire, 22 Jan. 1902; Cab. 37/60/32, B.'s memo of 6 Feb. and 37/60/37, B.'s memo of 11 Feb. 1902. See Munson, pp. 627–32 for Devonshire's approach.

Although Salisbury, Hicks Beach, and Chamberlain persistently sought to confine the measure to secondary education alone, the Duke of Devonshire began to impose himself at a cabinet meeting of 5 February. He argued that only his scheme, whereby those councils choosing to control elementary education would thus become *fully* responsible for all publicly financed schools in their area, could justify the abolition of School Boards and the enforcement of a uniform education rate in such areas. [115] According to Almeric FitzRoy, the Duke 'surprised his colleagues by displaying a complete mastery over the issues involved and unfolded his views in a speech of great cogency, not allowing himself to be disturbed by the interruption of Mr. Chamberlain'. Although Salisbury did not think that the Cabinet was ready to capitulate to the Duke, the latter had 'sensibly affected the views of his colleagues'; and, noted FitzRoy, 'much as they shrink from some of the consequences, they begin to see that there is no alternative that is not exposed to more damaging parliamentary criticism and does not threaten more imminent party disaster.' [116] Indeed, by Tuesday, 18 March, the Cabinet had finally decided to accept the Duke's scheme. Their mood was fatalistic. Both Balfour and the Duke thought the issue would 'wreck the Government'. [117] On Monday, 24 March, Balfour introduced the Bill in the House of Commons.

In so far as Balfour came into line with Devonshire on the more controversial details of the Bill, it may doubtless be accepted that the Duke was its principal ministerial author. But Balfour's underlying assumption that a scheme including elementary education could hardly be avoided went far to ensure that some kind of comprehensive solution would be attempted. While fertile and flexible in his search for the least disastrous political course, he gravitated to the Duke's side both in committee and in the Cabinet. When, on 13 December 1901, the Cabinet voted by 10 to 8 for secondary education alone, Balfour and the Duke were the leaders of the minority; and on 19 December Balfour told the Cabinet that he would not pilot—in FitzRoy's words—a 'narrow and half-hearted' measure. When, in February 1902, he abandoned his own scheme for universal, but partial, rate aid in favour of the Duke's adoptive proposal, he obviously helped to determine the outcome. [118] In sum, his role in framing the Bill of 24 March 1902, which was fundamentally changed by parliamentary process before it became law, was crucial, but secondary. Of course, his secondary role

---

[115] Munson, pp. 631–2.
[116] FitzRoy, i, 73–4 (5 Feb. 1902).
[117] Munson, p. 632; FitzRoy, i, 81.
[118] FitzRoy, i, 69 and 81.

befitted his position as First Lord of the Treasury and Leader of the House, just as the Duke ultimately fulfilled his own clear ministerial responsibility.

But what, then, of Morant? It has been written: 'Of all those concerned Morant had the greatest influence on the final form of the Education Bill of 1902.'[119]

It has been seen that, from August 1901, Morant established a special working relationship with Balfour; but inevitably Devonshire, having found Gorst and Kekewich wanting, also turned to Morant. By the end of September, Morant had become the principal adviser to the Duke as well as to Balfour.[120] Moreover, as Gorst's private secretary from 1899, Morant had worked for a comprehensive reform of the education system and had helped Gorst to lay the fuse leading to the Cockerton crisis of 1899–1901. Yet none of this can obscure the fact that, in the sphere of legislation, he could be no more than an expert adviser. Indeed, he received a reminder to this effect from Balfour early in January 1902. He and Thring were told to keep to their instructions; and Morant replied full of humble explanations.[121] Morant had no access to cabinet meetings. It was there that the key decisions were made, unmade, and made anew; and if it was Devonshire's scheme that eventually prevailed, it follows that Morant's work for the Duke was at least as important as his work for Balfour. Such was the position up to the final agreement of the Cabinet shortly before Balfour's introduction of the Bill in March 1902.

Of course, the clauses most discussed by the Cabinet were not necessarily those most important for the nation's future. Balfour, personally, is often credited with bestowing on his country a badly-needed system of secondary education; and when the whole parliamentary process of handling, and amending, the Bill is taken into account, his responsibility exceeds that of the other leading participants. But not only was Balfour's prior interest in the subject less than compelling. There are no indications that education, as an issue of long-term importance for the British economy, took up the time—or the fears and passions—of the Cabinet. So it is hardly surprising that when, on 24 March, Balfour had to introduce a bill so recently agreed and, by his own subsequent admission, so hastily drafted, he was glad to avail himself of Morant's briefing. To this extent it is fair comment that 'throughout his opening speech and in subsequent debates we can hear

[119] Eaglesham, 'Planning the Education Bill', p. 1.
[120] Ed. 24/14, ff. 79–81, 'Successive Stages of the Education Bill', unsigned departmental memo, late Oct. 1901.
[121] Ed. 24/17/130B, B. to Morant, 4 Jan. 1902; *B.P.* 49787, ff. 56–9, Morant to B., 6 Jan. 1902.

phrases of Morant's echoing down the corridors of Westminster.'[122] If the cabinet ministers, except perhaps for Devonshire, had not thought deeply about the direction to be taken by secondary education, this cannot be said of Morant. As indicated above, he was able on 1 August 1901 to compile a detailed set of questions a week ahead of the initial meeting of the original cabinet committee.[123] On the crucial subject of technical and commercial education, his views resembled those enunciated in the Bryce Report of 1895, the year when he joined the Education Department. On 1 August 1901 he wrote:

> Some say that, supposing the Technical Instruction Acts to be repealed, the conflict between the claims of Technical Institutes and Technical Evening Classes against Secondary Day Schools giving a *general education* will be very keen: that it is in an increase of good Secondary Day Schools, and an improvement of those that exist, that a real improvement of English Education can *alone* be found: that the plethora of classes giving specialised instruction to students of wholly inadequate general education is the curse of our system . . .[124]

It will be seen that Balfour, when introducing the Bill, followed a similar line. Morant himself would eventually suspect that, however plausible and generally accepted, his argument had reinforced a potentially damaging trend. Meanwhile, however, he was left free to develop secondary education largely along lines of his own choosing. Thus the new secondary system became a pale imitation of the 'Public Schools' with their pervasive anti-industrial bias.

In sum, then, Morant must certainly be accounted a major influence on the details of the Bill—and perhaps on those gaps in the details which left secondary education subject to the philosophy of the Education Department.

In so far as the Education Bill was the most important piece of constructive legislation with which Balfour was ever directly concerned from the drafting stage to its enactment, the inference must be that he was a constructive statesman only in a limited sense. In this cardinal instance, his motivation was primarily partisan. It was his sense of duty towards his party, with its denominational commitments, that fuelled his sustained parliamentary effort. As Sandars, quoting that fount of party-political

---

[122] Eaglesham, *The Foundations of 20th Century Education in England*, London, 1967, p. 43.

[123] Ed. 24/14/13a: 'Memorandum. Some questions to be considered before drafting the Education Bill for 1902', 1 Aug. 1901.

[124] Ibid., ff. 65–6.

wisdom, Captain Middleton, put it to Balfour on 8 March 1902, '*any* result is preferable to the failure to pass a Bill which is once introduced.'[125]

Likewise, if the party for lack of better called on him to lead, whether in the second or even in the first place, Balfour did not go so far as to refuse. Once he had, in July 1902, accepted the leadership of the Unionist coalition, he would not lightly abandon his task, any more than he had abandoned the leadership of the Commons in the early 1890s, though sorely tempted to do so. It was because Balfour was primarily a party man, except in extreme national emergencies, that he shared his uncle's unfavourable opinion of Peel. In essence, Balfour condemned Peel for placing his own view of the national interest above his duty to the Conservative Party. Yet it remains true, also, that specialists like Dilke and Haldane in defence, and Haldane in higher education, found Balfour more accessible to their ideas, across the party divide, than the leadership of their own party.

Balfour's opening sentences, when he introduced the Education Bill on Monday, 24 March 1902, give an exact account of the spirit in which he faced his task:

I rise on behalf of the Government to fulfil a pledge given in the King's Speech that a Bill should be introduced dealing not merely with secondary education or with primary education in their isolation, but dealing with both in one measure and with the view of their better co-ordination. Nobody can be more impressed than I am with the difficulty of the task which the Government have undertaken; and certainly no Ministry, and I think no House of Commons, would lightly engage in the controversies which any attempt like that on which we are engaged must necessarily involve. It is only because we feel that the necessity with which this Bill is intended to deal is a pressing necessity, it is only because we are of opinion that it cannot with national credit be much long delayed, that we have resolved to lay before the House our solution of the great problem.[126]

More than half way through his exordium, Balfour came to the delicate matter of the adoptive clause which was bound to annoy educationists, to say nothing of the powerful Anglican lobby. The limitation, he said,

requires more explanation. I recognise, and I am sure the House recognises, that whether they like the scheme we have proposed or whether they dislike it, it is, at all events, a far-reaching scheme. It touches an enormous number of controverted problems; it may rake up the ashes of many old controversies, and it may excite administrative disquiet, even alarm, in many portions of the country. I do not know that even now it has been brought home to the minds of everybody everywhere how vital is the need for some great reform, such as we propose; and we can hardly hope

[125] B.P. 49761, f. 16.
[126] *P.D.*, 4th, 105/846–7.

to succeed in our object unless we carry with us the local authorities on whom the burdens and responsibility of working the Bill will fall. We think it most undesirable to drive or force them, with but brief consideration, and possibly against their will, into accepting our plan. We therefore propose to leave it to the councils of the various districts to adopt the portion of the Act dealing with elementary education if and when they please.

He went on to recall the success of a similar permissive arrangement of 1876. This prepared the way for the Act of 1880, whereby attendance at school was made 'universal and obligatory' without any opposition at all. During the interval of four years, the objections had withered away. [127]

However, it was this adoptive clause which became the subject of a crucial amendment in committee on 9 July. In consequence, option gave way to compulsion and Nonconformist resistance to the Bill was heightened to a point where the Liberal Party realized that it had been presented with a great political opportunity. Why, then, did Balfour not oppose this risky amendment?

It will be remembered that the Duke of Devonshire's scheme, based on the adoptive principle, began to gain ground in the Cabinet of 5 February. On the 6th Balfour analysed the situation thus in a memorandum:

We are in a great difficulty over the Education Bill, and the difficulty is chiefly due to the following causes:-

There is a great reluctance among us to compel the Local authority to support Denominational Schools. There is great anxiety to prevent these schools from being squeezed out of existence. There is considerable apprehension that even if we could get round these difficulties, the ratepayer, as such, will object to having his burdens increased. And, above all, there is the fear that, if our Bill compels County and Borough Councils to mix themselves up in the denominational controversy, they may combine to denounce it. This would render our Parliamentary position untenable. [128]

The attitude of the Councils, then, would go far to decide whether the Government could move beyond the patchwork solution implied by the adoptive clause.

On 9 July Henry Hobhouse, a Liberal Unionist squire, moved the withdrawal of the adoptive clause. An established authority on local government, he numbered education among his special interests. By October 1901 he had been in touch with Morant who promptly passed on his

---

[127]   Ibid., 862–3.
[128]   Cab. 37/60/32, 6 Feb. 1902.

letter to Balfour. [129] While Hobhouse then saw 'great advantages' from a *'political* point of view' in a comprehensive measure, he sought ways of placating Nonconformist councils. Some of Balfour's suggestions at the drafting stage, such as retention of subscriptions for Voluntary Schools, may have been inspired by this communication.

On moving his amendment of 9 July 1902, Hobhouse observed that, when the Bill was introduced in March, 'it was almost universal opinion among the friends of the Bill that it should be optional'. But they now saw that a compulsory system would be better than perpetuation of the present chaos, and heightened agitation, in those areas opting out of the scheme for elementary education. He admitted that some authorities wanted the option to be retained, but said that 'the large majority of the County Councils, as represented by the County Councils Association, had expressed their general approval' of the scheme. (Indeed, according to a later speaker, 'only about seven' English counties had indicated their dissent from 'the general principles' of the Bill.) [130] Hobhouse pointed out that the option would leave the surviving School Boards 'threatened every three years with extinction'; and in any case their sphere of activity would now be restricted by the Cockerton judgement. As for the Voluntary Schools, where they were unlucky enough to be stranded in a dissenting area, they would have a new sense of grievance. [131]

In response, Balfour said he now felt that he could dismiss the likelihood of 'a rate war'. One reason for the greater willingness of county authorities to bear 'the administrative burden' of the Bill was the increase in government finance for councils undertaking elementary education. Secondly, he

was afraid it was more clear than it was at one time that, if this matter was left open as the Clause left it open, the result must be that they would introduce into County Councils and into the elections of County Councils elements of difficulty and friction which had never been introduced in these Councils or elections before.

Moreover, there had been, on both sides of the House, 'the profoundest interest' expressed in the training of teachers. This would suffer from 'a degree of confusion' if one of a group of counties did not 'adopt the Bill' or 'if important boroughs within the area of a county refused to adopt it'. Therefore the

changes in the position which he had indicated would induce him personally to vote

---

[129] B.P. 49787, ff. 26–8, Hobhouse to Morant, 23 Oct. 1901. Morant kept a copy: Ed. 24/16/100.

[130] *P.D.*, 4th, 110/1269.

[131] Ibid., 1233–6.

for his hon. Friend's Amendment. He would not attempt to make it a Government question, because it was one of those questions which might be very properly left to the judgement of the House itself. [132]

After the various arguments had been rehearsed and educationists of both parties had supported the amendment, the closure was applied and the adoptive clause was duly deleted by 271 to 102. In this free vote, Balfour was numbered with the majority.

A feature of this important debate was the absence of Joseph Chamberlain on account of a cab accident of 7 July, when he suffered an injury to the head. But, writing to Balfour on 4 August, even he seemed to accept the withdrawal of the option as politically unavoidable. Indeed, by opening 'My dear Arthur', he signified exceptional warmth (though he had reverted to 'My dear Balfour' by the 31st). He remarked on the 'surprising patience and resource' with which Balfour had been piloting the Bill. Latterly the (transformed) measure had, alas, 'brought all the fighting Nonconformists into the field and made of them active instead of merely passive opponents'. However, he admitted that 'many of my colleagues, including yourself, fully recognised the dangers ahead of us, but you thought, and very likely you were right, that any alternative course would lead us into still greater difficulties.' [133]

On 10 July, at a family dinner at 10 Downing Street, Balfour had revealed himself as far from jubilant after his big decision of the previous day. His sister Evelyn noted: 'A. said that owing to the debate on the education bill he was beginning to hate both Education and religion.' But his particular worry just then seems to have been not the Nonconformists, but 'our people' (the Unionists) who, through hatred of 'High Church Parsons', might give 'more power to the Education Authority in the management of voluntary schools than was just'. [134]

However, it was indeed a material achievement to have reached this point. The Government had not broken up. A Bill hamstrung by political circumstances had been developed into a measure of great potential merit. Yet the political consequences for the Unionists would prove severe. Not only was Nonconformist opposition much stimulated by the withdrawal of the option. The Liberals soon began to win by-elections and the working classes—comprising some two-thirds of the electorate—began to be more politically active. A shift away from the Conservatives, which had originated with the failures of the South African War and the Taff Vale

---

[132] Ibid., 1240–3.
[133] J.C.P. 11/5/5, Chamberlain to B., 4 Aug. 1902.
[134] Lady Rayleigh's Diary, 10 July 1902.

judgement against the trade unions, now attained a new momentum. Its scale was not revealed till January 1906.

However, even if the political cost of universality in the primary sector was high, there can be no doubt that order was imposed and standards raised. But what of secondary and technical education? What of the development of the country's human potential to meet the competition of German and American technology, applied science, and business management?

A short answer may be found in newspaper reports, for instance in *The Times* of 29 November 1979, six months after Mrs Thatcher came into office in quest of higher British industrial efficiency:

CALL FOR TECHNOLOGY TO HAVE PRIORITY IN ALL SCHOOL TEACHING.

Technology must be made part of the mainstream of education in schools, Mr. Neil Macfarlane, Under-Secretary of State for Education and Science, told a conference in London yesterday on education's contribution to Britain's economic recovery.

Technology should no longer be regarded as a poor relation, or something for the non-academic pupil, he said. It must both infuse the whole curriculum, being made part of the basic approach to literacy, numeracy and dexterity, and be encouraged in its own right.

Something has already been said about the Education Department's responsibility for this implicit damaging trend since 1902. But just what did Balfour himself have to say on the subject in that year?

According to his introductory speech of 24 March, Conservatives took special pride in the Technical Instruction Act of 1889. Under this Act, the recently established county and county borough authorities, working through technical education committees, had raised a rate and distributed a Treasury grant. They had done valuable work; but this had not met the need for secondary education in general. After the manner of Morant, he argued plausibly:

Higher technical instruction can only do its work—that is the belief and experience of every nation in Europe—it can only do its work well when that general work is based on a sound general secondary education. The very fact that you have given your authority ample power to assist technical education, has had, and could not but have, the effect to a certain extent of preventing and warping the natural growth of a sound education system. [135]

The difficulty presented by the non-county boroughs was relevant to

[135] *P.D.*, 4th, 105/849–50, 24 March 1902.

technical as well as to elementary education. At the cost of over-all damage to the system, the wish of Sir Albert Rollit and like-minded representatives of the smaller boroughs to retain control of their schools was duly met in the Bill. On 24 March, Balfour declared:

> We think it impossible to deprive Boroughs over 10,000 population, or urban districts over 20,000, of their existing jurisdiction over technical education; nor do we think they can be subordinated to the County in respect of primary education. We therefore leave them as they are with regard to the first; and make them autonomous with regard to the second . . . They retain their existing powers as to technical education, and they also become the authority for secondary education concurrently with the County Councils. The County Council of course is the authority over all the district outside the areas I have mentioned. [136]

Both from a general administrative viewpoint and for its effect on technical education, this superfluity of authorities was unfortunate. The elimination of these smaller entities was not accomplished till 1944. [137]

But the main damage was done by the clear-cut priority given to a 'general' education. A chance to save the country from 'gentrification' and the deepening anti-industrial tendencies of the social élite was entirely missed. Even more decisively than before, technical and commercial education was stamped with a working-class label. A working-class child bright enough to win a scholarship and enter the developing secondary sector often did not do what Balfour had presumably expected, namely qualify himself to go, say, to Birmingham University and become an engineer. Instead, if he found his way to such a university, he would aim to become a teacher, a lawyer, or perhaps a civil servant. Middle-class pupils, who had almost by definition attended fee-paying schools, were for their part less likely than before to gravitate towards occupations so effectively drained of social kudos. According to one Conservative MP, the situation did not improve during the next half-century. In a debate of 1956 he observed: 'The real trouble the Minister is up against is the spiritual one that technical education . . . is "servant's hall" if not scullery, whereas academic education is "drawing room" or "upstairs".' [138]

During Morant's time as Permanent Secretary (1 April 1903 to 28 Dec. 1911) the Education Department was staffed by men mostly of mature years, often of literary distinction, and 'almost without exception'

---

[136] Ibid., 858–9.
[137] G. A. N. Lowndes, *The Silent Social Revolution 1895–1965*, London, 2nd edn., 1967, pp. 64 and 219.
[138] Lowndes, pp. 321–2.

belonging to 'the academic school'. [139] Without Morant, the reform of 1902 might have been less comprehensive; but in his sudden ascent in the Department, he fell out, in 1903, with his former chief in the Office of Special Inquiries, Michael Sadler. Sadler was a gifted researcher—if allegedly a vain man—who understood what has been demonstrated since: that technical subjects can form part of a balanced education. [140] Indeed, it is ironical that, thanks to Admiral Sir John Fisher, just such a combination of subjects was successfully initiated at that very time (1902–1905) for cadets at the Royal Naval Colleges. [141] Of course the necessary workshops at Dartmouth cost money, but the result was a great state-financed technical school (though it has rarely been looked on in such a light) which showed what might have been achieved in the new secondary system. Morant, as it happens, was not irrevocably opposed to such a balanced culture in secondary education; but unfortunately he was shunted out of the Education Department just when his disciple, Frank Pullinger, was pressing for the incorporation of technical subjects in the curriculum of secondary day schools. [142]

During the debates of 1902, Haldane was among those who expressed some dissatisfaction with the lack of clear linkage between elementary school and university. He did not question Balfour's confidence in the new L.E.A.s. Both men evidently assumed that bodies which had shown such zeal for technical education since 1889 would continue to do so in the post-1902 environment. But Haldane commented during the initial debate:

I do not wholly appreciate the extent to which the permeating influence of the Universities is to come in. If I understand the scheme aright, the permeating influence . . . is to come in among the nominated members of the new local Committees. [Balfour: 'Where possible.'] That, doubtless, is the only way the Universities could be got under this Bill, although I almost think we are ripe for something more than that. It is important that these authorities for secondary as well as primary education should be animated by some common policy. [143]

Balfour clarified his own views when, during the second reading debate, he answered further criticism that the Bill threw no duty on the local authority to provide secondary education, but left action entirely to its discretion. Balfour replied that the Government had been 'most careful not to bind this authority instantly to produce a great scheme of secondary

[139] Ibid., p. 323.
[140] Ibid., p. 321; Eaglesham, *Foundations*, pp. 71 and 76–7.
[141] R. F. Mackay, *Fisher of Kilverstone*, Oxford, 1974, pp. 266–7, 273–5.
[142] Eaglesham, *Foundations*, pp. 71 and 107.
[143] *P.D.*, 4th, 105/901, 24 Mar. 1902.

education for their area'. But he said that Parliament could trust these bodies. 'We see what they have done under the Technical Education Act. We know the spirit which had animated them since 1889 animates them still.'[144] When the subject (Clause 2) was being debated in committee, Balfour said that while he could not, as some members demanded, 'accept absolutely mandatory words', he was prepared 'to make the Clause less neutral'. Finally the Clause emerged with words which did establish a duty with regard to secondary and technical education:

The local authority shall consider the needs, and take such steps as seem to them desirable, after consultation with the Board of Education, to supply or aid the supply of education other than elementary, including the training of teachers and the general co-ordination of all forms of education.

Yet in a later debate Balfour denied that he had made an important concession. The Clause, he asserted, 'did not throw on the Education Department the duty of declaring what were to be the adequate needs of secondary education in each county', nor would it be 'in the interests of secondary education' to do this. In other words, there was presumably to be no national system of secondary education![145] However, perhaps inevitably, the Education Department did determine the style of education adopted in the emergent secondary system.

Even the best-informed contemporaries were slow to perceive the inadequacy of British progress in technical education during Morant's regime at the Education Department. Philip Magnus, who had been the Director and Secretary of the City Guilds of London Institute for the Advancement of Technical Education since 1880, wrote in 1910:

The necessity of the higher scientific and technical instruction and of its specialisation to industry and commerce is generally realised. No one doubts it. The questions now engaging attention are the kinds of training that should lead up to it, the best means of providing avenues through which the children of our elementary schools may pass to the higher technical institutes, the character of the teaching most suitable for children after the elementary school age, and the relation between university and technological instruction.[146]

In fact, the extent and fundamental importance of the problem was not generally realized. Nothing short of a clear pro-industrial emphasis in the Bill of 1902 could have laid a basis for economic competitiveness with all

[144] Ibid., 107/1210, 8 May 1902.
[145] Ibid., 109/1481, 1486, 1545, 24 June 1902.
[146] P. Magnus, *Educational Aims and Efforts*, 1910, quoted by Roy M. McLeod in Gillian Sutherland (ed.), *Education in Britain*, Irish Universities Press, 1977, p. 216.

other states later in the twentieth century. How, it must be asked, has Japan, lacking even Britain's natural resources, contrived to emerge triumphant, if not by modernizing her people? Of course, a modern orientation of the British state education system in 1902 might not have succeeded in reversing the anti-industrial tendencies of the élite, as described in Martin Wiener's book. (See p.57 above.) But it must have helped.

It now remains to trace the story of the Education Bill after Parliament went into recess on 8 August. On that day the Board of Education was given a new President, holding the post as a single cabinet appointment. Devonshire having given up his education role, Balfour set aside Selborne's advice that Gerald Balfour—at the Board of Trade from 1900—would be suited to the Board of Education. Instead, Balfour named the Marquess of Londonderry, a 'Caligulan appointment' according to Chamberlain's biographer. [147] A few weeks later Morant, in a letter to Sandars, prepared the way for a further change of high personnel in the Education Department, namely the premature retirement of George Kekewich from the Permanent Secretary's post. According to Morant, 'Kekewich took the new regime to be a new lease of life and power for himself.' He had got one of his disciples appointed as private secretary to Gorst's successor, Sir William Anson. 'I cannot honestly conceal from you', wrote Morant, 'my own conviction that very great mischief will ensue under existing arrangements', a statement which he proceeded to bolster with much circumstantial detail. 'If and when I know', he concluded, 'that this is what is intended by the Chief, I will say not a word against it.' He then turned to the more immediate problem of Nonconformist onslaughts on the Bill's provisions for rate aid to Voluntary Schools and on the Schools' specified majority of denominational managers; and he confessed to 'feeling not a little perturbed as to the fate of the Bill'. [148] In September, Morant still feared that Balfour might 'yield to pressure' with regard to the managers. [149]

Balfour, for his part, wrote to Chamberlain on 3 September:

I confess to being in great perplexity about the whole subject. On the merits I think the Bill is a very reasonable one, not unduly favourable to the Church, and certainly not unduly favourable to the clergy, whom in its present form it in fact dispossesses.

I am further provoked by the extraordinary campaign of lies which has been set on foot against it, and by the total indifference to the interests of education which seems to be shown by the contending parties.

[147] Sandars P., C.736, Selborne to B., 30 July 1902; Amery, v, 75.
[148] B.P. 49787, ff. 73–6, Morant to Sandars, 28 Aug. 1902.
[149] Lady Rayleigh's Diary, Whittingehame, 28 Sept. 1902.

But regarding Chamberlain's sustained pleas for concessions—four Voluntary School managers to be appointed by the councils instead of two (and thus only two, instead of four, denominational managers for each school)—Balfour declined to give way. It would, he wrote, be futile to make 'the kind of concession which permanently conciliates no opponent, but does permanently endanger all confidence among your friends'. He noted that Chamberlain was 'disposed to entertain the view that the wishes of the Catholics' on this management issue might 'with advantage be ignored'. He could not agree. The Government's 'parliamentary difficulties would become even more formidable' than they already were 'if the Irish considered themselves at liberty to join their forces with Lloyd George in a warfare of obstruction'.[150]

On 9 October one particular political danger was ably confronted by Chamberlain when he met 105 leading Liberal Unionists in Birmingham. He emphasized the fact that, in Voluntary Schools as much as elsewhere, secular education would be wholly under popular control; and he argued that less should be heard of sectarian rivalry and more about the interests of British children. Balfour, in two major speeches at Manchester on 14 October, took a similar line. Stepping from the London train at 4 p.m., he went at once to address a meeting of Liberal Unionists. He deplored the 'extravagance of the accusations' of clericalism levelled against the Government and pointed to the 'political motive' underlying 'the storm of criticism'. He hoped that 'this eighth year of the Administration' would be 'marked by a great educational reform, a great educational departure'.

In the evening, he addressed a mass meeting of some 7,000 people in a packed St. James's Hall. Determined to boost support for the Bill before the imminent reassembly of Parliament, he made by far his most convincing statement to date of personal commitment to the constructive aspects of the measure. He alluded to the patriotism with which the country always reacted to easily understood challenges like the recent war in South Africa. The education issue was, he 'firmly and conscientiously' believed, 'no less intimately bound up with our greatness as a nation and with our Imperial position in the world'; but it was more difficult to explain. However, he had to recognize that 'the voice of the calumniator' had been 'too long uncontradicted'. Why, he was often asked, had the Government 'disturbed the social peace' by bringing forward the Bill?

The answer is this, that the existing educational system of this country is chaotic, is ineffectual, is utterly behind the age, makes us the laughing stock of every

---

[150] J.C.P. 11/5/9, endorsed 'Original missing E.D'.

advanced nation in Europe and America, puts us behind not only our American cousins, but the German and the Frenchman and the Italian, and that it was not consistent with the duty of an English Government—of a British Government—to allow that state of things longer to continue without an adequate remedy. (Cheers).

He traversed the sectarian difficulty, asserting that what mattered was not the 'managers' of the Voluntary Schools but the 'control' of these schools. This would be exercised by the Local Education Authorities who would also oversee the training of teachers.

Having spoken at considerable length and been generally well received, Balfour concluded by insisting that the Bill must be passed:

I tell you that there are at stake issues more important than the fortunes of any political party, be it what it may. (Cheers). There is at stake the education of your children for a generation (hear, hear) and if for that time we—I mean the members of the House of Commons, the majority of the members of the House of Commons—if we consent either through a desire to avoid a little extra trouble, or the fear of a few loud-mouthed speeches or mendacious pamphleteers, if we hesitate to do our duty and carry through this great reform, then I say we shall receive the contempt of the children living, and to be born, for the next generation, and that contempt which we shall receive we shall most justly and richly earn. (Loud cheers). [151]

Before the Bill received the Royal Assent on 18 December, a number of amendments were accepted. But these did not radically change the shape of the measure. [152] Thanks to the availability of the closure, Balfour at length brought his ship to port. Not only was it a triumph in parliamentary terms; his national reputation was brought to its zenith. In this outstanding episode in his career, he had shown himself a constructive statesman when placed, as a party leader, under the pressure of what he saw as a dire necessity. Education had not been his ministerial responsibility; but he had rescued his party from its extremity and, moreover, his name would always thenceforth be linked with 'a great educational departure'. If his successors failed to look critically at the direction followed, should he be blamed for that?

His own indecisiveness—or, it might be said, openness of mind— towards the whole question of the content of secondary education is illustrated in a speech of 1903:

I confess that, as far as I am concerned, I have never been able to make a theory satisfactory to myself as to what is or is not the best kind of education to be given in those great public schools which are the glory of our country, and which, in their

---

[151] *The Times*, 15 Oct. 1902, p. 5.
[152] Munson, pp. 637–8.

collective effect upon British character, I think cannot be overrated, but which are subjected, and perhaps rightly subjected, to a great deal of criticism as to that portion of their efforts which is engaged on the scholastic and technical side of education. I cannot profess myself to be satisfied with the old classical ideal of secondary education . . . But when I turn to the other side and ask what the substitute is, then I confess I am even less happy than when I consider the classical ideal; for I am quite sure—no, I am not quite sure, but I think—you will never find science a good medium for conveying education to classes of forty or fifty boys who do not care a farthing about the world they live in except in so far as it concerns the cricket field, or the football field, or the river . . . for only a few are capable at that age, and perhaps at any age, of learning all the lessons which science is capable of teaching . . . [153]

However, such uncertainty did not trouble Morant. In September 1904 he wrote to Balfour: 'It is almost a year now since I have ventured to trouble you with any serious matters on Education . . . knowing how beset you were with other matters.' His justification for writing at all was the need for a political decision on how to handle 'Lloyd-George's plan of campaign' in Wales. But Morant also took the opportunity to affirm:

The working of the Act in England proves its admirable qualities, from the education point of view. The developments from it in Secondary Education and in Pupil-teacher matters (one of the special aims of the Bill) are quite extraordinary; and in Elementary, too, the Act is absolutely justifying itself. [154]

[153]   W. M. Short, pp. 175–6: speech at dinner of Allied Colonial Universities, 10 July 1903.
[154]   B.P. 49787, f. 101, Morant to B., 17 Sept. 1904.

7

An Inevitable Prime Minister

1902–1903

ON becoming Prime Minister on 12 July 1902, Balfour inherited problems threatening the electoral future of the Unionist coalition. During the 1890s a struggle had developed between the trade unions and associations of employers. The latter believed, with good reason, that British industry was becoming less competitive. The unions, for their part, made increasing use of the strike weapon to improve their wages and conditions, while the employers resorted to lock-outs and appeals to the courts. Judgements adverse to the unions culminated in the ruling of 1901 in favour of the Taff Vale Railway Company, whereby the railway union was held liable for damages suffered by the company during a strike. This situation led to increased support for independent Labour representation in Parliament. However, no worsening of the electoral position of the Unionists had clearly manifested itself by July 1902. The 'pro-Boer' tendencies of the Liberal Party counted against it till the war finally ended in May 1902; and between the 'khaki' election victory of October 1900 and July 1902 the Unionists retained as many as nine seats at by-elections, otherwise gaining one and losing one. But the loss of a formerly safe Conservative seat at North Leeds a fortnight after Balfour's succession may be attributed to Nonconformist resentment against the Education Bill (now non-adoptive regarding rate aid to Voluntary Schools) as well, perhaps, as a change in labour feeling and the onset of post-war disillusion with the imperialistic policies of the Government. Lady Rayleigh records Balfour's political assessment as communicated to his family circle at Whittingehame on 4 October 1902:

After dinner tonight A. J. B. talked of the great wave of feeling against the govt. He said it was made up like all great waves of several small ones. There was the craving for excitement to which the nation during the war had become accustomed, suddenly left unsatisfied and looking for fresh food. This one said it was the Education bill; Midleton said it was all corn tax; another that it was income-tax;

another the natural see-saw—'give the other fellow a chance'—but in truth they all combined to produce it.[1]

However, Balfour seemed well established as the leader of the Unionist Party. Although he had taken care to consult Joseph Chamberlain before accepting the premiership on 12 July, he was already seen as an inevitable successor to his ailing uncle. Further to his able handling of the Education Bill, he had also in 1902 effected a further reform of the Rules of Procedure in the Commons. (His success in dealing with this subject in the 1895 Parliament was noticed in Ch. 5 above.) By 8 March 1902, Sandars was reminding Balfour that the pressures on parliamentary time had again become intolerable and that 'the Rules *must* be passed.' The position was such that 'as between the claims of Rules and Education, Rules must prevail.'[2] In fact, the New Rules were introduced into the House on 25 March, the day after the introduction of the Education Bill, and took up most of the available time till Friday, 2 May. (The second reading of the Education Bill began on the following Monday.) Henry Lucy commented:

Taking them altogether, the new Rules are admirably framed for the purpose of placing the House of Commons on a level in the matter of command of its own resources with lesser institutions, such as Town Councils or Boards of Guardians. A long stride has been taken in the desirable direction of delivering the House of Commons from the tyranny of the minority, frequently represented by an individual of the standing of Mr. Swift MacNeill or Mr. Channing.

He further remarked that the House had, in 1877, been 'imbued with fanatical desire to protect the rights of the minority', but the Parnellite party had flourished under these conditions and successive restrictions on debate had unavoidably followed.[3]

By 16 June, the diarist could vouch for the success of the New Rules. Substantial measures, notably the Education Bill, had been debated at times when the House was fresh; and the piling up of 'questions arising' no longer led to ministerial explanations of important bills being delivered to benches emptied by the approach of the dinner hour. 'Now everything goes like clockwork, the maximum of good resulting from the change being accompanied by an imperceptible minimum of evil.'[4]

But on assuming his prime-ministerial role on 12 July Balfour had no definite plans for constructive reform—apart, of course, from completing

[1]　Lady Rayleigh's Diary, 4 Oct. 1902.
[2]　B.P. 49761, f. 16.
[3]　*Balfourian Parliament*, p. 156, 2 May 1902.
[4]　Ibid., pp. 172–6.

the passage of the Education Bill. He certainly had no wish to change the law so as to strengthen the position of the trade unions, though had he foreseen the radical nature of the measure to be passed by a Liberal prime minister in 1906 (the Trades Disputes Act which conferred unparalleled immunity on British unions), he might well have considered pre-emption, following his uncle's example of 1891 when he largely abolished fees in elementary schools. True, in the sphere of defence policy, he had long meditated the improvement of high-level co-ordination. But understandably in the light of his recent commitments, he did not have a scheme ready in July 1902. Yet, as he would soon reveal, he possessed the necessary creative potential, once he was put under pressure to act by members of his own party-political circle.

When Salisbury was reconstructing his Government in October 1900, Balfour accepted the need for higher spending on defence. He wrote to his uncle deploring the continuance of Hicks Beach at the Exchequer. Beach, he remarked, 'will certainly go on dropping little grains of sand into the wheels of every department in turn. If, as I fear, we have to spend large sums of money on Army reorganization and naval construction I suppose he will describe our policy as "Jingo" and resign!'[5] Indeed Beach was much concerned about the financial implications of the policies—old age pensions and imperialism—associated with Chamberlain, and about the tendency of Balfour and other colleagues to travel in the same direction. In a memorandum of September 1901 envisaging the budget of 1902, Beach expressed alarm about rising government expenditure, which was by no means solely due to the war. For example, education was costing the taxpayer £2.5 millions more than in 1895. He suggested economies and threatened to resign if the Cabinet would not comply. Salisbury privately conveyed his sympathy to Beach and even went so far as to criticize the service ministers for surrendering to a 'Jingo hurricane'.[6]

When, in July 1902, Balfour began to form his own Cabinet, he signified basic continuance of his uncle's policies by pressing Hicks Beach to remain at the Exchequer![7] Beach yielded only to the extent that he offered to stay till October, and even then on condition that 'in the mean time the Cabinet should in no way be committed on Colonial preference', as Chamberlain wished. So Balfour ended by appointing C. T. Ritchie as Chancellor. But his determined attempt to retain Beach shows how closely Balfour's basic attitudes still conformed with those of his uncle. The largely unaltered

[5] Hatfield House MSS, 3M/Class E, B. to Salisbury, 20 Oct. 1900.
[6] Marsh, pp. 309–10.
[7] Sandars P., C.736, ff. 96–9, 100–3, 131–4.

composition of the Cabinet confirms the impression that no great changes of policy were intended; nor could the closely consulted Joseph Chamberlain suggest any youthful talent, apart from Austen Chamberlain and George Wyndham, which might with advantage be promoted to cabinet rank. [8] George Wyndham duly entered the Cabinet, continuing in the post of Irish Secretary to which he had been appointed in November 1900. Balfour had considered a switch of offices between Wyndham and another old friend, St. John Brodrick, who was making heavy weather of the War Office problem, and he was later to regret his failure to attempt the exchange. Austen Chamberlain entered the Cabinet as Postmaster General. So, as mentioned earlier, did Lord Londonderry as President of the Board of Education. Though Balfour was obviously pleased to clear Gorst out of the Education Department, it cannot be said that Londonderry's appointment strengthened either the Department or the Cabinet. But a basis was laid for Balfour's most useful and constructive work as Prime Minister by the continuance of Lord Lansdowne—Balfour's fagmaster at Eton—as Foreign Secretary (a post reluctantly surrendered by Salisbury, under pressure from Balfour and others, in November 1900) and by the reinstatement of Lord Selborne (who was married to Salisbury's daughter Maud) as First Lord of the Admiralty. Joseph Chamberlain, much unsettled by the Education Bill, remained as Colonial Secretary.

The implication of the whole arrangement was that Irish land purchase would be carried further; the fighting services, especially the War Office, would be overhauled with such expenditure of money as could not readily be avoided; that imperial ties would be strengthened where feasible; and that the education question would, if possible, be put to rest for a long time to come.

During 1902, however, pressure was gradually building up for action to be taken over the co-ordination of defence. Field Marshal Lord Roberts, who had succeeded Lord Wolseley as Commander-in-Chief, wrote as follows to Sandars on Sunday, 4 May 1902:

If Mr. Balfour has time, ask him to read the Second Article in yesterday's 'Times'. [A cutting of the article was enclosed. Dated 3 May, it foreshadows in some detail the scheme for a defence committee innovated by Balfour in December 1902, and also the further development thereof in May 1904. It expresses impatience with 'the curious detachment and unaccountable working of Mr. Balfour's mind' shown by his answers to Lord Charles Beresford's questions of

[8] Amery, v, 75–7.

Thursday, 1 May.] It deals with a very important matter—a Council of Defence—without the formation of which it will, I fear, be impossible for us to prepare for War.[9]

This succinct reminder produced no ascertainable result. What with the New Rules of Procedure and education, Balfour had been caught up in a whirl of activity unparalleled in his parliamentary experience. Moreover, in June he was pressed to institute the inquiry into the conduct of the South African War which had been promised in 1900. Brodrick indicated on the 12th that 'a small Royal Commission' would be appointed.[10] When Campbell-Bannerman, the Liberal leader, again raised the subject on 30 July, Balfour replied that he had 'not been able to get on with the formation of this Commission as quickly as could be desired'; but he had now secured Lord Elgin as Chairman. He envisaged not more than seven commissioners all told, mostly civilians. The terms of reference should be general, covering contracts made at any time during the war, the preparations for war, and 'military events' up to the occupation of Pretoria on 5 June 1900.[11] By 8 August he was able to furnish more names of appointees, including that of an old acquaintance, Lord Esher.[12] The latter's inclusion was to prove particularly fruitful.

Meanwhile, on 20 June 1902, the 'need for some reinforcement of the intellectual equipment' directing imperial defence had been affirmed in the Commons by H. O. Arnold-Forster, Financial Secretary to the Admiralty and a well-known writer on military subjects.[13] Then, on 8 August, Major J. E. B. Seely, a young Conservative MP recently decorated for services in South Africa, contrived during a debate on the Consolidated Fund Bill to ask Balfour when action on the co-ordination of defence might be expected. Although somewhat taken by surprise, Balfour replied at length. He at once rejected Seely's idea that a new 'joint Department' should deal with weapons and inventions, and also his suggestion that finance should be raised to meet the needs of defence as formulated by the new body. But, he continued,

let me say I entirely agree with him in thinking that we cannot pay too much attention to the larger problems of strategy, partly military, partly naval, which the defence of the Empire involves . . . I do not think any responsible statesman will now say that India can take care of herself, and all we have got to do is to see that we

[9] Sandars P., C.735, ff. 85–6.
[10] *P.D.*, 4th, 108/1540, 5 June; 109/499–500, 12 June 1902.
[11] Ibid., 112/127–8.
[12] Ibid., 1119–20.
[13] See the file Cab. 21/468, 'Committee of Imperial Defence: Constitution and Functions'.

have a sufficient Navy to look after these islands, and, when the storm breaks upon us, to protect our vast commercial interests in all parts of the world.

The problem of Imperial defence is one of the most difficult and one of the most complicated problems that any Government or any body of experts, can face . . . Everybody knows that while the problems of foreign Governments may be onerous in respect of financial contribution required, and may be difficult in consequence of the difficulty of providing an adequate force, the intellectual and speculative elements of those problems are incomparably below those of the problems presented by the British Empire. In these circumstances I entirely agree with my hon. friend that we cannot leave this matter to one Department, or to two Departments acting separately. It is a joint matter . . . the Government are fully alive, and have, if I may say so, for long been fully alive, to the difficulty of the problem which presents itself to his mind . . . It is one which we certainly do not mean to neglect to meet and grapple with to the best of our ability.[14]

Dilke, a long-standing advocate of radical reform in this area, expressed satisfaction with what he took as an acceptance of prime-ministerial responsibility 'to impose that co-ordination for the defence of the Empire which is so much desired'. However, Balfour gave no indication that he had settled on a remedy. By now the two departmental heads most closely concerned, namely Selborne at the Admiralty and Brodrick at the War Office, were becoming impatient for action.

In October 1902 Arnold-Forster furnished Selborne with a memorandum comprising detailed suggestions for a co-ordinating body. Among other things, the 'new Body' would inquire 'on what grounds the excess of expenditure upon the Land Forces is justified in a purely Maritime Empire'. This was printed as a cabinet paper.[15] The sequel was a joint memorandum written for the Cabinet by Selborne and Brodrick. It echoed Arnold-Forster's phraseology in being somewhat comically entitled 'Improvement of the intellectual equipment of the Services'.[16] It seems that the memorandum was associated with the less mirth-provoking threat of a dual ministerial resignation if action did not follow.[17] Foremost among the problems of concern to both services was the question of a possible invasion of the British Isles.

Once the South African War had ended in May 1902, Brodrick hoped to strengthen the Army and provide it with a striking force, based at home, of three army corps. Each corps would consist of 40,000 troops, mainly regulars. This force would be available either for home defence or for use

[14] *P.D.*, 4th, 112/835–9, 6 Aug. 1902.
[15] Cab. 37/63/145, 20 Oct. 1902.
[16] Cab. 37/63/152, 10 Nov. 1902.
[17] Earl of Midleton, *Records and Reactions*, London, 1939, pp. 140–1.

abroad, perhaps in Europe. There would also be three corps of selected auxiliary troops (militia, etc.) for home defence duties.[18] While Beach's departure from the Treasury favoured Brodrick's cause, the latter was not heartened by Balfour's advent as Prime Minister. Brodrick had 'become basically insecure, politically and perhaps emotionally', feeling that Balfour, caught up in education, was indifferent to his troubles.[19] He felt even more vulnerable when, in October 1902, Arnold-Forster's memorandum questioned the proportion of defence spending allocated to the Army. This move came on top of many public assertions to the 'Blue Water' theory that naval supremacy was the key to all British defence problems, including the invasion of the British Isles, and that the Army should be regarded as strictly subsidiary.

Brodrick wished to challenge the Blue Water argument in an appropriate forum; and Selborne, for the Navy, was equally determined to have the issue decided. Neither the end of the South African War nor Beach's retirement as Chancellor meant that money for the services would be abundant. If Selborne was to carry out his naval schemes, including those which he was concerting with Admiral Fisher (now Second Sea Lord), the Army Estimates would have to be kept as low as possible so that money would not be siphoned away from naval requirements.

Although Selborne did not dispute the established naval policy of building against France and Russia, he had sounded a warning note about the German Navy in a cabinet memorandum of 16 November 1901.[20] Salisbury had begged him not to press the issue then. But in the spring of 1902, Selborne informed Balfour: 'The question of our naval policy is more pressing now than it was when I wrote my memorandum in the autumn. I candidly admit that I had not then realised the intensity of the hatred of the German nation to this country.' Before bringing the matter before the Cabinet, he wanted a meeting with Balfour and Chamberlain, presumably believing that they would support him against Salisbury and Beach.[21] The outcome of the meeting was Selborne's decision to sanction the secret purchase of land for a North Sea base, as proposed by an Admiralty committee. While the base would provide for possible operations against Germany, it could be justified diplomatically as needed for general dockyard purposes.[22]

[18] L. J. Satre, 'St. John Brodrick and Army Reform 1901–3' in *Journal of British Studies*, spring 1976.

[19] Ibid., p. 130.

[20] Cab. 37/59/118.

[21] B.P. 49707, ff. 105–7, Selborne to B., 4 April 1902.

[22] Paul Kennedy, *The Rise of the Anglo-German Antagonism 1860–1914*, London, 1980, p. 252.

In July, however, when Balfour was forming his ministry, he sounded Selborne about his moving from the Admiralty either to the Colonial Office or to the War Office and taking Arnold-Forster with him.[23] This shook Selborne's confidence in Balfour's support for his naval plans. On 12 July he wrote to Balfour:

My dear Arthur,

I cannot tell you what pleasure it would give me to serve under you and of course I would do what you wished as to the moment for bringing my proposals before the Cabinet. At the same time I should not like to take office under you and find out afterwards that you did not approve of my policy. But I have never concealed my views from you; I have always told you just what I thought; I have nothing therefore to reveal to you. All I need to add to our previous communications on the subject of my shipbuilding policy is that, although I still think a margin of ten battleships is what we ought to work for in view of the rapid expansion of the German Navy, I would not press for more than the completion of my original margin of six by 31 Dec. 1907 if you did not think the German danger as great as I fear it is. I leave myself therefore in your hands to do just what you think best with me.

Yrs affly

Selborne[24]

Sandars noted in summary of the incident: 'Lord S most earnestly pleaded that he had initiated great reforms which it was most important in the public interest that he should superintend. Mr. Balfour believes this to be the fact.'[25]

After this exchange, Selborne remained in a particularly close political relationship with Balfour until, in 1905, he went to South Africa. Later in July 1902, Balfour discussed with him a number of the forthcoming government appointments. Selborne's preference for Gerald Balfour over Londonderry at the Board of Education has already been mentioned. But Balfour's experience of 1895 to 1902 seems to have left him with a curiously low view of that office for the rest of his political career. David Ogg has recounted how, in December 1916, Balfour raised an eyebrow on hearing that his friend, H. A. L. Fisher (the historian), was to accept the post from Lloyd George, and expressed concern that a man of ability should go to the Education Board.[26]

---

[23]   Sandars P., C.736, f. 1, shows that this suggestion originated with the King.

[24]   Ibid., ff. 119–20, 12 July 1902.

[25]   Ibid., f. 2, n.d.

[26]   Ogg, *Herbert Fisher*, London, 1947, p. 62.

It was against the inter-service background just described that the question of defence co-ordination was brought to a head by the joint memorandum of Selborne and Brodrick dated 10 November. But the two ministers were pushing against a half-open door—though Balfour handsomely acknowledged their initiative when addressing the Commons in August 1904. [27] If the reformed Defence Committee was thrust upon Balfour by Selborne and Brodrick, it was a forum congenial to the point of a self-indulgence. [28]

Balfour's hesitation seems to have been about the composition of the new committee. As to its work, he was uniquely well prepared and personally qualified. It has already been seen how, in his minute of 24 August 1895, he had asserted the value of keeping records of decisions and had suggested that the attendance of the professional service chiefs was essential. Otherwise, shortly before the first meeting of the committee, Balfour was in any case writing a substantial paper for the Cabinet on Britain's relations with Afghanistan. This paper, involving a subtle interplay of diplomatic and military reasoning, and bearing directly on the defence of India against Russia, was a classic example of the kind of study to be kept for reference by the future Defence Committee. Balfour's paper was finished on 16 December, the new committee first met on the 18th, and the paper was eventually printed for the fully-fledged Committee of Imperial Defence (C.I.D.) on 23 August 1904 so that it could be used at a meeting held two days later. [29]

At the initial meeting of the committee on 18 December 1902, Balfour fell in with the suggestions of Selborne and Brodrick about its composition. According to the minutes, Selborne led the discussion of the basic resolution (1): 'That the Memorandum on the constitution of the Committee submitted by the Secretary of State for War and the First Lord of the Admiralty, having been approved by the Cabinet, the Committee be constituted accordingly'. The effect of this resolution was that those then present were confirmed in the role of permanent members. By the second resolution, the Duke of Devonshire was confirmed as chairman under the new dispensation. Probably Balfour, so soon after his educational marathon, did not then envisage the dominant part which he was to take at the committee. Otherwise the members were: the two service ministers, the

[27]   *P.D.*, 4th, 139/617, 2 Aug. 1904.
[28]   See, for instance, Midleton, *Records*, p. 141 and Midleton in *The Post Victorians* (intro. V. Revd W. R. Inge), London, 1933, pp. 15–16.
[29]   Cab. 37/63/167, 16 Dec. 1902; 6/1/5D, P. 23 Aug. 1904; 2/1, 55th meeting of C.I.D., 25 Aug. 1904.

Senior Naval Lord (Admiral Lord Walter Kerr), the Director of Naval Intelligence (Captain Prince Louis of Battenberg), the Commander-in-Chief (Field Marshal Lord Roberts), and the Director of Military Intelligence (Lt.-General Sir William Nicholson). Finally, it was resolved that 'the existence and composition of the Committee' should be made public; and Balfour said he would make 'a statement to the House of Commons at an early date'.[30]

In consequence of the first meeting, Balfour arranged for the appointment of a secretary, namely W. G. Tyrrell (later Baron Tyrrell) of the Foreign Office. He was to keep the minutes and records. It had also been decided that, 'if possible, the Committee should meet once a fortnight (or oftener if the necessity arose), but at least once a month'—a commitment amply met during Balfour's term as Prime Minister. The subjects chosen for discussion at the second meeting, to be held on 11 February 1903, were distinctly Balfourian in flavour: (a) 'the military position in India on the outbreak of war with the Franco-Russian Alliance', on which Nicholson would prepare and circulate a paper before the meeting; and (b) the effect on Britain's 'naval strategic position in the Mediterranean of a Russian occupation of Constantinople and the Straits', on which a paper would be circulated by Battenberg.[31] Balfour's paper of 1892 on subject (b) has been extensively quoted in the previous chapter. As for (a), Balfour would direct much of the committee's attention to related topics during the next three years. Until the end of his time as Prime Minister, Russia would remain for him the main hypothetical enemy for purposes of defence planning and financial provision, especially with regard to the Army; and it was basic, in his view, that Russia had a military alliance with France.

The discussions at the second meeting of the Defence Committee were in the event confined to Battenberg's paper printed on the 7th.[32] Until the committee's reorganization in 1904, its minutes were simply a record of the resolutions passed; but Balfour's active role at the second meeting 11 February) is registered by his undertaking to prepare what turned out to be a major provisional report. By the evening of 13 February Balfour had arrived in Lancashire on a party-political visit. Yet his 'Report of the conclusion arrived on the 11th February in reference to Russia and Constantinople' had already been composed and would amount to five pages of print—somewhat longer than Battenberg's original paper![33]

[30]   Cab. 2/1, 18 Dec. 1902.
[31]   Ibid.
[32]   Cab. 4/1/2B, 7 Feb., and 2/1, 11 Feb. 1903.
[33]   Cab. 4/1/1B, 14 Feb. 1903.

On Saturday, 14 February, Balfour set out from Knowsley Hall with his host, Lord Derby, to visit the Liverpool Town Hall, the Exchange News Room, and the Cotton Exchange. Lancashire seemed still firmly 'Tory' then: he was everywhere enthusiastically received. His chief speaking engagement was at the Conservative Club and he took advantage of this opportunity to make a public statement about the new Defence Committee before Parliament met on the following Tuesday. He was doubtless motivated largely by enthusiasm for the work of the committee. However, he was also able to chalk up a party point in answer to Lord Rosebery's pronouncements on national efficiency.

Balfour said that he, too, wanted 'an ever-increasing standard of efficiency' in the public service. But how was this to be attained? Lord Rosebery seemed to have but one kind of suggestion. This was to place in government 'gentlemen who have been extremely successful in other and very different walks of life'. He had at first, in 1900, thought that Rosebery 'was joking rather'. Parliamentary and ministerial work required special training. But he had to look seriously at Rosebery's latest proposal, of 1902, that Lord Kitchener should not have been sent to India—to command 'the largest Army on a war footing' in the British Empire—but instead 'should have been made a member of the Cabinet for military purposes'. However, this proposal conflicted with 'the traditions of the British constitution' and was quite 'impracticable'. Balfour continued: 'Lord Kitchener is a very great soldier' but 'I have no ground for supposing that this great soldier has any special ability, as he certainly had no training, in the particular work which is thrown upon a Minister required to defend the proposals of his Government in the House of Lords or House of Commons.'

The Government had, however, been able to make 'a great change' of a practical nature. They had 'in the course of the last two months' made 'a great revolution in the constitution' of the Defence Committee. This was no longer, as it was before, 'a purely Cabinet committee to which on certain occasions the counsels of military and naval experts were called in'—a committee 'which made decisions indeed, or which came to provisional conclusions indeed, but of which no records were kept'. He delineated the ministerial and service membership of the new committee. Records would be kept of conclusions and 'of the reasons' (in practice largely embodied in memoranda) underlying those conclusions. The records would be passed on to successive governments and would provide 'an element of continuity' not seen before. Inter-service disputes would no longer be 'fought out by correspondence between the two Departments, but would be threshed out round the table by the most competent experts whose services we may command, associated with the most responsible Ministers belonging to the Cabinet'. Those listening to the speech may at this point have wondered how full membership for the service experts could be made compatible with constitutional practice; but Balfour continued: 'I need hardly say that this Committee does not bind the Cabinet. Their conclusions will come before the Cabinet, who will have the fullest opportunity of acting upon them or not acting upon them as they choose.' (Although this important point seems not to have clearly emerged at the inception of the committee in December—there is no trace of it in the early documentation of the body—what was later called the 'consultative' and 'advisory' role of the committee solved the problem of how to allow the service chiefs to participate on equal terms. It also opened the way for leading colonial politicians to attend.) Balfour finished by confiding that the new committee would measure up to 'the ever increasing gravity of the military and naval problems which this country has to face in all parts of the world'. [34]

On 5 March Balfour found an opportunity to make a fuller statement about the innovation in the House of Commons. [35] Points additional to those already mentioned include the committee's duty 'to survey as a whole the strategical military needs of the Empire, to deal with all the complicated questions which are all essential elements in that general problem, and to revise from time to time their own previous decisions, so that the Cabinet shall always be informed and always have at its disposal information upon these important points'. He emphasized that the committee would reconsider any question if new facts came to light. For the sake of 'continuity', there would be a 'fixed nucleus' of permanent members. But for the sake of efficiency, this membership would be kept down to ten. Other individuals, not necessarily ministers, would be asked to attend as and when appropriate. For instance, the Chancellor of the Exchequer was named in connection with problems of public expenditure; likewise, in view of Balfour's special preoccupations, it comes as no surprise to find mention of the Secretary of State for India (then Lord George Hamilton). The Foreign Secretary was also specifically mentioned. But it is perhaps noteworthy that Balfour did not name the Colonial Secretary. The omission was probably due to Chamberlain's absence, from November till mid-March, on a visit to South Africa. But in the immediate background to Balfour's speech was Ritchie's pre-budget threat to resign as Chancellor if Chamberlain's scheme—apparently agreed by the Cabinet before his departure—for retention of the wartime corn duty, with preferential reductions for the

---

[34] *The Times*, 14 Feb. 1903.
[35] *P.D.*, 4th, 118/1578–86.

colonies, were not abandoned. It was perhaps due to Balfour's sensitivity over his surrender to Ritchie that he failed to mention Chamberlain in connection with the Defence Committee. Chamberlain's natural interest in the body is emphasized by a decision taken at the committee's third meeting on 18 February. This was that 'the title of the Committee should be "Committee of Imperial Defence".'[36]

In the rest of his speech of 5 March, Balfour remarked on the 'experimental and tentative' nature of the new machinery—thus opening the way for the improvements suggested in 1904 by the Esher Committee. Balfour hinted at the possibility of attendance at the committee by colonial politicians. He also issued a judicious warning that

we are all liable to forget, that however well you constitute your Committee you must not expect too much from it . . . war is much too full of surprises . . . Constitute your Committee and your Intelligence Department as you will, you will have in any war in which you may unhappily be engaged, many surprises . . . no attempt, however successful, to bring the best brains of the Empire to deal with the Empire's problems will prevent difficulties arising in times of stress.

In many respects, the C.I.D. (Committee of Imperial Defence) resembled the committee suggested by Balfour in 1895. The basic difference lay in its advisory character. In 1895, Balfour had wanted the service chiefs to attend the meetings; yet he expected the committee 'to decide all questions of importance connected with Imperial Defence'. Under the new dispensation, the conclusions of the C.I.D. could be rejected by the Cabinet. While in practice this was unlikely to happen where the Prime Minister, the Lord President of the Council, and the service ministers had all agreed, the C.I.D. avoided, through its advisory status, the disadvantages of the cabinet committee which it replaced. Now that the new machinery existed, its value would depend on the assiduity and ability of the Prime Minister. In both these respects, Balfour gave full measure. In what general direction, then, did Balfour guide the deliberations of the C.I.D. in its early months?

Balfour's cardinal assumption was British naval supremacy. His comprehension of its meaning is exemplified in the third paragraph of his minute of 12 March 1892, quoted above. (See p. 62.) The Navy would both protect sea communications and prevent invasion of the homeland. Yet it could not preserve the jewel of the Empire—more prosaically labelled Britain's most valuable export market from 1875—against an overland invasion. That adequate military provision should be made to defend India

[36] Cab. 2/1, 18 Feb. 1903.

against Russia was Balfour's second assumption, and he held it almost as strongly as the first. Soon after becoming Viceroy, George Curzon wrote to Balfour: 'As long as we rule India we are the greatest power in the world.'[37] Near the end of 1901, Balfour put it more defensively: 'The weakest spot in the Empire is probably the Indian frontier.' Moreover, as he wrote in the same letter: 'A quarrel with Russia anywhere, about anything, means the invasion of India and, if England were without allies, I doubt whether it would be possible for the French to resist joining in the fray.' It was in such circumstances that the threat of invasion to Britain itself would become acute. Balfour therefore argued against the conclusion of a Japanese alliance which might place Britain in the worst conceivable situation. The alternative, in reality unattainable, of joining the Triple Alliance on acceptable terms would, he believed, be better.

It is a matter of supreme moment to us that Italy should not be crushed, that Austria should not be dismembered and, as I think, that Germany should not be squeezed to death between the hammer of Russia and the anvil of France. If therefore we had to fight for the Central European Powers, we should be fighting for our own interests, and for those of civilization, to an extent which cannot be alleged with regard to Japan.[38]

Nevertheless, the Anglo-Japanese alliance was duly signed in January 1902. While Russian strategic railways continued to creep ever closer to the border of Afghanistan, British weakness at the Dardanelles (in the event of a Russian coup), in Persia, and in Afghanistan, had become evident by the time the C.I.D. first met in December 1902. Over and above the Russian menace Selborne, by October 1902, was 'convinced that the great new German navy' was 'being carefully built up' for war with Britain; but he admitted that Britain could not afford a Three Power Standard.[39] Therefore, even from a naval viewpoint, the Government was anxious to minimize the possibility of a conflict. Peace, and especially an accommodation with Russia, were Balfour's diplomatic objectives; and the fact that he soon became dominant in the C.I.D. whereas Lansdowne was but a periodic attender strengthened Balfour's personal hold on foreign policy. However Lansdowne, though somewhat diminished in stature by his War Office connection with the reverses of the Boer War, worked easily and well with Balfour in the diplomatic sphere. In general influence with Balfour, he probably ranked second to Selborne till 1905.

[37] B.P. 49732, f. 35, Curzon to B., 31 March 1901.
[38] B.P. 49727, ff. 159–79, B. to Lansdowne, 12 Dec. 1901.
[39] Monger, pp. 82–3.

Before the end of February 1903, the C.I.D. had already begun serious study of the Indian defence problem. Balfour at once conveyed the gist of the fourth C.I.D. meeting, held on 25 February, to the Cabinet. Lord George Hamilton, who had attended at the C.I.D., remarked the impact of Balfour's comments on Lansdowne and Ritchie who had not. Now they more fully appreciated, thought Hamilton, the sheer magnitude of the British task in defending India against the Russians. Nor was Selborne unaffected by his participation in the study—still in its early stages. [40] Thus Balfour, as he had indicated at Liverpool in February and in the House of Commons in March, proceeded to use the C.I.D. for the enlightenment of the Cabinet. Although the C.I.D. was destined to survive the change of government in December 1905, the Liberal premiers would hive off its main investigations into sub-committees until, in 1912, Asquith reverted to that interaction with the Cabinet practised by Balfour. One advantage of the intervening system of sub-committees was that the radical contingent in the Cabinet did not have its attention unnecessarily drawn to such investigations, matters in which it was normally uninterested but which were liable to trigger off negative reactions if thrust upon it. Thus C.I.D. practice between 1906 and 1912 would provide an ironical sequel to Campbell-Bannerman's attributions, when in opposition in 1903–5, of unconstitutional tendencies to the Balfourian C.I.D. [41]

Why, then, was Balfour, who had established the C.I.D. with hesitation, prepared subsequently to invest in that body more time and thought than any of his prime-ministerial successors?

In the first place, he assumed that no part of the British Empire should be gratuitously surrendered. Any such concession without a *quid pro quo* would be seized on as a sign of weakness. Firm diplomacy must be backed by adequate force. But it would be quite erroneous to conclude that Balfour's sustained effort at the C.I.D. was therefore dissociated from party-political considerations. The Unionists were essentially a party of Empire. They were also a party of minimum state intervention in the domestic economy and of minimum taxation.

It has already been seen how, in October 1900, Balfour recognized without overt delight that 'large sums of money' would have to be spent 'on army organisation and naval constructions'. (See p.113.) At that time, however, he also deplored Hicks Beach's likely opposition to such expenditure. Yet again, on becoming Prime Minister, Balfour exerted himself to

[40]   Ibid., p. 111.
[41]   *P.D.*, 4th, 118/1586–91, 5 March 1903; 146/85, 11 May 1905.

retain the said Hicks Beach as Chancellor of the Exchequer. On party-political grounds, he preferred to have Sir Michael 'dropping little grains of sand into the wheels' of defence policy rather than lose a reputable figure firmly associated with the economies beloved of the taxpayer.

Balfour believed through his political career, at least until the great divide of 1914 to 1918, that private enterprise was the most likely source of economic growth and that government intervention was prone to do more harm than good. Therefore, the best contribution that government could make was to preserve the Empire from encroachment by the great protectionist powers. As he was to write in the summer of 1903, the politicians who had opted for free trade in the 1840s had made a 'double error'. 'They failed to foresee that the world would reject free trade, and they failed to take full account of the commercial possibilities of the British Empire.' This had resulted in Britain 'bearing all the burden, but enjoying only half the advantages, which should attach to Empire', as a consequence of permitting the colonies of white settlement to become protectionist in their turn. Elsewhere in the same pamphlet he argues:

It is in the last resort on military power that our diplomatic rights in some of these regions, and our territorial rights in others, ultimately depend. Without it, they would ultimately lapse; and sooner or later these areas would become absorbed by one of the great protective powers, and their markets be lost to us for ever. When we reflect how necessary these are to the full success of insular [i.e. unilateral] free trade, and remember how in many cases they have been originally won, and how in all cases they are now maintained, I marvel that small armaments, small responsibilities, a small empire, and a large external trade should ever have been considered as harmonious elements in one political ideal.[42]

Therefore, it was Balfour's task to ascertain the level of military provision which would ensure the safety of the Empire and keep the cost within politically acceptable limits. In so far as the Navy was geared to a two-power standard, the key question to be answered concerned the size of the Army. This question was by no means a simple one. There were interacting variables involved, such as length of service (long service being more essential for British troops in India than at home), ability to attract the permitted number of recruits, the quality of the intake, the kind and duration of training for regulars on the one hand and for auxiliaries on the other, to say nothing of the cost of the various permutations. Then there was the question of equipment, the need for new field and horse artillery having led to a War Office inquiry during the early part of the Boer War. By

[42]   *Economic Notes on Insular Free Trade*, London, 1903.

December 1902 trial guns had been supplied, and the relevant committee had recommended that trial batteries be ordered. These were tested from September 1903 onwards and, by the summer of 1904, a decision was reached on the types to be ordered.[43] As Brodrick informed the Cabinet in November 1902: 'A very heavy increase stares us in the face in respect of the rearmament'—and this at a time when reduced expenditure was regarded as a political necessity.[44]

Although he built up a reputation as an expert on defence policy, Balfour never saw himself as in any sense a professional—in the way, for example, that Winston Churchill was later inclined to do. His purpose was to extract from the army and navy chiefs the best expert opinion available, so that a sound political judgement could be made. Apart from what was said at C.I.D. meetings, expert opinion was recorded in the form of memoranda circulated before the relevant meeting. Some of these stood as basic statements of the position of one service or the other, and would provide points of reference for many discussions. The first of these basic memoranda written for the C.I.D. came from the War Office and was entitled 'Provision of Land Forces for the Defence of the United Kingdom.'[45] Dated 14 February 1903, it questioned the Navy's claim to be able to repel 'any attack' on the United Kingdom. This five-page document, the first stage in the C.I.D. investigation into the correct size and organization of the Army, was derived from a *magnum opus* produced by the War Office during the South African War. Entitled 'Military Needs of the Empire in a War with France and Russia' and extending to 66 pages in its printed form, it had originally been signed by Lt.-Colonel E. A. Altham, D.A.A.G., on 12 August 1901 and been updated by footnotes, in many cases dated 16 January 1903, provided by Altham and his superior, Lt.-General Sir William Nicholson, the Director-General of Mobilization and Military Intelligence.[46]

At the third C.I.D. meeting, held on 18 February 1903, the capable, sharp-tongued Nicholson began his tenacious defence of the army view that 350,000 regulars 'would suffice' to defend the homeland from invasion. The War Office memorandum of 14 February had relied thus far on the *magnum opus* of August 1901. It also raised the possibility of Germany entering a war against Britain on the side of France and Russia: 'We know

[43] B.P. 49722, ff. 261–7, a note by Arnold-Forster on the history of the new artillery, n.d., but c.3 Jan. 1905.
[44] Cab. 37/63/156, 15 Nov. 1902.
[45] Cab. 3/1/3A.
[46] Cab. 3/1/1A.

that plans for the invasion of England have been discussed in Germany, and deemed by some, even with our existing Home Defence Army, to be a not improbable enterprise.' But in so far as Balfour refused, from 1903 to 1905, to envisage for C.I.D. purposes a worse contingency than a war against France and Russia combined, the lack of reference in the minutes of the meeting to the German 'dash at our Eastern coast' envisaged by the memorandum need occasion no surprise. It was resolved that the War Office should next inform the committee as to the smallest force with which 'an enemy' would have landed (*a*) in England early in 1900 when 'most denuded' of regular troops, and (*b*) in Ireland to start 'an insurrection'.[47] While awaiting this information, the committee turned its attention to the other main object of military expenditure, the defence of India.[48]

Balfour's underlying determination to use the C.I.D. to promote economy was reinforced by the representations of C. T. Ritchie. In a cabinet memorandum of 21 February, the Chancellor stated that service expenditure, excluding the cost of the Boer War, was mounting at a rate certain to provoke a public outcry.[49] Moreover, by 23 February Brodrick was coming under heavy attack in the House of Commons. His proposed army scheme (of which some brief account was given above) sparked off some lively Liberal assaults on the Government, abetted by Winston Churchill and other restless Unionists. Nor did L. S. Amery's recent articles in *The Times*, suggesting a reformed Army at an annual cost of £23 millions against Brodrick's estimate of £34,245,000 for 1903–4, promote relief or comfort for the unhappy minister. According to Wilfred Blunt, 'Brodrick's Army Bill had frightened everybody by its extravagance, and when the Funds fell to 90 he had thought all was lost.' Indeed, at a time when more government borrowing was needed for Irish land purchase, concern was great for the Government's credit as well as for its level of expenditure. Balfour wrote to Lady Elcho that Brodrick's current unpopularity was 'the most serious menace to the Government'.[50] However, Balfour left army reform in the hands of the Secretary of State, although he seems to have considered setting up a sub-committee of the C.I.D. to provide an alternative scheme, as he was later to do when Arnold-Forster in his turn got out of his depth.[51] Meanwhile the political incentive to limit the role and thus the

[47] Cab. 2/1, 3rd meeting, 18 Feb. 1903.
[48] Cab. 2/1, 4th meeting, 25 Feb. 1903, etc.
[49] Cab. 37/64/15.
[50] Satre, pp. 132–5; Blunt, *My Diaries*, London, 1919–20, 2 vols., ii, 46 (31 Mar. 1903); Young, p. 229, for B. to Lady Elcho, 27 Feb. 1903.
[51] *B.P.* 49707, f. 118, Selborne to B., 25 March 1903.

cost of the Army remained a major ingredient in Balfour's approach to the work of the C.I.D.

How, then, does Balfour's announcement in the Commons on 5 March that a naval base was to be established at Rosyth fit into the economizing and mildly pro-German picture of his activities given above? Nicholson's memo of 14 February had been written against a background of anti-German agitation in the British press. Having been directed for some time at the growing German fleet, it reached a crescendo when, at the end of 1902, Britain was co-operating with the Germans in a blockade of Venezuela designed to recover debts unpaid to nationals of both countries and to prevent further molestation of Anglo-German shipping. At the Cabinet of 21 October 1902, joint action against what Balfour termed 'this disreputable little republic' had been agreed on the understanding that the United States would be informed beforehand.[52] But, by early February 1903, American opinion was turning hostile while the Germans, predictably, were making extreme demands. It was the threat to Anglo-American relations that particularly annoyed the British opponents of the joint enterprise. When the Venezuelans ended the dispute on 13 February 1903 by giving way to the Germans, the anti-German press in Britain thought it had won a victory. This was because, despite the disgust at the outcry privately expressed by Balfour, Lansdowne, and Austen Chamberlain, the Government had previously asked Germany to accept arbitration. However, it was not in fact the diplomatic sequel to this proposal that terminated the dispute.[53]

Meanwhile, on 9 February, Selborne had suggested to Balfour that questions were now bound to be asked in the Commons as to whether the Government intended to establish an (anti-German) east coast naval base. Selborne therefore wished to announce in his Navy Estimates statement that it had been decided 'to establish a Naval Base on the Firth of Forth'. 'Is it not much better', he asked, 'that we should forestall all this and gain the credit?'[54] Balfour himself did announce the decision on 5 March, too late for Selborne's purposes. Already on 16 February the self-styled victors of Venezuela had struck. At a public meeting held in the Westminster Palace Hotel, a campaign for a North Sea base was inaugurated. Amongst the assembled Germanophobe journalists was Leo Maxse, future author of the famous slogan of 1911 'B.M.G.: Balfour Must Go!' Therefore far from getting in first and gaining 'all the credit' the Government seemed to have

[52] Cab. 41/27/31.
[53] Monger, pp. 104–7; Kennedy, pp. 255–60.
[54] *B.P.* 49707, ff. 190–11.

conceded the base at Rosyth to anti-German clamour. In fact, however, very little money was spent on Rosyth in Balfour's time as Prime Minister. Some plans were made and surveys carried out; but when, in October 1904, Fisher became First Sea Lord he forcefully advised Selborne: '*Don't spend another penny on Rosyth!*' His successful intervention was scarcely due to pro-German feeling but rather to the zeal with which he carried into effect the Government's prescription of economy. In his case economy was, in a fashion most remarkable, combined with higher administrative efficiency. [55] It should be added that, while the absence of developed east coast bases was to prove a serious shortcoming in 1914, Balfour's attitude was not unreasonable in 1902 to 1905. In so far as the German Navy could not present a serious threat to the Royal Navy for some years yet, the preparatory work done at Rosyth from 1902 to 1905 might be deemed adequate. As will be seen in due course, Balfour's scepticism about Germany's aggressive intentions did not seriously distort British defence policy in 1903 to 1905. As far as the east coast bases were concerned, the trouble arose from lack of appropriate action by the Asquith Government after 1908, when the prospect of naval warfare with Germany became unmistakable.

However, from a retrospective viewpoint it is difficult to deny that the anti-German attitude of many journalists, servicemen, and civil servants was fully justified. In an era of social Darwinism, when colonial empires seemed both a badge of success and a commercial necessity, Germany's growing economic and military power made an eventual clash with a less progressive Britain and her ubiquitous Empire a distinctly possible contingency. That Europe's strongest military power should also be spending heavily on a fleet designed to fight in the North Sea gave substance to British fears, as did the manifestations of anti-British feeling emanating from various sectors of German opinion.

Nevertheless, for Balfour's Government in 1903, the imminent completion of the Russian strategic railways up to the border of Afghanistan seemed a more immediate and formidable threat. As long as Britain maintained a two-power naval standard and a state of instant naval readiness, the Germans would hardly risk a war in the North Sea. But in defending India Britain would have to act as a *land power* against a vast force of Russian conscripts—of uncertain quality till 1904–5. This presented a much more alarming prospect. Thus Selborne, despite his naval concerns, could write to Curzon at the beginning of 1903: 'we remain with

[55] Mackay, pp. 337–8.

all the difficulties and responsibilities of a military Power in Asia. That is the crux for us.'[56] Diplomatically, Russia continued to be at odds with Japan. France was the ally of Russia. Therefore Selborne found no reason to disagree with Balfour's approach to the rationalization of British spending on defence. As the argumentative memoranda on home defence began to come in to the C.I.D. from the Army and Navy, Balfour simultaneously went on investigating the defence of India.

Here, of course, there was limited scope for inter-service conflict; and—as will be seen in Chapter 9—Balfour was able to draft two sets of provisional conclusions on 30 April and 20 May respectively. By 5 April Selborne, who by now was quite absorbed in the Indian problem, was writing to Balfour that, after reading a memo by Lord Roberts on the South African garrison, a source of Indian reinforcement, he had seen 'the solution of all' their difficulties. 'For the cheapest way of finding 100,000 men to reinforce the North West Frontier is to provide 100,000 Militia which can relieve and so set free obligatory garrisons of regulars in India and the Colonies.' Such heady enthusiasm for the Militia would be conclusively deflated in the next few years. However, Selborne went on to remark with a mixture of insight and dramatic irony that Brodrick, at the War Office, was 'in some danger of being too sticky and not sufficiently resourceful or inventive; Chamberlain on the other hand doesn't know all his facts, and is impatient of those he doesn't like.'[57]

Chamberlain was indeed about to demonstrate the full force of his discontent and change the course of British politics. Balfour seems to have had no definite presentiment of the impending storm. During Chamberlain's absence, from November till mid-March, in South Africa, there had been signs of restlessness amongst the Unionist rank and file over Brodrick's approach to army reform; but otherwise it looked as though the protests against the Education Act would die down. From February to early May, the tone of Balfour's cabinet letters to the King was quietly confident.[58]

Some comments should here be made on the importance of Balfour's cabinet letters as a source for his term as Prime Minister. Looking back on these years his political associates would remark on his ingrained dislike of the physical process of writing and on the impersonal effect of his habitual recourse to dictation. More striking, however, from a researcher's point of view, is the disparity between the great volume of incoming and the

---

[56] Monger, p. 110.
[57] *B.P.* 49707, ff. 120–2, Selborne to B., 5 Apr. 1903.
[58] Cab. 41/28, Nos. 1–7.

comparatively small number of outgoing letters. The persistence of many unrequited correspondents is clearly due to Balfour's unwritten encouragement and his well-known openness of mind. This disparity of volume is, of course, particularly marked in the case of such subordinates and experts as Morant, but it is also marked where intimate ministers are concerned. For example, in Lansdowne's case the disparity can be readily glimpsed by looking at the footnotes on relevant pages of Monger's admirable monograph *The End of Isolation*. The same is true of Balfour's correspondence with Selborne. To take as an example Balfour's attitude to the growing German Navy (treated above), the historian must quite often turn to incoming letters for an indication of the recipient's view. But whenever Balfour did reply, his letter was usually of such high quality in terms of content and lucidity as to make it difficult for a future commentator to resist citation in full. This is especially true of his memoranda for the Cabinet and the C.I.D. Here dictation does not noticeably hamper the steady flow of the argument, the balance of the structure, or the general sense of objectivity. However, as a consequence of the spasmodic outflow to individuals, there is little continuity or general coverage to be found here—and this applies, of course, to his memoranda for the Cabinet and the C.I.D. Nor did he ever keep a diary though he would dictate accounts on returning home from meetings which he deemed critical. But the cabinet letters do provide a degree of continuity and in other ways represent a unique source for Balfour's premiership.

Apart from a few months in 1904, when he tried to get away with dictation, Balfour accepted the task of writing to the King as legibly as possible in his own hand, and his sense of humour often imparts life and humanity to his accounts. He specifies what he feels to be important. In contrast with his normal cool approach, his genuine enthusiasm for the developing C.I.D. shows through; and (as will be seen) he even gives vent to his acute personal distress and exasperation where he deals with the problem of Curzon. The letters are not, of course, a complete record of cabinet discussions; but compared with the offerings of his successor Campbell-Bannerman, they are a rich source of information and delight. [59]

An undated cabinet letter of early March serves to introduce the critical phase which began with Chamberlain's return to England some ten days

---

[59] Cab. 41/27–30 comprise B.'s letters to King Edward as Prime Minister. The whole series of cabinet letters (1868–1916) was made readily accessible to scholars when it was photocopied for the P.R.O. in the 1960s. B. had had experience of writing cabinet letters before he became Prime Minister—to Queen Victoria (Cab. 41/24, Nos. 32–5, Mar. 1898) and to King Edward (Cab. 41/26, Nos. 7–9, Mar.-May 1901 and No. 11, May 1901).

later, on 14 March. The Cabinet considered whether Britain should participate in the St. Louis Exhibition in the United States. In the background
was the somewhat discouraging fact that British industry had last exhibited
triumphantly in 1851. Balfour reported:

> The Cabinet took the view, with which Mr. Balfour heartily agrees, that this
> country ought to do all that befits the first commercial community in the World. The
> difficulty with which we have to deal, of course, lies in the fact that our manufac-
> turers are sick of exhibitions; and that they feel no small absurdity in asking them to
> shew their best products in a country which absolutely excludes them from its
> markets by their high tariffs. The Government however are prepared to do their best
> to give dignity to the occasion. [60]

This shows how irritated Balfour was with the protective policies followed
by the United States and, by implication, with those of other protectionist
countries such as Germany. Not much prompting was required to make him
consider tariff retaliation by Britain. The letter also implies that Balfour and
the Cabinet, in the face of the poor British showing since the Paris
Exhibition of 1867, did not look much beyond foreign protectionism for an
explanation. The notion that emphasis on the modernizing role of education
might have something to do with rising industrial efficiency abroad and that
a British government could strengthen domestic industry through a more
appropriate system of education—without any need to interfere directly
with the working of the economy—simply did not arise. Nor did it arise
with any real force in the thinking of any British government for more than
half a century, by which time it was deemed axiomatic that the highest
youthful talent should prefer Oxford and Cambridge to institutions of more
obvious technological orientation.

Joseph Chamberlain was soon to demand a stronger constructive lead
from government; but he could offer no policy better than the politically
divisive and economically dubious proposal of Tariff Reform. Yet Balfour
would be ready to support him, provided that he could demonstrate the
electoral viability of his policy. In so far as this policy would inevitably
entail food taxes, which could then be remitted in favour of the colonies, it
was destined, as Balfour always feared, never to be very popular in
Chamberlain's lifetime. Why, then, did Chamberlain undertake the political gamble of declaring unilaterally for Tariff Reform?

On 14 March 1903 Chamberlain returned to Southampton accompanied
by his beautiful third wife, Mary, and was greeted with something amounting to a hero's welcome. The 'Hotel Cecil' in the form of Balfour and

---

[60] Cab. 41/28, No. 4, n.d.—letter No. 5 being dated 10 Mar. 1903.

Selborne did homage to the Birmingham manufacturer. Selborne boarded Chamberlain's liner at Netley and the Prime Minister, with his sister Alice, headed a ministerial welcoming-party at Waterloo station. Moreover, as Mary Chamberlain recounted, her husband soon after had 'a most gracious reception' from the King. Yet by 25 March he was to be found at a cabinet meeting denouncing Wyndham's Irish Land Purchase Bill, due to be introduced in the Commons later that day. Apart from the Education Act, this may be accounted the most substantial piece of constructive legislation passed by the Balfour Government; but Chamberlain, with his rooted dislike of landlords, was no more favourable to the Irish bill than he had been to the Education Act. Such conflict was always inherent in the coalition of Conservatives and the Liberal Unionists with their Noncon-formist wing.

In a cabinet letter of 20 November 1902 Balfour had signified his personal satisfaction with the impending culmination of his attempts to bring conciliation and stability to Ireland. Wyndham, he wrote, 'gave an exceedingly lucid and interesting survey of his Irish land proposals, in relation to the present position of affairs in Ireland', which included a recurrence of land war and coercion. Land purchase under the existing Treasury scheme (wrote Balfour to the King) had almost ceased because it was not attractive enough to bring tenants and landlords together. The solution was to make 'a more liberal use of British credit' and to extend the term of the loans.[61] When the time for the Bill's introduction was drawing near, the Cabinet, in Chamberlain's absence, again discussed it on 10 March 1903. Apart from the new anxiety about the national credit—how could the country face up to a great war if its government could not borrow?—the Irish Bill filled Balfour with a rare enthusiasm:

> This is a very far reaching measure; and the Irish Government are sanguine that it will settle for all time the Irish land difficulty. The objections to it—and there are objections to all things—arise from the fact that it will make a heavy call on British credit, already handicapped by the great war loans and the Transvaal borrowings: and that it will be represented as a great gift to Irish tenants and landlords at the cost of the British taxpayer.

However, the Cabinet 'was clearly of opinion that in the interests of a great policy minor differences must be ignored'.[62]

While Chamberlain's old vendetta against the Irish landlords doubtless underlay his attack on Wyndham on 25 March, he appears to have

---

[61]　Cab. 41/27, No. 35.
[62]　Cab. 41/28, No. 5.

concentrated on the possibility that the tenant farmers, on finding themselves combined in a debtor's role, might collectively refuse to pay.[63]
Chamberlain's irascibility was due to a combination of causes. As
regards the Education Act, Lord George Hamilton later wrote in his
Parliamentary Reminiscences the oft-quoted opinion that 'the first change
propagated the second. If we had no Education Bill in 1902, we should have
had no Tariff Reform in 1903.' While this has been seen as less than a total
explanation,[64] Balfour's henchman Sandars provides specific first-hand
evidence of the importance of this causal factor. Writing in 1930, he holds
that it

undoubtedly influenced Mr. Chamberlain in becoming the evangelist of a new fiscal
gospel. The Colonial Secretary had been greatly perturbed by the political consequences of Mr. Balfour's Education Bill, which after a long and stormy passage
through the House of Commons, became law in 1902. He viewed with concern,
amounting to alarm, the havoc it had wrought in the ranks of nonconformity which
he himself had won over by his impassioned exertions to the cause of Unionism. The
Education Act had abolished School Boards—*ad hoc* bodies beloved of Birmingham and the chapels of the middle classes—and at the same time had undoubtedly
strengthened the decaying position of voluntary schools with all their clerical
apparatus. The country rang with cries to strike against the Education rate, and to
wreck operation of the new Enactment. Bye-elections were being lost to the
Government on the Education issue, and the ranks of Liberals, broken by the policy
of Home Rule, were rapidly reuniting. In more than one conversation with the
writer Mr. Chamberlain dwelt upon the paramount political necessity of what he
called 'changing the issue', by which he meant that it was essential to the Unionist
party to call off the electorate from the education question, and turn their attention to
a more attractive issue (as he was sure it would be), namely, a change in our fiscal
system. More than once Mr. Chamberlain referred to this aspect of his argumentative case, and there were occasions when he pressed his point upon the Patronage
Secretary, and the pundits of the Whips' room.[65]

But Chamberlain was also moved by other concerns. For long anxious
about imperial defence, he had, after the failure of his bid for a German
alliance in 1901, turned by late 1902 to a conviction of German enmity.
Already in September 1902, soon before the Venezuela issue led Balfour
and Lansdowne to co-operate with Germany, Chamberlain was telling

[63] Amery, v. 172. There is no cabinet letter for the meeting of 25 Mar. 1903 in the P.R.O.
series (Cab. 41), but B. himself later indicated in his letter of 27 Aug. to Devonshire that he
had written one. See Amery, v, 157 and 175.
[64] See for example R. A. Rempel, *Unionists Divided*, Newton Abbot, 1972, pp. 22–3.
[65] *J.C.P.* 18/16/28. 'For confidential reference: A Note on Mr. St. John Mildmay's letter
to the Editor of *The Times* referred to the Writer. J. S. S. 26th June 1930.'

Baron Eckardstein of the German Embassy that the Cabinet could no longer resist the strength of anti-German feeling in Britain.[66] Yet while he was visiting South Africa, the Government had acted against Venezuela in alliance with Germany; and the ensuing storm of anti-German protest confirmed that Balfour and Lansdowne were out of line with at least an articulate section of British opinion. By January 1903, Chamberlain wanted 'an entente cordiale' with France. In a letter of the 9th to his son Austen, he wondered if Lansdowne had considered the idea of a visit to England by the French President that year.[67] Indeed, the initiative leading to the French negotiations seems to have come from Chamberlain rather than from Balfour and Lansdowne who wanted, above all, an accommodation with Russia, and remained, as will appear, somewhat sceptical about the value of a French *entente*. However, the spread in Britain of anti-German views is denoted by the private opinion of the Liberal spokesman on foreign affairs, Sir Edward Grey who had, by January 1903, 'come to think that Germany is our worst enemy and our greatest danger'.[68]

Indeed, there are many pointers to Chamberlain's readiness, on his return to England in March 1903, to appeal to imperialist and anti-German opinion.[69] The case of Canada was central to his preoccupations. In 1897 Canada, for domestic reasons, had cut her tariffs by 25 per cent in favour of British goods, and this had led to retaliation by Germany. In 1903 this remained for British opinion a lively count against the Germans who were accused of hindering moves towards a British imperial federation. As far as Chamberlain was concerned, the Cabinet had decided on 19 November 1902 to retain the Corn Tax and make, in Balfour's phrase, a 'preferential remission' of it in favour of Canada.[70] Balfour's cabinet letter said that the remission would be given 'in favour of the British Empire'; but it was the unique preference given by Canada (but liable to be withdrawn if Britain did not offer a *quid pro quo*) that Chamberlain was anxious to retain as a point of departure for a whole system of imperial preference.

In the interval before Chamberlain returned from South Africa, C. T. Ritchie, the Chancellor of the Exchequer and a convinced Cobdenite free

---

[66] Monger, p. 107.
[67] Amery, iv, 206.
[68] Keith Robbins, *Sir Edward Grey*, London, 1971, p. 131, quoting Grey to Newbolt, Newbolt MSS, now at Bodleian Library.
[69] See Kennedy, pp. 254–62, for an account of the anti-German factor in the origins of Tariff Reform.
[70] Amery, v, 121 and 149; Kennedy, p. 262, for 'the tariff war' between Canada and Germany, 1897–1903, and for the imperialist outcry against Germany; Cab. 41/27, No. 34, B. to the King, 19 Nov. 1902.

trader, maintained the opposition to preferential tariffs which he had previously declared. Indeed, he wished to abolish the corn duty altogether, largely on Cobdenite grounds. But Ritchie's readiness to make an issue out of his opposition to the proposed tariffs was not revealed to Balfour till about 21 February 1903—the date of Ritchie's memorandum 'Our Financial Position' to which reference was made above in connection with the rising cost of defence. [71] Ritchie explained verbally to Balfour that unless the Cabinet gave up remission of the duty on Canadian corn, he would—just before the budget—resign as Chancellor. [72] There is little reason to doubt the accuracy of Balfour's statement of 1929 to Mrs Dugdale that he was 'perfectly horrified at what had happened', mainly on Chamberlain's personal account. [73] Yet already on 19 November 1902 Ritchie had indicated his definite opposition to preference, following from his cabinet memorandum of 15 November which objected to the principle of taxing British consumers to benefit colonial exporters. [74] Moreover, Ritchie had apparently been strongly backed by Lord Balfour of Burleigh (Scottish Secretary) and been supported also by Devonshire and Lord George Hamilton. [75] Why, then, did Balfour not perceive, at the Cabinet of 19 November 1902, that battle lines were being drawn on an important issue of principle?

The answer derives, at least in part, from Balfour's character as an intellectual statesman. Despite his beguiling diffidence on many occasions, such as the deference to professional opinion noticed in the sphere of defence, there was also in Balfour an underlying tendency towards intellectual arrogance. Selborne would write to Mrs Dugdale in 1934: 'I suppose I knew A. J. B. for forty years, and in early life he seemed rather cynical and intolerant of stupidity, but in later life he seemed to put up with almost anything and anybody, and was universally charming.' [76] This gradual evolution may be coupled with the painful process whereby he schooled himself during the 1890s to lead the House of Commons in a manner generally acceptable. When he came to preside in cabinet, he appears to have done so with patience, charm, and detachment. But when, in August 1903, he wrote at length to Devonshire on the fiscal question and touched on his own previous opinions, his diffident style cloaked a long-matured contempt for the Cobdenite approach:

[71] Cab. 37/64/15.
[72] Amery, v, 154.
[73] Dugdale, i, 345.
[74] Cab. 37/63/155, 15 Nov. 1902.
[75] Amery, v, 122–3.
[76] WHI/77, 23 Feb. 1934.

The question of 'fiscal reform', which has now burst into so violent a flame, is not new . . . I have not taken the trouble to search my own early utterances on the subject, though I accidentally came upon a very clear exposition of the views which I have consistently entertained on what is called 'retaliation' in a speech delivered twenty three years ago in the House of Commons. Unless my memory deceives me, Lord Salisbury has more than once adumbrated like opinions.[77]

In fact, a week earlier at Stanway, Lady Rayleigh had found her brother Arthur reading his own book 'Essays and Addresses (1893)'. This contained 'two essays' bearing on the tariff question 'which he said were excellent' and perhaps worth republishing.[78]

The most relevant of these essays had originally been published in the *Fortnightly Review* in January 1882. It was a highly critical appraisal of 'Cobden and the Manchester School', prompted by the publication of Morley's *Life of Cobden* in 1881. Its tenor is indicated by the comment that

Mr. Morley has taken care that his own opinions, while sufficiently enunciated, shall not occupy an unduly large share of space: a reticence for which his readers may be the more grateful, since, during the composition of his work, he would seem, from his occasional utterances, to have been in a frame of mind much more suited to the pamphleteer than to the historian.

Balfour's assessment of Cobden himself was scarcely more flattering:

Cobden was an honest, an able, and a useful public man, but not, I think, as his admirers claim for him, either a great politician or a great political philosopher. He was prevented from being the first by the mental peculiarity which made him a serviceable ally only when (as he says himself) he was advancing some 'defined and simple principle'; a limitation which, whatever its compensating advantages may be, is an effectual bar to the highest success in a career which requires in those who pursue it a power of dealing not only with principles, but likewise an infinity of practical problems which are neither 'defined' *nor* 'simple'. He was, on the other hand, prevented from being a great political philosopher . . . Much as he saw to disapprove of in the existing condition of England, he never framed a large and consistent theory of the methods by which it was to be improved. Outside the narrow bounds of the economics of trade he had political objects, but no coherent political system; so that if he was too theoretical to make a good minister of state, he was too fragmentary and inconsistent to make a really important theorist.

On Cobden's attitude to protection, Balfour commented:

It is absurd to ascribe corrupt motives to large bodies of men, merely because the

---

[77] *B.P.* 19770, ff. 66–141, B. to Devonshire, 27 Aug. 1903.
[78] Lady Rayleigh's Diary, 20 Aug. 1903.

economic theories they adopt are in accordance with their own interests . . . It may be said that the motives of the Protectionists were liable to suspicion because their theories were not only favourable to themselves, but were manifestly false. But at this moment the vast majority of the civilised world advocate false economic theories of precisely the same kind . . . Why are the English landlords of 1845 to be described in harsher language than the English manufacturers of 1821, or the French, American, German, Russian, Canadian, and Australian manufacturers of 1881? Their error may be a proof of stupidity, but if it be, the stupidity is too general to excite either surprise or indignation. [79]

In a world which, with the exception of Britain, had been protectionist since the 1880s, it seemed obvious to Balfour in 1902–3 that Britain should at least be able to retaliate against those countries that imposed duties on her export trade. To him this, at least, had been clear for more than twenty years. As for the particular issue of the imperial preference advocated by Chamberlain, it was a complex question whether it was practical politics; but it hardly occurred to Balfour that an ostensibly intelligent Chancellor of the Exchequer was going to make a do-or-die stand against a majority decision of the Cabinet in defence of Cobdenism as a matter of principle. Balfour's contempt for all slavish adherents of simple Cobdenism goes far to explain the ruthless manner in which he would cashier Ritchie and the other free-trade ministers—including his old familiar, Lord George Hamilton—in September 1903. Sandars would afterwards comment that Balfour 'parted without a trace of real regret from George Hamilton who for 29 years had been in close Parliamentary intercourse with him, and for more than 14 years his Colleague in Cabinets, and with the like indifference also from Balfour of Burleigh.' [80]

Once Balfour had carefully spelt out his views in his impressive *Economic Notes on Insular Free Trade*, [81] he had no compunction—in marked contrast, as will appear, with his handling of George Wyndham's fall— about hustling the Cobdenite ministers out of the Cabinet. To him, the soundness of his own reasoning was so evident that he believed it would make general headway, not only in the party but, given time, in the country. This helps to explain why he clung so surprisingly and tenaciously to office after the disastrous Unionist divisions of 1903.

[79] *Essays and Addresses*, pp. 185–223.
[80] *J.C.P.* 18/16/30, 'Alfred Milner', pp. 7–8. Sandars sent his memories of various political figures to J. L. Garvin in the early 1930s.
[81] Cab. 37/65/47 (1 Aug. 1903) comprises the cabinet paper on this subject. The published version of 1903 is cited on p. 126 above.

However, to revert to the actual sequence of events, on receiving Ritchie's threat to resign before the budget, Balfour passed on the information to Austen Chamberlain so that he could alert his father as soon as possible. This Austen did by writing on 24 February 1903 to catch the returning Colonial Secretary at Madeira. He indicated that no decision would be taken on the budget before he arrived back in England. Joseph Chamberlain, on receiving the news, considered resignation; but, knowing that Balfour and the majority of the Cabinet were on his side, he felt that it was Ritchie who should go. Meanwhile Gerald Balfour, involved in the issue as President of the Board of Trade, urged his brother to let Ritchie go; but the Prime Minister, oppressed by the attacks on Brodrick and on the Education Act, could not accept this blow to the ministry. Not only was the budget imminent. The embarrassment over finding a successor to Hicks Beach was all too recent.

At unreported cabinet meetings on 17, 25, and 31 March, Chamberlain fought for retention of the corn tax with preference for Canada. The majority of the Cabinet still supported his general position, but agreed with Balfour in not wishing to force the Chancellor's resignation at that moment. As Balfour wrote to Devonshire some months later, Chamberlain was 'rather ill, rather irritable, and very tired'; and he failed to insist that the Cabinet should choose between Ritchie and himself. Yet neither did he, after recouping his health and vigour during April, feel that he could let the matter rest. Already by the beginning of the month he was receiving complaints from the Canadian Finance Minister about Britain's failure to reciprocate Canadian tariff preference; and at about the same time Milner (who was backing preference from the South African angle) telegraphed his alarm at the British Government's 'apparent complete indifference' on the subject. Nor did Chamberlain favour Brodrick's scheme of army reform, especially as it offered to station only 15,000 British troops in South Africa, whereas Chamberlain preferred 30,000, on grounds of imperial strategy and of economy at home. That Chamberlain considered forcing the Cabinet to choose between him and Brodrick, when he had backed away from a show-down over Ritchie, testifies both to his interest in imperial defence and his general irritation with government policies.[82]

As if all this was not enough, early April also found Chamberlain embroiled in the sphere of foreign policy. Here he succeeded in causing a reluctant Government to make a third anti-German move in less than four months. This was over the matter of the Baghdad Railway. German

[82] *B.P.* 49770, ff. 66–141, B. to Devonshire, 27 Aug. 1903; Dugdale, i, 338–44; Amery, v, 154–75.

influence in Turkey had steadily increased since William II's visit in 1889 and in 1899 a concession was granted for extending the German-owned Anatolian Railway to the Persian Gulf. The Russians held as serious a view of the implications of a German railway through the Middle East as did Balfour and his advisers of Russian railways advancing towards India. Nor did the British care to see any rival power enter the Persian Gulf. However, the German bankers calculated that they alone could not raise the necessary capital for the projected railway and they therefore sought British and French investment. On the grounds that Britain could not, as Curzon wished, exclude other nations indefinitely from the Gulf, Lansdowne wanted Britain to take a share on the basis of the internationalization of the railway and especially of its terminal port at the head of the Persian Gulf. He was strongly supported by Balfour. But Leo Maxse learned of the Government's intentions in time to launch a fresh onslaught in the April number of the *National Review*. Moreover, he singled out 'our Mandarins'—presumably Balfour and Lansdowne—for scathing comment. The *Spectator*, edited by St. Loe Strachey, duly sprang once more into anti-governmental action, as did the *Morning Post*, *The Times*, and other right-wing papers. However, during the Easter recess, Lansdowne wrote to Balfour from Bowood: 'But for Joe's bile the opposition would not be serious. I hear from the F.O. that he *is* unwell and that you have given directions that he is not to be unnecessarily worried with papers . . . I am sorry for him as well as for myself.'[83]

Although Balfour despised the clamour of the press at least as much as he despised the adherents of Cobdenism, Lansdowne was more sensitive to these new attacks. He wrote again to Balfour, this time from Lancashire, on 17 April:

My dear Arthur,

. . . First let me say how sorry I am that you have again been on the sick list . . . I am very anxious to take stock with you of the situation as to the Baghdad Railway. Strachey and Maxse have proclaimed both in London and Paris that they mean to stop the whole thing, and they assert freely that they have 'nobbled' Joe.[84]

Lansdowne was convinced of the merits of British participation in the railway for the reasons already given and also because it would give him a bargaining counter with which to pursue his unvarying key diplomatic objective: a general settlement with Russia in Central Asia. Balfour was

---

[83] *B.P.* 49728, ff. 42–3, Lansdowne to B., 12 April 1903. For the Baghdad Railway episode as a whole see Monger, pp. 118–22 and Kennedy, pp. 260–1.

[84] *B.P.* 49728, ff. 45–6.

firmly associated with this aim. [85] But, despite Balfour's strong support over the Baghdad Railway (which was, however, seen as a fairly minor issue by the Prime Minister), [86] Lansdowne late in April gave way before the combination of Chamberlain and the anti-German press. [87]

If, as Mrs Chamberlain reported to her mother in America, ministerial depression had touched even the normally serene Balfour before the Easter recess (8–12 April), [88] the succeeding weeks held even less joy in store for the Prime Minister. During the recess, Chamberlain apparently made up his mind to declare for 'imperialism' in the shape of Tariff Reform. He was due to address his Birmingham constituents on 15 May and he discussed the content of his speech with his election agent. The latter vehemently agreed with Chamberlain's suggestion that his audience would welcome preferential tariffs as a way of hitting back at Germany. [89]

Meanwhile on 23 April Ritchie introduced his budget and announced the abolition of the corn duty. There was some dissatisfaction in Unionist ranks and the protectionist ex-minister Henry Chaplin arranged to meet Balfour with a deputation on 15 May—the day of Chamberlain's Birmingham speech, as it happened. On 12 May Balfour wrote to the King that the Cabinet 'was almost entirely preoccupied with a discussion of the present position of the Corn Tax'. There was no question of restoring it that year but, Balfour wondered, what should be said to the delegation about the future? He felt that he should speak

in such terms as would indicate the possibility of reviving the tax, *if it were associated with some great change in our fiscal system*. Such an announcement may cause disquiet in certain circles; but in view of possible eventualities such as the necessity of retaliating on foreign countries or of the expediency of a closer fiscal union with our Colonies, it seems desirable to make it. The Cabinet unanimously assented. [90]

Chamberlain, for his part, understood that retaliation represented the common ground between him and Balfour, as can be seen by reading the Birmingham speech of 15 May. [91] Likewise Balfour subsequently pointed out to Devonshire that at the cabinet meeting of 12 May, 'Chamberlain, if you remember, took the occasion to observe that *he* proposed to say at

[85] See, for example, Cab. 41/28, No. 2, B. to the King, 19 Feb. 1903.
[86] *B.P.* 49770, ff. 66–141, B. to Devonshire, 27 Aug. 1903.
[87] Monger, p. 122.
[88] Amery, v, 176.
[89] Ibid., pp. 176–8.
[90] Cab. 41/28, No. 8, 12 May 1903.
[91] Amery, v, 184–94.

Birmingham much the same as what *I* proposed to say to the deputation, *only in a less definite manner.'* [92]

As far as specific indications of future government policy were concerned, Chamberlain kept his word. After stressing the unique value of the Empire, and playing on the theme of German interference therewith, Chamberlain—having earned loud applause for his demand for freedom of action and negotiation over tariffs—moved towards his peroration: 'I leave the matter in your hands. I desire that a discussion on this subject should now be opened. The time has not yet come to settle it . . .'. Such words could almost have been taken from Balfour's mouth. But the sense of urgency communicated by Chamberlain, the conviction that a fleeting opportunity to save the Empire must be grasped, led Leopold Amery to remember it as 'a challenge to free trade as direct and provocative as the theses which Luther nailed to the Church door at Wittenberg'.

[92] *B.P.* 49770, ff. 66–141, 27 Aug. 1903.

8

Chamberlain Rocks the Boat

1903

IT was the response to Chamberlain's speech of 15 May that was crucial.
There is every indication that Devonshire was justified in remarking a
couple of months later that he was 'confident that Chamberlain had not
given the least sustained thought to the consequences of his theories'.[1]
Indeed Chamberlain himself was much surprised by the amount of excitement generated. But, as his biographer observes, the Rubicon had been
crossed. The forceful tone of the speech electrified those who had been
concerned about Britain's relative decline as a world power and who, in the
tradition of Sir John Seeley, looked to the Empire as a source of renewed
strength. Again, in a year of economic recession, there were industrialists,
especially in declining industries, whose interest was at once aroused by
any such sign that protection might emerge as a political possibility. Even if
he had had second thoughts about the political viability of his proposal,
Chamberlain could hardly have retreated.[2]

The political world breathlessly awaited the fiscal debate in the Commons on 28 May to discover whether Chamberlain's views conflicted with
those of the Prime Minister. If they did conflict, the Unionists were split.

In the debate, Balfour spoke before Chamberlain. Not only was tenacity
concealed beneath the Balfourian grace and charm. His intellectual contempt for outright Cobdenites and straight protectionists alike may be
readily discerned in the following passage, even if his tactical purpose was
to calm the situation and play for time:

Mr. Speaker, I always regret the manner in which political economy is treated in
this House and on public platforms. It is not treated as a science, or as a subject
which people ought to approach impartially with a view to discovering what the
truth is, either from theory or experience. Not at all. They find some formula in a
book of authority and throw it at their opponents' heads. They bandy the old
watchwords backwards and forwards: they rouse old bitternesses, wholly alien, as

---

[1] FitzRoy, p. 143 (30 July 1903).
[2] Amery, v, 225–6; Kennedy, pp. 261–2; and see his Ch. 15: 'Economic Transformation
and Anglo-German Trade Relations'.

far as I can see, to any modern question; and our controversies are apt to alternate between outworn formulae imperfectly remembered, and modern doctrines imperfectly understood . . . I should hope . . . that the country will devote itself . . . to a consideration of the real economic position in which we stand . . .³

Having, however, paid a tribute to Chamberlain's work in strengthening the bonds of Empire, he declared that Britain must in such a case as German action against Canadian preference, be able to defend those imperial bonds, if necessary, by 'retaliatory tariffs'. As for Britain establishing a system of preferential tariffs, he accepted Chamberlain's demand for an inquiry. In so far as such a system involved Britain in taxing food, he did not know whether the British people would accept it. Similarly, he did not know whether the colonies would accept a modification of their tariff systems in exchange for Britain's action. He urged patience while the complicated position was properly investigated. 'Remember—this question is not a question that this House will have to decide this session or next session or the session after. It is not a question that *this* House will have to decide at all.'

But Chamberlain, speaking later in the debate, was not content simply to agree, as he did, that fiscal reform might be an issue at the next election. He confirmed that imperial preference, the policy which he advocated, *did* entail a tax on food. For good measure he added that, as the working classes would pay three-quarters of such a tax, the resulting 'very large revenue' should be used for social reform, such as Old Age Pensions. While Chamberlain had not gone far enough to make it certain that he was in conflict with the Prime Minister, he had gone too far for Ritchie and the free-trade ministers. Worse, from Balfour's viewpoint, Chamberlain had gone too far for the Duke of Devonshire.

However, assisted by three of his intimate friends in the Cabinet (the Liberal Unionists, Lansdowne and Selborne, and the Conservative George Wyndham) Balfour succeeded in getting the Duke to remain in the Government while the promised inquiry was carried out.⁴ The Duke's adherence to free-trade principles was by no means clear and definite. Sir Henry James (of the Crawford divorce case) had not forgiven Balfour for dropping him from the Cabinet in July 1902; and his repeated visits to Devonshire House in the summer of 1903 were, Sandars believed, directed at reviving the Duke's resentment at not being consulted before Balfour's succession to 'the purple'. Yet, by dint of tact and assiduity, Balfour could at

³ *P.D.*, 4th, 123/162–3, 28 May 1903.
⁴ Rempel, pp. 37–8.

least hope to retain this prestigious member of the Cabinet. But though he might also be able to persuade ministers to refrain from speaking publicly on Tariff Reform while the government inquiry was carried out, it could hardly be for long. Already in the debate of 28 May, backbench free traders had declared their opposition to Chamberlain's proposals. Winston Churchill, the scourge of Brodrick, unerringly observed that Chamberlain's preferential policy would end up as full protection. Indeed, much of Chamberlain's support would come from industrialists in declining industries who wanted just that. Churchill also forecast that the

old Conservative Party, with its religious convictions and constitutional principles, will disappear and a new Party will arise like perhaps the Republican Party of the United States of America—rich, materialist, and secular—whose opinions will turn on tariffs, and who will cause the lobbies to be crowded with the touts of protected industries. [5]

But from Balfour's point of view, it was the split in the family group itself which was to prove the most traumatic feature, not only of the debate, but of the whole long-drawn-out Tariff Reform saga. 'I cannot tell you how deeply I feel it, or how much pain it has given me', Balfour would write some years later. [6] Speaking after Balfour in the debate, Lord Hugh Cecil—perhaps the most brilliant of Balfour's Cecil cousins—declared strongly for the fundamental merits of pure free trade. [7]

It was suggested in the previous chapter that Balfour genuinely expected his doctrine of retaliation to provide an acceptable basis for the restoration of party unity. But it can also be said that the sheer difficulty of bringing this about possessed for him a peculiar fascination.

A crucial cabinet meeting was to be held on 9 June. Lord Esher (still serving on the Elgin Commission and also, as ever, busy at Court) wrote on that day to his son Maurice: 'A. Balfour saw the King yesterday, and did not seem very hopeful of being able to keep his team together.' And on the 10th, after Balfour had succeeded in getting a pledge of public silence from the Cabinet during the tariff inquiry, Esher commented;

I had a talk with Mrs. Chamberlain who was in great form. She says Joe will not speak at present for fear of provoking more disunion. This *pax* I don't think can continue. It is hardly practical. The Duke of Devonshire very nearly left the Government. They will break up this year. There is little doubt of it. [8]

⁵ *P.D.*, 4th, 123/194, 28 May 1903.
⁶ Bodl. MS, Selborne 1, B. to Selborne, 6 Mar. 1908.
⁷ *P.D.*, 123/170–5; Amery, v, 231, 237.
⁸ E.P., 7/16. (cf. Lord Esher, *Journals and Letters*, 1934, i, 412–13).

Esher was a shrewd judge on such matters. So was Almeric FitzRoy who noted on 10 June that a parliamentary respite had been gained but it did 'not seem that the Prime Minister's idea of drawing a mantle of indecision over their differences can materially prolong the life of the Administration'. [9]

But Henry Lucy picks out a strong strand in Balfour's motivation: 'The apparently impossible, the certainly difficult has for him irresistible attraction.' [10] It has already been seen how, since Cambridge and the following years at Whittingehame, Balfour had loved games, whether intellectual or sporting. In these, he delighted to excel. It was, perhaps, the challenge of the parliamentary game which had brought him into serious politics. Thus it is piquant to find a specific reference to the said 'parliamentary game' in his account to the King of how he negotiated, in the Cabinet, the crucial meeting of 9 June:

The whole time of the Cabinet was occupied by a discussion of the present position created for the Government by Mr. Chamberlain's and Mr. Balfour's recent utterances on the subject of retaliation and the Colonial preferences. On these subjects, as Your Majesty knows, the Cabinet is not agreed. And though they do not involve immediate action, in as much as no one suggests any variation from our traditional fiscal policy till the country has had an opportunity of expressing its opinion, still the fact of divisions among us, greatly weakens our position, and gives the Opposition a new and unexpected advantage in the parliamentary game.

Mr. Balfour has used and is using, every effort to avert any rupture among his colleagues; and he is very loyally supported by all the other members of the Cabinet. He hopes that it may be found possible to avert, or if not to avert, at least to defer, any crisis which may threaten the existence of the Government. [11]

But Lucy often registers, as did so many others, a sense of higher motivation underlying Balfour's sublime gamesmanship. Commenting on the Prime Minister's transition from languid criticism of Gladstone's Irish Land Bill of 1881 to the second reading of Wyndham's Bill in May 1903, he observes 'how odd a thing is politics, even when practised by the highest-minded.' [12] Balfour was so devoid of pomposity and autobiographical self-interest that it is difficult to find quotable illustrations of this high-mindedness. But when Wyndham, acclaimed for his Irish Bill, wrote to Balfour in July 1903 asking whether, as a minister still in office, he should accept a proffered knighthood, he received a revealing answer. It was couched in diffident language, leaving it entirely open to Wyndham to make

---

[9]   FitzRoy, p. 135.
[10]   Lucy, *Balfourian Parliament*, p. 408.
[11]   Cab. 41/28/10.
[12]   *Balfourian Parliament*, p. 256, 4 May.

his own decision, but it included the following unvarnished affirmation: 'I regard Cabinet rank as the highest sphere in which any man can be called upon the serve the King. It is laborious, and, no doubt, often unpleasant, yet the honour is so great.'[13]

In terms of specific measures, there can be no doubt of Balfour's continuing determination to pre-empt Home Rule by entrenching the policy of Irish land purchase. FitzRoy felt (10 June) that the threat posed by Tariff Reform to the continuance of Balfour's Irish policy would make him 'do his utmost to keep the Cabinet together for the remainder of the Session'.[14] And retrospectively, when Home Rule was being seriously mooted in 1916, Balfour (as was not his wont) seemed at a private luncheon to be 'much depressed' and 'the admitted reason was that he greatly lamented the fate which had overtaken the political purpose of his life, namely the preservation of the Union.'[15]

The sequence of Balfour's manœuvres before and during the inevitable cabinet crisis of September 1903 has been so much studied that it is unnecessary to follow it in detail.[16] Amid accounts of discussion in the Cabinet of various subjects (the need for new legislation on licensing, a difficult war in Somaliland, Russia in Manchuria, Russia threatening the British position in Persia, the beginning of the negotiations for a French *entente*) the progress of the fiscal theme is told in Balfour's own words to the King:

(23 June 1903) The subject of tariff reform, on which as Your Majesty knows the Cabinet is much divided, again came up for discussion: and though there is a certain natural impatience at the anomalous position which the question at present occupies, Mr. Balfour was able, he believes, to mitigate acute divisions.[17]

(14 July) [The 'character and number of returns' on the fiscal subject to be made public were discussed.] Mr. Balfour, with the consent of the Cabinet, resolved to give no special opportunities this session for the discussion on 'tariff reform' unless they are asked for in connection with a vote of censure.[18]

(14 August) There was some little disagreement at the end of *Tuesday's* Cabinet [11 August] as to whether a *final decision* should be come to at *Thursday's* Cabinet

[13]   B.P. 49804, f. 140, 25 July 1903.
[14]   FitzRoy, p. 136.
[15]   Sandars P., C.769, Sandars to Frank Mildmay (holo. draft) *c*.17 July 1916.
[16]   Many of the documents are printed in the biographies of Chamberlain and Devonshire by Julian Amery and Bernard Holland to which reference has been made above—especially in the former. Alfred Gollin, *Balfour's Burden*, London, 1965, is largely devoted to this particular topic. Alan Sykes, *Tariff Reform in British Politics 1903–1913*, Oxford, 1979, is a comprehensive, intensively researched, treatment of its subject.
[17]   Cab. 41/28, No. 12.
[18]   Ibid., No. 14.

[of the 13th] on the subject of 'Fiscal Reform'. Mr. Balfour however subsequently laid it down that a final decision was *not* required until the Cabinet again meets to consider the subject on Sept. the 12th. It was subject to this ruling that the discussion took place on Thursday. It was not very satisfactory. Mr. Balfour does not feel justified in entertaining any very confident hope that he will retain the co-operation of all his colleagues for the scheme which he himself favours. But if (as he does not doubt) Mr. Chamberlain shows a readiness to accept Mr. Balfour's scheme and to modify some of the plans which he has from time to time put forward rather hastily, Mr. Balfour is of opinion that the majority of the Cabinet will cordially support him in the moderate, yet important suggestions which he (Mr. Balfour) is prepared to recommend.

There cannot be anything in the nature of a Cabinet crisis till the middle of September at the earliest; and, whatever then happens, Mr. Balfour is confident that he can carry on the work which Your Majesty has entrusted to him. In any case he will do his best to steer between the opposite dangers of making proposals so far-reaching in their character that the people of this country could not be expected to acquiesce in them—and (on the other hand) of ignoring, in a spirit of blind optimism, the danger signals which indicate approaching perils to our foreign and to our colonial trade.[19]

As expected, the cabinet crisis came in mid-September. The next cabinet letter provides an admirable summary of Balfour's own position. It reinforces the impression (as his accompanying 'Notes on Insular Free Trade' do in more detail)[20] that he did believe in his own policy of 'retaliation'. Indeed, he could hardly have prolonged his defence of it for so long if he had not. At the same time, it is highly unlikely that he would have proposed it as part of his legislative programme if it had not been for the crisis brought on by Chamberlain. Even 'retaliation' was too uncertain in its effects, above all politically.

Here, then, is the major part of his cabinet letter of 15 September:

Mr. Balfour can perhaps most easily make clear a very complicated position if he begins by describing his own views on fiscal reforms—views to which he proposes to give full expression at Sheffield on Oct. 1, and the economic basis of which [is] set forth in a Pamphlet which he begs respectfully to send with this letter.

The root principle for which Mr. Balfour pleads is *liberty of fiscal negotiation*. Hitherto it has been impossible for us to negotiate effectively with other governments in respect of commercial treaties because we have neither anything to give which they wish to receive nor anything to take away which they are afraid to lose. Our negotiations are therefore barren; and we have been obliged to look on helplessly while in all the most advanced countries a tariff barrier is being built up

[19] Ibid., No. 18.
[20] Cited on p. 126 above.

against our manufactures which is an ever growing obstacle to our legitimate trade development. Mr. Balfour does not contemplate that at this stage the evil can be removed: but if there are any means of mitigating it, those means should be tried . . .

There are, however, two quite different shapes in which this 'freedom to negotiate' may be employed—one against Foreign Governments—the other in favour of our own Colonies. In dealing with Foreign Governments we may threaten—and if need be employ—'retaliation'. In dealing with our own Colonies we can only offer 'Preference'. The second is perhaps the most imporant; *if*, that is, a really good bargain could be struck between the Mother Country and her children. But . . . it is hard to see how *any* bargain could be contrived which the Colonies would accept, *and which would not involve some taxation on food in this country.*

In Mr. Balfour's opinion there are ways in which such taxation *might* be imposed, which would in no degree add to the cost of living of the Working Classes. But he is also of opinion that in the present state of Public feeling no such plan would get a fair hearing; to make it part of the Government Programme would be to break up the Party and to endanger the *other* half of the Policy—that which authorises retaliation—for which the Country is better prepared. Mr. Balfour, therefore, as at present advised, intends to say that, though Colonial preference is eminently desirable in the interests both of British Commerce and Imperial Unity, *it has not yet come within the sphere of practical politics.* Mr. Balfour believes that the policy thus indicated is the right one for any Statesman to recommend who is responsible to Your Majesty for carrying on the Government. He believes that the great majority of the Unionist Party—Conservative and Liberal—will accept it. But he cannot conceal from himself, and he ought not to conceal from Your Majesty, that in all probability several members of the Government will feel unable to accept it, either because it goes too far or because it does not go far enough . . . But he may perhaps say at once (1) that the course he advises will cause *less* disruption than any other, (2) that he believes it to be *right in itself* and (3) that he entertains no doubt of being able to make proposals for filling up the vacant places which will enable Your Majesty's Government to be carried on with credit so long as it retains the confidence of Parliament. [21]

What, then, of the charge reiterated against Balfour that he was out of touch with public opinion and totally ignorant of the wishes of 'the common man'? In this basic matter of public attitudes to food taxes, who was to be proved the better judge, the intellectual Prime Minister or the Unionist 'Tribune of the People', Joseph Chamberlain?

Meanwhile, at the cabinet meeting on the previous day (14 September) Balfour had virtually dismissed both Ritchie and Balfour of Burleigh because they had each circulated Cobdenite memoranda irreconcilable with Balfour's 'Notes on Insular Free Trade' and with a cognate 'Blue Paper',

[21] Ibid., No. 19, B. to the King, 15 Sept. 1903.

both of which had been before the Cabinet on 11 August. [22] By 15 September, Balfour held letters of resignation from Ritchie and Lord George Hamilton. There was only a technical delay in the case of Balfour of Burleigh who was then in waiting on the King at Balmoral. [23] But the Prime Minister privately reassured Devonshire that there would be no commitment to preference in his Sheffield speech and this sufficed to make the Duke stay his hand *pro tempore*. Meanwhile, it had been privately agreed between Balfour and Chamberlain that if the free trade ministers (apart from Devonshire) did in fact resign, then Chamberlain's own provisional resignation (unknown to the said Cobdenites) would become effective. Chamberlain would embark on a crusade in the country to see if he could sway public opinion in favour of imperial preference. Meantime his son Austen would remain in the Cabinet to maintain an intimate link with the Prime Minister. [24]

In so far as Balfour appeared to have separated the Duke of Devonshire from the more irreconcilable free traders, he had pulled off a dazzling coup. 'My dear Willie Selborne', wrote Sandars on 21 September, 'I telegraphed you this morning that the Duke stays on. This was finally settled at . . . Devonshire House on Wednesday evening [the 16th], when the Chief returned radiant. He left the next day for Balmoral.' Having received instructions from Balfour by cipher on Saturday, Sandars had sent by King's Messenger to Lord Milner at Carlsbad 'a warm invitation to accept post of Colonial Secretary and also a personal message from the King warmly urging acceptance'. Valuable though this appointment would be, Sandars thought that the War Office was a 'perhaps greater outstanding difficulty'. 'Alick Hood' (the Chief Whip) quite agreed with Sandars that the War Office would be their 'heaviest burden next Session' in the wake of the report of the Elgin Commission, published in July 1903. The King disliked the idea of appointing the tactless Arnold-Forster, but it was important to avoid choosing someone whom critics of the Government would describe as a 'hack'. Esher, having emerged as an informed critic of the existing regime, was a possibility; but this would mean having the heads of both the 'great spending departments' in the House of Lords. 'I need not say,' he commented, 'how anxiously I am awaiting the result of today's colloquy at Balmoral.' [25]

[22] Sykes, p. 45.
[23] Amery, v, 408 and n.
[24] Amery, v, 405–20.
[25] Bodl. MS Selborne 1, ff. 20–25, Sandars to Selborne, 21 Sept. 1903.

Selborne himself received stark messages from Balmoral on the 23rd and 25th. Balfour, desperately searching for recruitable ministerial talent, reported:

> Milner has refused Colonies by telegram . . . I may have to ask you to take them . . . Chamberlain strongly presses for [Arnold-Forster] for War Office. The King feels very strong objection . . . am hesitating now between Esher, Wyndham [and Akers-Douglas]. There are very strong . . . arguments against all . . .

Then, two days later, he intimated: 'Esher refuses office . . . Chamberlain suggests Lord Cromer but . . . it would seem that W. O. must be in Commons . . . I think possibly Milner might be induced to reconsider.'[26] Chamberlain, also, tried to persuade Milner, but in vain.

If Selborne remained Balfour's most important confidant within the Cabinet, Chamberlain, outside it, retained for the moment something of the virtual co-prime-ministerial position which he had held since 1902—or even since 1895. Austen, who might otherwise have usefully filled the War Office post, was to be promoted from the Post Office to the Chancellorship of the Exchequer.[27]

However, no announcement of the new ministerial appointments had been made by the time that Balfour found himself addressing a packed meeting at the party conference held at Sheffield on the evening of 1 October. Although, following the lines of his above-quoted cabinet letter of 15 September, he offered nothing more than the possibility of 'retaliation' and omitted colonial preference altogether, a telegram from the Duke of Devonshire reached him before breakfast at the New Club in Edinburgh the next morning (Friday, 2 October). The Duke—who was, it seemed, unable to understand Balfour's 'Economic Notes' and was much plagued by Ritchie and Co. who claimed him as their leader—had discovered in the Sheffield speech a pretext for resignation. Balfour was shaken out of his customary *sang froid*. He rushed off a long letter to the Duke before breakfast, complaining bitterly of the illogicality and destructive timing of his decision.[28] Coming at a time when he was struggling to fill four vacancies in the Cabinet, but had just made his unifying speech at Sheffield, it was galling to learn that a crucial part of his intricate contrivance had buckled. Just before midnight he wrote to Selborne in his own barely legible hand:

[26] MS Selborne, 1, ff. 26–7, 32.
[27] Dugdale, i, 358–9.
[28] Holland, ii, 363–6.

My dear Willie,

I enclose the King's reply . . . and a copy of my reply to him which I have just written. I am dog tired after Sheffield and so may have written great nonsense.

I am here till 12.45 p.m. tomorrow Sat. I then motor to Whittingehame . . . I have a cypher of course.

Yrs affly
A. J. B.

I fear the King does not quite realize that the Public will soon get impatient—and that if a suspicion gets around that he is fighting [Arnold-Forster] it will be very unfortunate . . . The worst of it is that if I force A. F. down his throat, he may (quite unconscious of harm) make that young man's life a burden to him. [29]

Despite his fatigue and extreme disappointment over Devonshire, Balfour clearly had no thought of giving up office and his attempt to reunite the party. Having returned to Whittingehame on the next day, he was able to joke at the dinner table about the Duke's resignation. [30] Meanwhile in London, as Sandars later recalled, Devonshire 'asked me what he (Balfour) would do as he had lost five members of his Cabinet, and I told him I was sure Balfour could carry on. He looked, and was, frankly amazed, and jerked out: "Well, I think he is the boldest man I have ever known in politics." ' [31]

Before the five new cabinet appointments could be announced on 6 October, Balfour was involved in difficult transactions behind the scenes. Chamberlain had conferred on the Colonial Office post more prestige than it deserved politically in the deflating circumstances, aggravated by the recent publication of the Elgin Report. Balfour's old friend Alfred Lyttleton (of cricketing fame and brother of May Lyttleton) was remembered by Sandars as 'probably the most popular man of his time in any circle', and filled the place without discredit: 'his universal popularity and Balfour's affection, which was a devotion, sustained him as far as possible in the difficulties he encountered.' [32] Selborne remained First Lord—the King had opposed his being transferred from the Admiralty 'under any circumstances'. [33] The fact that Admiral Fisher (then Commander-in-Chief at Portsmouth) was at Balmoral at the time was due to the King's close interest in the continuing reformation of the Navy. [34] Balfour, as in July 1902, seems to have tended to under-estimate the value of what Selborne and Fisher had

[29] Bodl. MS Selborne 1, '11.45 p.m. Friday' [2 Oct. 1903].
[30] Dugdale, i, 362.
[31] J.C.P., 18/16/17.
[32] Ibid., 18/16/26.
[33] Sandars P., C.719, Knollys to B. (cipher telegram) 30 Sept. 1903.
[34] Mackay, pp. 288–9.

still to offer in the way of reform. Certainly, the senior service was not a subject of recurrent political embarrassment in the way that the Army was; and the need for reform of the War Office itself had been re-emphasized in July by the Elgin Report. Moreover, the King insisted on action here. [35]

By the time that Balfour, on 4 October, offered the War Office to Arnold-Forster, he had accepted the idea that Esher (whose additional note had given depth to the Elgin recommendations on the subject) should with others form a committee to assist the new Secretary of State to reconstitute the War Office. This involved such radical steps as the abolition—so long overdue—of the Commander-in-Chief and the establishment of an Army Council along the lines of the Board of Admiralty. Balfour wrote to Arnold-Forster: 'I think such a Committee would be of great assistance, would act as a buffer to diminish the violence of the personal shocks which all such official revolutions involve, and would in no way hamper you in the general discharge of your duties.' [36] On this basis, the ministerial post was filled—with considerable misgivings on Balfour's part. [37] With hindsight, he would probably have done well, both on the side of the Irish policy and of Army reform, had he plumped for the transfer to the War Office of Wyndham mooted on 23 September. Certainly, Brodrick could not be retained at the War Office, and he was shunted into Hamilton's place at the India Office. The other appointments announced on 6 October were of Austen Chamberlain to the Exchequer, of Lord Stanley in his stead at the Post Office, and of Andrew G. Murray as Scottish Secretary instead of Balfour of Burleigh. The dismal ministerial picture was completed by the elevation of Londonderry to Lord President of the Council in place of Devonshire—the Board of Education incongruously remaining in Londonderry's charge. What proved to be quite a useful addition to the Cabinet (12 October) was that of Balfour's cousin 'Jim' (who had succeeded his father Salisbury in August) as Lord Privy Seal. Balfour noted, a shade optimistically, that 'the old "Hotel Cecil" cry' was unlikely to be raised as the post—which he himself had held jointly with his other offices since July 1902—'carries with it no emoluments, and nobody else expects it'. [38]

If Balfour's principal objective was to reunite his party before being

---

[35]   Peter Fraser, *Lord Esher*, London, 1973, p. 91.

[36]   Arnold-Forster P., 50335, ff. 4–5.

[37]   Bodl., MS Selborne 1, 23 Sept. 1903; also E.P., 10/32, B. to Esher, 30 July 1904: 'I have always been anxious about A.F.'

[38]   Sandars P., C.719, B. to Knollys, 15 Oct. 1903. Sir Robert Ensor, in *England 1870–1914*, Oxford, 1936, p. 611, seems to be responsible for the hardy tradition that Londonderry had been Lord Privy Seal.

forced to go to the country, how was he to achieve it? While Chamberlain was arousing more enthusiasm in Unionist circles than Balfour, the latter persisted in believing that reason in the form of his 'Economic Notes on Insular Free Trade' would prevail, if given time. They were published in September by Longman, Green and Co. and in his Preface Balfour wrote in characteristic style:

These Economic Notes were circulated to my colleagues in the first days of August . . . Though the argument is occasionally somewhat abstract, and occasionally somewhat compressed, I think that perhaps a larger circle than that for which the paper was originally written may like to have an opportunity of reading it. Hence its publication.

It is one of the difficulties inherent in the present controversy that some important points can hardly be made interesting, or even intelligible, on the platform without an amount of expansion and illustration which would render it impossible to put them in their proper setting within the limits of a single speech . . .

Having, however, rather unsuccessfully attempted to get his message across to the conference at Sheffield on 1 October, he was abruptly confronted with the above-mentioned incomprehension of the Duke of Devonshire![39] But he hoped that eventually light would penetrate even such dark recesses. Meanwhile, Balfour's object was to provide firm, economical, and efficient government and hope that the electorate would not be wholly ungrateful.

Certainly, as far as this study of Balfour is concerned, the question of his constructive achievement is central. It will therefore be appropriate, in the next chapter, to turn away from the constant threat of his removal from office by the largely uncontrollable tariff issue and see how far his main constructive work, in the sphere of foreign and defence policy, confers retrospective value on the continuance of his administration.

[39]   Dugdale, i, 360–1.

9

In Defence of Empire

1903—1905

THE conclusion of the Anglo-French *entente* has inevitably impressed historians as one of the most significant achievements of Balfour's administration. However, such an ultimate historical judgement was hardly anticipated by Balfour. While he certainly approved of Lansdowne's positive, if scarcely eager, response to the French initiatives, he does not seem ever to have referred to them with the enthusiasm detectable in his references to Wyndham's Irish Land Bill or even, at times, to his own policy of 'retaliation'—let alone the Committee of Imperial Defence. Typical is the following comment, in a cabinet letter, on the 'early progress of the French negotiation' of 1903:

It is moving, though but slowly. The great obstacle seems to be connected with the Newfoundland fisheries, and the position in Egypt. As regards the latter, Lord Lansdowne is in constant contact with Lord Cromer who is deeply interested in the whole transaction.[1]

A series of letters written during November by Sandars to Balfour's brother Gerald, who was unwell, gives an excellent idea of Balfour's daily round and the foci of his attention. 'There was no Cabinet on Saturday [7th] and so the P.M. was able to do a little at his paper on Home Defence, which is his present main occupation.'[2] Indeed, Balfour had been keeping a persistent hold on the deliberations of the C.I.D. and, despite the fiscal distractions, the work of defining the roles of the fighting services had gone steadily ahead on the assumption of a war with Russia and France. This work at the C.I.D. amounted to the first attempt to devise a coherent defence policy for Great Britain.

As mentioned earlier, the object was to establish principles in the sense of eliminating Army responsibilities beyond what seemed essential. On the defence of the Indian North-West Frontier, Balfour produced papers on

---

[1] Cab. 41/28, No. 20, 6 Nov. 1903.
[2] WHI/122, 9 Nov. 1903.

30 April and 20 May 1903[3] which were adopted by the C.I.D. as a
provisional report on 11 June.[4] Together they amounted to some 19 pages
of print and constituted an indication of 'the broad lines of strategy which it
would be desirable, if possible, to adopt'.[5] On 25 June 1903 it was decided,
having provisionally set a figure on the need for British troops in India
during the first year of a war with Russia, to pass on to the case of Egypt,
'leaving the defensive needs of the United Kingdom to be taken last'. 'The
cost of each [Egyptian] alternative was considered.'[6]

It was, of course, always assumed that Indian defence represented the
biggest single call on the British Army, so Balfour wrote a memorandum to
cover his two-part draft report.[7] This invited Curzon and Kitchener
(Commander-in-Chief in India) to comment on the report—thus initiating a
series of exchanges which failed to provide the C.I.D. with an *agreed*
number of Indian reinforcements in Balfour's time as Prime Minister. The
position was not dissimilar after the change of government! However, from
the point of view of the Balfour Government, reinforcements of 30,000 on
the outbreak of war and of 70,000 later represented a working basis for
holding the Russians on a line between Kabul and Kandahar. This figure of
100,000 regular troops to be sent during the first year of 'a war on the
frontier of India' still held good at the C.I.D. in October 1908.[8]

That much having, for practical purposes, been clarified, the Committee
proceeded during July and August to direct continuous attention to Home
Defence: that is, attention punctuated but not seriously diverted by such
lightweight bagatelles as a critical rejoinder, amounting to nine pages of
print, from Curzon and Kitchener, and preparation by the Committee of a
suitable response![9] At the fourth of these meetings on Home Defence, 'the
Prime Minister undertook to draw up during the holidays a Memorandum,
similar to that on Indian Defence, recording the progress of the discussions
up to the point which had now been reached.'[10]

By 17 November Sandars was able to inform the still absent Gerald
Balfour that he was about to circulate the Prime Minister's 'finished paper'
on Home Defence to the Cabinet, 'and also the elaborately constructed

[3] Cab. 6/1/12D and 6/1/19D (corrected version 6/1/21D).
[4] Cab. 2/1, 16th meeting. And see John Gooch, *The Plans of War*, p. 204, for comment.
[5] Cab. 2/1, 38th meeting, 14 Apr. 1904.
[6] Cab. 2/1, 18th meeting.
[7] Cab. 6/1/28D approved by C.I.D., 2 July 1903, Cab. 2/1, 19th meeting.
[8] Cab. 16/3A, 'Final Conclusions' of Report of Sub-Committee on Invasion, 22 Oct. 1908.
[9] Cab. 6/1/30D, 7 Aug. 1903 (9 pp.) and W.O. 'Observations' on that memo, Cab. 6/1/31,
3 Oct. 1903 (7 pp. plus map).
[10] Cab. 2/1, 22nd meeting, 5 Aug. 1903.

papers on Indian Defence, together with Curzon's and Kitchener's criticisms on it'. This illustrates the way in which Balfour continued to use the C.I.D. for the enlightenment of the Cabinet on defence policy in a way that his Liberal successors were, before 1912, unable to do, because of the fundamental disagreement in the Cabinet on the subject. As Sandars went on to remark, these C.I.D. reports would determine the framework within which Arnold-Forster would devise 'his War Office schemes, and the estimates of next year'. [11] Balfour's report on Home Defence, the 'invasion paper', [12] was indeed a landmark in the history of modern British defence policy. It took France as the possible invader, not because diplomatic relations were bad but because Balfour considered them irrelevant. As he remarked before a Sub-Committee of the C.I.D. in May 1908, in language which reflects his evaluation of the Anglo-French agreement of 1904, 'I imagine that the Committee of Imperial Defence would not consider that they were doing their duty if they supposed that the safety of the country could depend upon some paper instrument or a mere *entente*, however *cordiale* it might be.' The factors to consider were, at all times, 'of a military and naval character'. [13] From the viewpoint of practical policy, Balfour did, of course, take account of a *military alliance*, such as the Franco-Russian or the Anglo-Japanese. But it was mainly on account of her proximity and military capability that France was accepted as the hypothetical invader in 1903.

British naval superiority was assumed. It would be effective in preventing invasion, provided that the invader's preparations were on such a scale that they could not be concealed. To ensure this scale of enemy activity, the British home army would have to be such that the invader would not come with fewer than 70,000 troops. It was considered that, when the British home forces were at their lowest ebb of the South African War, the French would not have come with anything less than an army of 70,000. Provided that a completely secret embarkation of such a force was manifestly impossible, the invasion of the United Kingdom would not be attempted as long as Britain maintained (*a*) a Two-Power Naval Standard, [14] and (*b*) a minimal, trained, home defence force, equivalent to that of March 1900 when most of the trained regulars (normally earmarked for reinforcement

[11] WHI/122, 17 Nov. 1903. The important defence memoranda to which Sandars refers do not appear in the list of Cabinet Papers (Cab. 37) but only among the C.I.D. Papers; so Sandars's letter adds usefully to knowledge of the procedure followed.

[12] Cab. 3/1/18A, Draft Report on the Possibility of Serious Invasion, 11 Nov. 1903.

[13] Cab. 16/3A, B.'s evidence at Invasion Sub-Committee, 29 May 1908, on p. 249.

[14] B. announced on 1 March 1904 that Britain would maintain a Two-Power Standard plus a margin, and from Nov. 1904 the Admiralty envisaged this margin as 10% in battleships.

of India) had been sent to South Africa. The key component of the home defence forces of March 1900 had been 17,000 trained regulars (1 cavalry brigade, 1 brigade of Guards, and 1 (old-style) Infantry Division). Otherwise, there were some 80,000 untrained regulars, 50,000 Militia, 6,000 Yeomanry, and 225,000 Volunteers—but all these were accounted of little immediate value in the face of fully-trained continental conscripts.[15] Therefore Balfour had succeeded in establishing the principle that, apart from 100,000 regular troops assigned to Indian reinforcements, the equivalent—in the language of 1906—of one 'great' fully-trained regular division was to be retained for the defence of the United Kingdom. This would be supplemented by the auxiliary forces.[16]

After the 'invasion paper' had been considered at the C.I.D. on 18 November, Sandars on the 21st reported to Gerald Balfour:

> The Committee of Defence were much pleased with the P.M.'s Memorandum on Home Defence, and the sailors declared that it suggested some novel problems which had not occurred to them . . . St. John [Brodrick, as ex-army minister, but now Secretary for India] and the military intelligence officer [Nicholson] have undertaken to work out the technical detail of isolated attacks on these shores, independently of the main idea of an invasion in force . . .[17]

The C.I.D. meeting of 18 November was, incidentally, the first to come under Balfour's chairmanship—the Duke of Devonshire having presided until his resignation from the Cabinet. However, the change seems to have had little practical significance. As long as Balfour himself was a constant attender,[18] the other ministerial members did not fail to come, and their work was guided by the Prime Minister.

As indicated in Sandars's letter above, the C.I.D. agreed on 18 November that Brodrick and Nicholson should try to find a weakness in Balfour's invasion paper. Arnold-Forster, of course, as a keen 'blue-water' man was not likely to be as critical of navalist argument as his predecessor at the War Office, a situation which did not augur well for relations between a tactless minister and his professional advisers at the said Office. On 12 December, the suggestion that 30,000 invaders of Ireland might divert sufficient naval force to open up London to a separate invasion was duly rebutted by the

[15] These figures had been given in the W.O. paper, 'Liability of United Kingdom to French Invasion during the South African War', 28 Feb. 1903, Cab. 3/1/7A.
[16] Owing to the shortcomings of Arnold-Forster's regime at the W.O., the decision to organize the regular Army in large divisions of 18,000–20,000 men was not taken till June 1906. See Ian F. W. Beckett and John Gooch (eds.), *Politicians and Defence*, 1981, p. 76, etc.
[17] Cab. 2/1, 23rd meeting; WHI/122.
[18] It is not quite true that he never missed a meeting. Lansdowne deputized as Chairman on 8 Feb. 1904 when B. was ill; Cab. 2/1, 31st meeting.

naval members, Lord Walter Kerr and Prince Louis of Battenberg. The meeting is also of interest for the fact that Balfour pointed out that 'raids with small forces had not yet been dealt with.' He asked for professional information about possible raids on places on the east coast. Consistently with his principle of looking at military capability rather than current diplomatic relations, he assumed for his purpose German raids in 'a war against Germany and Russia combined'. But the conclusions reached on raids were unlikely to affect Britain's over-all military provision. [19]

While it remains to take note both of the work of the Esher Committee for reform of the War Office, and of the naval reforms associated with Fisher, it can certainly be argued that Balfour had already completed his main direct contribution to defence policy by November 1903. In essence, his achievement consisted in placing the defence of Britain and her Empire on a basis of logical provision consistent with the need for economy. At a meeting of the Cabinet on 6 November, just as Balfour was finishing his 'invasion paper', the need to cut government (and thus especially defence) expenditure received much emphasis. The new Chancellor, Austen Chamberlain, 'reviewed the financial situation'. This, Balfour commented to the King, was 'most unsatisfactory'.

The expenditure is great and the revenue less than was anticipated: and the prospects for next financial year are by no means reassuring. The unexpected sources of expenditure are 1st the Navy (due to the rapidity with which the contractors are doing their work) and 2nd the Somali war—which is, financially, a running sore. [20]

And again, on 16 November:

There was some further talk about Army Estimates, which *must* apparently be reduced if fresh taxation is to be avoided—a contingency which would be disastrous considering that the war taxation has not yet been taken off! [21]

In the last of his series of four letters to Gerald Balfour, Sandars enlarged on the financial problem:

Our whole trouble is finance. Austen has the worst possible outlook before him: and how to avoid fresh taxation he knows not. The revenue for the current year will probably be short by a million—I understand—and then next year? Ritchie's budget seems to have been almost a fraud. The corn tax brought in more than he calculated; and I expect he took 1d more off the income tax than he should have done. [Ritchie

[19]   Cab. 2/1, 27th meeting.
[20]   Cab. 41/28, No. 20.
[21]   Ibid., No. 21.

brought it down from 1/3d to 11d. In 1899–1900, it had been 8d.] The P.M. the other day said to me that he thought he might even now be driven to taxation on Joe's lines of some import duties: but I don't think this was more than a chance observation.

Anyhow our financial situation and a Budget of an unpopular character might turn us out early next session. Of course we had been hoping that A.F. [Arnold-Forster] would get Army Estimates down to 28½ millions—the more or less normal figure— but, struggle as he will, and reduce as he will certainly do—they must *slightly* exceed 29 millions . . . [22]

Yet in the wider world Russia and Japan had been steadily drifting towards a conflict which, owing to the alliances, might well result in Britain having to fight against Russia and France. The financial reasons for avoiding such involvement were brought home to the Government by the incident of the Chilean battleships. On 27 November the Cabinet was faced, in Balfour's words, with 'two matters of very great and pressing difficulty'—the second of which was the question of Chinese labour on the Rand, of which more anon.

The first related to an offer suddenly made by Russia to the Chilean Government to purchase two battle ships belonging to the latter, and now lying, nearly ready, in the Tyne. These ships Chile is obliged to sell under the award given by Your Majesty in connection with the Chile – Argentine arbitration.

Lord Selborne had been 'constantly urging the Japanese to buy them'. But it seemed that the Russians were prepared to outbid the Japanese. If they did, 'the balance of naval power in the Far East' would be 'seriously modified'. So should the British buy them? One reason against a British purchase was the design of the ships which did not suit the existing British 'battle squadrons'; but more fundamental was the state of the national credit. Balfour lamented

we do not see how to find the money. There is, or rather will be, a heavy deficit on this year's budget. It seems almost impossible to avoid fresh taxation next year. The money market is in so depressed a condition that even the smallest fresh borrowing upsets it. The matter was so suddenly sprung on the Cabinet that it was absolutely necessary to give the Chancellor of the Exchequer a few hours to consider the situation with his advisers and the Cabinet therefore reassembles tomorrow at 3, to make its decision. [23]

Balfour's cipher dated 30 November informed the King that a cabinet

---

[22] WHI/122, 29 Nov. 1903.
[23] Cab. 41/28, No. 23, 27 Nov. 1903.

committee had arranged to buy the ships on special terms. [24] The money involved amounted to some £1,600,000. [25] The two ships subsequently comprised the *Swiftsure* class: they were both rated too weak to count as battleships.

From the point of view of Balfour's constructive guidance of defence policy, it was fortunate that there was no autumn sitting of Parliament in 1903. Within the parliamentary party, Balfour's initial difficulties derived more from the free traders. Winston Churchill, for example, indicated his actual severance from the Conservative party in December. By the time that Parliament met in February 1904, it was quite sufficient for the Liberals to move an amendment to the Address of an appropriately fiscal nature (i.e. condemning food taxes) for Unionist free traders to be forced to choose between party and principle.

The constitution and composition of the Esher Committee required Balfour's intermittent attention between the first moves at Balmoral in September and the announcement of its appointment on 7 November. Once the soldiers at the War Office realized that they were threatened with a reforming committee of 'blue-water' complexion (represented in the alarming form of Admiral Fisher) there was 'a great palaver' at Buckingham Palace (according to Arnold-Forster); and there was constant 'arguing and discussing' (according to Esher) with General Kelly-Kenny, the Adjutant-General, to the fore on the one side and 'Jacky' Fisher on the other—all most 'unedifying'. [26] Balfour, however, after initial hesitations in early September about the value of Esher's ideas, steered a steady course once he had accepted the principle of a radical-reforming committee. It was, in the end, appointed for its special purpose by the Prime Minister. Unprecedented in its constitutional origins, it finally consisted of Esher as chairman, Sir John Fisher, and (to the further dismay of Kelly-Kenny *et al.*) Sir George Clarke. This ex-Colonel of the Royal Engineers and former secretary of the Colonial Defence Committee (1885–1892) and the Hartington Commission (1888–1890), was currently Governor of Victoria. Something of a master-mind and a publicist, he had made no secret of his 'blue-water' convictions. [27]

Esher was in no doubt about the importance of the work already done at the C.I.D. from the viewpoint of his committee. He and Fisher (working

[24] Ibid., No. 24; and WHI/122, Sandars to Gerald B., 29 Nov. 1903.

[25] Cab. 41/28, No. 24.

[26] A.-F.P. 50335, Arnold-Forster's diary, 26 Oct.; E.P. 7/16, Esher to Maurice Brett, 27 Oct. 1903.

[27] Gooch, pp. 36–41; Fraser, pp. 90–5; Mackay, pp. 288–92.

together in advance of Clarke's arrival) understood, as he wrote to Balfour on 25 November, that the C.I.D. had 'agreed upon certain definite principles, on which Mr. Arnold-Forster and the new War Office Organization' were henceforward 'to act'. It would therefore help the committee if it could be officially informed about these principles. [28] Indeed, Balfour not only thus made the work of the Esher Committee possible. After the reports had been compiled in double-quick time, he sanctioned their publication in February and March 1904 and gave indispensable backing to the removal of the 'old gang' from the War Office, to the initiation of a General Staff, and to the establishment of an Army Council on Admiralty lines instead of the notorious dual system of Secretary of State and Commander-in-Chief. At last, the Augean stables had been cleansed!

The Committee also recommended the establishment of a secretariat for the C.I.D. There was to be a secretary—prospectively Sir George Clarke—who, while not a member of the C.I.D., would attend its meetings and keep its records. He would also act as a remembrancer to the Prime Minister and help him to foresee developments affecting defence policy. Esher had wanted to develop the secretariat into a kind of inter-service general staff but Balfour, writing from Whittingehame on 14 January 1904, queried the 'portion of your scheme' relating to the 'Defence Committee'. It should, he insisted, be made clear that the six or eight 'subordinates' in the so-called 'permanent nucleus' were not part of the Committee itself. Again, what was the position of the Secretary and his staff *vis-à-vis* the First Military Member (Chief of the General Staff) and the First Sea Lord and their staffs?

I presume [wrote Balfour] the First Military Member, the Head of his Intelligence Department, the First Sea Lord, and the Head of *his* Intelligence Department will, as now, be usually summoned to the Defence Committee . . . Will not the creation of a *third* expert body, different from both and in closest relation with the Defence Committee, be very difficult to work successfully, except under a very strong Prime Minister? [i.e. not under such as Campbell-Bannerman?] Is there not a danger of creating, under this system, *two* Headquarter Staffs, who, from the very fact that they are two, and not one, will tend to polarise into a natural opposition, just as the Army and Navy now . . .?

This, of course, would not happen under the present system . . . Points are constantly raised on which either the Naval or the Military Intelligence Departments are asked for reports and calculations. With the help of these the Prime Minister finally drafts a report, which in its turn is the subject of discussion and examination. This system is likely to bear better fruit as the Intelligence Departments are better trained and equipped. But would it be improved by introducing into it a new set of

[28]   Sandars P., C.747.

experts, officially independent of both Army and Navy, yet dependent on the Army and Navy for all their information[?] [29]

That same day (14 January) Sandars reported to Balfour that he had just 'had a long innings with Esher' who had 'handsomely done a great deal of softening' in the relevant report. [30] The fact was that the C.I.D. could only discharge its co-ordinating role under the attentive presidency of a Prime Minister of Balfour's calibre. The alternative was a Ministry of Defence— fleetingly advocated by Sir John Fisher in the autumn of 1903. [31] However, a Ministry of Defence would have excluded the imperial possibilities of the C.I.D. as envisaged, well ahead of Esher's reports, by Balfour in early December 1903. On 4 December, Balfour wrote to the King, at a length and with an enthusiasm that was quite exceptional:

Mr. Balfour with his humble duty to Your Majesty begs respectfully to say that perhaps the most interesting thing *in principle* to which the Cabinet assented at today's sitting, related to a new development of the Defence Committee which, unimportant at the moment, may have important results. Mr. Balfour pointed out to his colleagues that the Defence Committee was a body summoned by the Prime Minister to aid him in regard to those larger questions of military and naval policy which lie outside the departmental work both of the S. of S. for War, and the First Lord of the Admiralty. Elasticity is given by the power which the Prime Minister for the time being ought to possess of selecting the person to be summoned to each meeting.

'No one', he continued, in contradiction of his statement to the Commons of 5 March 1903 about 'a fixed nucleus in this Committee', 'has a *right* to come: though of course the advice of the Committee would carry no weight unless it was representative of the best military and naval opinion.' This implied diminution of the standing of the two service ministers in the C.I.D. followed quite naturally from Balfour's assumption of the chairmanship after Devonshire's resignation. Warming to his subject, Balfour continued:

Now a body so constituted has an extraordinary flexibility of adaptation to varying circumstances. It may be made, on occasion, *to include representatives of the Colonies*—which is true of *no other element* in our ordinary constitutional machinery. It thus contains the potentiality of being an 'Imperial Council' dealing with Imperial questions. If indeed representation of the over-sea Empire were there *as of course*, the Committee would become unmanageably large for its ordinary work. But as, at each meeting, the council is (so to speak) constituted afresh

[29]   B.P. 49718, f. 60, B. to Esher, 14 Jan. 1904.
[30]   B.P. 49762, f. 19.
[31]   Mackay, pp. 289–90.

according to its business *for that meeting*, this will not happen. Mr. Balfour has been for some time on the lookout for an occasion to put the theory, thus explained, into practical operation: and the occasion has now presented itself. The War Minister of Canada [Sir Frederick Borden] is coming over here to recommend some modification in the constitution of the Canadian Militia. With the consent of the Cabinet, and he trusts with Your Majesty's approbation, Mr. Balfour proposes to summon him (next Friday) to the Defence Committee, *not* as a witness, or even as an adviser, but as a *member . . .*

Despite Balfour's own tact and charm, it seems not inconceivable that this representative of a young but progressive nation detected a hint of condescension on his admission to the meeting. Balfour nicely suggests an atmosphere of that effortless English superiority, often noticed by visitors from 'the Colonies', when he adds:

He [Borden] will be associated, that is to say, for this particular purpose, and on this particular day, with all the other members of the Committee on equal terms. Unfortunately it appears that this particular gentleman is of rather inferior quality—and we shall be careful what we say before him! The compliment to Canada remains the same. A new precedent of great imperial significance will have thus been set. [32]

Whatever Borden may have felt about his reception when he duly attended the Committee on 11 December, the fact is that this move to strengthen the bonds of Empire bore little fruit. The Dominions, as they would soon be commonly designated, suspected that some surrender of independence might result from attendance at the C.I.D.

However, Balfour had by the end of 1903 brought the C.I.D. to a point where, despite its shortcomings, it had transformed the Government's ·means of controlling defence policy and he had played a central part in preparing the way for sensible economies. Because the Esher Committee had such a dramatic and largely beneficial impact on the War Office, there has been some tendency to exaggerate its contribution to the machinery of the C.I.D. This contribution was comparatively small. Nothing of great importance was accomplished by the C.I.D. after the publication of the Esher reports which could not have been done under Balfour's previous arrangements. During 1903 there was every indication that inter-service co-ordination was being steadily improved. The introduction of Clarke as Secretary [33] in May 1904 strengthened the doubtfully constitutional influence of Esher (and, for a short time, of Fisher, who did not become a

---

[32] Cab. 41/28, No. 25, 4 Dec. 1903.
[33] See John Gooch, 'Sir George Clarke's Career at the C.I.D., 1904–7', *The Historical Journal*, xviii (1975).

member of the C.I.D. till November); but Balfour had made it clear that Clarke was not a member of the Defence Committee and that his staff, seconded from the services for only two years in each individual case, was restricted to collative duties. In so far as Clarke had harboured more grandiose ideas, it is not surprising to find that, as long as he was Secretary, he was restive under the constraints watchfully maintained by the professional service chiefs. Indeed, his principal achievement, before reverting in 1907 to his career as a colonial governor, was to heighten Fisher's resentment of the C.I.D. after January 1906 and thus to contribute to the partial retreat from co-ordination that marked the period of Liberal government before 1912. However, the strengthened secretariat did provide the Prime Minister with useful assistance and helped to ensure continuity of existence for the C.I.D. itself. Moreover, in 1916 Lloyd George was to convert it into a secretariat for the War Cabinet, and subsequently for the Cabinet in time of peace.

On 14 December 1903 Balfour presided at the last cabinet meeting before the Christmas holidays. 'Mr. Arnold-Forster explained his general views with great ability', but, wrote Balfour to the King, 'any judgement would be premature on a scheme which is really not in being.' The original forecasts of Arnold-Forster's unwillingness to modify his schemes, even when they were shown to be unworkable or politically unacceptable, were unfortunately to be amply justified by his subsequent conduct. Indeed, he was hardly to advance beyond advocacy of his initial step: a new system of recruitment which would produce two separate armies. One would be for long service of nine years (with fewer regular battalions than had previously been possessed by the regular army) and the other for short service of two years (consisting of 30 battalions always with the colours and accumulating a trained reserve which could supplement the long-service army in wartime).[34] But the implications of this scheme for long-service recruitment, for the number of fully trained and uniformly organized troops actually ready for war, and for economy, were not pellucidly clear. According to Balfour's cabinet letter of 14 December, the tone of the 'long discussion' was 'critical but not unfriendly'.

What are in Mr. Balfour's opinion the objects to be aimed at may be roughly summarised as follows. We want an army which shall give us sufficient force for at least any immediate needs of Indian defence—and, in conjunction with the Auxiliary forces, for Home defence; which shall be capable of expansion in times of national emergency; which shall, if possible, be less dependent on men in civil

[34] Beckett and Gooch: 'H.O. Arnold-Forster and the Volunteers' by Ian Beckett, p. 52.

employment (i.e. the reservists) for filling up the ranks on mobilisation; and which shall throw a smaller burden on the taxpayer. This last is of peculiar importance, not merely because the demands of the Navy are so great and so inevitable, that the *total* cost of Imperial Defence threatens to become prohibitive. [35]

There is certainly no sign here that Balfour had an inkling of Fisher's plans for reducing the cost of the Navy though he may well have hoped that he would enhance its efficiency. However, he had overcome Selborne's objections to Fisher's being on the Esher Committee by suggesting that its meetings should be held at Admiralty House, Portsmouth (so that Fisher could still attend to his duties as Commander-in-Chief there) and correspondence from Fisher, sometimes reciprocated by the Prime Minister, had begun to flow by the end of 1903. On 29 December, Fisher sent one of his vivid Admiralty House prints, 'The Effect of Submarine Boats', to Sandars—obviously hoping that it would be shown to Balfour. Its relevance to Balfour's work at the C.I.D. on the invasion problem is clear. The new type of vessel, wrote Fisher, 'must revolutionize Naval Tactics'. Moreover:

It affects the Army because, imagine, even one Submarine Boat with a flock of transports in sight loaded each with two or three thousand troops. Imagine the effect of one such transport going to the bottom in a few seconds with its living freight. Even the bare thought makes invasion impossible! Fancy 100,000 helpless, huddled up troops afloat in frightened transports with these invisible demons known to be near. Death near—sudden—awful—invisible—unavoidable! Nothing conceivably more demoralizing! . . . an order for 25 more Submarines would cost less than one Battleship. Which is the more pressing?

Balfour responded in person on 3 January 1904, registering his 'deepest interest'. He was pleased to see how Fisher's argument supported his own view on submarines and invasion: 'indeed, my paper on Home Defence, which I think was shewn you, is largely based upon the considerations to which you refer.' But Balfour was quick to perceive what Fisher for long would not acknowledge, that the submarine was pre-eminently a weapon of the weaker naval power:

I am very little consoled by an observation which occurs on page 3 of Appendix A, where you point out that the Submarine may be used for offensive, as well as for defensive purposes. On the whole, this seems to me to be greatly to our disadvantage. I take it that Portsmouth for instance is more accessible than either Brest

[35] Cab. 41/28, No. 27.

or Toulon, and the game you propose to play at the latter could be played by the French even more effectually at the former.[36]

While Fisher had hoped that naval expenditure would be maintained at the expense of drastic cuts in the Army, his radical suggestions to Selborne since 1902 had included the scrapping of obsolete vessels. Retrospectively, Balfour was particularly appreciative of this reform. In a speech of January 1905 at Glasgow he would praise the way that so many 'useless' vessels, costly to maintain, had been removed from the list 'with one courageous stroke of the pen', and his support for the measure was later acknowledged by Fisher. As Second Sea Lord in 1902, Fisher had already established a common entry for officer cadets; and he had also innovated 'nucleus crews' which allowed ships to be placed in reserve and yet be kept ready to fight at short notice. The latter reform, like scrapping, smacked of economy; and in his speech of 1905 Balfour would say: 'of all the reforms that have taken place since the time of Nelson this is, perhaps, the biggest that has yet been made.' What with Balfour's exposure to Fisher's ideas from the end of 1903, it may be concluded that, when Selborne on 11 May 1904 requested Balfour's approval of Fisher's selection as the next First Sea Lord, the Prime Minister did realize that the Admiral might be able to help the Government out of a deep financial hole. The need for economy was impressed on Fisher by Selborne there and then: 'it is necessary, for the influence of the Admiralty over the House of Commons, and for the stability of the national finances, that we would show a substantial decrease.' But even Selborne hardly realized that he was going to be able to offer the Cabinet a cut of some three and a half million pounds in the estimates following Fisher's actual arrival at the Admiralty on 20 November 1904.[37]

Of course, the totally unexpected elimination of Russia as a major naval power, though not completed till May 1905, was crucial to the naval economies. Certainly, the outlook had been less encouraging when Balfour wrote his aforementioned cabinet letter of 14 December 1903. As his quoted words indicate, he was concerned about the Army's powers of expansion in a major war with Russia and France, and had not yet set his face against Arnold-Forster's intention to replace the (cheap) Militia and Volunteers with (more expensive) short-service regulars. However, as far back as 5 August, the C.I.D. had laid down for the benefit of the Norfolk Commission, the numbers of Militia and Volunteers 'which should, in the

[36] Mackay, pp. 299–303.
[37] Ibid., pp. 308, 344; A. J. Marder (ed.), *Fear God and Dread Nought*, London, 1952–9, 3 vols., i, 322n., 444.

opinion of the Defence Committee, be taken as the basis of the discussions of the Commission'. Appointed in March 1903, this Commission's recommendations, which did not become available till May 1904, were bound to have some influence on the reform of the country's military establishment. It will be seen that Balfour, during 1904–5, was willing to back Arnold-Forster up to the point where his proposals either threatened to alienate the Government's precarious parliamentary support or to come up against strong military or economic objections. When Arnold-Forster duly failed to adapt to these circumstances, the simple solution would have been to sack him. But, as seen above, no alternative minister sprang readily to mind. Moreover, politically speaking, there had been enough sackings of late. Meanwhile, therefore, Balfour ensured that Arnold-Forster did no irreparable harm to the country's military capacity. One of his comments on Haldane's proposals of 1906 explains his own attitude when Prime Minister: 'I, of course, strongly disapprove of Army reductions made before we have any working scheme of Army expansion, and one of the most serious aspects of the change is that it makes us less than ever able to meet possible Indian demands.' [38]

Always subject to feverish colds at the onset of winter, Balfour succumbed soon after the cabinet and C.I.D. meetings of 14 December 1903. He was then visiting Lord Derby at Knowsley Hall; and Knollys wrote on the 22nd to say that the King was 'very sorry to hear' that he had been 'obliged to keep to his bed'. [39] However, with persistent indications of a coming war between Russia and Japan, Balfour had already on the 21st begun writing to Selborne and Arnold-Forster about the probable course of the conflict, [40] and by the 22nd he was involved in a series of exchanges with Lansdowne, ending on the 29th. The question was: Should Britain intervene (as Lansdowne wished) to secure the mediation of France or the United States, on a basis of Russian moderation in Manchuria in exchange for British pressure on Japan to back down in Korea? Or should Britain openly back the Japanese, as some of the soldiers wished? [41] As usual, Balfour had thought his position through and followed a firm, clear, logical line of argument, which probably stemmed from a cabinet meeting of 11 December. He then wrote to the King:

The position in the Far East is necessarily a cause of anxiety . . . Lord Lansdowne was authorised to speak unofficially to M. Cambon, and point out to him that a war

[38]   B.P. 49719, ff. 55–6, B. to Esher, 6 Oct. 1906.
[39]   Sandars, P., C.719.
[40]   B.P. 49707, ff. 152–7.
[41]   Monger, pp. 147–51; B.P. 49728, ff. 109–136.

between Russia and Japan might draw *us* in: and that if we were drawn in France might find it difficult to keep out in the face of her treaty obligations. It was impossible to contemplate anything at once so horrible and so absurd as a general war brought on by Russia's impracticable attitude in Manchuria. The present condition of the Russian Foreign Office—which is so well known to Your Majesty—adds to the danger of the situation: and it seems almost possible that the Emperor of Russia, the advocate of peace and disarmament, may without knowing it, become the occasion and author of a widespread conflagration. We must hope better things . . .[42]

Balfour's fear of Russian power was genuine. On 29 December he wrote for the Cabinet: 'Russia's strong point is her vast population and the unassailable character of her territories. Her weak point is finance.' He knew about Britain's own financial weakness and would receive insistent reminders of it from Austen Chamberlain. If Lansdowne (as reported by Balfour on the 11th, above) was hoping to get France to restrain Russia, Balfour was probably more interested in dividing France from Russia. Certainly, by the time that he embarked on his sick-room correspondence before Christmas he was clear that the Japanese should be allowed to start fighting the Russians if they wished. If they took the initiative that was their look-out.[43] While the Russians would probably defeat the Japanese on the mainland of Asia, they would not be able to invade Japan herself. Russia would over-extend herself and that would be to Britain's advantage.[44]

What, then, was Balfour's attitude to the incipient French *entente*? There is no reason to doubt that he agreed with at least one of Lansdowne's arguments in its favour, that it was worth having in itself. But evidence that he also sought it as a likely bridge, as is commonly argued, to a settlement with Russia is difficult to find. In this critical situation of late December he attached more importance to the fact that France was the *ally* of Russia than that she was engaged in colonial negotiations with Britain—wherein she was driving a fairly hard bargain![45] The point is made, both implicitly and explicitly, in the memorandum which he wrote for the Cabinet and 'the naval and military authorities' on 29 December. Besides developing his argument for British non-intervention in the Far East, he makes pointed references to France:

10. It is true that Masampo [the Cheju Island off the southern tip of Korea] would

---

[42] Cab. 41/28, No. 26, B. to the King, 11 Dec. 1903.

[43] Balfour would not even allow a loan to Japan. Monger, p. 153.

[44] See Cab. 37/67/97 for B.'s substantial memo. of 29 Dec. 1903—also quoted below.

[45] Cab. 41/28, Nos. 26 and 27, 11 and 14 Dec. 1903; 41/29, No. 1, 24 Jan. 1904—where 'something like deadlock' had been reached.

fall into hostile [Russian] hands. If I were a Japanese I should greatly dislike it. As an Englishman, I regret that France possesses a fortified port at Cherbourg, within 80 miles of Portsmouth. But if *we* survive a fortified port within 80 miles of our chief arsenal, I do not see that the Japanese need be ruined by one which is, at least, 160 miles from theirs . . .

14. I submit, then, the following proposition as a summary of the preceding argument:

(a) We are not bound in law, in equity, or in honour, to join Japan in a war against Russia single-handed . . . Our policy . . . must be dictated solely by a cool calculation of national interests.

(b) The risk and loss inevitably attending a world-wide war, in which Britain, Russia, and France (for France could scarcely abstain) would all take part, are incalculable. The only Power that would certainly gain by so unexampled a calamity is Germany.

(c) The risk on the other side is that, if we do not go to her assistance, Japan will be 'crushed' [as Selborne had put it to Balfour on 21 December].

(d) But it is very doubtful whether Japan will even be beaten, and it seems quite certain that, in any event, she will not be crushed.

(e) Even if we assume Russia to get the best of it, we can by no means assume that she will come out of the fight stronger than she went in. Stronger in the Far East for many purposes she may, perhaps, be. But we have to fear her chiefly as (a) the ally of France; (b) the invader of India; (c) the dominating influence in Persia; and (d) the possible disturber of European peace. For these purposes she will be not stronger but weaker after over-running Corea. Weaker because she will have diminished her financial resources . . . weaker because her fleet will not only be diminished by war, but, bound to the East by the necessity of watching Japan, will be unable to take part in strategical combinations against Britain in the West. Though her value to France in a war with Germany might thereby be little affected, her value to France in a war with us would be greatly reduced . . .[46]

Balfour's arguments for non-intervention were decisive. In this important crisis, Lansdowne was overruled. It is therefore not entirely adequate to say that Balfour and Lansdowne worked as a team. Once it is accepted that Balfour attached prime importance in foreign affairs not just to Anglo-Russian relations, but to *Russia in military alliance with France*, light is thrown not only on which of the two ministers ultimately controlled British

[46] Cab. 37/67/97, 29 Dec. 1903.

foreign policy but also on its intellectual basis. In Balfour's mind the ascertainable military facts, together with the considered judgements on them (as articulated at the C.I.D.), and the available diplomatic and foreign information were all arranged in one orderly, coherent system. As George Monger has correctly observed, [47] no other member of the Cabinet—and, it might be added, no other member of the C.I.D.—could rival Balfour in this kind of intellectual performance. Even the talents assembled under Asquith's premiership would be outshone at a unique meeting of 1908. In May of that year Esher would report to the King on Balfour's appearance before a Sub-Committee of the Liberal Government's C.I.D. The ministers attending were Asquith, Lloyd George, Grey, Haldane, McKenna, and Crewe; and Sir John Fisher and Sir William Nicholson (by then Chief of the General Staff) were among the professionals present. This array of ministerial and professional talent was astonished by 'a statement, lasting about an hour, quite perfect in form and language, and most closely reasoned, of the views which he has formed upon the question of national defence'. And in his private journal Esher noted: 'Not a question was put to him. Asquith, Grey, Haldane, Crewe, Lloyd George. All were equally dumbfounded.' [48]

Balfour wrote his cabinet memorandum of 29 December 1903 to stand up to scrutiny not only from his own colleagues, most of them of unremarkable intellectual capability, but also from the service chiefs and their Directors of Intelligence (Nicholson and Battenberg, both very able men). And it did. The assumptions which Balfour had previously established at the C.I.D. are all there: the most probable major war in which Britain might become involved was against Russia and France. If Russia (with her strategic railways and ill-defined expansionist aims) was the obvious menace, France was likewise a danger *as long as she remained Russia's military ally.* Moreover, from the viewpoint of geo-military capability, France was best placed to invade the British Isles. Then there was Germany. Her navy, though still small, was apparently designed to fight the British in the North Sea and she had the best army in Europe. But she would not risk conflict with the vastly superior Royal Navy unless it had been gravely weakened in war with France and Russia. Therefore, a British decision not to intervene (either to appease Russia or to reinforce Japan) could result in diminution of the strength of Russia and France combined, as Balfour had explained in his above-quoted memorandum of 29 December. That was the policy to follow.

---

[47] Monger, p. 233.
[48] Esher, ii, 317–18, 29 May 1908. For the Journal entry see E.P. 2/11, 29 May.

As far as the Anglo-French negotiations were concerned, they could lead to a useful improvement in the British situation in Egypt, where international control of the finances had been a thorn in Britain's side since Gladstone's time. 'We must earnestly hope that these promising negotiations will not wholly break down', Balfour wrote to the King on 24 January 1904. 'It would be lamentable, especially from the Egyptian point of view.'[49] But, even if attained, the Anglo-French *entente* would hardly be a bond of equal strength to that represented by the military alliance of France and Russia. The correctness of this judgement was to be substantiated by the Kamranh Bay crisis of April 1905. There was, even at that date, a distinct danger of Britain's having to fight France and Russia, despite the fact that the Kaiser's landing at Tangier had already conferred on a flagging Anglo-French *entente* an importance which it had never previously possessed.[50] In so far as, in his paper of 29 December 1903, Balfour saw Russia as 'the possible disturber of European peace', he clearly did not see Germany as a more probable menace to that peace. Therefore, he could not think in terms of an Anglo-French military combination against Germany without compelling evidence of the Germans' hostile intent.

What, then, was Balfour's view of Germany up to the time of the Kaiser's pronouncement at Tangier on 1 April 1905? So far, it has been indicated that Balfour recognized the existence, design, and growth of the German Navy. Indeed, on 1 March 1904 he informed the House of Commons that Britain would not only maintain a Two Power Standard but would provide an additional margin of strength. This margin remained undefined; but it was clearly aimed against the growing German Navy, in a situation where Britain might suffer serious losses—by implication at the hands of France and Russia.[51] Balfour had also agreed that the C.I.D. should study the problem of raids by the French (sic) or the Germans on the British coast. The evolution of his attitude to Germany during 1904 must be examined in the context of the French *entente* and German diplomatic reactions to that agreement. Unbeknown to Balfour, the Anglo-French *entente* blasted the secret ambitions of Germany's ruling clique.[52]

Shortly before the Anglo-French agreement was happily concluded on 8 April 1904, Balfour reported to the King on a cabinet meeting. The

[49] Cab. 41/29, No. 1.
[50] Monger, pp. 91–2.
[51] Marder, *The Anatomy of British Sea Power 1880–1905*, Hamden, Conn., 1964, reprint, p. 510.
[52] See Kennedy's *Rise of the Anglo-German Antagonism* for the German side of the matter.

'anxious question' which took pride of place—spilling over into an afternoon session—was not the French treaty but the budget. It looked as if an increase in income tax was, as feared, unavoidable—and it went up by 1d to 1/− in the horrific event! But Balfour did include a laconic reference to the imminent *entente*. Lansdowne 'reported that the French negotiations were proceeding satisfactorily', though difficulties, such as the tiresome matter of the 'treaty shore' of Newfoundland, had yet to be settled. That was all.[53]

Germany first signalled her dislike of the *entente* by withholding her assent from the Khedivial Decree which was to institutionalize the British ascendancy in Egypt. Balfour, informing the King of the cabinet discussion of the matter on 4 May, noted that the assent of 'the Great Powers' had to be obtained 'before England can reap in Egypt the full advantage of the treaty' with France (to which there had been British military and diplomatic objections). He commented light-heartedly: 'Hence an opportunity for "black-mailing" us, of which, it is unnecessary to say, Germany proposes to take full advantage!!' But a solution, he thought, could be reached by the Foreign Office. The aim was 'to isolate Germany in this matter by inducing Russia, Italy, and Austria to give their assent by small diplomatic concessions, believing that Germany, if left alone, will be obliged to abandon her dog-in-the-manger attitude'.[54] In much the same vein, the subject reappears on 19 May. A German communication had to be answered.

It was agreed that we should decline to treat the Egyptian question *as part* of a general settlement; that, though the suggestion of a general settlement should not be rejected, it should be approached with caution, and that any demand for commercial rights in Egypt should be met by a corresponding demand for commercial rights in German Colonial possessions. The dispatch was so framed as not to express any enthusiastic eagerness to meet the German views—views which, in their original form, savoured too much of blackmail![55]

Again, on 14 June, the Cabinet agreed on 'the avoidance of anything in the nature of a treaty with Germany which could be compared with the recent Anglo-French agreement'. In Egypt Britain would concede, commercially, 'most favoured nation treatment for 30 years and small concessions as regards schools, etc.'. But as soon as Germany settled on these terms, Britain would 'offer them at once to the other powers' and deny any special advantage 'to the Nation that has attempted to drive a hard bargain, as compared with the Nations which acted with generosity'.[56]

53	Cab. 41/29, No. 10, 30 Mar. 1904.
54	Cab. 41/29, No. 14.
55	Ibid., No. 16, 19 May 1904.
56	Ibid., No. 19.

There is no hint, in Balfour's cabinet letters during 1904, of serious anxiety with regard to Germany. No more does he express concern about any possible German resentment of the *entente*. Parliamentary difficulties apart, his real worry, registered on and after 2 June, arose from the evident intention of the Russians to send their Baltic fleet out to restore their fortunes in the Far East. (It was still generally believed, even in the highest naval circles, that the Russians would ultimately defeat the Japanese.) Balfour held detailed discussions, in the Cabinet and the C.I.D., about the problems which might arise under international law from Russian requests for coaling facilities for the Baltic Fleet—also from the implications for the Anglo-Japanese alliance. What if British colliers took private action to supply the Russians? And again, what would Britain do if the remnants of the Russians' eastern fleet escaped from Port Arthur and sought refuge in the British port of Wei-hai-wei? A number of Cabinet and C.I.D. meetings focused on these problems. [57] On 3 August Balfour informed the C.I.D. that the Russians had been warned that the 'ships from Port Arthur were not to enter Wei-hai-wei' and that the Russian Ambassador had 'offered no objection'. [58]

The danger of war with Russia became imminent when news reached London on 23 October of British fishing boats being sunk in the North Sea—having been mistaken by the Baltic Fleet for Japanese torpedo boats! Balfour required from Russia satisfactory assurances of an inquiry with a view to reparation before allowing the Russian fleet to proceed. Unless the Russians gave such assurances in time for Balfour's speech to a party conference at Southampton on the 28th, it was likely, according to some sources, that he would have to announce that Britain was at war with Russia. [59] What would then be the relevance of the *entente*? Certainly, even if the French might, in fact, have found a pretext for neutrality on this extraordinary occasion, there is no sign that Balfour paid heed to the possibility. However, his cabinet letter of 29 October casts doubt on whether 28 October did mark a deadline for Balfour:

A great many suggestions were made [on the 28th] as to what Mr. Balfour should or should not say at Southampton last night—the difficulty being to steer between a speech which should fall short of public feeling *here*, and a speech which should render the course of further negotiation difficult at St. Petersburgh.

---

[57] Cab. 41/29, Nos. 17 and 29 of 2 and 28 June 1904; Cab. 2/1, 45th, 46th, 49th, and 51st meetings of the C.I.D., 9, 13, and 17 June and 27 July 1904.
[58] Cab. 2/1.
[59] Monger, pp. 170–4.

The Cabinet decided *neither* to mobilise the fleet—*nor* to warn the colonies that they must take exceptional precautions to protect the landing places of the telegraphic cables and other critical points. We may hope [in view of the Russian assurances] that these measures may now be indefinitely postponed.[60]

Even if there was no naval mobilization on this occasion, it is important to note that the Cabinet considered it.

Although it was the Dogger Bank crisis that brought Britain to the edge of war with Russia, Balfour was constrained to prepare for such incidents throughout the episode of the Baltic Fleet's passage to the Far East (October to April)—and, indeed, before it. And as long as this tension persisted, France remained for Balfour more of a potential enemy than a secure friend. On 11 August 1904, more than two months ahead of the Dogger incident, he conveyed to the King the line which he would follow with regard to Russia as long as Russian maritime activity continued. The meeting of the Cabinet was 'wholly occupied' by discussion 'on the eternally recurring question of neutral rights', and they agreed the dispatches that Lansdowne was to send to Russia.

The line taken is a strong one, but Mr. Balfour is of opinion that this is on the whole likely to conduce to peace rather than war. The Russians are sometimes under the delusion that a *conciliatory* attitude is a *weak* attitude and that Great Britain is prepared to make any concession rather than defend her rights by force. So lamentable a misconstruction of the real feeling of this country is a serious menace to good international relations; and the sooner it is dissipated the better.[61]

After the easing of the Dogger Bank affair, there were continuing alarms about the possible depredations of the Russian ships. In November, the question arose: What orders would be given to the Baltic Fleet if the Russian government received news of the fall of Port Arthur to the Japanese? Investigation of such possibilities once again illustrates the way in which Balfour used the C.I.D. to assist the deliberations of the Cabinet. On 18 November (as Balfour informed the King)

Mr. Balfour explained to the Cabinet the suggestions to which the Committee of Defence had agreed respecting the course to be pursued if, by chance, the Russian battleships now going out by the west coast of Africa were, in the event of Port Arthur falling, to adopt some course hostile to British interests—for example, the occupation of a port in the Persian Gulf.

Lansdowne (Balfour commented) had already issued a warning against

---

[60] Cab. 41/29, No. 33, 29 Oct. 1904.
[61] Cab. 41/29, No. 31, 11 Aug. 1904.

such action, and Russia would, in addition, be asked 'to abstain from anything in the nature of a landing'. Meantime Britain would order 'a superior force of battleships' to Bombay. If the Russians refused to give the required assurances, Balfour thought 'it would be necessary' to recall the British 'Ambassador from St. Petersburg, and, should this be insufficient, to take ulterior steps'. [62]

Two C.I.D. meetings in November discussed the British naval dispositions needed to deal with a variety of possible developments. The second meeting, held on 16 November, was marked by the initial attendance at the Committee of Sir John Fisher. To judge by the unusually long and detailed minute devoted to his contribution, he must have made a considerable impression. Although he has usually been rated low among naval strategists on account of his lurid utterances, it should be appreciated that he often played for pure psychological impact. This applies to his personal correspondence, his 'secret' prints on naval policy, and even his statements directed at the public press. At the meeting on 16 November, he assumed the mantle of professional strategist, giving coherent and detailed reasons, based on knowledge and calculation, for overturning the plan agreed at the previous meeting. [63] Likewise, when he returned to the Admiralty as First Sea Lord in 1914–15, he proved himself a cautious strategist when it came to the operational point, in wartime, whatever wild schemes, such as the notional 'Baltic Plan', he may have dangled before politicians to show them that he was a war-winner. [64]

On his arrival at the Admiralty on 20 October 1904, Fisher intended to concentrate British naval power nearer to home, though he still placed its strategic centre of gravity in the Mediterranean. The underlying assumption was, as before, that the most likely war was with Russia and France. But during the Dogger crisis, which came within a week of his appointment, he sprang to the conclusion that it was 'really the Germans behind it all', [65] and it is true that Germany was angling for closer relations with Russia at the time. [66] Fisher and Battenberg (still D.N.I.) then worked out a scheme of redistribution aimed against Russia and Germany. However, this had already been modified by 14 November. The distribution was now based on a dual principle. As Battenberg put it in a memorandum dated 14 November:

[62] Cab. 41/29, No. 38, dated 19 Nov. 1904; Cab. 2/1, 56th and 57th meetings of C.I.D., 12 and 16 Nov. 1904.
[63] Ibid., 16 Nov. 1904.
[64] Mackay, pp. 468–85.
[65] Ibid., pp. 314–16.
[66] Kennedy, pp. 271–2.

The Atlantic Fleet being the reinforcement of either of our main battlefleets in the north or in the south, according to where the principal enemy is located, both of these will get the benefit of specially powerful ships when they specially need them. [67]

This certainly seems to imply a strategic shift in an anti-German direction on Balfour's part. But how far, in fact, had he changed his basic assumptions?

In his key memoranda on the Army during 1904 and early 1905, Balfour continued to assume that the fundamental and 'most formidable of probable' contingencies was a war with Russia in defence of India, and he refrained from naming the potential European invader of the British Isles (in deference, doubtless, to the *entente*). It was implied that the minor provision of regular troops for home defence would, together with British sea power, deter either a French or a German invasion. [68] In general: 'A struggle with Russia being the most formidable of probable wars, calculations based upon it will suffice for any war of lesser magnitude.' [69] Likewise, Fisher's naval dispositions after 14 November 1904 (until June 1905) continued to meet the requirements of a war with Russia and France, even if they also envisaged a German possibility. Fisher wrote for Balfour in the margin of an Admiralty print of February 1905:

the Gibraltar Fleet is the 'germ' of the new scheme! We have arranged it with our best and fastest battleships and cruisers and our best admirals . . . it is always instantly ready to turn the scale (at the highest speed of any fleet in the world) in the North Sea or the Mediterranean. [70]

Confirmation of the wisdom of this agreed flexible strategy is implicit in a letter written by Fisher to Balfour on 22 April 1905. After a very slow voyage, the Baltic Fleet had at length dropped anchor in Kamranh Bay on the coast of French Indo-China. This raised some big questions.

The fact of the Russian Fleet sending their vessels out of the French harbour of Kamranh to search passing vessels, and utilizing that harbour as they are for an indefinite time to perfect their fighting arrangements . . . seems the most flagrant and outrageous breach of neutrality possible to conceive! I suppose we have impressed all this on the French Government. Suppose the Japanese attack . . . Kamranh Bay, as they are justified in doing. Will France fight Japan? If so, we fight France! What pickings for the German Emperor! [71]

[67] Mackay, p. 318.
[68] Cab. 4/1/26B, 22 June 1904; 3/1/28A, 19 Dec. 1904.
[69] Cab. 17/3, 24 Feb. 1905.
[70] Mackay, p. 318.
[71] Ibid., pp. 318–19.

The Kamranh incident came up during the Easter recess, but because the appropriate naval dispositions had been made long since, Balfour apparently decided that no crisis action was needed. 'I hope', he replied to Fisher, 'the incident will pass off without any serious trouble, as far as we are concerned.' [72]

A glance through the list of subjects discussed at the C.I.D. during the relevant period suffices to confirm that Balfour's sights were steadily set on the danger of war with Russia until the Kaiser's speech at Tangier on 1 April 1905, and beyond. By late December 1904, Selborne had told him of Fisher's suggestion of a preventive attack on the German fleet at Kiel. 'He meant it', wrote Selborne on the 26th. [73] Balfour certainly deplored such ideas. There is direct evidence of his views on Anglo-German relations at about this time, as will be seen in due course.

In sum, while the modified naval distribution of November 1904 does mark a shift on Balfour's part, it may be regarded rather as a small tactical concession to a surge of anti-German feeling than a fundamental change in his main strategic assumptions. As far as the Army went, the emphasis on India remained substantially intact when he left office in December 1905. Indeed, he held to this view of the Army's role in a Commons debate of 12 July 1906 and in a letter written to Esher as late as 25 March 1908. [74]

In December 1904 Anglo-German relations had reached a low point. It was not only Fisher who thought of preventive attack on the German Navy. *Vanity Fair* and the *Army and Navy Gazette* openly advocated the idea and there was fear and top-level complaint on the German side. Even Balfour wondered in January whether German naval manœuvres near the Shetlands implied ultimate hostile intent. [75] The question of raids, based on the Franco-German assumption, came up from time to time, for example in Balfour's important memorandum of 22 June 1904; [76] and at the C.I.D. on 23 February 1905 it was agreed that the figure of 5,000 previously mooted, should be taken as the size of the raiding force, despite Fisher's protest that, with nucleus crews ready to go to sea, 'a raid by 5,000 was, in his opinion, out of the question.' [77] As will shortly transpire, Balfour agreed with this assessment. Having constantly given close personal attention to the defence of India, he left office in December 1905 without completing his report on raids.

[72] Fisher Papers, doc. no. 154, 26 Apr. 1905.
[73] Mackay, pp. 316–19.
[74] P.D., 4th, 160/1162 and B.P. 49719, ff. 71–2.
[75] Monger, p. 176.
[76] Cab. 4/1/26B, 'A Note on Army Reform and the Military Needs of the Empire.'
[77] Cab. 2/1, 63rd meeting, 23 Feb. 1905.

However, he had not forgotten it. After resigning as Prime Minister on 4 December, he settled down to finish the report in order to encourage the Liberals' continuance of the C.I.D. Dated 12 December 1905, it analysed the hypothesis of French and German raids in a vein of mounting incredulity. For instance, in the case of a German raid on the Tyne, the Channel fleet would need to be located 'at least 300 miles from the mouth' of that river 'and 600 miles from [the German Admiral's] return course to the Skagerrack or Cuxhaven, if he is to avoid a fleet action on his return journey'. Yet it was 'evident that if there is the smallest friction between Great Britain and Germany, the fleets of the former will be so placed as to make the adventure impracticable'. His view of the magnitude of the 'friction' occurring between Britain and Germany during 1905, including the Moroccan crisis, is implied in the following remarks:

On the hypothesis, therefore, most favourable to the invader, the danger run by the maritime portion of the supposed expedition would be of the most serious kind. But how extreme this hypothesis is! There are plenty of cases of war being begun before it is declared. There are plenty of cases where a country, though involved in some controversy with a neighbour, has yet been taken unawares. It will not be easy to find a single case where relations of unruffled amity have been suddenly broken off by an unprovoked invasion. [78]

Yet in April 1905, at the height of the Moroccan crisis, Britain was prepared to back the French against Germany. Just what was Balfour's view of the situation?

He evidently agreed with Lansdowne's view that it was 'a bad thing' that Germany should, by putting effective pressure on the French Foreign Minister, have discredited the *entente*. [79] But it is easy to exaggerate the intention behind the Government's telegram (drafted on the 23rd by Balfour and Lansdowne) telling Bertie in Paris that Britain would join France in offering 'strong opposition' to any demand made by Germany for a port in Morocco. [80] Balfour treated the whole Moroccan 'crisis'—which it certainly was for Germany, France, and the *entente*—as one among many of the diplomatic incidents deserving prime-ministerial attention, but as less than a real crisis for Britain. He took no crisis action of the kind already noticed in connection with the Russian naval movements in 1904–5. *Then*, as has been said above, the dangers were constantly discussed, both in the Cabinet

[78]   Cab. 3/1/34A, 'Possibility of a Raid by a Hostile Force on the British Coast', 12 Dec. 1905.
[79]   B.P. 49729, f. 117, Lansdowne to B., 23 Apr. 1905.
[80]   See for example, Monger, p. 190. The evidence adduced could support a more modest evaluation of the British telegram.

and in the C.I.D., and naval dispositions were agreed. If, in Balfour's opinion, the Moroccan 'crisis' had involved the slightest real danger of war between Britain and Germany, there would certainly have been something similar to show for it at the C.I.D. or in his cabinet letters, especially those for July 1905. However, at the C.I.D. a special sub-committee was formed in July—of which more below. But in the memorandum on raids quoted above, Balfour implies the absence of serious tension between Britain and Germany during 1905.

It is evident that if there is the smallest friction between Great Britain and Germany, the fleets of the former will be so placed as to make the adventure impracticable. If, on the other hand, the political atmosphere is without a cloud, and the raiding expedition is a mere buccaneering attempt to weaken a Power with which Germany has not the smallest quarrel, then it may, no doubt, conceivably happen that the Channel fleet [the fleet nearest of the three to the North Sea] will be at the extremist point of its annual orbit—at Lagos, 88 hours' steam at 15 knots from the direct course of the German fleet. But the smallest scrap of information reaching the Admiralty, the observation of unusual measures, such as those required to turn commercial steamers into transports, would arouse suspicion; suspicion would immediately suggest the recall of the Channel fleet to home waters, and if this return were not realized in time by the German Admiral, his Government would be caught in the very trap they had set for others, and they might lose not merely their 10,000 troops [which *might* be acceptable], but the fleet that was employed to escort them.

No one seems to have published evidence of any British naval or military alert of consequence in 1905.

However, after the great Japanese naval victory at Tsushima on 28 May 1905 had conclusively eliminated the Russian Navy from the Admiralty's two-power standard of comparison, there was a considerable redistribution of British naval power in favour of the Channel Fleet, though the Atlantic and Mediterranean Fleets (based at Gibraltar and Malta) continued to exist. In July 1905, Fisher brought before the C.I.D. a proposal for the 'Formation of a Permanent Sub-Committee of the Committee of Imperial Defence to Consider and Elaborate Schemes of Joint Naval and Military Expeditions'. With the Russian Navy out of the way, the Admiralty could see only the German Navy as a potential threat; and Fisher, building on the ideas of Admiral Sir Arthur Wilson, wanted the sub-committee to frame strategy on the supposition of a war between Germany on the one hand and Britain and France on the other. If Germany attacked France, Britain would (*a*) command the sea and (*b*) influence the war on land by threatening to put a British striking force ashore in Schleswig-Holstein. The case for such a revolution in strategic policy was persuasively argued in a paper (probably

In Defence of Empire

written by Captain C. L. Ottley, now Director of Naval Intelligence, and destined to succeed Clarke as Secretary of the C.I.D. in 1907). Fisher sent it to Balfour before the C.I.D. meeting of 20 July at which it was agreed to form the Sub-Committee. Although it bears no date, it was on internal evidence written after Delcassé's second and definitive resignation, under German pressure, on 6 June. The paper argues, tactfully enough, that the strategic assumptions on which Balfour had been acting at the C.I.D. (at which, of course, Fisher and Ottley were in regular attendance) are now out of date:

It is presumed that under existing circumstances, should Germany attempt to push France to extremes over the Morocco imbroglio, Great Britain would almost perforce have to come to France's assistance. Remote as is the contingency, the events of the last few days do indicate it as a possible one. We have, therefore, to consider what British action would be possible under these special circumstances.

Previously (the paper continues) the Admiralty has never been able to assume anything better than French neutrality in a major war—with Russia. It has always been supposed that Germany would await 'the moment of utmost embarrassment to Great Britain before she threw her sword into the scale'. Now, however, the plight of Russia has relieved Germany of the threat to her eastern frontier. 'But Germany appears to have forgotten, in her present outrageous defiance of France, that it is not only *France's ally* that has been weakened in the Far East, but also *England's most dreaded possible enemy.*' The threat to India has receded. 'This is a condition of affairs which could scarcely have been hoped for 12 months ago.'

There follows an optimistic scenario of Anglo-French operations against Germany, featuring 'the magnificent French Navy, with its splendid force of "defense mobile" torpedo craft and submarines' (which Fisher was to scorn in 1906–1910). Not only would the combined fleets bottle up the German North Sea estuaries, but 'the whole of the German carrying trade, so laboriously built up, would have passed into other—probably British—hands.'

Every German colony would fall into the possession of the allies, and this, be it observed (so long as Russia remained neutral), without any power on Germany's part to retaliate . . . Russia would at least be neutral, if not actually hostile to Germany . . . Every British soldier, except for those needed for police and obligatory garrison duties, should, therefore, be available to strike a blow in Europe. A well-equipped British army, acting in Schleswig-Holstein, would undoubtedly create a substantial diversion in France's favour, if such action should commend itself to the British military authorities . . .

The writer seems then to have asked himself: How should we argue the case if Balfour is not instantly enthused by such beguiling prospects? He launches into a paragraph that might have been written by Sir Edward Grey:

The changes in the political balance of power in Europe occasioned by the Russian losses in the present war have rendered it imperative to consider the probable consequences of a second overthrow of France by Germany. Briefly it may be said that such an event would end in the aggrandisement of Germany to an extent which would be prejudicial to the whole of Europe, and it might therefore be necessary for Great Britain in her own interests to lend France her active support should war of this nature break out . . .

If Britain were to support France, 'it would become obligatory upon us to decide how we could best furnish the support required'; and 'the over-whelming extent of our maritime supremacy would permit us to undertake operations' which otherwise 'would be unjustifiable, such as close approaches to hostile ports and attacks on defended positions'. It was for 'our War Office authorities' to decide whether this sea supremacy should be used to land troops 'at some point on the North Sea', or perhaps 'on the German Baltic coast'. It was asserted that the mere embarkation of the British force 'would compel Germany to place troops all along her coasts, and thus perhaps appreciably reduce the strength of her army on the French frontier'.[81] The paper also suggests that, if Britain should happen to fight *alone* against Germany, 'operations on these lines' might be the best answer.

At the C.I.D. meeting of 20 July 1905, Balfour inaugurated the special Sub-Committee. Although he and the other ministers had considered the possibility of a French request for support against Germany,[82] he appears to have made no direct reference at the meeting either to France, or to Germany, or to the *entente*. He explained the need for a 'Sub-Committee to consider and prepare such schemes for joint naval and military operations as might be found practicable or desirable'. The C.I.D. as a whole could not find time for this.

To enable this to be done the Admiralty and the General Staff ought in peace time to be brought into the closest communication . . . and it was important that machinery should be provided not only to frame schemes, but to subject them to constant review, in order that they might always be in harmony with the conditions of the moment.

[81] B.P. 49711, ff. 65–9, 'British Intervention in the event of France being suddenly attacked by Germany'.
[82] Williamson, pp. 41–2.

In so far as Neville Lyttleton, the Chief of the General Staff, agreed to draw up (with Fisher) a constitution for this Sub-Committee, it may be doubted how far the general then understood Fisher's covert intentions which amounted to reduction of the Army to a small amphibious force. However, the brief of the Sub-Committee was settled at the next C.I.D. meeting, held on 26 July. It would consider 'What objective could be assigned to joint expeditions with a view to bring the maximum pressure to bear upon any Power or Powers, war with which must be regarded as possible . . .', and draw up a list of possible operations. As to composition, the president of this 'permanent' Sub-Committee was to be the Prime Minister. Otherwise, the membership would be professional: First Sea Lord, D.N.I., C.G.S., D.M.O. (i.e. Director of Military Operations, the post having been established, like that of C.G.S., as part of the General Staff recommended by the Esher Committee in 1904). Clarke was to be Secretary, this time with the status of a member. As for procedure, the Sub-Committee would draw up a list of possible operations for consideration by the whole C.I.D. When approval had been given, the Sub-Committee would associate the designated commanders with the relevant operational planning. Where the Prime Minister could not attend, the senior officer present would deputize for him. [83]

Interest has tended to centre on the implications of this Sub-Committee for the debate between the advocates of a maritime (or amphibious) strategy on the one hand and of a continental strategy of direct support for the French Army on the other. For this study the main questions are: How far was Balfour in sympathy with the implied switch from war (in association with Japan) against Russia and France, to war (either in association with France or singly) against Germany as the basic underlying assumption of defence policy? What did he *now* feel about Germany and about the *entente*? What did he think of the amphibious strategy? And why did he, in the event, decide not to convene the sub-committee at all for its intended purpose?

It will be seen that Balfour had reservations about the Fisherite strategy of coastal landings but that—to take the last question first—his reasons for not convening the Sub-Committee after the summer holidays were mainly political. As will be shown in the next chapter, his tenure of office could not for much longer be prolonged. Therefore the question of the future of the C.I.D., in the hands of the apparently hostile Campbell-Bannerman, was anxiously debated behind the scenes.

[83]   Cab. 2/1, 76th and 77th meetings, 20 and 26 July 1905.

In early October 1905 there were talks at Balmoral involving the King, Balfour, Esher, Knollys, and latterly Haldane, whose political sights were, however, set on the Woolsack rather than the War Office.[84] Esher had, since his triumphant though controversial transformation of the War Office, kept in close touch with Balfour on the reform of the Army itself and on the attempted use of the C.I.D. to that end.[85] Balfour, after interminable cabinet discussions on Army Reform, had tried to break the double-sided deadlock (1) between Arnold-Forster and the Cabinet on the issues of the Militia and economy, and (2) between Arnold-Forster and the Army Council on the recruitment[86] and the strength of the Army. But no definite progress had been made by the time of the Balmoral conclave.[87] Thanks to the fact that between June 1904 and June 1905 Arnold-Forster would not compromise over his recruitment proposals, other pressing problems— such as a proper system of selection and training for the embryonic General Staff—had remained unsolved. Although a limited experiment with recruiting was then agreed, time was running out for effecting any other army reforms.

Esher had been complaining, with support from his fellow 'triumvirs' of the Esher Committee, about the failure to develop the General Staff which was so far limited to some posts at the War Office.[88] He had also urged the sacking of Arnold-Forster, though he evinced scant enthusiasm when asked to undertake the job himself. Instead he agreed with Sandars (17 September) that it was too late in the Government's life to make 'any such change'. Moreover, as he wrote to his son Maurice on 4 October, he was sure that the

[84] E.P. 7/18, Esher to Maurice Brett, 6 Oct. 1905, for reference to Haldane.

[85] See B.P. 49718, f. 116 to the end and 49719, up to f. 51 for Esher and B., 17 June 1904—2 Dec. 1905; also Esher's *Journals and Letters*, ii, 53—122 and Fraser, chs. 4—7, for further information on Esher's activities at that time; but Fraser seems too sympathetic to Arnold-Forster, on whom see Beckett and Gooch, Ch. 3.

[86] A.-F.'s short-service scheme would, in the view of the Military Members of the council, destroy all prospects of long-service recruitment.

[87] Cab. 41/29, No. 9, 15 Mar. 1904: 'As regards Army Reform, Mr. Balfour impressed upon the Cabinet the need for speed.' See also Nos. 11, 12, 13, 14, 15, 16, 18, 20, 23, and 25—which last is dated 13 July 1904. At this point the subject was left in a fluid state, with doubts about expense. Soon after, Unionist outrage at the proposed abolition of the Militia ensured that A.-F.'s scheme could not pass. But he indicated that he preferred resignation to compromise. Cab. 41/30, No. 7, 10 Mar. 1905: B. had put forward 'an alternative scheme', hoping to settle this 'ever-recurring question'; but the estimates for 1905—6 could not now be changed, so neither plan could 'in the immediate future' be brought into effect. Nos. 18 and 24 (16 May and 23 June 1905) end the series of relevant cabinet letters with the system unchanged, except for recruitment. Long service of 9 years was the rule, instead of Brodrick's 3 (with re-engagement for 5—insufficient in the event); and A.-F. was allowed to experiment with his 2 years short service on a small scale.

[88] See p. 163 above, and Gooch, pp. 84—6.

Government could not 'stand another resignation, or dismissal'. He may have been aware that the Sub-Committee which 'Jack Fisher wanted' for 'strategic questions' was running into stiff opposition at the War Office on the grounds of the impracticability of landings on the German coast. But he had also hit on the idea, which he had already broached with Balfour on 16 September, that the Sub-Committee could have its scope enlarged to cover such matters as provision 'for naval and military *expansion* in the event of a great war'. Indeed, as he indicated to Sandars, he saw the Sub-Committee undertaking '*Organisation* whether naval, Military or Indian; the policy of sea and land fighting' which could no longer 'be left to the old Departments'.[89]

During the first phase of the talks at Balmoral, Esher compiled a memorandum (dated 5 October) about how to meet the 'risk of the partial or total collapse of the Defence Committee' under the next Government. He suggested that, before 'quitting office', the Prime Minister 'should by numerically strengthening the permanent element' in the C.I.D. 'give fresh assurances of its continuity'.

> The proposal is [he continued] that two permanent sub-committees should be formed, under the presidency of Mr. Balfour, specially constituted to deal with (a) certain scheduled recommendations made by the Elgin Commission. [Listed in a letter to Balfour of 3 Sept. 1905, these featured especially (1) up-to-date analysis of military needs, along the lines of B.'s 'Note on Army Reform printed for the use of the Cabinet' in June 1904[90] and (2) the development of the General Staff.] (b) certain strategical questions raised last summer by Sir John Fisher.
>
> A change of Government, taking place while these Sub-Committees are engaged upon work of the kind suggested, would not threaten (for reasons which appear obvious) their continuance, and consequently the existence of the Committee itself.[91]

The King was soon urging that, if political circumstances precluded Esher's appointment as War Secretary, he and Milner should be made permanent members of the C.I.D.; but Esher thought that Balfour was against this answer to the continuity problem.[92]

Esher had for some time cultivated close relations with Sandars (addressing him in correspondence as 'My dear Jack', etc.). Haldane having arrived at Balmoral on the night of 5 October, Esher on the 7th wrote for Sandars a

[89] B.P. 49719, ff. 15–16, Esher to B., 16 Sept.; ff. 17–20, Esher to Sandars, 17 Sept.; E.P. 7/18, Esher to Maurice Brett, 4 Oct. 1905.
[90] Cab. 37/71/84 and also, for the C.I.D., Cab. 4/1/26B, 22 June 1904.
[91] B.P. 49719, ff. 27–8 (Esher, ii, 114–15).
[92] E.P. 7/18, Esher to Maurice Brett, 6 Oct. 1905.

brief account of the proceedings—including the respective decisions on Arnold-Forster and on the Sub-Committee:

Results of conferences here.

1. Nothing can be done about A.F. *It is too late*. The PM says 'we have made our bed' etc.
2. Re the Defence Committee
   (a) The Chief inclines to leave things as they are.
   (b) Haldane says C.B. [Campbell-Bannerman] . . . is secretly hostile to the Committee. Asquith, Grey and he are strongly in favour of it only they want to give it a more 'scientific' and less 'political' complexion.
   (c) The King wants to strengthen *while you are in office* the permanent element. He thinks Lord Roberts and one or two others should be appointed 'permanent nucleus' for 3 years. This is a guarantee of the stability of the Committee . . .

   They fear that C.B. will let it die of *inanition* . . . the Committee will revert to what it was, a spasmodic meeting of Cabinet Ministers . . . Think out these alternatives . . . I helped the Chief as much as I could, but he ought to have someone with him when he comes here. He cannot cope with papers.[93]

With regard to the final remark, in so far as Balfour wanted to leave the C.I.D. as it was, he probably preferred not to have too many papers (e.g. written by, or wanted by, Esher) too readily available. However, it may well be true that he did his best work when recumbent, thinking and dictating, rather than at a desk. In any event, the clear implication of Haldane's remarks was that establishment of one or more 'permanent' sub-committees, with what might be construed by Liberals as sinister powers, would be the surest way of ensuring the abolition of the C.I.D. by what Balfour regularly termed 'the Radical party'. While Balfour might well have enjoyed a C.I.D. investigation into possible landings on the German coast, he evidently concluded that the military case for such activities was outweighed by political considerations bearing on the C.I.D.'s survival. Also British top-level concern about the Kaiser's volatile anti-British stance had ebbed, once it seemed clearer (by late October) that the latter's meeting with the Czar at Bjorko in July had failed to bring into being a coalition of Germany, Russia, and France against Britain. Consequently, the special Sub-Committee never was reconvened.[94]

[93] B.P. 49719, ff. 23–4.
[94] B.P. 49730, f. 205, Lansdowne to B., 27 Oct. 1905; F.O. 800/130, f. 122, Lansdowne to Lascelles, 31 Oct. 1905. See also F.O. 800/129–30, for the Kaiser's animosity towards Britain, 1904–5.

Knowing that the C.I.D. represented a material addition to governmental institutions, Balfour can perhaps be forgiven for feeling resentment at the apparent danger represented by the leader of the Liberal Party. While it did transpire that the Liberals, with their large radical wing, could not wed the C.I.D. as closely to the work of the Cabinet as Balfour had done, and that their foreign policy might have been more firmly oriented, after 1909, towards a French alliance, the over-all performance of the Liberal governments was hardly irresponsible by Balfourian standards. But this was not easy to anticipate at the time when Balfour made his notorious statement, in January 1906, that 'the great Unionist Party should still control, whether in power or whether in Opposition, the destinies of this great Empire.' Judging by the aforementioned Balmoral conclave, the King himself must have shared the Unionists' mistrust.

By 3 October, the Admiralty had been informed that the War Office was opposed to the idea of landings in Germany. [95] While this did not necessarily rule out the joint investigation of all such amphibious projects, it provided scant encouragement. Fisher, however, having got wind of the War Office's increasing interest in direct British support for France or Belgium, sent a new memorandum to Sandars on 10 October. At the C.I.D. (he wrote) it had been established that a cardinal

point was to be borne in mind—often emphasized by the Prime Minister himself— that under no circumstances was it contemplated that Great Britain could or would undertake single-handed a great military continental war, and that every project for offensive hostilities was to be subsidiary to the action of the Fleet, such as the occupation of isolated colonial possessions of the enemy, or the assistance of an ally by threatening descent on the hostile coast, or otherwise effecting a diversion on his behalf. [96]

Balfour's caution is discernible in this version. Fisher does not claim his support for an actual landing 'on the hostile coast'.

However, even if not seriously alarmed, Balfour certainly did not refuse to look seriously at worrying aspects of German policy. In April, Clarke had raised the question of German designs on the Dutch East Indies and by June, Balfour was investigating, through the C.I.D. and the Foreign Office, the desirability of an international guarantee of integrity being offered to Holland itself. But he appears to have lost interest in this matter by August. [97] Meanwhile, however, the question of Dutch vulnerability had led

[95]   Mackay, pp. 333–4.
[96]   Ibid., p. 332.
[97]   Monger, pp. 208–9.

Clarke, by mid-July, to ask Balfour to investigate the situation in Belgium.[98] After asking the War Office whether 'there would be a strong inducement', in a 'Franco-German' war, 'for either of the belligerents to violate the neutrality of Belgium', Balfour further inquired: 'In what time from the order to mobilize could two British Army Corps be disembarked in Belgium?' On 23 September the War Office replied that a calculation had recently been made, 'on data supplied by the Admiralty, of the time required to mobilize and transport a British force to Belgium'. For two Army Corps, the answer was twenty-three days.[99] But Balfour evidently saw no need, by then, to look further into preparedness for a German war.

As for Britain's obligations toward France, Balfour's attitude during his final year in office is illuminated by his remark at Asquith's invasion inquiry of 1907–8, already noticed above, that the C.I.D. would be failing in its duty if it let the 'safety of the country' hang on 'a mere *entente*, however *cordiale* it might be'. On that occasion, he proceeded to discuss the danger of a German invasion on a basis of pure military capability, as updated by the relevant C.I.D. memoranda recently given to him. He argued convincingly against the practicability of Colonel Repington's hypothetical German bolt from the blue. But he admitted that significant changes had taken place on the Anglo-German scene since he had personally investigated the invasion question. What is notable, however, is that he still, in May 1908, presupposed Britain at war, in the first instance, with a power *other than Germany*.

The trend of events [he said] has been to give the Germans some advantages in respect of invasion which were never possessed by the French, and if we were seriously involved with some other great naval and maritime Power and felt ourselves obliged to denude ourselves of any large portion of our military force, I should feel that we were in a more perilous position than we have been for some generations. Personally, I was one of those who was most reluctant ever to believe in the German scare. But I cannot now resist the conclusion that every German thinks that 'the enemy is England'; that while the more sober Germans probably admit to themselves that they will never be able to deal single-handed with the English navy, the German Staff and, what is much worse, the German nation, have ever before them the vision of a time when this country will find itself obliged to put out its utmost strength in some struggle with which Germany is not at all connected, and that then the opportunity will come for displacing the only Power which stands between it and the universal domination of Europe, or hinders the establishment of a colonial Empire.[100]

[98] B.P. 49701, ff. 268–73, Clarke to B., 11 and 15 July 1905.
[99] Cab. 4/1/65B, 'Violation of the Neutrality of Belgium', 29 Sept. 1905.
[100] Cab. 16/3A, p. 253, 29 May 1908. See also pp. 158 and 172 above.

If, by May 1908, he had come so lately to the conclusion that a German war was possible (but still remote), it is certain that he did not regard Germany as an inevitable enemy before he left office in December 1905. Moreover, there is further evidence to the same effect. Firstly, there is a letter which he drafted for transmission to Lascelles, the British Ambassador in Berlin, in the sequel to the aforementioned calls for preventive attack on the German Navy in December 1904.

In the middle of January 1905 Balfour wrote to Lascelles that he had read his letter to Lansdowne mentioning that, in 'important quarters' at Berlin, 'the idea had found expression that England was seeking a pretext for an attack on the German Empire.' It was 'astonishing', wrote Balfour, that such a 'misconception', both of English public opinion and of the views of English statesmen' should have been entertained even for a moment. He and Lansdowne had often discussed the matter. 'I have, as you know, never at any time been anti-German; and I have often regretted the vehemence with which some sections of the English Press have expressed their suspicions of German intentions.' He went on to declare that the article in the *Army and Navy Gazette*, to which Count Bülow, the German Chancellor, had referred, was quite exceptional. 'I have not read it, and I have not met anyone who has.' The *Gazette* was a specialist journal, appealing to a small audience.

However, Balfour continued, he could not deny that there was in Britain some mistrust of Germany. This was not principally due, as many Germans seemed to think, 'to commercial jealousy'. There were doubtless Englishmen who conceived themselves 'to be suffering from German competition, and are therefore the less disposed to look sympathetically upon German ambitions or methods. But this is a trifle.' His own analysis was as follows:

I believe that situation to have been created by the co-operation of three separate causes. The first is to be found amongst certain diplomatic episodes which have produced a painful impression on a public opinion embittered by the character of the attacks on the British Army made during the Boer War. The second is to be found in the arguments by which the German Fleet was brought into being. The third is to be found in the fact that a whole school of political thinkers in Germany have not merely denounced in violent language the role which Britain has played in universal history, but have preached the doctrine that Colonies were necessary for German expansion, that it was Britain alone who stood between Germany and the realisation of this German ideal, that it was only, therefore, out of the fragments of the British Colonial Empire that a German Colonial Empire could be built up.

In so far as 'this school of anti-English thinkers' found 'a wide hearing in

Germany', it was hardly surprising that British people who knew of this should 'regard with suspicion every movement of German diplomacy'. They thought that Germany sought strife between Britain and other powers so that Germany might 'profit by the exhaustion consequent on a conflict which she has occasioned but not shared'. This was the true explanation, he believed, of this unhappy phenomenon. A proper understanding of it was the best cure for the disease. [101]

Balfour never denied that German diplomacy was abrasive, and a jesting reference to it may be found in a cabinet letter of 11 April 1905, though the German activities here concerned not Morocco, but Uruguay. [102] Nearly two months later, after Germany had forced Delcassé's second resignation, Balfour does at last refer in a cabinet letter to the Moroccan affair. The Cabinet, he wrote, held 'an important, if brief, discussion'. However, he did not, on the evidence of his letter, dwell upon Germany as the cause of damage to the *entente*. The lesson he conveyed to the Cabinet was a different one, namely that French diplomacy was weak and undependable:

Mr. Balfour pointed out that M. Delcassé's dismissal or resignation under pressure from the German Government displayed a weakness on the part of France which indicated that she could not at present be counted on as an effective force in international politics. She could no longer be trusted not to yield to threats at the critical moment of a negotiation. If therefore Germany is really desirous of obtaining a port on the coast of Morocco, and if such a proceeding be a menace to our interests, it must be to other means than French assistance that we must look for our protection. [103]

In fact, Balfour had earlier written to Fisher on the subject of the Moroccan port: 'The Germans are behaving abominably, and we must do what we can to prevent them squeezing any illegitimate advantage out of the situation they have endeavoured to create.' But he doubted the value to them of such a port, from a naval viewpoint. It would be expensive to develop and difficult to hold against a stronger maritime power. [104]

In a cabinet letter of 22 June 1905 Balfour hints at the remote possibility that 'the German Emperor means serious mischief.' This aside may be linked with Clarke's prior advice that the Moroccan question might,

[101] B.P. 49747, ff. 155–162, B. to Lascelles, draft, n.d., acknowledged in 49729, ff. 77–9, Lansdowne to B., 18 Jan. 1905.
[102] Cab. 41/30, No. 14.
[103] Ibid., No. 21, 8 June 1905.
[104] Fisher Papers, doc. no. 154, 26 Apr. 1905.

judging by warlike matter being published in Germany, become exceedingly serious. [105] But the general tenour of the cabinet letter of 22 June, and that of the 28th (where Balfour clarifies his previous reference, queried by the King, to a British policy of following the French lead over Morocco) is that Britain will act 'in strict conformity with the principles of the "entente cordiale"'—that is, giving support to French diplomatic policy towards Morocco, but no more than that. [106]

The extent to which, between July and November 1905, Balfour had settled into a conviction that the German Emperor did *not* mean 'serious mischief' is shown by the episode of the new field guns. As mentioned in the previous chapter, the War Office was ready to place orders for the new field and horse artillery (18½ and 12½ pounders) by the middle of 1904. [107] However, actual manufacture was delayed. Meanwhile, from September 1904, Esher had been urging Balfour to keep intact the 'striking force' established earlier by Brodrick at Aldershot—'the one successful "coup" which St. John effected'. [108] This 'corps' of some 40,000 men was commanded from 1901 to 1907 by Sir John French with whom Esher was on very friendly terms. Esher not only feared that Arnold-Forster would remove key personnel from Aldershot before the rest of the Army had been properly reorganized but discovered that French's corps, hypothetically ready to fight, was ill provided with artillery. [109] 'As regards the guns', wrote Clarke to Sandars in December, 'now that Lord Esher has stirred up the whole matter, you will be able to get the contracts placed at once.' [110] This brought the gun question to the fore, as far as Balfour was concerned—not less because parliamentary criticism was to be expected when the 1905 session got under way. On 16 December 1904 Balfour informed the King that the Cabinet had 'resolved, with absolute unanimity, that artillery rearmament should proceed as fast as Woolwich and the Private Firms could conveniently turn out the guns and limbers'. [111] Balfour's anxiety that a change of government might occur before substantial numbers of the new weapons had actually been delivered has been recorded by Mrs Dugdale. She is certainly justified in naming this as one reason for Balfour's continuance in office during 1905 and it is an interesting point

[105] B.P. 49701, ff. 233–5, Clarke to B., 17 June 1905.
[106] Cab. 41/30, Nos. 23 and 24.
[107] B.P. 49722, f. 264, note by Arnold-Forster. See also A.-F.P., 50314, 'New Field Guns'.
[108] B.P. 49718, ff. 122–23, 25 Sept. and 31 Oct. 1904.
[109] Ibid., ff. 128–9, Esher to B., 31 Oct. and ff. 134–5, Esher to Sandars, 21 Nov. 1904.
[110] B.P. 49700, ff. 263–4, 14 Dec. 1904.
[111] Cab. 41/29, No. 43, 16 Dec. 1904.

that the King's eagerness, in May, to see some of the first batteries uncovered the vulnerability of the ammunition tubes to jolting on a hard pavé. Remedial action could thus be taken long before they were duly shaken on the road to Mons. [112]

However, Balfour had no concern, in 1905, that the guns should be ready for a *German* war. As they were progressively handed over to the Army, they were all duly dispatched to *India*, until Arnold-Forster intervened over a batch of field guns held up in Britain at the beginning of November. He suggested that, as long as there was a chance of the Kaiser opting for war in Europe, these remaining guns, at least, should be retained. Brodrick (as Indian Secretary) thought they should all go to India, as arranged. Lansdowne, when consulted, apparently saw little likelihood of real trouble with Germany; and Balfour agreed. However, Arnold-Forster pressed his point at the C.I.D.—there being few meetings of the Cabinet between 8 August and Balfour's resignation from office on 4 December. On 21 November Brodrick proposed at the C.I.D. that as the guns in question had been delayed, 'they should go to the Army Corps at Aldershot, so that the artillery there could be trained to use them.' At Balfour's final C.I.D. meeting, held on 24 November, Arnold-Forster explained why the guns had not already gone to India. 'All the guns on the Indian order except fifty-four had already been dispatched, and he desired to retain these latter guns' for the Aldershot corps. If they were sent to India as originally intended, they could not 'be placed in the field' because they lacked limbers and waggons. He added that £1,213,000 had been allocated, in the Army Estimates for 1905–6, to the continuing programme of artillery rearmament. The C.I.D. then agreed to Arnold-Forster's suggestion—'unless the Indian Government strongly oppose the change'. [113]

It seems clear enough that, even if Grierson and his Operations department at the War Office had begun to mull over a strategy of direct support for France in a German war, this cogitation had made little political headway by November 1905. There is no sign, at the level of the C.I.D., that there was real concern about the readiness of the 'striking force' to operate on the Continent in a sudden emergency. As long as Balfour presided at the C.I.D., no one was disposed to challenge the approach to over-all strategy which he had so ably and systematically established since February 1903. Perhaps the most succinct exposition of his approach is to be found in a speech he made on the Army estimates as Leader of the Opposition on 12 July 1906. Replying to Haldane, Balfour stated: 'The

[112] Dugdale, i, 425–8.
[113] Monger, pp. 231–3; Cab. 2/1, 81st and 82nd meetings, 21 and 24 Nov. 1905.

right honourable Gentleman has based his whole scheme upon his power of immediately mobilising 154,000 men.' He commented:

The contingency requiring such an expedition might occur, but it is not very easy to imagine that it would. We might be asked to land 150,000 men on the coast of Europe, but I do not know that I should sacrifice much money or take enormous pains so to organise my force that it could be done straight away and immediately. What is required, so far as I am able to see, is the power of sending continuous reinforcements to India in a great emergency.

He went on to explain that, 'in case of trouble on the North-west frontier of India', the need was not for '150,000 men ready at a moment's notice, but a force of more than that' which could be sent out over a period of time. The same reasoning, he indicated, should be applied to 'any of these difficulties which, however remote, are of a character which we cannot exclude from our view'.[114]

[114] *P.D.*, 4th, 160/1161–4.

10

On A Fiscal Needle's Point

1904–1905

WHILE Balfour's underlying purpose in clinging to office after the Tariff Reform crisis of 1903 had been to rebuild party unity before the next election (not due, under the Septennial Act, till 1907), his main administrative effort had gone into foreign and defence policy. Much of this has been covered in the previous chapter, but there remains the renewal and extension of the Japanese Alliance. This will here be treated as part of the pre-election sequence of 1905. In general, Balfour hoped that Unionists would lose interest in the contentious advantages of Tariff Reform, especially once by-election losses pointed to its lack of popularity in the country. As ever, he correctly saw that food taxes were bound to arouse great opposition. It was surely more important for Unionists to unite to resist radicalism and higher taxes, and yet maintain the Union and the Empire. Even in an unreasonable world, Balfour hoped that the primitive instinct of self-preservation would prevail.

On the parliamentary level, the rift between the Tariff Reformers and the Unionist Free Traders led to a critical debate at the opening of Parliament on 8 February 1904. As noted above, Balfour was prevented by illness from attending a C.I.D. meeting on that day. Indeed, he had never fully recovered from his feverish cold of Christmas 1903 and he also had to miss cabinet meetings on 4 and 8 February. The fiscal debate of the 8th, precipitated by John Morley's amendment to the Address condemning food taxes, gave the Liberals an eagerly awaited opportunity to expose the variegated opinions held by Unionists on that subject. The ordeal of the Unionist ministers ended only with the termination of the debate on 15 February. It fully demonstrated that only Balfour could balance, with inexhaustible dexterity and resource, on the needle's point of the doctrine enunciated by him at Sheffield the previous October. Even if the Sheffield policy was clear in outline—freedom to negotiate with foreign powers about tariffs and to retaliate where appropriate—great agility of mind was needed if the cut and thrust of debate were not to expose inconsistency on the government side.

Great was the consternation of the party leaders at having to face the fiscal debate without Balfour. George Wyndham, whose stock had risen since 1903, and the unhappy Home Secretary, Bob Akers-Douglas, who had to deputize for Balfour in the Commons, did their best to prepare their strategy, but something of a shambles was inevitable. At the outset, however, Henry Lucy thought that Douglas would pass muster in his own fashion.

Mr. Akers Douglas is a model man for the post at the present juncture. Some men, even some Ministers, assuming ignorance with respect to an awkward topic, destroy the effect by looking as if they knew all about it. With fine art, the greater because it is concealed, the Home Secretary, questioned by unreasonable members opposite, absolutely looks as if he knew nothing on the particular subject submitted, or indeed on any other . . . Mr. Balfour, questioned as to his views on Fiscal Reform, sometimes lost, or affected to lose, his temper. Mr. Akers Douglas, surveying inquisitive members opposite as if they were a field of buttercups and daisies, with childlike blandness says he doesn't know. And there the matter ends.[1]

But as the debate progressed, opposition hearts were gladdened by symptoms of confusion and disarray on the government side. Gerald Balfour could not conceal that Colonial Preference seemed less impractical to him than it did to his brother; while Alfred Lyttleton sounded even more like a true Tariff Reformer than Gerald Balfour—as did Andrew Bonar Law, Parliamentary Secretary at the Board of Trade since 1903. In winding up the debate on Monday, the 15th, the unfortunate Akers-Douglas made an appeal to party unity. But Morley's motion garnered as many as 276 votes against the Government's 327—the over-all Unionist majority at the 1900 election having been 134. On 15 February 1904, only 14 of the 52 Unionist Free Traders voted with the Government, while 26 voted against it, and 12 abstained. On the 16th Sandars sent Balfour an account of 'last night's finish to the long Debate'.

Asquith excellent from his point of view and quite light-hearted: George Wyndham good, effective, serious: in the evening C.B. [Campbell-Bannerman] as bad as ever, full of notes, dull, inconsequential and ignorant. Douglas wound up. His speech reads better than it was delivered. He never broke down, or anything like it, but the failure was in trying to make a speech partly from notes and partly without, and in his lack of experience as a speaker to deal with a highly strung assembly expecting the debating vigour of the last speech . . . He was dreadfully mortified by his conviction that he had not risen to the occasion, and that he was not worthy to stand, even for a few minutes, in your shoes, but his popularity was

[1] *Balfourian Parliament*, p. 293 (8 February 1904).

evident on all hands, and his only accuser is himself . . . He worked hard, indeed far too hard at the speech. We were at it Saturday, Sunday and part of yesterday. The fact was that he had written too much and thought too little, and he was not adroit enough to make the most of what he had on his paper. [2]

A few days later, on 21 February, Sandars wrote at considerable length to his 'Chief' about 'the general tone of Parliament with regard to the fiscal question' over the previous fortnight. He doubted whether 'the mere reports—I do not suppose you have read them—why should you?' effectively registered the feeling of the House.

It is perfectly clear to me [he continued] that the only thing which has saved us from disaster has been the most rigid adherence to your Sheffield policy: and while affirming that policy in your language it has been necessary to disclaim any idea of protection, any idea of the taxation of food or raw material, and any idea of diminishing the control of the House of Commons over our fiscal arrangements . . .

There is no doubt that a great change has come over the spirit of [Chamberlain's] dream. The majority of our men can hardly bear a sympathetic toleration to be expressed for the aspirations of the advanced Birmingham; and we have certainly not, *in your absence*, a speaker who can hold our men on the Sheffield lines, and yet avow a modicum of sympathy with Colonial Preference and food taxation. The moment a man says he is for the Government policy, but that with public opinion in its present state, the taxation of foodstuffs is not within the range of practical politics, then he is dubbed a Protectionist in disguise . . . I do not say that there is no answer to it. On the contrary there is a very good one; and in your mouth an admirable debating reply . . .

However, Sandars continued, despite the sniping of 'Winston and Jack Seeley' the party had subsequently rallied on the contentious subject of 'Chinese labour'. (Churchill, having lined up with the Liberals on free trade, was fast establishing himself as a particular *bête noire* in Sandars's eyes and was soon to be stripped of the familiar appellation 'Winston', as far as Sandars was concerned.) But on the central topic of fiscal policy, the balance of factions which Balfour had hoped to establish through his Sheffield policy could be clearly discerned. 'Joe's men', Sandars continued, 'are behaving well. They see it is no use to force the pace, and they trust time will help on *their* policy: and they also see they must back us for all they are worth. Austen quite realizes the situation.' Indeed, in the words of Joe Chamberlain himself, the Tariff Reformers had 'nowhere else to go'; and their own unity could be preserved only by looking to Balfour for adoption of their policy in a parliamentary context.

[2]   B.P. 49762, ff. 57–8, 16 Feb. 1904.

As for the conduct of the Unionist Free Traders, Sandars felt sure that enough of them could be kept in line, despite Liberal hints at co-operation in the constituencies. On the one hand, according to Sandars:

The recalcitrants in the Lobby in the Fiscal Debate were much more numerous than we expected. [But in fact] the division was a great disappointment to the Opposition . . . If we avoid either frightening or irritating these 25 [loyal] Unionists we shall carry on. If, on the other hand, we alarm or annoy them on the fiscal question, they can turn us out at a moment's notice. The large majority of them I do not believe want to have us out . . . They are torn by Linky [Lord Hugh Cecil] and Winston and Geordie Hamilton with the old Duke [of Devonshire] in reserve.

His (the Duke's) advice to them last week to vote against the Government determined many of them: and the dramatic way it was given at the meeting was engineered by Winston.[3]

All this served to confirm in Balfour's mind the soundness of his tactics. During the recess he had received a letter from Sir Samuel Hoare, a free-food Conservative and the father of the future Viscount Templewood, appealing to him to insist that loyalty to the party must come before opinion on Tariff Reform.[4] Balfour replied very characteristically on 5 November 1903:

In my view, differences on Fiscal Questions ought, if possible, not be allowed to split the Party. I have given expression to my own views at Sheffield, and, if there were a general election tomorrow, these are the views I should put in my Address. But I have neither the desire, nor the power, to reduce the views of every Member of the Party to a particular shape, although that shape be the one which, in the present state of public opinion, seems to me most likely to serve the interests of the Country.[5]

This stance proved tenable throughout 1904. While, on the one hand, some eleven Unionist Free Traders, including Churchill and Jack Seely, actually defected to the Liberals between February 1904 and the beginning of 1906, the rest of the free-Trade group continued to support the Government.[6] The Chamberlains, for their part, felt increasingly frustrated; but, despite the large following for Tariff Reform in the party, they failed in the course of 1904 to capture Balfour. Joseph Chamberlain, who was recuperating his health in France from February to April, wrote to Austen on 11 March. He noted the set-backs to Tariff Reform in the February

---

³ B.P. 49762, ff. 75–80, 21 Feb. 1904.
⁴ B.P. 49855, ff. 288–91, 30 Nov. 1903.
⁵ B.P. 49856, f. 11, 30 Nov. 1903.
⁶ Rempel, p. 92.

by-elections, and had also to recognize that Balfour had 'plainly pledged himself to go to the country on retaliation and *nothing more*'. But he was not prepared to launch a direct attack on Balfour. 'In no case', he wrote, 'am I going to fight against Balfour's government. I would much rather go out of politics.'[7]

It was of the essence of Chamberlain's stance that he challenged the old Conservatism. Somewhat after the manner of his onslaughts, when a Liberal, on the Gladstonian Whigs, he could be seen by Conservatives as still fundamentally hostile to the landed classes and the Established Church. While many Unionists found inspiration in Chamberlain's dynamic approach to Britain's economic and imperial problems, when it came to leadership of the party most backbenchers would still prefer Balfour. Balfour, unable or unwilling to impose a constructive programme of his own, continued to balance skilfully between the Free Traders and the Tariff Reformers. He was the best champion the Free Traders had. Many of the latter were deeply traditionalist, like Lord Hugh Cecil, and their influence in the party would end as soon as Balfour ceased to be Prime Minister. Therefore it was only Chamberlain who was likely to force Balfour to go to the country.

Chamberlain sought through his own speeches, and through letters written to Balfour by the strategically placed Austen in August and September, to push the Prime Minister into public acceptance of some distinctive item in the whole-hog Tariff Reform programme. Such an announcement would affront the Unionist Free Traders. Then Balfour, lacking a reliable majority in the Commons, would have to go to the country. The general election would be lost by the Unionist Party; but within that party, Tariff Reformers would be returned in overwhelming numbers. Consequently Balfour would finally have to embrace the whole programme.[8]

But Balfour was not easily caught. Writing at length to Austen from Whittingehame on 10 September, he argued that his Sheffield scheme, if unexciting, was logical and self-contained. However, he was prepared to take up Austen's suggestion of a colonial trade conference to follow a Unionist victory at the polls. It has just been noted that such a victory was, in any event, recognized as being most unlikely. However, Balfour proposed further to hedge his commitment by announcing that a trade conference should not affect British policy till endorsed at a second general

[7] Richard Jay, *Joseph Chamberlain: a Political Study* (Oxford, 1981), p. 295, citing J.C.P.

[8] See Sir Austen Chamberlain, *Politics from Inside: an Epistolatory Chronicle 1906–1914* (London, 1936), pp. 22–34, for his exchanges with Balfour in 1904.

election. Any class of goods could be discussed at the conference; but he would declare that 'true protection' had no place in Unionist policy. This last item offered little cheer to the Chamberlains who, whatever their original intentions, were being forced progressively to give ground to agricultural and industrial protectionists. So the disappointed Austen replied on the 12th that, while he would remain loyal to Balfour during the current parliament, he could not be expected to conform with the latter's policy at the next general election.[9]

As related in the previous chapter, Balfour had been closely watching the Russian Fleet, expected soon to sail from the Baltic for the Far East; and evidence of his distrust of the Liberals' ability to handle foreign policy and defence has been duly noted. However, his exchanges with his closest confidants, Selborne and Sandars, do not indicate that such considerations were predominant in the Prime Minister's mind near the middle of the long parliamentary recess. On 15 September, he wrote to Sandars:

I talked to Willie Selborne before leaving London about the Navy Estimates. I know he is desirous of making a reduction, and he begged me to ask Austen for a figure on which he could work . . . Austen, however, has refused at present to give such a figure. But I do not think this need be taken as at all indicating that on this point we are likely to have difficulty in the Autumn. Our main difficulties are when to 'cut the painter', and *how* to cut it.[10]

Sandars quickly replied: 'I trust I am right in thinking that no matter what line Austen and Co. should decide to take after your forthcoming speech at Edinburgh [stipulating the double election] we should still carry on.' He then proceeded to rehearse the considerations apparently to the fore in Balfour's small inner circle:

If I am [right], and you decide to meet Parliament I think you may trust to Alick [Hood] and me to find you the opportunity for resigning. That need not be a difficulty; though I am not sure that there may not be a real hardening in our ranks, if our men realized [*sic*] a strong lead which avoided food taxation; which pulled us together against the Welsh Mutiny against the Education Act; and which declared against Home Rule in any guise.

He then rounded off with a reference to 'the irritation' caused by MacDonnell in connection with Dunraven's 'devolution scheme' for Ireland and 'uneasiness' in the party about the latter.[11]

---

[9] Ibid., pp. 27–34.
[10] B.P. 49762, ff. 123–4, 15 Sept. 1904.
[11] Ibid., ff. 125–6, 16 Sept. 1904; i.e. B's letter from N. Berwick, dated the 15th was answered by S. from Torquay on the 16th.

So far so good. Even if there is no sign of a constructive programme and no reference to the achievement, six months before, of the French *entente*, the current problems (Lloyd George's 'Welsh Mutiny' and the rumblings over Ireland) are to be manipulated as deftly as possible, and above all there seems to be a fair chance of holding off the Chamberlains and fostering party unity.

Meanwhile Selborne had asked Balfour whether, as a Vice-President of the Liberal Unionist Association, he should agree to help Chamberlain's autumn campaign. Balfour, responding on 19 September, did not see how he could refuse, if the campaign was 'conducted on lines with which' Selborne could agree. 'I should', wrote Balfour, 'have been disposed to think such agreement quite easy had it not been for Austen's letter, which you have just seen.' By implication, Balfour regarded his own forthcoming speech at Edinburgh as a test of the practicability of remaining in office.

If Joe, speaking at Luton on the 5th (two days after I speak at Edinburgh) says nothing to make co-operation difficult, your course will be clear. If, on the other hand, he expresses the view that my plan is so utterly inadequate that, from his point of view, it amounts to an indefinite shelving of the question, you may have to reconsider the line you will take. This contingency is, however, I hope unlikely; and it is unnecessary now to make provision against a misfortune which may never occur.

On 2 October Balfour, *en route* from Balmoral to Whittingehame, had lunch at Aberdeen with Esher who, for his part, was on his way to the royal residence. As Esher reported to his son Maurice, Balfour was 'in some trepidation' about his Edinburgh speech. While his double-election plan would reassure those who feared food taxes, the Tariff Reformers would not be best pleased. Balfour was face to face with his deepest fear—that after all his subtle balancing, he would split his party. [12]

The speech, duly delivered on 3 October to the Scottish Conservative Club in Edinburgh, seemed to such of Balfour's intimates as George Wyndham to have provided, in fact, a basis for unity. [13] But Joseph Chamberlain, though he felt powerless, was consumed with fury. [14] However, Balfour's offer of an imperial conference did constitute a concession. Chamberlain and the Tariff Reformers now looked a few weeks ahead to the forthcoming Conservative Party Conference at Southampton. It was agreed that the agricultural protectionist Henry Chaplin ('the Squire')

[12] Esher, ii, 65.
[13] J. W. Mackail and Guy Wyndham, *Life and Letters of George Wyndham* (London, 1925), ii, 482: W. to his sister Mary (Lady Elcho), 19 Oct. 1904.
[14] Amery, vi, 634.

should try to pass a strong Tariff Reform resolution, going further than Balfour wished, first through the Council of the Conservative National Union and then in the full Conference.

Chaplin duly reported to Chamberlain (on holiday in Italy) the successive stages of his mission. By 22 October, his resolution had been unanimously passed by the Council, a slight verbal amendment apart. Then he went down to Southampton for the Conference and on the 28th the meeting evidently carried the resolution with a show of enthusiasm. When the Free Traders moved an amendment specifically conforming with Balfour's Edinburgh doctrine—that is, Sheffield plus a double election before a conference—they were severely rebuffed. However, what might have been seen in the press as a humiliation for Balfour was masked by a happy coincidence. This was the Dogger Bank crisis. As related in the previous chapter, the public awaited Balfour's speech of 28 September to find out whether Britain would, or would not, go to war with Russia. Balfour, at his best in this situation, did not need, when winding up in the evening, even to refer to the Tariff Reform resolution. Chaplin's triumph died with the afternoon. It was scarcely reported. [15]

But Balfour could find no position of stability on his fiscal needle's point. Just before the potentially mortal trials of Edinburgh and Southampton were successfully negotiated, Milner wrote from South Africa (2 October) asking to be relieved as High Commissioner. [16] This raised issues of the first importance in high Unionist circles. Milner had not been able to achieve his aim of anglicizing the colony; yet his successor would have to handle the establishment of a representative assembly in the Transvaal. Milner suggested that Balfour's old friend, Alfred Lyttleton, who had replaced Chamberlain at the Colonial Office, should be the new High Commissioner. Balfour agreed that this would not be a step down for Lyttleton. However, at a time when he might at any moment be forced into a general election, he did not relish having to find someone to replace Lyttleton who had been in office for little more than a year. [17] Indeed, he might have added, Milner himself had refused to provide a solution to this particular problem in September 1903. That Balfour's choice fell upon Selborne possesses much significance.

Curzon had been in England on leave during the summer and autumn of 1904. There seemed a good chance that he would resign as Viceroy and that a replacement would have to be found. Apparently, it was understood that

[15] Ibid., 638–40.
[16] B.P. 49697, ff. 112–17, Milner to B., 2 October 1904.
[17] Judd, *Balfour*, pp. 192–3.

Selborne would go out to India.[18] However, Curzon went back to India in November; and, now that South Africa was falling vacant, Balfour asked Selborne to be the new High Commissioner. After several months, Balfour wrote to Milner that Selborne had agreed to go. He would 'be a dreadful loss to the Government and the Party. He goes reluctantly, and out of a sheer sense of public duty.'[19] Indeed, on the face of it, the choice of Selborne at a time when Fisher was just beginning his great reforms as First Sea Lord is surprising. Again, Selborne (married to the late Lord Salisbury's daughter, Maud) was a member of Balfour's family circle and had been closer to him politically even, it would seem, than Lansdowne since the reconstruction of the Government in July 1902. It is a mark of the weight given by Balfour to imperial matters that, by February, he was still insistent that Selborne should go to South Africa.[20] Also, Balfour's exchanges with Milner and Selborne show that the problem of making official appointments of a kind likely to survive the advent of a Liberal government was already well to the fore.[21]

On 26 January 1905, not long before the parliamentary ordeal of 1905 was due to begin, Balfour responded to a challenge from Morley and summarized his fiscal policy on 'a half-sheet of notepaper'. It was ably done—Sheffield plus Edinburgh, but omitting any reference to a double election.[22]

Parliament duly opened on 14 February. Balfour was soon under pressure from three directions: firstly, the troubles of George Wyndham which culminated in his resignation; secondly, a series of no less than five fiscal resolutions tabled by the Opposition to put the Unionists on the rack; and thirdly, the increasingly discontented Tariff Reformers apparently on the verge of revolt. Yet, in the later part of March, the Cabinet showed true Balfourian resilience in embarking on the negotiations which resulted in the renewal and extension of the Anglo-Japanese Alliance.

As Sandars long afterwards wrote for Garvin's edification, Wyndham had been Balfour's 'most intimate friend' up to the time of the Irish

[18] Bodl., Selborne MS 191, 'Some Memories and Some Reflections in my old age' (written in late 1932 and early 1933), p. 52: it had been Curzon's suggestion, and 'St. John and Arthur both agreed and asked me if I would go.'

[19] B.P. 49697, ff. 134–5, B. to Milner, 23 Feb. 1905; 49708, f. 28, Selborne to B., 26 Nov. 1904: 'My Dear Arthur, I repeat that if you think I ought to go to South Africa I will go . . . I say [Balfour of Burleigh] is the man.'

[20] Ibid., f. 77, Selborne to B., 19 Feb. 1905: 'As you think we can be of use in South Africa we are quite willing to go.'

[21] See, for example, B.P. 49697, ff. 118–28, B. to Milner, draft of Oct. 1904—not sent.

[22] Amery, vi, 651.

Secretary's resignation in the spring of 1905. In terms of 'political confidence', indeed, Sandars rated Wyndham closest of the Unionists to Balfour until he was placed at the Irish Office in August 1902. Sandars however confirms that, thenceforward, Wyndham played no significant part in the 'transactions of the Inner Cabinet'. This apparently consisted of Balfour, Selborne, Lansdowne, and Akers-Douglas, with Sandars himself playing an influential though necessarily subordinate role. Lyttleton, though always a close friend of Balfour's, was not of great political weight. After Wyndham's fall, the mutual affection between him and Balfour gradually declined. [23]

Yet Wyndham had seemed, from 1903, to be the rising star of the Unionist Party. However, by the autumn of 1904 drink was getting the better of him and he failed to exercise sensible control over the activities of Sir Anthony MacDonnell. Wyndham had succeeded, despite the misgivings of Balfour and Lansdowne, in having the Roman Catholic MacDonnell appointed as his Under-Secretary at the Irish Office and then, through inattention or befuddlement, allowed him to co-operate with Dunraven's scheme of devolution for Ireland. This could easily be mistaken for a move towards Home Rule—and therefore meant almost certain political death for Wyndham as soon as it was thus interpreted by Unionists. It would also do little to ease the Prime Minister's anxieties.

On 31 January Balfour, who always thought of himself as an optimist, wrote to Wyndham: 'My dear George, Do not be distressed about Sir A. MacDonnell . . . We may possibly have a tightish time in the House over it, but I do not think you need worry yourself . . . Yours ever . . .' [24] But by the end of February, 'the brilliant Chief Secretary' had been 'knocked out of the ring'.

Forced to publicly censure the colleague [MacDonnell] who, rightly or wrongly, believed he was acting in accordance with his chief's views, he withdrew from the Parliamentary scene, leaving the Ulster men triumphant. He was in his place on Monday [27 February], with feverish irritation answering fresh questions about Sir Anthony MacDonnell. On Tuesday morning he left town . . . and questions addressed to him were replied to by the Irish Attorney-General, who is as much out of sympathy with his generous broad views of Irish government as is that truculent Orangeman, the English Solicitor-General (Sir Edward Carson). [25]

[23] As indicated on p. 139, the interesting pieces written by Sandars in his last years (1933–4) on most of Balfour's political associates are to be found in J.C.P. 18/16/17–30. They were for J. L. Garvin's use in writing his life of Joseph Chamberlain. The piece on Wyndham is quoted in Amery, vi, 671–2.

[24] B.P. 49805, f. 18.

[25] Lucy, *Balfourian Parliament*, pp. 367–8 (6 Mar 1905.)

By 3 March, when Balfour was dictating a letter to Wyndham, he had received the latter's offer of resignation. Balfour doubted whether he should accept it. It would probably be interpreted 'as a practical admission that you encouraged a Home Rule, or quasi Home Rule, agitation' and 'perpetual questions' on the subject could be expected. Moreover, quite aside from his 'particular affection' for Wyndham, Balfour disliked caving in to 'pressure from outside'.[26] But no viable alternative suggested itself. On 6 March Wyndham's resignation was announced in both Houses of Parliament. As Sandars wrote for the benefit of J. W. Mackail after reading *The Life and Letters of George Wyndham* early in 1925, Wyndham had, since 1903, 'been marked out as certain of the party leadership'; but he allowed himself to be won over to 'large schemes of policy' which 'in his sober moments he should have realized were anathema' to Balfour, 'his friend and patron'.[27]

Fast on the heels of this blow to the Government came the merciless stream of fiscal motions, initiated by the turncoat Winston Churchill on 8 March. By the 18th Sandars was telling FitzRoy that this onslaught had brought relations between Balfour and Chamberlain near breaking-point. Chamberlain's Tariff Reform League had recently evinced open contempt for Balfour's Sheffield doctrine of retaliation, and Chamberlain had pointed publicly to the imminence of a General Election. As Sandars indicated, Balfour had been able hitherto to lead the party on a basis of greater discontent amongst the Free Traders, a relatively small group with no generally acceptable refuge other than the Unionist party. Now, Sandars thought, the crash could be expected at any time, once Chamberlain had had the satisfaction of seeing Austen introduce his second budget. Meanwhile, Balfour felt that he had done well by his party by preserving it from the deadly taint of protectionism. He was aggrieved by Chamberlain's harassing tactics, which included pressure on Free Fooders in the constituencies and open demands for an early election; and he was veering towards Hicks Beach and the Free Traders. FitzRoy concluded from Sandars's remarks that Balfour was facing a General Election with the party in grievous disarray but that, in the circumstances, the blame would inevitably fall on Chamberlain.[28]

Such considerations underlay a cabinet meeting held on 21 March. Winston Churchill's fiscal motion of the 8th, condemning preference, had been negotiated by moving the previous question and finding adequate

[26] B.P. 49805, ff. 33–6.
[27] Sandars P., C.771, S. to Mackail, holo. draft, Mar. 1925.
[28] FitzRoy, pp. 244–6, 18 Mar. 1905.

support when it came to a vote on that.[29] On the 21st the Cabinet's attention was completely engrossed by a motion, in the names of a Liberal and a Liberal Unionist, aimed directly at Chamberlain and thus threatening a major Unionist split. It was to be closely followed by three others, directed in turn at Balfour's retaliation policy, at Chamberlain's Tariff Reform policies, and at various implications of the policies of both. Of the first motion, which had to be faced on the following day, Balfour reported to the King in his cabinet letter of 21 March that it condemned

a proposition laid down by Mr. Chamberlain in 1903 at Glasgow, to the effect that an average ten per cent all round duty on manufactured goods shall be imposed, varied in the case of each class of goods by the amount of labour required to produce it. In the eyes of most people this amounts to protection: and it certainly would be impossible to induce the party not to vote against it—even by suggesting that they should avoid voting on it at all by supporting the 'previous question' as they did (at Mr. Balfour's request) a fortnight ago. It is certain therefore that the motion will be carried—and that thereby a portion of Mr. Chamberlain's policy will be condemned.

In these circumstances, wrote Balfour, the Chamberlains were pressing for the previous question to be moved 'and made a matter of life and death to the Government'.

This, however, Mr. Balfour absolutely refused to consent to do. Rather than adopt a course which would (however illogically) lay open the whole party to the charge of being protectionists, and would have forced a dissolution under these unfavourable circumstances, Mr. Balfour informed the cabinet that he would, this afternoon, have placed his resignation in Your Majesty's hands. Finally it was agreed that it was not necessary on any of these fiscal motions to endeavour to repeat the struggle victoriously terminated a fortnight ago; but that the proper policy was to treat with contempt [for which term 'neglect' was substituted] these abstract resolutions which deal with no problem with which the present Parliament is concerned, and which are only designed by their framers to embarrass and if possible to divide the Government and the Party.[30]

The debate of the 22nd presented the lobby-correspondents with delicious fodder. Henry Lucy compared Balfour's tactics with those of the disappearing Cheshire Cat in *Alice in Wonderland*.

Interposing at the earliest moment, [the Prime Minister] announced his intention of walking out before the division and invited his followers to imitate his example.

---

[29]   Amery, vi, 674–5; Sykes, p. 87.
[30]   Cab. 41/30, No. 10, B. to the King, 21 Mar. 1905.

Courteous to the last, he remained to hear the vigorous speech [Campbell-Bannerman] delivered across the table. Then, with smiling countenance, languorous grace, and lingering step, he fared forth, followed in single file by his colleagues on the Treasury Bench. Simultaneously a strategic movement to the rear was made by the rank and file of the party, their steps hastened by the fact that Sir Howard Vincent [noted for his hearty Unionist shouts of 'Hyah! Hyah!'], in a white waistcoat and a loud voice, had commenced what threatened to be a long speech.

However, Vincent was alert enough to get out before the locking of the doors. Through a combination of misjudgement and misfortune, two of his Unionist colleagues were trapped in the chamber. The Clerk of the House 'did full justice to the opportunity. "The Ayes to the right," he said, "were 254. The Noes"—here a dramatic pause—"Two."''[31]

While Sandars, like many Unionists, felt that the walking-out manœuvre had succeeded brilliantly, there was discontent amongst the Tariff Reformers. As Parker Smith informed Joseph Chamberlain, Balfour had confided his belief that it was better for the country if the Unionist Government handled South Africa and foreign affairs for the time being. Balfour thought that opinion was becoming more favourable to the Government on education and on Chinese labour in South Africa.[32] But Chamberlain disagreed with this assessment. He thought that the longer Balfour held on, the worse the position of the Unionists in the country would become.[33]

Meanwhile, the question of the Japanese Alliance had been brewing since 13 January, when Lord Percy, Under-Secretary at the Foreign Office, broached the matter with Balfour. He wrote that Lansdowne had already shown interest in his suggestion of renewal of the Alliance at once—before the Government could fall. In the continental press it was rumoured that a Liberal government, seeking a Russian *entente*, would back out of the Japanese connection. 'Why not', Percy continued, 'at once put a stop to such a campaign by taking time by the forelock and binding ourselves for another five years?' He also suggested that the Americans might join the alliance.[34] Balfour generally favoured working as far as possible in tandem with the United States—and nowhere more than in the Far East. However, soundings in this regard proved unfavourable. But encouraging signs were made by the Japanese that they might welcome not just a renewal of the

[31] Lucy, *Balfourian Parliament*, pp. 329, 372–6 (22 March 1905).
[32] Amery, vi, 685–7.
[33] Ibid., p. 688.
[34] B.P. 49747, ff. 143–4, with a typescript copy (ff. 145–6) indicating B's interest in the project. Incidentally, the writer was Earl Percy (1871–1909), and not Lord Eustace Percy, as has sometimes been stated.

existing alliance, but its extension.[35] This was just what Balfour wanted. He thought a bare renewal would be too generally construed as deliberate pre-emption of the Liberals.[36] However, on 23 March, the day after Balfour had led his party out of the Commons, the Cabinet settled down to a discussion about the Alliance. The idea of renewal on the strengthened basis of a British guarantee of the Japanese position, after the peace, against Russian encroachment in the Far East, balanced by a Japanese obligation to defend the British position in Afghanistan and India, received serious consideration. Balfour told the King that such an idea, 'even if acceptable to the contracting parties', would 'require the most careful thinking out in detail. In the meanwhile the cabinet authorised Lord Lansdowne to sound the Japanese minister unofficially.'[37]

As far as Balfour was concerned, the next step was to examine the subject in the C.I.D. On 12 April, he opened a meeting of that body by observing that 'the Cabinet desired' its opinions. There seems to have been agreement that 'the defensive character of the Treaty should be strictly maintained' and that the 'scope of the existing Treaty might be extended so as to make it operative in the event of either Contracting Party being attacked by a third Power'. These requirements were effectively written into the new treaty. An interesting point recorded was that it was 'of primary importance to ascertain the views of the Indian Government as to the desirability of the troops of another Asiatic Power co-operating with our native Indian troops'. (This proposition did prove repugnant to the Indian authorities.) However, the idea of Japanese assistance for the maintenance of Afghan independence remained a prime objective of Balfour's.[38]

This, of course, was a time of anxiety about the outcome of the naval war in the Far East. As Clarke, with whom Balfour was working on all sides of the Alliance proposal, wrote to the Prime Minister on 29 April: 'If Kamranh Bay had been nearer to the Japanese bases, and if the Japanese had attacked the Russians there, an awkward situation would have arisen.' As for the general naval prospect, Clarke believed that Togo lacked 'force enough for a great victory'. What he needed was 'two more battleships'. Clarke argued that it was battleships, not destroyers with their 'speculative' torpedoes, that counted.[39] However, despite the contrary views of most British experts, Balfour seems never to have wavered from a fairly

35 Ian H. Nish, *The Anglo-Japanese Alliance 1894–1907*, London, 1966, pp. 300–1.
36 B.P. 49747, ff. 152–4, B. to Percy, 15 Jan. 1905.
37 Cab. 41/30, No. 11, B. to the King, 23 March 1905.
38 Cab. 2/1, 70th meeting of C.I.D.
39 B.P. 49701, ff. 168–70 and 114–15, Clarke to B., 29 Apr. and 26 Apr. 1905.

optimistic view of Japanese chances of victory in the war. Therefore he sought, a few weeks before the naval issue was settled at Tsushima, to make some deserved political capital out of the C.I.D. and unobtrusively to prepare opinion to give credit to the Government if the Japanese negotiations succeeded.

Already, in June 1904, Balfour had sounded cabinet opinion as to whether his memorandum on invasion (11 November 1903)[40] should be published. Of course, his desire for publication was not solely due to the feeling that he should get some political kudos for his solid personal contribution within the C.I.D. Publicity could also serve as a material deterrent to any continental power which might happen to be maturing plans for the invasion of the British Isles. (As Professor Paul Kennedy has made clear, the idea of rushing an invasion force across from the Scheldt to southern England, before the Mediterranean Fleet could be brought home, had been examined in Germany as early as 1897.)[41] However, the Cabinet 'felt that there were grave difficulties in the way of making Defence documents public property: and that it would not be easy to draw a distinction between one such document and another. In the meanwhile', Balfour reported to the King, he would 'take no steps in the matter'.[42]

On 11 May 1905, Balfour felt that the moment had come to make a statement. If it achieved no lasting electoral effect, Lucy indicates that it made a distinct impression on those parliamentarians who heard it.

That the Premier took a special interest in the work of the Defence Committee is a fact not unfamiliar to the House. Certainly the Prime Minister's personal appearance and manner do not irresistibly suggest a man of war. There is something incongruous in the idea of his presiding over a Board of Military and Naval Council, charged with the task of preserving by force of arms the safety of the empire. This afternoon the crowded house, listening in silent amazement, discovered in him an absolute master of the naval and military situation at home and abroad, a pellucidly clear exponent of its intricacies.

The statement in the form presented came as a surprise. The vote for the salary of the Secretary of the Defence Committee cropping up in the Civil Service Estimates, it was recognized that the opportunity was convenient for making a few remarks promised some time ago . . . When Mr. Balfour rose the House was by no means full. Members gathered in anticipation of an ordinary dull sitting devoted to discussion of the distribution of shillings and pence in the most miscellaneous of

---

[40]   See pp. 156–9.
[41]   'The development of German naval operations plans against England, 1896–1914', *E.H.R.*, (1974), pp. 50–1.
[42]   Cab. 41/29, No. 18, B. to the King, 9 June 1904.

Estimates. What it found itself treated to was a statement full in detail, positive in purpose, Bismarckian in bluntness, imperial in range of interest.

The Premier was conscious that his audience spread far beyond the circle of members listening with breathless attention, loth to break the thread of the discourse by a cheer. Outside all the nations of the world were within hearing, whilst not defiantly, without a touch of blatancy, in quiet, businesslike manner, he demonstrated the inviolability of these islands from invasion, and quashed the bogey of Russian descent on India . . . warning . . . Russia in the matter of attempting to build strategic railways in Afghanistan. It would, he quietly said, be regarded as an act of direct aggression.[43]

In treating the Indian problem at some length, Balfour made full use of Clarke's arguments about the severe logistical difficulties facing a Russian invasion of Afghanistan. As if with an eye for the events of the 1980s, he added to his comments on the Russian need to build new railways in that country:

I may observe that the Afghans are not likely to welcome these railway makers in their fastnesses. I quite agree that the Ameer would probably find it quite impossible to resist in detail the attacks of the disciplined forces of Russia; but they would become very formidable opponents indeed when the approach was made to their mountain fastnesses . . .

He argued that 'India cannot be taken by assault' but that Britain's defence against Russian incursion 'must be certainly a very long one'; and Kitchener's demands for reinforcement by 'eight divisions of infantry and other corresponding arms' were 'not too great'. He thought the House could 'take it as a most safe estimate that not more than that would be required during the first year of hostilities with Russia', but the matter was still under investigation.[44]

This speech certainly focused attention on the manpower problem. Balfour and Clarke evidently thought it would be a political master-stroke to cap the speech with an announcement that Japan would, in case of need, make good any shortage of British troops for the defence of India.[45]

Esher, appreciative of Balfour's performance in the Commons, wrote the next day:

My dear Arthur,
    After reading your wonderful speech, I am extremely proud of two things

---

[43] *Balfourian Parliament*, pp. 383–4, 11 May 1905.
[44] *P.D.*, 4th, 146/63–81, 11 May 1905.
[45] See also Nish, pp. 305–7 and 317.

(a) that I was the first to suggest to you a 'permanent nucleus' for the Committee which *you* founded . . .

(b) much more proud of the fact that for 25 years I have been honoured with your friendship.

That is a solid fact, which leaves everything else rather in the shadow.

Yours ever affectionately,

Esher [46]

Balfour's shortcomings as a party leader have already been encountered; but his speech on defence illuminated in clear relief the difficulty of finding in Unionist ranks a worthy substitute for him—assuming always that it would not be Joseph Chamberlain.

Before the end of May, and before Tsushima, the Japanese had agreed to the basic British proposals, including extension of the agreement to cover India in return for British support in Korea. Partly to justify the Government's continuance in office and partly to give public reassurance to the Japanese, Lansdowne intimated to a Conservative rally on 1 June that the only question about the Japanese Alliance was, not that it would be renewed, but to what extent it would be strengthened. [47]

On 2 June, the day following Lansdowne's speech, Balfour was to address the National Union at the Albert Hall. There he made a strong appeal for party unity. However, far from being able to move ahead from an eleventh-hour consensus in the party to triumphant completion of the Japanese negotiations, and thus a fair electoral prospect, [48] Balfour was faced with the scarcely veiled hostility of Chamberlain. In May, Chamberlain had demanded that Balfour should publicly accept the need for a general tariff to make retaliation effective and that he should drop his double-election pledge. Balfour had apparently conceded the first demand and, in part, the second; but he had reverted to his former position to appease his outraged Free Traders, hoping that his elevation, on 2 June, of imperial preference to the forefront of the Unionist party's concerns would satisfy Chamberlain. But Chamberlain was far from satisfied. While not

---

[46]   B.P. 49718, f. 193 (Esher, ii, 87), 12 May 1905.

[47]   Cab. 37/77/98, B.'s memo of 27 May on the Anglo-Japanese Treaty. This is supplemented by a note of the 31st, including: '. . . there are obvious difficulties—not to say absurdities—in allowing Australia and other Colonies to treat our Japanese allies as belonging to an inferior race . . . There is much to be said for trying to get this question put on a satisfactory basis before the Treaty is signed, though, on the other hand, it may be one of the difficulties which it is best to ignore . . .'. See also Nish, p. 311.

[48]   See Bodl. MS, Selborne 2, Brodrick to Selborne, 26 May 1905, for Unionist expectations of success if elections followed hard upon a new Treaty.

On A Fiscal Needle's Point

going so far as to challenge Balfour openly for the leadership of the party, he decided to press their disagreement on fiscal policy to the point where Balfour would have to resign or ask for a dissolution. He set out, by degrees, to build up Tariff Reform pressures till Balfour was tumbled from his fiscal point of balance. Whereas Balfour believed that recent by-election losses were due to a widespread fear of food taxes, Chamberlain designated Balfour's endless ambiguities as the cause. [49]

Meanwhile, Balfour's parliamentary traumas continued until the session at last came to an end on 11 August. But his manner scarcely betrayed his growing emotional exhaustion. On 22 May, he calmly refused to respond to probing from Campbell-Bannerman about his fiscal attitudes, 'lolling with studied negligence on Treasury Bench'. When Alfred Lyttleton tried to temporize at the dispatch box, bedlam broke out on the opposition benches and was 'incessant for full forty minutes'. Balfour at last got to his feet and, the din having subsided, he said: 'It is not consistent with usage or ideas of justice that the criminal in the dock—and that is the situation I am supposed to occupy—should offer his defence before he has heard the whole of the accusation.' Flabbergasted silence reigned for a few moments. Then Lyttleton reappeared at the dispatch box. He was greeted by an uproar which continued for half an hour. On five occasions Lyttleton could be heard embarking on a statement; but he never progressed beyond the words 'The Prime Minister' before roars of protest cut him short. Balfour, reclining on the Treasury bench 'with affected ease', made no further overt response. The Deputy Speaker, J. W. Lowther, finally adjourned the House. [50]

On the night of Thursday, 20 July, the Government actually suffered a defeat in the Commons on a detail of the Irish estimates. According to Sandars, this resulted from 'an exceedingly able manœuvre'. The Opposition did not disclose its strength 'until the very last moment' and the government whips had no inkling of this midnight foray. 'After the Division', Sandars noted, 'Sir Michael Hicks-Beach rushed breathlessly into my room, and in agitated tones exclaimed, "The Prime Minister must accept defeat and resign."'

Later on [Sandars continued] the Prime Minister came in [with] Gerald, Alfred Lyttleton, Walter Long, Arnold-Forster and others. Beach forced his way into the room and, much to the Prime Minister's disgust, repeated his opinion already expressed to me in language of no less heat . . . the Prime Minister . . . was by no

49   Sykes, pp. 88–95; Amery, vi, 690–713.
50   Lucy, *Balfourian Parliament*, pp. 384–9 (22 May 1905).

means disposed to accept his reasoning . . . [He] exhibited perfect calmness, and never moved from his opinion that the division . . . should not be treated as decisive of the tenure of the Government.

In default of a cabinet letter, the upshot can likewise be traced in Sandars's note. On the 21st Sandars himself saw the King who 'insisted that every effort should be made by Mr. Balfour to maintain himself in office'. He gave as reasons: '(1) the Anglo-Japanese Treaty [not signed till 12 August], (2) the Moroccan Conference [demanded by Germany to determine the future of Morocco], and (3) the [Russo-Japanese] Peace Conference at Washington'. Sandars added: 'I undertook to represent His Majesty's strong opinion on these points to Mr. Balfour.' That afternoon the Cabinet unanimously resolved to hold on. Balfour communicated this decision to the King in person at 6.30 p.m. that Friday, 21 July. It was announced in the Commons on the following Monday. [51]

Interwoven with these events was the culmination of Balfour's anxieties about Curzon and India. The pros and cons of Curzon's regime in India (1898–1905) have been much studied and his relations with Balfour at this time have been latterly well treated in Lord Egremont's biography of the latter. [52] Suffice it here to say that the imperious Curzon—like Balfour in having been a leading member of the 'Souls' of the nineties, but quite unlike his fastidious senior in his earthy pursuit of women—found it difficult to accept that the Viceroy of India should be treated as anything less than a mighty sovereign autocrat. In 1902 he had sought Kitchener's appointment as Commander-in-Chief in India. Unfortunately, Kitchener did not slip easily into the reverential posture expected of him. Once he had decided that the existing system of dual control of the Indian Army was inappropriate, the General did not hesitate to appeal to Brodrick and the Cabinet. The Government, to Curzon's outraged astonishment, not only sided with Kitchener but went so far as to assert its ultimate control over its illustrious pro-consul in India. A brief report in *The Times* of 19 July indicated that Curzon had given free vent to his feelings about the Government of the United Kingdom in a speech to the Indian Legislative Council. Balfour, in turn, went much further than usual in exposing his own private wounds in a letter to the King. The Cabinet had instructed Brodrick to await 'a full telegraphic report of the speech' before replying; but Balfour thought *The Times* must be correct in conveying the 'deplorable taste and temper' of the

[51] Sandars Papers, C.749, 'Note on Some Events of the Crisis', 24 July 1905.
[52] Egremont, pp. 168–74.

Viceroy's speech. Indeed, he wrote, 'no such public exhibition of dis-
loyalty to the Home Government has ever yet been made by an Indian
Viceroy.' Balfour's further remarks indicated how acutely he felt this blow
inflicted on him by an old friend at a time of maximum political tribulation.

> Mr. Balfour looks forward to the development of this incident with the gravest
> anxiety . . . how the Government are effectively to defend against an unanswerable
> charge one who has left no means unused, legitimate or illegitimate, to deflect their
> policy, it is difficult to see. On personal, even more than on public grounds Mr.
> Balfour is deeply grieved.[53]

However, it did look for a few days as though Curzon had finally come at
least to an accommodation with Kitchener.[54] But this possibility was
foreclosed by Curzon's resignation, telegraphed on 5 August.

On the 8th, the Cabinet discussed the final stage of the Japanese negotiation, but then turned to the less encouraging subject of the Raj. As Balfour
recorded, the 'very painful subject of Lord Curzon's position was then
brought under consideration'. Balfour had already drafted 'a very conciliatory telegram in answer to his message of resignation, and it was agreed that
this could be sent'. But Curzon's 'proposal for dividing Bengal' had raised
'a tremendous storm' in India. This, in addition to 'his relations to Lord
Kitchener and the Home Government', might 'induce him to grasp at any
expedient for relieving himself of his task'. Curzon's 'extreme sensitiveness to even the gentlest comment, and the violence of his own language
towards those who differ from him can only be due, in Mr. Balfour's
opinion, to the combined effect of overwork, climate, and ill health'.
Balfour felt that these factors engendered 'in so masterful a mind' a
'somewhat overbearing style of diplomacy'. This threatened 'unnecessary
trouble with the Amer of Afghanistan—a calamity the magnitude of which
it would not be easy to measure'.[55]

But this ultimate misfortune, at least, did not befall the Government. On
21 August Curzon's resignation was formally accepted. But further
encounters, even more directly gladiatorial in character, lay ahead for 'dear
Arthur' and 'dear George'.

Meanwhile, the parliamentary session of 1905 had at last come to an end
on 11 August. Lucy observed:

> The most striking thing about the session is that it should have closed today. There
> are few members among the crowd who met in February who would have put their

[53] Cab. 41/30, No. 28, B. to the King, 19 July 1905.
[54] Ibid., No. 29, 25 July.
[55] Ibid., No. 32, 8 Aug. 1905.

money on the duration of the session to such a date . . . That what is deemed the impossible should have happened is due directly and solely to the stubborn will of one man. None but Mr. Arthur Balfour would have carried the Government through the past session and, it may be added, in the peculiar circumstances of the case, none other would have desired to prolong its life . . .

It must be admitted that up till May 1903, he trod the primrose path of Premiership. Popular in the country and the House, facing a disorganised Opposition with well disciplined phalanx, he was autocrat of the position. The starting of the Fiscal Reform campaign changed the face of all things. Surveying a suddenly riven party, he set himself the task of preventing widening the fissure. Whether the course he adopted was the wisest is not here discussed. Once taken, it has been followed with a dexterity and resource illimitable in their range, unfailing in their fertility . . .

He has answered at question time, made speeches in successive debates, and never committed himself by an embarrassing admission. That may not be the highest form of statesmanship. As an intellectual feat it is unparalleled. [56]

But such parliamentary effort, together with sustained administrative work, had taken their toll. 'The incessant labour of official life, the constant worry of the leadership' had 'during the last six weeks obviously told upon the Premier's light heart and dauntless courage'. [57]

On 10 August, the day before the ending of the parliamentary session, Balfour had been furnished with a memorandum nominally written by Acland Hood, the Chief Whip, but apparently attributable to Sandars, giving arguments for and against an autumn election—the alternative being to hang on till Parliament met in the New Year. [58] At this stage, Balfour accepted the disinclination of the rank and file of the party to face an early election. The Opposition's campaign to keep public opinion incensed 'with their stories of the horrors of Chinese labour' (dating from the Government's acceptance of Milner's insistent suggestion in 1903) [59] was, said the memo, draining away Liberal party funds and should be allowed to continue. It was believed by some Unionists that the prejudice against Chinese labour was already rapidly subsiding 'in consequence of the undoubted success of that experiment in South Africa'—though a devastating Milnerite shock was about to demolish these hopes. It was also argued that, 'though it cannot be contended that the Education Act is popular, the opposition to it in many parts of the country is undoubtedly

---

[56] *Balfourian Parliament*, pp. 408–11, 11 Aug. 1905.
[57] Ibid., p. 411.
[58] Cab. 37/79/145. See Sandars P., C.750, ff. 62–5, for a print of this memo endorsed 'Written by me for Sir A. Acland Hood. J.S.S.'
[59] See Cab. 41/28, Nos. 21, 23 of 16, 27 Nov. 1903.

much less acute than it was.' This assessment was probably accurate. But the Act had done its work in rallying the Liberal Party both before and after Tariff Reform had burst upon the political scene.[60]

However, as the memorandum of 10 August claimed, the Unionists had 'a very creditable record in respect of the management of foreign affairs, including the conclusion of a popular alliance with the Japanese'. After some six weeks recuperation at Whittingehame, Balfour asked Sandars for his opinion of 'a plan of action' which had 'occurred' to him.

We have now [wrote Balfour] been in office ten years. In my opinion, our record in all the great departments of legislation and administration is a good one. But it is never considered *as a whole*, and public attention is entirely occupied with some momentary sub-issue of the perennial political controversy. What I should rather like to do, if it were thought practical, is to devote each of a series of speeches to one phase of our governmental activity—Ireland, Foreign Affairs, Colonial Policy, Education, National Defence, Social Reform, would be the great natural compartments into which the subject might be divided, and one, or at most two, of these topics would supply material for a speech. There are two objections to the idea. One is that more trouble will be required to look up the subject than is usually necessary when we are only dealing with contemporary incidents: the other is that the great audiences which I am obliged to address might think anything in the nature of a historical retrospect dull, and not sufficiently relevant to present issues . . .[61]

Sandars thought it would be very difficult to make such a survey 'sufficiently attractive from the platform' but that it was not beyond Balfour's capability.[62] However, Balfour evidently decided to wait until the Conservative Party Conference, to be held at Newcastle in November, to make a last supreme appeal to the Government's record and to rally the dissident semi-faithful. But it comes as a surprise that his list of *electorally useful* achievements should have passed beyond Ireland, Foreign Affairs, Education, and National Defence to Colonial Policy and, least credible of all, Social Reform.

Whatever might have been claimed for the Government's record in South Africa had already been undermined by what Balfour saw as 'the quite inexplicable illegality of which Milner seems to have been guilty, in permitting, before he left, overseers in the [South African] mines to inflict corporal punishment'. Balfour was not mistaken in deeming this embellishment of the Chinese Labour theme the 'worst rock ahead, from a purely

---

[60] Cab. 37/79/145, memo by Acland Hood; A. K. Russell, *Liberal Landslide*, Newton Abbot, 1973, pp. 104–8, 192, 196–8.
[61] B.P. 49763, ff. 227–9, 27 Sept. 1905.
[62] Ibid., ff. 230–4, 30 Sept. 1905.

electioneering point of view'. (Of course, he had not yet despaired of restoring unity on the fiscal question.) Milner's act was, he thought, an 'amazing blunder, which seems to violate every canon of international morality, of law, and of policy.'[63]

As for social reform, there must inevitably be a feeling that the Government should have passed a moderate, but tangible, amendment of the law relating to trades disputes as established by the Taff Vale judgement. The consequence of that judgement was payment by the railwaymen's union, in 1903, of £23,000 in damages and costs. This had such a galvanizing effect on the trade union movement and its support for the incipient Labour Party that the upshot was the far-reaching Trades Disputes Act, passed by the Liberals in 1906 and regretted by business interests and conservative politicians ever since. However, to be fair to Balfour (who is commonly accused of being exceptionally blind to all social trends) the Liberals in the Commons, for their part, advocated a very moderate approach to the question from 1903 to 1905—and were just as astonished by the extent of the electoral landslide of 1906 as were the Unionists.[64]

The course of the general election of 1906 leaves an impression that the Unionists might have benefited by having no social policies at all. Labour and the trade unions were so far prejudiced against the Unionists by the threat of food taxes and so disappointed about employment opportunities in South Africa, promised by the Government early in the War but denied by its approval of 'Chinese slavery', that reasoned defence by Balfour and others of the Government's record merely presented critics with an unmissable target.[65] Indeed, Balfour's cabinet letters from 1903 to 1905 show that he was not insensitive to the political importance of working-class opinion.

On 19 April 1904 Balfour consulted the Cabinet about the proper response to a Labour-sponsored Trade Union Bill. This bill, he wrote to the King, sought to render 'what it terms "peaceful picketing" legal; and it desires to prevent Trades Union Funds being liable for the improper action of Trades Union Officials.'

On the first of these points it has to be observed that 'peaceful picketing' is, or may be, a most serious form of intimidation: and, as such, can scarcely be permitted unless surrounded by precautions which the bill does not contain. As regards Trades Union Funds, it may be perfectly right that the portion of those funds which is

[63] Bodl., MS Selborne 1, ff. 66–7, B. to Selborne, 21 Sept. 1905.
[64] See Henry Pelling, *Popular Politics and Society in late Victorian Britain*, London, 2nd edn., 1979, pp. 76–9.
[65] See A. K. Russell, *Liberal Landslide*, for B.'s courageous but ill-fated speeches in Jan. 1906.

devoted to charitable purposes (pensions and so forth) should not be liable to seizure; but it can hardly be right that the funds employed in promoting strikes should possess privileges which *no other corporate funds in the Kingdom* are allowed to enjoy.

But the electoral importance of the issue by no means escaped the Cabinet, as the rest of Balfour's letter shows. In Balfour's opinion the bill 'ought not to pass'. But unfortunately 'it seems impossible to defeat its second reading next Friday. Members are afraid of the Trades Union element in their constituencies; they are tolerably confident that even if the second reading is passed, the bill can never become law in the course of the session; and they will abstain from voting, or vote wrong. In the circumstances Mr. Balfour does not propose to make the subject a government matter—but himself to vote and perhaps speak against the measure'.[66]

However, by 11 November, the problem had not receded. The Cabinet again discussed 'certain demands for legislation made by the Trades Unions in this country'. Complications stemmed from 'the fact that the House of Lords, acting as a Court of Appeal has made one or two decisions which, though excellent law and excellent sense, are very distasteful to the trades unions'. Balfour referred specifically to 'the "Taff Vale" decision' which

simply puts the Trades unions in the same position as every other Company or corporate body, such as a Railway or a Bank, and makes them subject to the ordinary law of the land. Mr. Balfour has no doubt that this is in substance right, and that the singular freedom of the Country from unnecessary trade disputes is largely owing to it. Nevertheless, from a purely electoral point of view, it will no doubt put those Members of the Unionist Party who have a large trades union element in their constituencies (as Mr. Balfour himself has) in a considerable difficulty, and may lose them many votes. The Cabinet were very clearly of opinion that, in spite of electoral considerations, it was our duty in the interests of the country at large to resist any demands which we conceive to be contrary to justice and sound policy.[67]

So the case could hardly be more clearly stated. Balfour was by no means unaware of the political hazards involved in this area. In March 1905 he felt constrained to allow a free vote on the principle of non-liability and the second reading of a Labour-inspired bill was actually passed; but no statute resulted. Meanwhile, more positive action was taken on the other issue of great concern to the unions, namely measures to relieve unemployment.

[66] Cab. 41/29, No. 12, n.d., but copy in Bodl., Sandars P., C.716, is dated 19 April 1904.
[67] Ibid., No. 37, B. to the King, 12 Nov. 1904.

Acting, as always, on the assumption of strict economy on the part of central government, Balfour here pursued a two-pronged strategy. On the one hand, an 'Unemployed Bill' was promoted, first under the auspices of Walter Long and then of Balfour's brother, Gerald, who took over at the Local Government Board when Long succeeded Wyndham as Chief Secretary for Ireland in March 1905. On the other hand, in the matter of alien immigration, there was no financial objection in the way of complying with demands for restrictions made by the Trade Union Congress from 1892 onwards. It was the number of Jews coming in from Russia and Poland that made an impact on employment, especially in the East End of London, and also aroused a degree of anti-Semitism. At the 'khaki' elections of 1900 promises of legislation to restrict immigration did no harm to the fortunes of Unionist candidates in the East End. [68] A Royal Commission was appointed after the war and reported in 1903. When the Cabinet discussed the proposed bill in November, Balfour thought the subject 'full of difficulty'. The bill failed in 1904; but, after redrafting, passed as the Aliens Act in 1905. Not only was the labour market protected, but also the ratepayer—in so far as immigrants had now to prove that they could support themselves. [69]

As far as the direct relief of unemployment was concerned, recognition of the need for government action was growing in the country at large. But the Unionist alarm—on electoral grounds—which has been noticed in the areas of trade union legislation and alien immigration, did not obtrude here. Balfour and the Cabinet were concerned that the system might be abused and that the relevant distress committees might constitute a threat to the ratepayer. On 28 February 1905:

> The cabinet discussed this long and anxiously. There can be no doubt [wrote Balfour to the King] that if the machinery which is now at work in London could be rendered permanent, and could be trusted to deal in the future with each separate case of the 'unemployed' with the severe yet kindly conscientiousness which they have hitherto displayed, that much good would be done, and many persons who would otherwise sink into pauperism and become a charge on the rates, might be enabled to tide over the season of commercial depression and wait for better times. But, on the other hand, it would be a social calamity if these labour committees were to make such use of the penny rate, placed by the draft bill at their disposal, as to create a new class of semi-paupers (so to speak)—i.e. of labourers who got employment in the ordinary way during the summer months, and each recurring winter claimed from the local authority to be provided with work out of public

---

[68] Pelling, p. 94.
[69] Elie Halévy, *Imperialism and the Rise of Labour*, London (1961 edn), v, 371–5; Cab. 41/28, Nos. 22, 25 of 20 Nov., 4 Dec. 1903.

funds. These persons would have the privileges of pauperism, while retaining the full rights of citizenship—they would even have votes for the municipal authorities on whose favour they partially subsisted . . . Mr. Long promised to reconsider the bill with Mr. Balfour, and see if anything could be done to guard against the abuse of the new powers he proposed to call into existence. [70]

The result was that, very late in the session, what Balfour called 'a "machinery" bill' was devised, empowering the Government to set up committees in the large provincial towns to find work for the unemployed. To get the measure on to the Statute Book it was decided 'to cut out of it everything which involved the payment of wages out of rates'. [71] However, on 6 November, a cheerless encounter between Balfour and a delegation of unemployed, duly publicized in the *Labour Leader*, indicated that the working-class electorate derived little joy from the Government's economical approach. [72] No more effective, from an electoral viewpoint, was the Cabinet's decision to set up a Royal Commission on the whole contentious question of the Poor Law and the relief of distress caused by unemployment. [73] The selection of the commissioners was the 'subject of most anxious deliberations' in the Cabinet on 23 June 1905. 'It is certain', Balfour commented, 'that every name selected will be scanned with malevolent criticism.' [74] In the event, the eighteen commissioners represented a variety of views, mainly conservative, but were well qualified by experience and ability, including Beatrice Webb of the notable Minority Report eventually issued in 1909. The tactful, but hardly expert, Lord George Hamilton afterwards wondered why he was ever chosen as Chairman. [75] The answer is that Gerald Balfour considered the possibility of Rosebery; that Sandars thought Rosebery would 'get out of it before the Commission' finished its work and represented to the Prime Minister that 'George Hamilton' should 'earn his first class pension' as an ex-Secretary for India; that Balfour decided first to ask Devonshire (with whom he was trying to mend fences before the election) though expecting him to refuse; and that he then duly turned to Hamilton. [76]

It should be added here that, apart from the Education Act of 1902, Balfour had personally, while Prime Minister, made a substantial contribution in a quite different area of domestic reform. This was in licensing.

[70]   Cab. 41/30, No. 5, B. to the King, 28 Feb. 1905.
[71]   Ibid., No. 30, 1 August 1905.
[72]   Russell, p. 31.
[73]   See Michael E. Rose, *The Relief of Poverty 1834–1914*, 1972, pp. 43–4.
[74]   Cab. 41/30, No. 24.
[75]   Maurice Bruce, *The Coming of the Welfare State*, 4th edn., 1968, pp. 200–2.
[76]   B.P. 49764, ff. 21–7, Sandars to B., 9 Oct. and ff. 31–8, B. to Sandars, 10 Oct. 1905.

Drunkenness had been recognized as a major social problem during the later Victorian period and the Royal Commission on the Licensing Laws had reported in 1899 in favour of a big cut in the number of public house licences. The recommendation that compensation should be found by the trade rather than the taxpayer was in line with Unionist—and Balfour's— thinking. [77] The measure led to drafting difficulties which apparently proved too much for Balfour's colleagues on the relevant cabinet committee. This sad state of affairs may be glimpsed in Balfour's cabinet letter of 4 December 1903; [78] and Austen Chamberlain, a member of the said cabinet committee, has testified to the fact that Balfour's draft was quite unlike that of the committee and was entirely his own work. He has also praised it for providing an Act (of 1904) that worked well in practice for many years. [79] Sandars believed that the Bill 'would have stood but poor chance of life had it not been carefully nursed through the House of Commons by the Prime Minister'. [80] But, like Balfour's other constructive work, the measure conferred scant electoral benefit. [81]

As November of 1905 and the Party Conference approached, Balfour wrote at length to the Duke of Devonshire in an eleventh-hour attempt to recruit him to the cause of party unity. Taking the ex-minister Lord James of Hereford as an example of one who 'regards himself as a Free Trader first, and as Unionist second', Balfour tried to persuade the ageing Duke not to conform with so misguided an example.

Every school among the political prophets seems to agree that the Unionists are to be defeated. Is it wise for any Unionist, whatever his views on the Fiscal Question, to contribute to that defeat? No doubt the precise dangers which we have to face in a Radical Administration are still partially hid from us because they have announced no programme, and are apparently incapable of agreeing upon one . . . Nevertheless, it seems plain that with the Irish in undiminished strength, with the Welsh acting as a more or less independent party, with 40 Labour Members constituting a separate and powerful organisation, a Radical Administration will be forced to conciliate one section of its supporters after another by legislative projects of the most dangerous description. The unjust increase of direct taxation, the taxation of ground rents, a perilous diminution of our military strength, payment of Members, Home Rule all round, Welsh Disestablishment, and so forth, are all evils which we

---

[77] Donald Read, *England 1868–1914*, London, 1979, pp. 110–12.

[78] Cab. 41/28, No. 25.

[79] Sir Austen Chamberlain, *Down the Years*, London, 1935, p. 209. See B.P. 49762, ff. 35–6, 17 Jan. 1904, for some of B.'s cogitations about how to outmanœuvre temperance critics.

[80] Sandars P., C.771.

[81] See Russell, pp. 30, 183, on licensing at the 1906 elections.

must contemplate as within the region of practical politics . . . It is for these reasons that I venture, though with much diffidence, to express the hope that any economy campaign [against Chamberlain] which you may think necessary . . . shall . . . do as little damage to Unionism as possible. [82]

This forecast proved remarkably accurate in some respects; and it was indeed on a basis of 'anti-socialism' that Balfour was able to restore a semblance of cohesion to his party by 1909. But his appeal failed utterly of its immediate purpose. The Duke's aloofness during the elections seems to have swayed many middle- and upper-class voters against the Unionists. [83]

Although Balfour may well have hoped, till the end of October, at least to deny the Liberals an over-all majority, his position swiftly deteriorated in November. On the 1st, Londonderry, speaking at Sunderland, deplored the divisive effect on Unionism of the Tariff Reform movement. [84] Chamberlain at once launched a scathing public counter-attack and Austen duly remonstrated privately with Balfour. [85] 'But the Prime Minister's ingenuity' once more proved 'equal to reconciling the irreconcilable'. As FitzRoy recorded on the 8th, after a stressful cabinet meeting the episode ended with ministers 'content to remain bound in the gossamer web of their chief's dexterities'. [86]

Having rejected a last-minute plea from his brother Gerald that he should accept a low general tariff 'levied in the first instance for revenue purposes'—'should I not go very near to Joe's methods of bribing each class of the community in turn?' [87]—Balfour made his final appeal for unity at Newcastle on 14 November to a Conference that had already endorsed Chamberlain's policies. The Tariff Reform resolution had been moved by Chaplin in the afternoon, while Balfour was getting ready to go from Alnwick Castle by train to Newcastle, with Earl Percy and Lady Betty Balfour, to deliver his culminating addresses in the evening. If Chaplin had been robbed of his triumph at Southampton the previous October, his success at Newcastle was complete. Not only was his own resolution carried almost unanimously. A Balfourite amendment, based on the premier's 'half sheet of notepaper', was specifically and overwhelmingly rejected. Small wonder that Joseph Chamberlain, the former hammer of the landed classes, achieved unique intimacy henceforth with the man symbolically known as 'the Squire'. From now on, they were 'Joe' and 'Harry'

[82] WHI/108, 27 Oct. 1905 (copy).
[83] Rempel, p. 165; Russell, p. 176.
[84] *The Times*, 2 Nov. 1905.
[85] B.P. 49735, ff. 203–6, 3 Nov. 1905.
[86] FitzRoy, p. 267; B.P. 49735, f. 207, B. to A. Chamberlain, 3 Nov. 1905.
[87] WHI/117, Gerald B. to Goschen, 9 Nov. (copy).; WHI/108, B. to Gerald B., 10 Nov. 1905.

for purposes of political correspondence.[88] If fiscal Balfourites, to say nothing of Unionist Free Traders, now faced deep disaster in the coming elections, the Tariff Reformers could expect to hold a fair number of seats on a programme clearly differing from that of the Liberals. Therefore, after the elections, Balfour would evidently have to conform with the wishes of the prospective Chamberlainite majority in the Unionist parliamentary party. Or so it seemed to Tariff Reformers.

However, there was no sign of defeatism on Balfour's own part up to and including delivery of his own speeches. That morning (Tuesday the 14th) *The Times* indicated that the speeches had 'been looked forward to with a good deal of curiosity' and commented that there were 'no signs that the country hails the advent of a Liberal Ministry with enthusiasm'. However, the paper noted that Colonel Haig had just succeeded (the disappointing) 'Captain Wells in the difficult post of Chief Agent' and that the organization, like the party as a whole, needed the inspiration of Tariff Reform.

On arriving at the Conservative Club, Balfour said that their opponents had in the past proffered 'showy schemes of social reform' but that 'the more the public get to see upon whom they have to rely for the steady maintenance' of British 'foreign policy (loud cheers) and for steady progress—the steady but not rash or futile progress—of social reform', the more they would trust the Conservatives.

After dinner, he went to address three thousand people at Olympia and was accorded 'a splendid reception'. Having there delivered his major speech, he went on to an overflow meeting at the Drill Hall. Here he passed his major points more briefly in review. The Liberals had made 'obscure and shallowy suggestions' entailing higher government expenditure. He quite agreed with opponents of high taxation that since 1895 the country's spending on the Army, Navy, and education 'had increased in an enormous manner'. However, it was known that military expenditure was largely determined by Lord Kitchener's needs in India. Moreover, by redistribution of the fleets and 'abolition' of vessels 'useless in a great war with a great navy', the Government had both reduced the cost and raised the efficiency of the Navy in an unprecedented fashion. Could expenditure now be cut in any of these three spheres? The Liberal proposals for education would 'throw an even heavier burden upon the ratepayers in country and town, an even heavier burden than that which has already assumed proportions which I quite admit are of a most serious character'. So he returned to his original theme. In the electoral struggle before them he called upon

[88] *The Times*, 15 Nov. 1905, pp. 6 and 9; Amery, vi, 752–3.

Unionists to unite and to exercise 'the common sense, the courage, and patriotism to sink minor and insignificant differences and opinions' in the face of a threat to valuable policies.[89]

It seems that on the following Saturday, 18 November, Balfour travelled by train to Windsor in the same compartment as Chamberlain and his wife, and that he was at least provisionally persuaded of the need to dissolve or resign at an early date.[90] However, Chamberlain was taking no chances. At Bristol on Tuesday, 21 November, he delivered a direct attack on Balfour's handling of the fiscal question.[91] The following day, Sandars drew up a memorandum for Balfour in which he concluded that all hope of reuniting the Party on the Prime Minister's speech at Newcastle had 'been completely shattered' by Chamberlain at Bristol. If Balfour decided to meet Parliament in the New Year, he faced the 'disastrous' possibility of falling on a Liberal amendment 'skilfully' insinuating a Unionist 'desire to tax the food of the people'. Sandars therefore came down on the side of early resignation: 'Nothing is more calculated to restore harmony in our ranks than the presence in office of a Government whose whole career will promise to be the very opposite of that which will command the approval of our Party.'[92]

However, Balfour's cabinet letter of 24 November shows that his colleagues 'were greatly divided in their opinions'; but he himself was inclining 'to the resignation alternative', in part because it would 'enable the Radical Ministers to make some acquaintance with their offices and with pending questions of public policy before enunciating their programme'. Yet he was still 'carefully watching the trend of public opinion, and endeavouring to estimate the degree of success which his appeal for unity at Newcastle was likely to meet among his supporters. At present', he remarked, 'the success seems but moderate!'[93]

In view of the extraordinary Liberal renaissance and Unionist defeat registered at the coming elections, it is not without interest to try to date Balfour's actual decision to resign in relation to Rosebery's speech against Home Rule for Ireland delivered at Bodmin on Saturday, 25 November. Campbell-Bannerman had announced on the 23rd that his party would move step by step towards Home Rule. Rosebery, unaware that Asquith and the other leading Liberal Imperialists had come to a private accommodation with Campbell-Bannerman, denounced the party leader's speech. As

[89] *The Times*, 15 Nov. 1905, p. 6.
[90] Amery, vi, 755; Cab. 41/30, No. 33, 23 Nov.
[91] Amery, vi, 756–60.
[92] B.P. 49764, ff. 109–14, memo by Sandars, n.d., but 22 Nov. 1905 on clear internal evidence.
[93] Cab. 41/30, No. 33, B. to the King, 24 Nov. 1905.

Julian Amery has shown, Balfour finally decided by 28 to 30 November to override dissension in the Cabinet and resign on Monday, 4 December. The signs are there that Balfour must have hoped for more of a Liberal Imperialist revolt than in fact occurred.[94] But on Saturday, 25 November, before he could have known of Rosebery's speech, he had compiled a substantial paper for the Cabinet which shows that his determination to resign had already hardened considerably. The only trace of continued inclination to delay his decision occurs three-quarters of the way through his lengthy argument for 'a resignation in December':

> I have made an appeal at Newcastle for that enthusiastic party unity without which the Parliamentary embarrassments of next Session cannot possibly be surmounted. By all means let us suspend judgement until we can fully judge of its effects. What has subsequently occurred, still more what has subsequently *not* occurred, does not leave me hopeful. The utmost that I now dare expect is that my exhortation may improve our prospects at a General Election. That it will renew the youth of a Parliamentary party [still in office] seems beyond expectation. But let us by all means wait a little and see. If, however, I be right in my unfavourable forecast, is not the most obviously 'straightforward' course to resign place, which has ceased to be power, in time to allow the other side to form their Government, to become acquainted with their various offices, and agree, if they can, upon a policy?

Even in this passage, Balfour's own impatience for agreement in favour of resignation is surely apparent.[95]

The story of Balfour's last days as Prime Minister may be left to Esher. Esher's original journal includes some interesting details, especially regarding Sandars, which were understandably excluded from the published version. On Friday, 1 December:

> I went early to Sandars' house, and drove him to Downing St. I told him that I had spoken to the P.M. about him, and was quite frank about what had been said on both sides.
>
> On arriving in Downing St., I saw A.J.B., who was not dressed, and talked to him while he finished his toilet. There was a Cabinet at 12. He will ask the King to make S. a Peer, and he will put it on the footing of a Life Peerage, as S. has no children. In this way he hopes to get over the bogey of a 'precedent'.
>
> The P.M. was in excellent spirits, and determined to hold his own at the Cabinet. Walter Long is the only man, who matters, who is violently opposed to resignation. [Long wanted time to reassure the Ulster Loyalists who feared a resurgence of Home Rule.]

---

[94] Amery, vi, 760–2.
[95] Cab. 37/81/175, memo by B., 25 Nov. 1905, 6 pp.

At the last moment, the P.M. spoke to me about Lord Roberts' retirement from the Defence Committee, and my going on it. I stuck out for Sir John French, on the ground that it would strengthen the Committee, and that I, alone, was no substitute for Bobs.

The King, who was asked, has agreed . . .[96]

The rest of the entry refers to Balfour's 'talks with Asquith' and strongly implies that the Prime Minister knew the drift of events in the Liberal camp—that it would not be split by Rosebery.

Finally on Monday, 4 December Esher noted:

The King arrived this afternoon, and the Prime Minister drove up to the Palace within a few minutes. He was with the King a quarter of an hour, and then came down into Knollys' room. He seemed a little moved, which was not strange, on relinquishing his great Office, but his spirits revived almost immediately.

A.J.B. and I then drove, in his motor, to Downing St. We went in at the garden entrance. Alfred Lyttleton came into his room, and Jack Sandars [who became a P.C.—not a peer], but no one else. And so he ceases to be Prime Minister.[97]

[96] E.P. 2/10. Cf. Esher, ii, 121. From 1904 Roberts, though no longer Commander-in-Chief, had continued to attend the C.I.D. when invited. After 1905, Esher and French were in a similar position. They were 'permanent' in the sense that they were continuously eligible to be summoned, irrespective of any official post they might hold.

[97] E.P. 2/10. Cf. Esher, ii, 122–3.

11

The Toils of Opposition

1906–1911

IN the general election of 1906, polling began on 13 January. Balfour soon heard that he had lost his seat at Manchester but he continued to speak on behalf of other candidates. Meanwhile, when answering various letters of sympathy on the 17th, he recognized the advent of a significant Parliamentary Labour Party as the start of a new era in British politics. Responding to Austen Chamberlain, he played down the Tariff Reform versus Free Trade issue. To him it seemed 'quite obvious' that

we are dealing with forces not called into being by any of the subjects about which parties have been recently squabbling, but rather due to a general movement of which we see the more violent manifestation in continental politics, and I cannot help fearing, therefore, that the new Labour issue may carry away seats in the Midlands which, under other circumstances, would have been practically safe . . . [However it] will end, I think in the break-up of the Liberal Party . . . [1]

Indeed, Dr Russell has concluded that the last great Liberal victory resulted from a confluence of developments, such as 'the climax of the movement of opinion against imperialism, the development of the movement for social reform, the Ulster revolt against Irish reformism', as well as the commonly cited cries such as the 'big loaf' and 'Chinese labour' which, with Nonconformist agitation against Balfour's Education Act, put heart into the Liberal Party and its organization. [2] For Balfour, Sandars thus listed the causes of the defeat:

1. The Pendulum with its doubly-strong swing—i.e. arrested in 1900 only to come back the harder.
2. Chinese Labour—as potent in the country as in town.
3. The organisation of labour and the socialist vote.
4. Nonconformist activity over Education. [3]

Only 157 Unionists were returned to the Commons, despite an increase

[1] B.P. 49735, f. 216–17, B. to Austen Chamberlain, 17 Jan. 1906.
[2] Russell, p. 206.
[3] B.P. 49764, ff. 143–8, Sandars to B., 21 Jan. 1906.

of more than a third in the total Unionist vote since 1900. The Liberals had won 377 seats. Labour had 53, counting Lib-Labs., and the Irish Nationalists numbered 83. So Ulster Protestants breathed again. At the same time, Balfour was robbed of a half-expected opportunity to rally his decimated party against Home Rule.

Balfour was therefore faced with the problem of reasserting his leadership of the Unionists. Not only had he lost his own seat while both Chamberlains had won theirs, but there was now a majority of Tariff Reformers in the parliamentary party. However, most Unionist members still sought 'to be as Balfourite as they could' and varied right down the line in the strength of their commitment to Tariff Reform. The Free Traders had plummeted to only about a dozen.[4]

While arrangements were being made for Balfour to find a seat in the City, Joseph Chamberlain wanted a party meeting at which Balfour would be constrained to declare conclusively for Tariff Reform. Meanwhile, Lansdowne was emerging as something of a key figure on the Unionist scene. He had been the Unionist leader in the Lords since 1903. Now, the huge Unionist majority in that House enhanced his standing in the party as a whole. By 28 January he was taking the initiative with Balfour in a way which he had not done previously. Although a Liberal Unionist, he was concerned that Chamberlain should be effectively subordinated to Balfour. No commitment to protection should be incurred.[5] After Chamberlain had extracted from Balfour his 'Valentine' letter of 14 February—which hinted beguilingly at the possibility of a non-protective general tariff—it was at Lansdowne House that the party meeting was held. Although the Tariff Reformers were jubilant, they had really gained little of substance from Balfour. As Chamberlain knew, Conservatives still preferred Balfour to him as leader because he stood for traditional values.[6]

Still, Balfour's fortunes had reached a low ebb. When Parliament opened on 19 February Chamberlain—inevitably—deputized as Leader of the Opposition and gave the Unionists a taste of the aggressive stance to be expected of him. On 27 February Balfour was duly returned for the City; but that very day, both he and Chamberlain went down with influenza and the leadership went into commission until mid-March. When Balfour then reappeared in the Commons, he seemed to the mass of his newly-elected opponents something of a futile anachronism, with his subtle evasions on

---

[4] Sykes, p. 100.

[5] B.P. 49729, ff. 208–11, Lansdowne to B., 28 Jan. 1906.

[6] Sykes, pp. 101–12; Amery, vi, 796–851; Lord Newton, *Lord Lansdowne*, London, 1929, pp. 348–52.

the question of tariffs. A few months before, he had been deemed the greatest parliamentarian of the day. Now he could scarcely gain a hearing. Yet, imperturbable and unshaken, he had by the end of the year regained, in Austen Chamberlain's opinion, the respect of all his opponents.[7]

Meanwhile, there remained a good deal of dissatisfaction among Unionists with Balfour's leadership of the party (still encompassing Liberal Unionists with their own organization as well as Conservatives). But the position was, and remained, that no successor to him could be discerned. In this regard, he was further safeguarded by the stroke which felled Joseph Chamberlain on 11 July 1906. The admirable Mrs Chamberlain managed to conceal the nature of this calamity in the hope of a material recovery; but by October the truth—that Chamberlain was finished as an active politician—was known in parliamentary circles.[8]

While there was widespread anticipation of conflict between the great Unionist majority in the Lords and the big over-all Liberal majority in the Commons, it was Lansdowne who proposed on 5 April that some machinery should be established for co-ordinating the attacks of the two Opposition front benches on the more radical or partisan legislation emanating from Campbell-Bannerman's Government.[9] In his reply of the 13th Balfour agreed with the proposed strategy. He assumed that moderate members of the Cabinet would expect the House of Lords to excise extreme proposals from Liberal bills, while the more radical members would be pleased to accumulate a case for modifying 'the constitution' of the Lords which could in due course be put before the electorate. In making this crucial assumption, he evidently believed in the existence of an agreed Liberal strategy along these lines. He wrote: 'This scheme is an ingenious one, and it will be our business to defeat it, as far as we can.' While tactics would have to be left flexible, he thought that Unionists should 'fight all points of importance very stiffly in the Commons, and should make the House of Lords the theatre of compromise'.[10] It will be appreciated that Balfour's assumption about Liberal strategy fortified his own subjective moral position—otherwise open to charges of grave inconsistency in a self-declared House of Commons man.

Certainly, up to 1908, these Balfour—Lansdowne tactics enjoyed considerable success. The (Nonconformist) Education Bill of 1906 was, in

[7] Chamberlain, *Down the Years*, p. 216; Amery, vi, 855–61; Lucy Masterman, *C.F.G. Masterman*, London, 1939, p. 72.
[8] Amery, vi, 908–11; FitzRoy, p. 300 [19 Oct. 1906].
[9] Newton, p. 353.
[10] B.P. 49729, ff. 228–30, B. to Lansdowne, 13 Apr. 1906.

accordance with Balfour's detailed recommendations, subjected to such amendment in the Lords that it was abandoned by the Government in December. Having something of a fresh mandate for the measure, Campbell-Bannerman might perhaps have dissolved there and then; but he did no more than protest against such flouting of the electoral will.[11] However, the inadequacy of such a Lords-based strategy for fulfilling the aims of the Opposition in the House of Commons is apparent in the case of the Trades Disputes Act. Although Campbell-Bannerman had, as early as 30 March, declared for the immunity of trade union funds on the thorough-going lines demanded by Labour, and although this conflicted sharply with Balfour's previous attitudes as well as those of Asquith and many Liberals (thereby lending plausibility to Balfour's dubious assumption of 13 April), the Bill passed through the Commons virtually unopposed. On 3 December Lansdowne pointed out to the Lords the danger of blocking so popular a measure in the upper house, though he also saw the Bill as 'conferring excessive privileges upon the Trade Unions'—'privileges fraught with danger to the community and likely to embitter the industrial life' of the country.

However, although the Government passed a fair amount of useful legislation during the years 1906 to 1908, including the Old Age Pensions Act, it suffered cumulative frustration from the Balfour–Lansdowne system. In 1906 a Plural Voting Bill suffered outright rejection by the Lords. In 1907 attrition in Commons and Lords combined to scupper five out of nine prospective major measures.[12] Campbell-Bannerman, meantime, refused to be side-tracked by proposals to reform the composition of the Lords or to provide for joint sittings of the two Houses. In June 1907, he passed a resolution in favour of limiting the Lords' power to veto a bill to less than the life of a Parliament. During 1908 five bills fell by the wayside, though seven (including Old Age Pensions) went through.[13]

Meanwhile, the preoccupation of his party with the divisive Tariff Reform issue was giving Balfour much food for thought. Even before Joseph Chamberlain's retirement from the fray had been confirmed Balfour told Beatrice Webb that he was thinking of writing a treatise on economics.[14] He also began in December 1906, to discuss the question of fiscal reform with Professor W. A. S. Hewins, an economist, who had, since 1903, devoted himself to the role of Secretary of Chamberlain's Tariff

---

[11] Roy Jenkins, *Mr. Balfour's Poodle*, London, 1968, pp. 37–45.
[12] Peter Rowland, *The Last Liberal Governments (1905–1910)*, London, 1968, p. 122.
[13] Ibid., p. 166.
[14] *Our Partnership*, p. 354, 16 Sept. 1906.

Commission. Balfour seems never to have revealed to his political intimates the fact that he worked on his economic treatise, off and on, from 1907 to 1928—a period extending beyond the limits of his fully active political life. [15] Parallel with his interviews and correspondence with Hewins during 1907–8, [16] Balfour moved closer to a Tariff Reform position and the Tariff Reformers moved closer to him. Now that the Reformers had effectively lost Joseph Chamberlain, they were ready to come to terms with Balfour. Against a background of economic recession, Tariff Reformers argued that protection would save jobs. Balfour, though not going as far as that, was by November 1907 promising to impose duties to increase revenue. This meant that he could, at last, be fairly dubbed a Tariff Reformer, though a very moderate representative of that species. He rightly emphasized that the future well-being of the community depended on productivity rather than on distribution of income. But his ideas of how better to attain such basic objectives did not advance beyond the protection of private property. However, in view of growing socialistic manifestations (such as the independent socialist Grayson's by-election victory over Liberal and Conservative opposition at Colne Valley), the defence of private property, for Balfour's party-political purposes, was enough. [17] But the need for additional revenue supervened with more of a bang than politicians on either side of the Commons had anticipated.

As mentioned earlier, Balfour's authority in defence matters had been recognized when the Government invited him to give evidence, in May 1908, at the invasion inquiry of the C.I.D. (see pp. 172, 189). In March he had queried the adequacy of the Navy Estimates in the face of a possible acceleration of the German dreadnought programme. Asquith (deputizing for the ailing Campbell-Bannerman) reasserted the Two-Power Standard

---

[15] See B.P. 49945–56, consisting of 12 bundles of manuscript and typescript. Bundles 1–10 (B.P. 49945–54) apparently belong to 1907–14. The last of those bundles consists of 182 pp. of proofs and a note by Short refers to 'the bound (book) proof' (49954, f. 1). The text is entirely theoretical and concerns the interrelations of productive 'groups'. The terms Land, Labour, and Capital receive sophisticated attention. B.P. 49955–56 show that B. worked, from Oct. 1926 till Feb. 1928, to complete an essay of some 10,000 words, largely extracted from the pre-war 'book'. It was, however, never finished. B.P. 49955 shows that Balfour was inclined to make comparisons with a communist economy. Otherwise, his discussion is entirely in terms of free enterprise. J. S. Mill is the classical economist most subjected to critical analysis.

[16] B.P. 49779 contains the correspondence which consists almost entirely of letters from Hewins. These arose from discussions with B. and contain comment from a Tariff Reformer's viewpoint on the changing financial and economic scene, 1907–11. The last of the few subsequent items is dated 29 Jan. 1917. See also W. A. S. Hewins, *The Apologia of an Imperialist*, London, 1929, 2 vols., i, 185–9, etc.

[17] See Sykes, Ch. 6.

and, for the moment, public confidence was restored. [18] But, as Balfour remarked to Hewins in June, 'the increasing tension' between Britain and Germany gave him 'profound anxiety'. [19] By March 1909, there was a first-class scare over a rumoured German acceleration—Liberal economies having cut the British lead too fine for comfort. Balfour, apart from genuine patriotic concern, must have seen some party advantage in emphasizing the situation, but he little knew where this short-term advantage would lead. For the unexpected need for money to build dreadnoughts was to combine with the under-estimated cost of Old Age Pensions.

On 29 April 1909, Lloyd George introduced his famous 'People's Budget' to meet the enhanced need for revenue. In due course, it was rejected by the Lords; two General Elections followed in 1910; the powers of the Lords were considerably reduced in 1911; and Balfour resigned from the leadership of the Unionist party. Moreover, the way was now open for a Home Rule bill to be passed. So why did Balfour consent to the Lords' fatal rejection of the budget?

A cogent analysis has recently clarified the reasons. [20] Towards the end of 1908 the Lords had rejected a Licensing Bill. Lloyd George envisaged turning the tables by taxing the trade in his next budget. Indeed, he was already seeing the budget as the engine of a grand design which would defeat the Balfour—Lansdowne strategy. He would show how additional revenue could be found without Tariff Reform, thus opening the way for further social reform, such as the projected national insurance scheme. At the same time, he could get round the Lords' veto on such Liberal issues as land valuation and licensing. [21] While the general tendency of the 'People's Budget' was to be redistributive on an unprecedented scale, it did not bear harshly on the lower reaches of the middle class. Therefore, it presented a comprehensive party-political challenge to the Unionists.

Although the land taxes were aimed specifically at the class which had assured Balfour of the succession to Salisbury as Unionist leader, he was at first (like Lansdowne) against rejection of the budget, unless a general and definite revulsion against it occurred. [22] But Lloyd George's Limehouse speech of 30 July transformed the whole picture. This demagogic masterpiece ridiculed the gentlemen of England, and especially the dukes, for demanding higher naval expenditure and then wanting the ordinary,

[18] Marder, *From the Dreadnought to Scapa Flow*, i, 139–40.
[19] B.P. 49779, f. 173, B. to Hewins, 17 June 1908.
[20] Bruce K. Murray, *The People's Budget 1909–10: Lloyd George and Liberal Politics*, Oxford, 1980.
[21] Ibid., pp. 108–10.
[22] Ibid., p. 109.

industrious people of the country to pay for it. The Balfour—Lansdowne strategy had aimed at a great electoral recovery; and this had seemed likely from the standpoint of 1908. Now, however, as J. L. Garvin (the editor of the *Observer* and a powerful proponent of Tariff Reform) was arguing by August 1909, the popular tide was running so strongly for the Liberals that capitulation in the House of Lords would presage electoral disaster. Further doses of redistributive taxation would follow and Unionist demoralization would be completed. Rejection, however, would hearten Unionists and, at the following election, up to 300 seats would be won, leaving the Irish holding the balance of power. The consequent Home Rule threat would be grist to the Unionist mill. Acland Hood, who was still the Unionist Chief Whip, also assumed rejection and emphasized the need to boost Tariff Reform as the answer to unemployment. Agents in the country, he reported, thought that tariffs should be everywhere promised as an alternative to the budget. [23]

By 13 August, Balfour had concluded that rejection was unavoidable. Continuing parliamentary discussion of the Finance Bill made it clear that the budget was intended to outmanoeuvre the Lords' inevitable opposition to land valuation. He saw the whole of the Unionist political position beginning to disintegrate. Lansdowne at first preferred amendment to rejection in the Lords; but, before the end of September, Balfour and Sandars won him over to rejection, with a view to a material Unionist recovery and a minority Liberal government. [24]

On 22 September Balfour, in a speech at Birmingham, duly argued for Tariff Reform as the best substitute for 'socialism'. Tariff Reform would protect jobs, but 'socialism' would merely provide a few palliatives for poor people while tending to destroy the private enterprise system and thus employment. [25] Even Unionist Free Traders could agree to fight Lloyd George's 'socialism'. At last, Balfour had reunited his party.

The lack of a definite statement by Balfour about rejection was due to tactical reasons—he kept the Government guessing as long as possible. [26] On 2 October Lansdowne doubtless expressed Balfour's view as well as his own in responding to Balfour of Burleigh's fears of a permanent diminution of the Lords' powers if they went ahead with rejection. He thought that, in the circumstances, it was in effect a justified gamble: a second election would be required before 'destruction or reform' of the Lords could be

[23] Ibid., pp. 212–14.
[24] Ibid., pp. 214–18.
[25] N.U. No. 863—a National Union pamphlet.
[26] Murray, p. 223.

accomplished, and by then the electorate would be cooler about the budget and clearer that it wanted a proper Second Chamber.[27] While this prognosis would, notoriously, prove incorrect, yet it cannot be taken for granted that, even had Balfour been able to see as far ahead as the rather disillusioning result of the second election, he would have decided against rejection of the budget in 1909. Even if (and this was in the event uncertain) Asquith would by November 1910 have obtained the King's guarantee to create sufficient peers, and consequently a Parliament Act had to be assumed, the definitive reunion of the Unionist party would then take place on the issue of Home Rule. It was on this issue that Balfour had built his political career and enlisted a maximum of Unionist enthusiasm.

The actual course of events was that the House of Lords overwhelmingly rejected the budget on 30 November 1909, a general election was held with a record turnout in January 1910, and the Unionists achieved a net gain of 116 seats. With a total of 273 (against the Liberals' 275) they were just below the 280–300 range posited by Garvin the previous August and duly left the Government dependent on Labour and especially Irish Nationalist votes (amounting to 40 and 82 respectively). Balfour was ill during most of December but issued a printed address at the beginning of the election campaign (10 December 1909) which concentrated on constitutional jus-tification of the Lords' action. This left the Liberals with ample targets but, owing to the exceptional duration of the campaign, staleness had set in before the New Year. Whole Hoggers, inspired by the publication of Joseph Chamberlain's election address, then started to make the running. In January Balfour, coming freshly into the contest, was naturally the focus of press attention. However reluctantly, he put new life into the Unionist campaign, just before polling began, by spelling out some details of the Tariff-Reforming stance adumbrated in his speech at Birmingham the previous September. On the 12th at York he promised a duty on foreign wheat, together with industrial protection against undue inroads by foreign manufacturers.[28] However, it was, and is, disputable how far the electoral swing to the Unionists was due to this commitment. The over-all picture is that, despite Lloyd George's lenient taxing of middling incomes, the middle classes in the South reverted to Unionism while those in the North (evidently still wary of Tariff Reform and its implications for their com-petitive position in textile manufacturing) did not. The industrial working classes remained substantially loyal to the Liberal – Labour alliance, seeing

[27]   Newton, p. 379.
[28]   Neal Blewett, *The Peers, the Parties, and the People: the General Elections of 1910,* London, 1972, pp. 113–23.

the forthrightly redistributive budget as more favourable to their interests than a combination of 'black bread' and a chancy screen of tariffs against unemployment—especially when advocated by 'dukes'.[29]

Having fought on such favourable ground, the Liberal Cabinet was disconcerted by the result. There was a mandate for the budget but for little else. Asquith remained indecisive throughout 1910 on the shape to be given to the Parliament Bill; but, to his discomfort, Redmond's Irish Nationalists insisted that such a bill must be passed to open the way for Home Rule.

Balfour, for his part, was quite heartened by the result of the election but was aware that the pendulum had been checked by an anti-Unionist consolidation of opinion in the North. By mid-February, though he felt committed still to vote against the (1909) budget in the Commons, he was discussing the possibility of 'a Tory socialist policy' at some length with such as Esher. In like vein, at a Unionist meeting on reform of the House of Lords held at Lansdowne House early in March, he wanted the party to accept an elective element in order to shift the anti-Unionist consensus in Yorkshire, Lancashire, and Scotland. He specifically recognized the democratic trend in those areas.[30] But it was to prove impossible to devise an agreed constructive alternative to Liberal policies apart from those Tariff-Reforming nostrums advocated by Balfour himself in January. While Balfour tried to find a way out of that morass, King Edward died in May; and the Liberals suggested a constitutional conference to see whether a compromise could not be reached with the Unionists on the House of Lords. This might save the new King, George V, from having to respond to a Liberal demand for guarantees on the creation of peers.

Long-drawn-out discussions between the parties took from June to November. From Balfour's viewpoint, there was no reason to feel that disunity was a Unionist prerogative—Lloyd George's remarkable scheme for a coalition hinted at Liberal restlessness under the Irish yoke. Both sides played for time, with Asquith showing the public his consideration for the new King and Balfour waiting for false moves and splits amongst the Liberals. On 16 October Balfour suggested that, after two rejections by the Lords, a Home Rule bill should 'go to a plebiscite'. While Lloyd George saw this crucial proposal as not unreasonable, he indicated that political necessity bound the Government to reject such a concession.[31] The Unionist

[29] Ibid., pp. 404–9.
[30] B.P. 49765, ff. 111–13, B. to Sandars, 29 Jan. 1910; 49758, ff. 231–2, B. to Salisbury, 4 Feb. 1910; Esher, ii, 451 (16 Feb. 1910); Sir Charles Petrie, *The Life and Letters of Sir Austen Chamberlain*, London, 1939, 2 vols., i, 251.
[31] Newton, p. 403.

leaders therefore broke off the negotiations. By 16 November Asquith had secured his guarantees from the King. The fact that the latter had agreed to secrecy later pained him—and Balfour. For the latter had little option but to persevere with a policy of rejection by the Lords of the Parliament Bill until, in July 1911, he was informed of the King's pledge. [32]

Meanwhile a General Election had been held in December 1910. Although it had been expected throughout the year, Asquith managed to catch the Unionists in some disarray by announcing on 18 November that the dissolution would be on the 28th and that polling would begin on 3 December. Proceedings were dominated by Asquith and Balfour in a way not seen in January. However, the latter did not succeed in shifting the focus of attention away from the class-cleavage to Home Rule. There was again a high turnout, though the financial burden of a second election within a year reduced the number of contests. Over-all there was a swing to the Unionists of 0.8 per cent in the constituencies contested in both elections. This scarcely changed the parliamentary situation (the Unionists winning 271 seats and the Liberals 272). [33] Though still fearing the effect of food taxes on working-class opinion, Balfour had felt bound to stand by them, after his pledge of January, against all intra-party criticism right up to 17 November; yet in the twelve days elapsing before his electioneering speech at the Albert Hall on 29 November, he was converted to making an unconditional offer of a referendum before proceeding to the implementation of Tariff Reform. This late-hour switch was decided by Balfour without much consultation, on the prompting of the Unionist press and finally of Lansdowne, with the idea of swaying opinion in Scotland and the North of England. Only thus, it seemed to him, could the Unionists escape an indefinite period in the political wilderness. But it was Andrew Bonar Law, then crusading for Tariff Reform in marginal North-West Manchester, who probably did more than anyone to induce Balfour to gamble on the referendum. In the event, the referendum bid had a slightly favourable effect in the North and Scotland; but many Tariff Reformers were infuriated, and their discontent was a major factor in the events leading to Balfour's resignation from the leadership of the Unionist party in November 1911. [34]

After this third successive electoral defeat, unrest was even greater amongst the party enthusiasts in the constituencies—many of them wholehog Tariff Reformers—and in the Unionist press. The result was a reform

[32] Harold Nicolson, *King George the Fifth*, London, 1952, pp. 133–9; Newton, p. 417.
[33] Blewett, pp. 168, 192, 379, 387–8.
[34] Ibid., pp. 170, 177–87, 410–11; Sir Austen Chamberlain, *Politics from Inside*, pp. 298–312.

of the party organization. By June, the ennobled Acland Hood had been succeeded as Chief Whip by Lord Balcarres. Part of Hood's functions went to the holder of the new post of Chairman of the Party, the thirty-five-year-old Steel-Maitland. Henceforth Balfour would have to communicate with the party through him, rather than through Sandars. Steel-Maitland was to be of cabinet rank.[35] However, within the parliamentary Opposition there was no challenger in sight for Balfour's position as leader; and the process of opposing the Parliament Bill in the Commons and the Lords continued in earnest until Balfour heard that the Government held the King's guarantees. At once, on 7 July, he summoned a shadow cabinet, and there were signs of a rift, though the majority agreed with Balfour that there was no point in continued rejection. The Bill left the Unionist Lords with the power to delay a Home Rule Bill for two sessions, and this power should not be thrown away. What particularly upset Balfour was the fact that, after Lloyd George had at last, on the Government's behalf, informed him about the guarantees,[36] the shadow cabinet of 21 July divided, with eight members obdurately backing the Diehard peers, despite a majority of fourteen concurring with Balfour's policy of sudden tactical retreat. Among the eight were three members of Balfour's intimate circle: Selborne, Salisbury, and George Wyndham. The normally loyal Austen Chamberlain and the new Chief Whip, Balcarres, were also among the rebels. Soon afterwards Balfour told Sandars that he saw this dissension as being on a more basic level than that associated with Tariff Reform. He deemed the line to be taken over the Parliament Bill a question 'of mere party tactics', not of 'principle'. In cabinet meetings, 'the majority must prevail' and an irreconcilable majority must resign. Here, the minority had 'gone into the world proclaiming their differences'. 'I confess', said Balfour, 'to feeling that I have been badly treated.' He concluded, with unusual 'intensity of feeling', that he could not continue as leader under such circumstances.[37]

On 10 August, before the Parliament Bill was acrimoniously passed by the Lords, Balfour went abroad to Bad Gastein. This was correctly interpreted in some quarters as signalling his intention to resign.[38] After returning in September from Gastein, Balfour was confronted at Whittingehame by Steel-Maitland who emphasized the need for a decisive lead

[35] John Ramsden, *The Age of Balfour and Baldwin 1902–1940*, London, 1978, pp. 56–61.
[36] B.P. 49730, ff. 243–4, 'Note of Conversation with Mr. Lloyd George in Mr. Balfour's Room, July 18th, 1911'.
[37] B.P. 49767, ff. 281–311, 'A Note on the Events leading to Mr. Balfour's Resignation', 8 Nov. 1911; Dugdale, ii, 66–71, 84–85.
[38] Sykes, p. 246.

to quell the dissatisfaction in the parliamentary party and the constituencies.[39] But if Balfour could 'hang on till the Home Rule Bill', he would be
secure.[40] On the 29th, Short wrote to Sandars: 'He [Balfour] seems a little
sick of the situation . . . The Chief this morning again referred to his
unwillingness to retain the leadership if the Party were so much dissatisfied
with him, and he read out to me certain extracts of one of Steel-Maitland's
Memoranda.' Short, however, took due note of Maitland's suggestion that,
if Balfour could stave off the criticism, he would be saved by 'the Home
Rule campaign'.[41]

Sandars wrote to Balfour from Torquay in an attempt to dissuade him
from his privately declared intention. If his health really was inadequate,
that was one thing. But Sandars was 'confident that the vast majority of the
Party' would be 'unable to reconcile themselves' to his resignation. No
successor was visible. Only 'the enemy' would rejoice if he did not stay to
fight Home Rule.[42] But Balfour was already set on resignation by 30
September. He then told Steel-Maitland and Balcarres that the 'faculty for
readiness in debate is not one which the country necessarily demands in a
Leader' and a 'slower brain would often be welcome to the Party as a
whole'—someone who did not 'see all the factors in a situation'. He could
not contemplate taking office again as Prime Minister, so it was better for
him to go on health grounds, thus avoiding schism in the party—as he did
on 8 November—rather than await the Home Rule contest.[43]

On 9 November Esher noted in his journal: 'I have just written to A.J.B.
that personally I can never forgive those who (whatever he may say) have
caused his retirement, and the disaster of it.'[44] To Almeric FitzRoy on the
same day 'Lloyd George expressed himself with heartfelt regret, avowing
his admiration for the way he [Balfour] had conducted a difficult and
thankless task.' FitzRoy weighed up the matter thus:

There is no question that the loss to the Unionist Party is in a sense irreparable; no
doubt a leader fit to do the ordinary House of Commons work will be found among
the men who stand around Mr. Balfour, but the qualities which lifted statesmanship
out of the ruts of party scheming will no longer illuminate the counsels of the
Opposition. There have been moments when he seemed to lose strength in sup-
pleness, and even to sacrifice prudence to dexterity; but in the attributes of mind, the
force of logic, the courage of endurance and high purpose, patience and dignity

---

[39] Ibid., p. 249.
[40] B.P. 49861, ff. 329–33, memo by A. Steel-Maitland, 20 Sept. 1911.
[41] Sandars P., C.764, 29 Sept. 1911.
[42] B.P. 49767, ff. 273–5, Sandars to B., 8 Oct. 1911.
[43] B.P. 49767, ff. 281–311, 'Note', 8 Nov. 1911.
[44] Esher, iii, 69.

under defeat, he displayed resources of the highest order and adorned them with a charm and courtesy of fence which justified the Prime Minister's description of him this evening as 'the most distinguished member of the greatest deliberative assembly in the world'.[45]

[45] FitzRoy, p. 468.

12

A Not-So-Philosophical Retirement

1911–1914

EVEN Balfour's celebrated 'detachment' was not entirely proof against disenchantment with politics in the late summer and autumn of 1911. Yet his interest in philosophy, actively continued since publication of his *Foundations* in 1895, lay ready to hand and he had already started work on an article about 'Bergson's Creative Evolution' before his return from Gastein.[1] When, on 30 September, he told Balcarres and Steel-Maitland of his intention to resign the leadership, they asked who could succeed him. He thought that Austen Chamberlain would emerge as leader in the Commons and that Curzon would ultimately lead in the Lords. In order, doubtless, to preserve party unity he said that he would continue to support the party line in the Commons and would continue to sit on the Unionist front bench.[2] When Bonar Law became leader (as a compromise between Austen Chamberlain and Walter Long) Balfour could hardly have been overwhelmed by the intellectual calibre of his successor; but he duly gave support and advice when this was requested. It was not long, indeed, before Bonar Law, though a Tariff Reformer himself, found the issue of food duties as troublesome to party unity as had his predecessor. As Mr Sykes has commented, by March 1912 it had become 'increasingly clear that any statement upon the subject would cause a split in one direction or the other. Like Balfour before him, Law found refuge in silence.'[3]

In these circumstances, Balfour found solace in philosophy at Whittingehame. An invitation to give a course of Gifford lectures within the sphere of 'Natural Religion' afforded Balfour an opportunity to develop further that intellectual justification of a theistic philosophy which he had attempted in his *Defence* and *Foundations*. During 1912 he gave fairly continuous attention to his new task, but by no means to the exclusion of music, games, and entertainment. The era of the nephews and nieces was well under way at Whittingehame and Balfour delighted in this aspect of his

---

[1] Dugdale, ii, 83; Balfour, *Essays Speculative and Political*, London, 1920, pp. 103–47.
[2] B.P. 49767, ff. 281–311, 'Note', 8 Nov. 1911.
[3] Sykes, p. 265.

life. Until the German war came, he was also still engaged in his habitual round of country houses. At Whittingehame and at Carlton Gardens he entertained a much wider circle of people than he had in the 1880s. Overt opposition to Conservatism was certainly no bar. The Webbs have already been mentioned. Another remarkable instance of his interest in a sharply dissenting mind was Alice Stopford Green, widow of the historian J. R. Green. Daughter of an Archdeacon in the Church of Ireland, she had become a passionate supporter of a separate Irish political identity and had made a name for herself by publishing *The Making of Ireland and its Undoing* (1908). As far as Balfour was concerned the essential marks of acceptability were her qualities of wit, charm, and intelligence.[4] However, he was not unaware of the progress through Parliament of Asquith's Home Rule Bill and, in September, he duly subscribed to a Unionist message of support for the Ulster Covenant.[5]

Of course, Home Rule had at least provided the long-awaited cause on which Unionists could unite, without disputing amongst themselves over Tariff Reform or indeed any constructive programme. Bonar Law was proving a somewhat crude but effective hammer of the Government in this mounting crisis and the stream of Conservative by-election victories continued till the advent of the War in 1914.

It was, indeed, an intimation of war that came nearer to luring Balfour away from his philosophical cogitations of 1912 than did the issues of Home Rule and party politics. In December 1911 he had received a friendly letter from Winston Churchill, newly appointed First Lord of the Admiralty. Balfour reassured him on the matter of resentment for old political injuries. He had never, he wrote, 'been the least tempted to allow public differences to destroy private friendships'; not did he think that Churchill had 'the smallest reason to reproach' himself. He was glad to see him placed at the Admiralty—and took the opportunity to point out the advantage which submarines conferred on the weaker navy.[6] Churchill, under the influence of Fisher's persistent adulation of the submarine, rejected Balfour's clear-sighted view and argued that it was Britain that stood to gain most from further development of submarines.[7] Sandars, who continued to send Balfour gossip damaging to Churchill on the assumption that he was relishing such accounts, was staggered when, in May 1915, he was

[4] Lyons, p. 323.
[5] Sydney H. Zebel, *Balfour*, Cambridge, 1973, p. 181.
[6] Randolph S. Churchill, *Winston S. Churchill*, London, 1969, Companion Vol. ii, pp. 1358–9, B. to Churchill, 16 Dec. 1911.
[7] B.P. 49694, ff. 64–5, 6 Jan. 1912.

confronted with Balfour's affectionate consideration for the loathsome renegade.[8] Meanwhile, Balfour's grasp of the U-boat threat was to bear spectacular fruit in 1913 when he convinced that afficionado of the submarine, Lord Fisher, that unrestricted submarine warfare against merchant shipping was inevitable, should war break out with Germany; and Fisher thereupon wrote a brilliant paper to that effect, but his contention was rejected as unthinkable by Churchill and the Admiralty.[9]

To revert to 1912, however, Balfour turned down an offer from the Government in January to put him on the C.I.D.,[10] but Churchill kept him posted with information about the development of a naval staff and shook him in March with evidence of Germany's warlike intentions. Balfour replied:

> A war entered upon for no other object than to restore the Germanic Empire of Charlemagne in a modern form, appears to me at once so wicked and so stupid as to be almost incredible! And yet it is almost impossible to make sense of modern German policy without crediting it with this intention.

He disagreed with French observers who thought that war would come that spring. Only, he felt, when the Germans had reduced Britain's naval margin would they dare to fight. 'But', he concluded, 'imagine it being possible to talk about war as inevitable when there is no quarrel, and nothing to fight over! We live in strange times!'[11]

In view of the much enhanced threat presented by the new German Navy Law, Churchill had since February been proposing a radical redistribution of British naval strength from the Mediterranean to the North Sea. By late June he was struggling to get his plan through the Cabinet while outside it Esher (still a member of the C.I.D.) and a group of Unionist peers (including Lansdowne and Selborne) all denounced this 'evacuation' of the Mediterranean and the implied British reliance on France in that traditionally crucial sea.[12] However, apparently unbeknown to Esher—even he could not know everything!—Balfour had already aligned himself with

---

[8]   R. S. Churchill, pp. 1357–8, 1653–4, 1654–5 for the gossip. On discovering that Churchill and family were being allowed to live pro tem at the Admiralty, Sandars thenceforward dissociated himself entirely from B.—and after B's death he returned a dusty answer when asked by Austen Chamberlain whether he would assist B.'s biographer. See Sandars P., C.768, ff. 69 and 107, and C.771, ff. 341–4.

[9]   Mackay, pp. 447–53.

[10]   B.P. 49768, ff. 14–17, Sandars to B., 11 Jan. 1912.

[11]   B.P. 49694, ff. 75–6, B. to Churchill, 22 March 1912. (See also Randolph S. Churchill, Companion Vol. ii, pp. 1530–1.)

[12]   Samuel R. Williamson, Jr., *The Politics of Grand Strategy*, Cambridge, Mass., 1969, pp. 264–78.

Churchill. On 12 June he wrote to the Foreign Secretary, Sir Edward Grey, that Churchill had indicated that he (Grey) 'would like to see formally developed a line of thought' which Balfour had put to the First Lord at Grey's dinner at the Foreign Office on the 10th. In his accompanying 'Memorandum on Anglo-French Relations', Balfour referred to the naval build-up of the Triple Alliance and to the strengthened 'public sentiment' which would no longer brook a gratuitous attack upon an *Entente* partner. In these circumstances, he deprecated either building enough ships to meet Britain's exigencies in a single-handed war with the whole of the Triple Alliance ('a most costly operation') or abandoning the Mediterranean till the British were 'safe in the North Sea' (a policy which would endanger trade routes in war and weaken diplomacy in peace). Therefore, in order to 'secure the co-operation of the French Fleet' against Austria and Italy, they should seek 'the substitution of a formal alliance for an informal Entente'. To avoid attribution of an offensive character to the alliance, the partner calling for assistance could be committed to offer to go to arbitration, 'say at the Hague?'. [13]

On the 16th Grey wrote thanking Balfour for his suggestion. He added that the 'Mediterranean position' would make the Government give very careful consideration to relations with France. [14] The outcome was a strengthening of the *Entente* on its naval side—but there was still no formal commitment to fight.

Although disconcerted to find that Balfour was backing Churchill's approach to the problem of the Navy and the Mediterranean, Esher found common cause with Balfour in the matter of the Garton Foundation. Inspired by Norman Angels's famous book *The Great Illusion* (1911), the Foundation aimed to educate opinion internationally as to the dire economic consequences of a large-scale conflict. Although concerned that the Foundation's propaganda might be misrepresented as defeatist, Balfour apparently consented to join Sir Richard Garton and Esher on the board of trustees. [15] He received an appeal from Esher, in a letter of 4 October 1912, to comment on Angell's book in such a way that the true aim of the Foundation could be generally understood. His name would not be used; but Esher wanted to publish something to encourage German and other thinkers to take part in discussion of the book's main contention. [16]

[13]   F.O. 800/105, B. to Grey, 12 June 1912.
[14]   B.P. 49731, f. 12.
[15]   Peter Fraser, *Lord Esher*, London, 1973, pp. 275 and 434.
[16]   B.P. 49719, ff. 232–4, B. to Esher, 4 Oct. 1912.

Balfour's mounting anxiety about German intentions had recently led him, despite his ingrained contempt for such ephemeral writing, to accede to a request from the editor of the periodical *Nord und Süd* for an article on 'Anglo-German Relations'. The article is, in effect, a tactful version of the acute concerns expressed in his above-quoted letter to Churchill of 22 March and in his memorandum for Grey. He points to British doubts about why 'the greatest military Power and the second greatest naval Power in the world is adding both to her army and to her navy'—to say nothing of 'increasing the strategic railways which lead to frontier states'.[17] It was with similar concerns in mind that, on 12 October, he composed a statement for Esher's use

The Garton propaganda could be 'of the utmost value to humanity', but only if its objects were not misunderstood. He gathered that the Foundation desired 'to impress upon the civilised nations of the world' that 'aggressive warfare, undertaken for the purpose of making the aggressor happier, wealthier, more prosperous', was 'not only wrong but silly'—a proposition with which he heartily agreed. But the doctrine of the Foundation must not be seen as a plea for ' "peace at any price" '. If it was, 'it would do much more harm than good.' But he entirely agreed with Angell's 'business' argument. Victory could not repair the damage done by war to national interests.

He concluded with a paragraph which sheds considerable light on the spirit in which he would before very long reassume the mantle of an active statesman:

Nevertheless, the nation is something more than the individuals who at any given moment compose it. Its corporate reality is not a fiction. It can suffer as a whole. It has duties and responsibilities extending to an indefinite future; and we, its citizens, who temporarily constitute it, must never allow ourselves to lapse into a selfish individualism. Patriotic feeling, even in its most perverted manifestations, has in it a root of something which is noble and unselfish; and if I thought this was to be crushed out of existence by the business calculations which Mr. Norman Angell most rightly presses upon our attention, I should fear that his efforts might do more harm than good. It is, however, probably sufficient to point out the danger in order to avoid it. In any case, it will, as I suppose, be the duty of the Trust to see that in furthering one of the greatest of all causes—the cause of peace—they neither endanger national defence nor weaken national sentiment.[18]

Esher wrote back the same day from Callander to Wilfred Short: 'I am

17 *Essays Speculative and Political*, pp. v–vii, 195–207.
18 B.P. 49719, ff. 235–8, B. to Esher, 12 Oct. 1912.

infinitely obliged for the draft memo. sent by Mr. Balfour. It is perfect.' [19]
He indicated soon after that he would have it printed and shown to people
privately. [20]

There ensued a year or so of superficially easier Anglo-German relations
while the German Army prepared for pre-emptive war with France and
Russia. Meantime, the British naval manœuvres of 1912 had suggested the
possibility of German troops descending on the British coast in greater
numbers than had previously been accepted. Knowing that the War Office
was aiming to send all six divisions of the Expeditionary Force (B.E.F.) to
France in the event of war with Germany, Asquith, who had begun in 1912
to use the C.I.D. in closer conjunction with the Cabinet, decided to institute
a third invasion inquiry. By January 1913 Balfour had agreed to serve on
the relevant Sub-Committee of the C.I.D. In the same month he was the
chosen spokesman for the Opposition in moving rejection of the Home Rule
Bill on its third reading; and even before the autumn he was becoming
increasingly involved in Unionist moves against the reintroduced Bill. [21]
Philosophy took a back seat for the first seven months of 1913.

Having missed the first two meetings of the Invasion Committee, Balfour
attended on 10 April 1913 and went to ten further consecutive meetings—a
series of attendances which ended on 10 July. Lord Morley (who, as
editor of *The Fortnightly Review*, had published an extract from Balfour's
Defence of Philosophic Doubt before it came out in 1869) admired
Balfour's performance at the Invasion Committee on 10 April where the
latter at once 'brought to the discussion those qualities of rapid grasp and
luminous insight which quicken and adorn his thought'. [22] Of the eight
meetings remaining after 10 July, Balfour attended only three, but was kept
posted, and consulted, by Captain Maurice Hankey (Secretary of the
C.I.D. since 1911) with whom he would be much associated during the rest
of his political life. [23] The effect of the Report was that 'in the event of the
despatch of an Expeditionary Force oversea, the equivalent of two divisions
of regular troops' would—much as in 1908—be retained for home defence.
Together with ten Liberal ministers, Esher, and seven leading servicemen,
Balfour signed the Report on 15 April 1914. [24]

[19]   Ibid., ff. 236–7, Esher to Short, 12 Oct. 1912.
[20]   Ibid., f. 238, Esher to B., 14 Oct. 1912.
[21]   Zebel, p. 182.
[22]   FitzRoy, p. 508, 11 April 1913.
[23]   See B.P. 49703, ff. 1–21, concluding on 20 Mar. 1914 with a revised proof of the Report submitted to B. 'for any final remarks'.
[24]   Cab. 16/28A.

During the autumn Balfour was informed and consulted by Bonar Law as the resistance of Ulster to the Home Rule Bill, due to become law in the spring of 1914, mounted in intensity. The trend of Balfour's advice accorded with the views he had formed after Gladstone committed the Liberals to Home Rule in the 1880s. Irish nationalism should be reconciled within the existing framework of the United Kingdom. If it was not, Catholic Ireland should be offered independence. Now that Ulster Protestants in effect demanded to be as independent of Dublin as Nationalists wished to be free of Westminster, Balfour strongly supported the Ulstermen in letterS to Bonar Law, advice to the King, and public speeches.[25]

However, with his capacity to switch his attention away from disturbing matters which he could not control,[26] he was able during the autumn of 1913 to finish preparing his course of ten Gifford Lectures. He delivered them at Glasgow University in January and February 1914. One much-discussed feature of his *Foundations of Belief* had been the chapter entitled 'Authority and Reason'. This had suggested to Esher that Balfour was ripe for conversion to Roman Catholicism![27] If this theme had reappeared against the background of the Ulster crisis, it might have attracted comment—but it did not reappear.

Balfour does not aim in his Gifford Lectures (any more than in his previous work) to carry the theory of knowledge beyond the position reached by David Hume.[28] What he does try to demonstrate is that God must be central to the most reasonable of all the perpetually evolving systems of belief. As a firm believer in science and an ordered material world, Balfour compares his standpoint with that of Descartes. 'Descartes rests the belief in science on a belief in God. I rest the belief in God on a belief in science.'[29] God himself, he finally concludes, is

the condition of scientific knowledge. If He be excluded from the causal series which produces beliefs, the cognitive series which justifies them is corrupted at the root. And it is only in a theistic setting that beauty can retain its deepest meaning, and love its brightest lustre, so these great truths of aesthetics and ethics are but half-truths, isolated and imperfect, unless we add to them yet a third. We must hold that reason and the works of reason have their source in God; that from Him they

[25] Wilfred Scawen Blunt, *The Land War in Ireland*, pp. 303–5 (diary, 4 Sept. 1887); Balfour, *Opinions and Argument from Speeches and Addresses, 1910–1927*, London, 1927, pp. 71–81: 'On Nationality and Home Rule'—based on a speech at Nottingham, 1913; Zebel, pp. 183–7.

[26] See WHI/81: Parry, p. 21.

[27] Esher, i, 183 (11 Feb. 1895).

[28] *Theism and Humanism*, London, 1915, p. 170.

[29] Ibid., pp. 253–4.

draw their inspiration; and that if they repudiate their origin, by this very act they proclaim their own insufficiency. [30]

But the second series of Gifford Lectures was to be postponed for some eight years. As Balfour would write on 24 May 1915 (three days before replacing Churchill as First Lord of the Admiralty): 'No one who took any part in public affairs between March 1914 and the outbreak of the war, or between the outbreak of the war and the present moment, is likely to regard these months as providing occasion for quiet thought and careful writing.' [31] On 30 January 1914, before Balfour had quite finished delivering his course of lectures, Bonar Law asked him, in lieu of attendance at a shadow cabinet, to consider the idea that the Lords should amend the Army Annual Bill, thus forcing a General Election. [32] Although Balfour had for long argued that the Government should go to the country before trying to impose Home Rule, he made clear his dislike of this particular proposal. The result might well be that 'the party of law and order' would hamper the use of the Army in that very regard—for instance to defend Belfast Catholics against Orange bigotry or to control Labour unrest in Britain. [33] This letter probably represents Balfour's most important contribution during the Ulster crisis. His advice, with that of Curzon and Lansdowne, may well have been decisive in discouraging this unwise, and indeed unpatriotic, expedient. However, the Curragh incident (20 March) in any event rendered the proposal obsolete. [34]

The final, and most dangerous, phase of the Home Rule controversy extended from February to July 1914. The Home Rule Bill started on its third and final parliamentary round, accompanied by much contention about the terms on which Ulster might be excluded from the operation of the Act. Balfour actively supported Carson's rejection of a time limit and sought means of forcing the Government to hold an election on the Irish issue. [35] When, in mid-July, an all-party conference was to be held at Buckingham Palace, Balfour was specifically excluded. Although the King had asked for his inclusion, and although Asquith had in March deemed Balfour 'the only quick mind in that ill-bred crowd' of Unionists in the

[30] Ibid., p. 274.
[31] Ibid., Preface, p. viii.
[32] B.P. 49693, ff. 139–40.
[33] B.L.P. 31/3/7, B. to Law, 3 Feb. 1914.
[34] Robert Blake, *The Unknown Prime Minister: the Life and Times of Andrew Bonar Law 1858–1923*, London, 1955, p. 181. See Law's memo of 18 June 1914 in B.L.P., 39/4/38.
[35] Zebel, pp. 189–91.

Commons, the Prime Minister firmly declined to have him at the conference. On the Home Rule question, he told the King, Balfour was 'a real
wrecker'.[36]

Even on such a count, therefore, it remains unclear that Bonar Law was
better qualified to be the fighting leader of the Unionist Party than
Balfour—once the Home Rule sequence was started in earnest. But quite
suddenly, on Wednesday, 29 July, the Cabinet for its part found that it had
more pressing business on hand than the Irish conundrum. On the previous
day Austria-Hungary had declared war on Serbia. Asquith realized that
the long-dreaded Great War was actually imminent. For Balfour, too, the
whole perspective was soon transformed.

[36] Roy Jenkins, *Asquith*, London, 1964, pp. 310 and 320.

13

Resurrected by War

1914–1916

IN previous summers Balfour had escaped to Whittingehame, as soon as parliamentary duties permitted. But in 1914, July found him firmly based at his house in Carlton Gardens, though he scarcely realized how much time he was destined to spend there during the next four years. Nor, when he encountered Admiral Fisher outside the Admiralty and expressed warm regard for Winston Churchill as First Lord,[1] did he imagine that, within nine months, he himself would be graciously waiving his own right to occupy the First Lord's accommodation—primarily because Churchill and his family had no other home in London, but also, doubtless, through preference for his own neighbouring establishment.

On Saturday, 1 August, Germany declared war on Russia. That morning found several of the Unionist leaders, but not Balfour, out of London. However, Bonar Law, Balfour, and others gathered at Lansdowne House that evening and sent word to Asquith that they were available to discuss the crisis. On Sunday the 2nd, the Cabinet began to unite on a basis of keeping the German Navy away from the French Channel coast (thus underscoring the British fear of the maritime threat ultimately presented by a German victory over France and Russia) and of taking Belgium's side against a German invasion. Meanwhile, at Austen Chamberlain's instance, Bonar Law assured Asquith that he and Lansdowne, together with their 'colleagues', would support the Government in upholding France and Russia against Germany.[2]

On Monday, 3 August, the Cabinet moved closer to war as alarming news came in from Belgium. Haldane (still Lord Chancellor but also in charge of the War Office since the previous day) announced British military mobilization—the Fleets having already steamed to their war stations. That afternoon, Grey made his famous pro-Belgian speech in the House of Commons. Then it became known that Germany had declared war on France. On Tuesday the 4th, as the hours before expiry of the British

[1] Martin Gilbert, *Winston S. Churchill*, London, 1971, iii, 17.
[2] Blake, p. 220; Dugdale, ii, pp. 112–15.

ultimatum to Germany steadily melted away, Balfour wrote to the acting
War Secretary:

My dear Haldane,
   The fact that we worked together upon the Sub-Committee [on invasion] up to
February 9th of this year, combined with the fact that the Unionist Party are most
anxious to aid to the very best of their ability the Government in their present crisis,
emboldens me to write to you on the subject of the Expeditionary Force.
   As you are aware, I was altogether opposed, as a matter of general policy, to
completely denuding these Islands of regular troops, and I certainly have no
predilections for a policy of military adventure on the Continent, but surely there
are overwhelming reasons at this moment for giving all the aid we can to France by
land as well as by sea.
   (1) as regards Germany, we have burnt our boats. We have chosen our side, and
must abide by the result.
   (2) the sort of British force we could send, after leaving 2 Divisions at home, is no
doubt a very small fraction of any Continental Army; but it is probably *not* a very
small fraction of the troops immediately available for field operations in the
North-East of France.
   (3) If Germany could be 'stalemated' in her advance through Belgium and N.E.
France her position becomes very perilous with the menace of Russia on her eastern
frontier. If, on the other hand, the Germans are in sufficiently overwhelming
numbers to inflict on France a crushing defeat, the whole future of Europe may be
changed, and changed in a direction which we should regard as disastrous.
   (4) Is it not a fundamental principle of strategy, in a crisis of this particular kind,
either to keep out of a conflict altogether, or to strike quickly, and to strike with your
whole strength?

I know that you will forgive me for troubling you with this note: but the circumstances are unique, and a course which would be otherwise unjustifiable will, I
know, be forgiven.

> Pray believe me,
> Yours very sincerely,
> Arthur James Balfour.[3]

   This letter carries overtones of Balfour's reluctance to accept the idea of
war with Germany, together with British military limitations in such a
context. There is also a hint of the common overestimation of Russian
potential. But most characteristic of all is the sense of tenacity and
commitment: 'We have chosen our side, and must abide by the result.'
Haldane wanted to talk to Balfour about the letter; and they were discussing
its contents when the British ultimatum ran out at 11 p.m. Haldane indicated

---

[3]   National Library of Scotland, Haldane P., 5909, ff. 242–8.

that it might be wiser to keep the Expeditionary Force as a nucleus for a much bigger army of true continental proportions. He also thought that its retention would set the Fleet free—a reversion to the old invasionist argument which left Balfour far from impressed. [4]

Asquith held Councils of War on 5 and 6 August at which the size of the B.E.F. and its zone of concentration were decided. Kitchener having been appointed War Secretary on the 5th, it was agreed that four divisions of infantry and one of cavalry were to go (instead of the six infantry divisions, plus cavalry, so insistently demanded over recent years by General Henry Wilson); and Haldane was prompt to inform Balfour that the troops should be embarked by Sunday, the 9th. [5] By 23 August they were actually in action near Mons—a remarkable triumph for the pre-war trainers and planners.

A party truce was soon established in the interests of national unity, but the Government's enactment of Irish Home Rule did not fail to anger the Unionist leaders. In the House of Commons, Balfour was 'petulant and shrewish' according to Lloyd George. [6] However, Balfour's old links with the Liberal Imperialists held good. On 12 August, Grey wrote from Haldane's house at Queen Anne's Gate, which he described as familiar and congenial ground for Balfour, inviting the latter to come and talk with them about Home Rule over lunch. Balfour duly went. Sandars, temporarily acting again in a secretarial capacity, sent Grey a record of the discussion after Balfour's return to Carlton Gardens. 'Sir Edward Grey proposed that the Home Rule Bill should be put on the statute-book, accompanied by a one-clause Bill which should provide, not merely that the Bill should not come into operation, but that nothing should be done under it until . . . the war was over . . .' Balfour had pointed out that 'this might be very unfair to Ulster.'

Ulster was at the moment War broke out fully prepared for all eventualities. The result of the War [and Ulster's patriotic response thereto] would inevitably be to shake her organisation to its foundations.

Balfour therefore wanted a moratorium added whereby Home Rule would not be effective till three months of peace had elapsed. [7] The matter was settled, for the time being, along Grey's lines rather than Balfour's.

Meanwhile Balfour had already written to Hankey, who was to play a crucial role at Whitehall throughout the War, about the country's food

---

[4] B.P. 49724, ff. 170–7, notes of B.'s conversation with Haldane, 5 Aug. 1914.
[5] Ibid., f. 178, 6 Aug. 1914.
[6] Cameron Hazlehurst, *Politicians at War July 1914 to May 1915*, London, 1971, p. 137.
[7] B.P. 49731, ff. 20–2.

supply. Hankey was able to reassure him; the current position was sound. [8]
In September, Hankey sent a ten-page memorandum in proof, designed to
enlighten the C.I.D. on invasion, for Balfour's scrutiny and comment. [9] He
was glad to hear, by 3 October, that Balfour would attend at the C.I.D. on
Wednesday, the 7th; and that he would go to 'the christening' that afternoon
and meet Hankey's wife. Hankey had asked for this, the first C.I.D.
meeting since July, to clear up confusion in the naval and military plans for
home defence. [10] The meeting also dealt with 'Instructions to Local Authorities in the Event of Belligerent Operations in the United Kingdom'. [11]
Balfour, working closely with Hankey, was busy with this subject right
through to Christmas. [12] A by-product was a memorandum of 26 October by
Balfour on 'Attack on the British Isles from Oversea', printed the next day
for the C.I.D. and reminiscent of his classic paper of November 1903. The
situation was

that in Lord Kitchener's opinion a military deadlock might easily occur within the
next few weeks, when both parties, in strongly entrenched positions, might go into
an informal sort of winter quarters. In that event it might be possible for Germany
silently to withdraw 150,000 men or so . . . for transport across the North Sea . . .
As I understand the matter, the North Sea . . . is in . . . joint occupation by the
submarines of both countries. The Admiralty appear to have informed Lord
Kitchener that they could not engage to bring the main fleet to . . . where a landing
was being attempted for thirty-six hours from the moment the news reached
Admiral Jellicoe . . . Personally I find it very difficult to believe that such an
operation is likely to be attempted, or if attempted is likely to be successful.

However, Balfour continued, the trouble stemmed from German submarines and would persist, even if the High Seas Fleet were totally
destroyed. Jellicoe 'would still have to remain thirty-six hours away from
the threatened coast'. Balfour therefore made a number of suggestions for
local measures to hinder landings in the more likely places, including mine
laying (for which the Navy was unfortunately ill-prepared, as it happened). [13]
    As it became apparent that cabinet government on the peacetime model
could not cope with the escalating demands of the war, a War Council was
formed to advise the Cabinet on national strategy. The first meeting was

[8] B.P. 49703, ff. 39–40, Hankey to B., 13 Aug. 1914.
[9] Ibid., ff. 41–6, Hankey to B., 10 Sept. 1914.
[10] Ibid., ff. 47–50.
[11] Cab. 2/3/3, 129th meeting, 7 Oct. 1914.
[12] Ibid., ff. 51–125; see also Cab. 3/3/1A/83A, 'Instructions to Local Authorities . . .',
minute by Balfour, 9 Nov. 1914, 4 pp.
[13] Cab. 3/3/1A/82A, 4 pp., 26 Oct. 1914.

held on 25 November. At this point there were only nine members but among them were ministers of such high standing that their advice was almost certain to be taken by the Cabinet. However, the fact remains that it was a two-tier system, and delays did result until Lloyd George gave full executive authority to his small War Cabinet from December 1916. Balfour was the only representative of the Opposition's shadow cabinet who attended the War Council, apart from a single meeting mentioned below. On 25 November Asquith took the chair. The other Liberal ministers were Lloyd George (Chancellor of the Exchequer), Lord Crewe (Secretary for India), Churchill (First Lord), and Grey (Foreign Secretary). Lord Kitchener, as Secretary of State for War, spoke for the Government in the House of Lords, but can hardly be labelled a 'Liberal'. The role of the remaining two members was unfortunately not specifically defined. They were Admiral of the Fleet Lord Fisher of Kilverstone, lately brought back to the post of First Sea Lord by Churchill, and Lieutenant-General Sir James Wolfe ('Sheep') Murray, Chief of the Imperial General Staff. Fisher was to argue, after the naval failure at the Dardanelles, that he had been constitutionally debarred at the War Council from volunteering his view that Churchill's plan was impracticable. [14]

By 16 December, when the War Council met for the third time, the rush of volunteers to join the Army at Kitchener's behest had been on such a scale that industry was facing serious disruption. At the same time, Allies and wavering neutral states were applying to Britain for loans. Although diffident about his position on the Council, Balfour, the only person present who had, however secretively, made a serious study of economics, [15] gave lucid expression to the growing realization that

if such large financial demands were to be made on this country, it was essential that our economic position should be well maintained. In order to secure this it was essential that a large part of the population should continue in their normal employments. It appeared desirable to ascertain how far, and in what trades, it was safe to continue recruiting, and when the point was reached beyond which our economic position would be weakened by continuing enlistment.

THE PRIME MINISTER agreed that this was a most important question.

MR. BALFOUR undertook to write a paper on the subject. [16]

Thus Balfour was first to emphasize in the War Council industry's crucial role in the total war effort. He had also foreshadowed the stance to be

[14] Mackay, pp. 487–8.
[15] See pp. 230–1 above.
[16] Cab. 22/1/1, 16 Dec. 191.

adopted by the anti-conscriptionists the following summer, when demands grew for an Army of 70 divisions on the Western Front. Hankey, who was now Secretary of the War Council as well as of the C.I.D., had been against conscription before the War.[17] By 19 December, he was reminding Balfour—enjoying his last family gathering during the war for Christmas at Whittingehame—of his promise to write a paper on the danger presented to the economy by excessive recruiting.[18] This was duly completed by 1 January 1915 and was printed in good time before the C.I.D. met to discuss it on 27 January. Both in his paper, entitled the 'Limits of Enlistment', and at the discussion, Balfour emphasized Britain's need to keep up her volume of exports. Only thus could she pay for the essential imports and, in particular, retain the ability to borrow abroad. Therefore the need to restrain enlistment extended well beyond procurement of enough labour to make munitions. Kitchener, who certainly took a long view of his man-power needs and had lost recruits through having to brake the inrush in September, said it 'would be a dreadful thing at this stage to put a limit on recruiting'.[19] So nothing very effective was achieved. The supply of munitions, in particular, remained a problem too revolutionary in scale for Kitchener and the War Office.[20] But already Balfour was becoming a leading spokesman of a political group fearful that the Army might waste lives at the expense of Britain's longer-term strength.

Meanwhile Hankey had been even busier than usual. The result was his famous Boxing Day Memorandum. Contemplating the stalemate which had by now developed on the Western Front, he emphasized the dispropor-tionate losses suffered for small gains in that theatre. Either special equipment had to be produced in aid of a break-through or opportunities for an offensive had to be found elsewhere. Germany was thus far surviving all the economic pressures. Perhaps she could be weakened most effectively by the capture of Constantinople? Three British army corps might become available by the spring. Then the Balkan states might be persuaded to attack the Austrians while the Germans were held to their eastern front by the Russians. On 29 December he sent a copy of his paper to Balfour for an opinion—explaining that he had written it for the Prime Minister.[21]

Balfour replied from Whittingehame on 2 January. He agreed with Hankey about the Western Front. Offensives should be avoided until some

---

[17]   Stephen Roskill, *Hankey: Man of Secrets*, Vol. i, 1877–1918, London, 1970, pp. 95–6.

[18]   B.P. 49703, ff. 121–2.

[19]   Cab. 4/6/1/200B, 1 Jan. 1915; Cab. 2/3/4, 27 Jan.

[20]   Peter Simkins, 'Kitchener and the Expansion of the Army', in Beckett and Gooch, pp. 99–102.

[21]   B.P. 49703, ff. 126–36.

new way of effecting a deep penetration at a vital point could be found. If the Russians could only live up to their claimed strength, they would have that room for manoeuvre which was unavailable in the West. But as for Constantinople, he feared that the Balkan states would squabble over the spoils. Moreover, Germany was 'perfectly indifferent to the fate of her Allies' unless a direct threat to her own security was entailed. Such operations, 'however successful, must be regarded as merely subsidiary'. However, he wondered if the Austrians could be weakened if British troops went up through Montenegro.[22] Meanwhile Lloyd George had also weighed in with a powerful memorandum condemning western offensives. He advocated a thrust through the Balkans, abetted by Serbs, Roumanians, and Greeks, against the Austrians. This, he argued, should involve 600,000 British troops. A further 100,000 might be landed in Syria behind the Turks if they advanced on Egypt.[23] As Hankey remarks, he and Lloyd George thus discovered an unsuspected affinity of ideas; and, though Lloyd George had not hit (as Hankey had) on 'caterpillar' driven vehicles (i.e. tanks) as the key to the break-through which both of them recognized as necessary in the West, they were destined to work together on the project after the Welsh-man had moved from the Exchequer to the Ministry of Munitions.[24]

However, the more immediate upshot of discussions in and out of the War Council was the decision (in the Council) on 13 January that preparations should begin for a purely naval attack on the Dardanelles. This was confirmed on 28 January, after an inarticulate show of opposition by Fisher had apparently been resolved by Churchill. Fisher afterwards blamed Balfour for clinching a disastrous decision by his irresistible persuasiveness on the 28th. But it seems clear from the records that Balfour was justified in thinking, as most, or possibly all, Council members did at the time, that troops were *not* available for the attack and that, if the Navy failed to get through to Constantinople, the whole enterprise would be abandoned. It was surely the subsequent decision, of mid-February, to send troops to the area just when a systematic naval bombardment was about to begin, that contained the seeds of real disaster. (The Turks had, indeed, already been alerted by naval bombardment of the outer forts as far back as 3 November.) For if the Navy alone failed to get through, but troops were on hand, there was danger that a landing would *then* be undertaken. Meanwhile surprise, the basic requirement for an amphibious assault, would have been entirely and disastrously lost. Yet already by 16 February, an incomplete War

[22] Hankey P., 4/7, B. to Hankey, 1 Jan. 1915.
[23] Cab. 24/1/G.2, 1 Jan. 1915.
[24] Hankey, i, 250–1.

Council (Balfour being back at Whittingehame) had decided to send various army and marine elements to Lemnos 'to be available in case of necessity to support the naval attack on the Dardanelles'.[25] The main naval attack duly failed on 18 March. A small War Council was called by Asquith on 6 April. Churchill and Kitchener were the only other participants, apart from Hankey in his usual secretarial role. Despite Hankey's warnings (which overstepped strict constitutionality) a military assault was endorsed.[26] This was the only semblance of a War Council meeting before the landings of 25 April. The expenditure of many lives for minimal gains continued at Gallipoli till the New Year. If it has already been indicated that Balfour did not share responsibility for the most damaging formal decisions, exactly what was his role in the causal sequence?

Before his return to Whittingehame for Christmas, Balfour had finished interviewing the Lord Lieutenants about civil defence; and the three War Council meetings which he had attended did not seem to imply much involvement for him in the running of the war. But Hankey called him down for the meetings held on 7 and 8 January, thinking that the discussions would be 'of great importance'. There was a general feeling, he wrote, that they must find some new way to hit Germany.[27] Nothing very significant did occur at those meetings. Balfour, however, realized that he might 'in Council give an opinion in favour of some course of action which, in the event, would lead to a disaster more or less serious'. So he sought the agreement of Bonar Law and Lansdowne to his remaining on the War Council.[28]

It was at the Council of 13 January that Churchill explained the plan for a naval attack on the Dardanelles without troops. He was at once backed by Lloyd George and by Kitchener. As the latter said: 'We could leave off the bombardment if it did not prove effective.' This important observation attracted no recorded comment from Balfour. However, when discussion turned to the Western Front, Balfour queried whether Sir John French had the strength to embark on an offensive.[29]

After his return to Whittingehame, Balfour's correspondence with Hankey registered his continuing interest in munitions and labour problems connected therewith. Hankey mentioned that Fisher was failing to speak up

[25] Cab. 22/1/2.
[26] Cab. 22/1/2.
[27] B.P. 49703, ff. 142–3.
[28] B.P. 49730, ff. 272–4, B. to Lansdowne, 9 Jan., and 49693, ff. 201–4, B. to Law, 30 Jan. 1915.
[29] Cab. 22/1/2.

when he disagreed with Churchill's statements at the War Council.[30]
Munitions were to bring Balfour closer to Lloyd George in March and
April. However, there is no firm evidence (or likelihood) that Balfour
wanted Asquith's displacement.[31]

Balfour was back in London for the C.I.D. meeting of 27 January on
enlistment.[32] On the 28th, the War Council confirmed that the naval
campaign at the Dardanelles should go ahead. There were three meetings
on that day. In the morning, Balfour at once expressed relief after hearing
Kitchener explain that a proposed advance along the Belgian coast could not
be undertaken. He deprecated 'an early advance by our troops against the
enemy's entrenched positions'.[33] When the subject of the Dardanelles was
reached, Fisher indicated that the Prime Minister knew he was not ready to
endorse the naval attack. Asquith replied to the effect that the Russians had
already welcomed the idea and it 'could not well be left in abeyance'.
Kitchener thought the naval scheme 'vitally important' and noted (as has
been mentioned) that it could be broken off if unsuccessful. It was then that
Balfour analysed the advantages flowing from success in the manner that
Fisher thought so fatally captivating.[34] At 4 p.m. Balfour took part in a
small sub-committee of the Council with Kitchener in the chair. It was to
examine possibilities of using troops in another theatre if the spring found
stalemate on the Western Front. After some discussion, during which
Lloyd George expressed his usual interest in the Balkans, Balfour concluded 'that the Adriatic should be ignored' (on account of Austrian
submarines); 'that the naval bombardment of the Dardanelles should be
attempted; and that in any case a force should be landed at Salonica'.[35] The
full War Council, now numbering ten, reassembled at 6.30; and after
hearing the recommendations of the sub-committee, they were informed by
Churchill 'that the Admiralty' (meaning presumably Churchill and Fisher)

[30] B.P. 49703, ff. 151–2, 21 Jan. 1915.
[31] B.P. 49692, ff. 222–31, B. to Lloyd George, 5 March; Hazlehurst, pp. 197–8; Stephen
Koss, *Asquith*, London, 1976, p. 179.
[32] Cab. 2/3/4, 27 Jan. 1915.
[33] Cab. 22/1/2, 28 Jan. 1915, p. 4.
[34] Ibid., pp. 5–6. Most of the records relevant to these discussions are to be found in Martin
Gilbert, *Winston S. Churchill*, Companion Vol. iii, London, 1972. (However, the extract
from Hankey to B. on p. 425 should be dated 17 Feb. 1915—not 17 Jan. See B.P. 49703, ff.
167–8.) See Cab. 19/33, p. 195, for Fisher's evidence (11 Oct. 1916) to the Dardanelles
Commission about B. on 13 Jan. 1915: 'He was beautiful! He has got the brain of Moses and
the voice of Aaron. He would talk a bird out of a tree, and they were all carried away with
him . . . I was very angry with him all the time.'
[35] Cab. 22/1/2, 4 p.m., p. 2.

'had decided to push on' with the naval attack on the Dardanelles 'approved at the meeting held on 13th January'.[36]

Back again at Whittingehame, Balfour received from Fisher a copy of his 'Memorandum by the First Sea Lord on the Position of the British Fleet and its Policy of Steady Pressure'.[37] It dwelt on the cumulative damage suffered by Germany as long as Britain ensured her continued supremacy in most of the North Sea and avoided costly coastal operations such as those latterly discussed in the War Council. In his covering letter to Balfour, dated 29 January, Fisher wrote:

This is the paper I wished to circulate to the War Council and which I handed to Winston five days ago. However they don't wish it so I say no more but in view of my cordial and close relations with you I send it for your private eye asking you kindly to return it to me.[38]

As far as Balfour was concerned, this memorandum was Fisher's considered argument against the naval attack at the Dardanelles. Neither here nor, it would seem, in any of his official discussions of the question, did Fisher specifically challenge the practicability of the operation.[39] He thought (according to his utterances) that the Navy *would* succeed in getting through to the Sea of Marmora. What bothered him, it always appeared, was the number of ships and trained men that would be lost. This, he argued, posed a threat to British predominance in the North Sea. While he was surely entitled to complain about Asquith's decision not to circulate the paper to the War Council, it seems very doubtful whether he would have argued against the *practicality* of the naval attack *if* the Council *had* asked him to develop his views. The Council would still have concluded that, in view of the far-reaching consequences of success, high losses of largely obsolete vessels together with some loss of trained men could, if necessary, be accepted. Balfour was seen by Fisher as the ablest expositor of the prospective advantages waiting on a naval success. Fisher's animus against Balfour, when the latter now proceeded to demolish his memorandum, can be understood—however unreasonable such animus may have been. So Balfour's response to Fisher's memorandum is important for the story of the naval attack and for Fisher's subsequent behaviour. Entitled 'Notes on

[36] Ibid., 6.30 p.m.
[37] The full text of this memo, in which Hankey and Julian Corbett had a hand, has been published in Gilbert, Companion Vol. iii, 452–5 and elsewhere. Fisher had a number of copies printed in Feb. 1915. See Fisher P., 4343 and 4901.
[38] B.P. 49712, f. 136. The memo of 25 Jan. 1915 (ff. 137–43) has a note at the head by Short, pointing out that the references to the War Council are omitted from subsequent prints.
[39] Mackay, pp. 481–2.

Lord Fisher's Memorandum of January 25', it also remains a cardinal statement of Balfour's general approach to strategic policy. It was dated 1 February and was sent, initially, to Hankey:

The main objects we have to keep in view at the present moment in their order of importance seem to me to be as follows. (I assume throughout that we now possess, and can retain, ocean control, so far as commerce is concerned; and on this I propose to say nothing.)

(1) Our first national necessity is to keep our Grand Fleet to such a point of efficiency that, when it is at its weakest, it should be overwhelmingly stronger than the German Grand Fleet at its strongest. To this supreme necessity everything else must give way.

(2) Second in importance to this, but only just second, is the duty of checkmating the German advance in France and Flanders.

(3) If, and when, these two objects have been amply secured, we may properly take in hand operations of secondary importance. Although, for various reasons, it may be impossible to carry these out at once, they should be considered at once, and prepared for at once.

(4) Among such secondary operations there is, however, one already decided on, which can be begun with little delay—namely, the bombardment of the Dardanelles. If the naval views laid before the War Council be accepted, the risk to the ships does not seem great; while the advantages of success—military, political, and economical—would be enormous. The Turkish Empire and the Turkish Army would be cut in two; the Balkan States, whose foreign policy is in the balance, would come down on the side of the Allies; a way would be opened towards Central Europe from the South; and Russian corn would be released from Odessa to the immense advantage both of the Russian seller and the British consumer.

These advantages are far in excess of any which would be gained by the mere reduction of an ordinary maritime base—like Zeebrugge. Nor do I think that the two operations should be put in the same class. They belong to a different order of magnitude; and even if the greater operation were more perilous than the former (and the reverse appears to be the fact) some risk might well be run if there seemed a reasonable prospect of obtaining its great results.

Let me incidentally remark that the loss of a ship at the Dardanelles by a lucky shot ought not to involve the loss of its crew. Assuming that the Admiralty are right in believing that there is no risk from submarines, the personnel of a sinking ship could surely be rescued.

No doubt it would be very desirable, if only it were possible, to have a land force—Greek or British—co-operating with the Fleet at Gallipoli. But I understand the Admiralty view to be that with our 12/15 in. guns all the Turkish heavy artillery could be silenced; and that, when silenced, such light field guns as the enemy possessed would be insufficient effectually to obstruct the passage of an armoured Fleet. If this be so (and it is a purely technical question) the co-operation of a military force is not absolutely necessary; and the Fleet may for this operation be regarded as self-sufficing. I do not remember any close parallel in naval history; but it has rarely, if ever, happened before that guns mounted in ships have markedly outranged guns mounted in fortresses.

I need not say that I entirely agree with you in thinking that we should keep a considerable margin of strength to meet the unforeseen; including in the unforeseen the possible action of Neutrals. But I gather that in the opinion of the Admiralty our strength in capital ships relative to Germany is increasing; and that in a very few months the Russian Fleet in the Baltic will be very far from negligible. If that is so, we may be fairly content with the maritime situation—except indeed, as regards the submarine menace. [40]

By 3 February Hankey was reporting that he had shown Balfour's 'Notes' to the Prime Minister. Asquith had instructed him to show the paper to Kitchener and Churchill. Hankey suggested omission of the heading and the final paragraph to avoid letting Churchill know that Fisher had sent a copy of his Memorandum to Balfour, thus contravening the ban imposed by Asquith and Churchill on its distribution to other members of the War Council. Hankey continued:

I asked Lord Fisher this morning if he agreed in this view, and he pressed me very strongly not to send it to the First Lord [in its present form]. Lord Fisher, however, quite agreed that it was most desirable that the substance of your Memorandum should be communicated to the First Lord, as it presents questions of principle in a clear form in which they have not yet been stated. [41]

Such, indeed, was Balfour's forte. Moreover, even Fisher seems to have been temporarily mollified by Balfour's reasoning. 'I believe your suggestion may solve all difficulties', Hankey reported soon afterwards. 'If the P.M. will go to the heart of things himself he may be able to arrange matters between Churchill and Fisher.' [42]

As indicated above, crucial decisions about the Dardanelles were brewing in and around the War Council in the first half of February. Balfour, however, remained at Whittingehame until after the meeting of six members suddenly called on the 16th (see p. 255). On 30 January he had hinted to Bonar Law that he was still uneasy about his politically ambiguous membership; [43] and by 10 February Hankey was writing that 'there is not much doing in the C.I.D. to justify me in asking you to return to town.' He could not promise Balfour 'continuous work'. He mentioned that he

[40] B.P. 49712, ff. 144–7, B.'s 'Notes on Lord Fisher's Memo. of Jan. 25', 1 Feb. 1915.
[41] B.P. 49703, ff. 157–8, 3 Feb. 1915.
[42] Ibid., ff. 160–1, n.d.
[43] B.P. 49693, ff. 201–4.

disliked a War Council decision of the 9th to take up with the Greeks and French the idea of sending British troops by way of Salonika to help the Serbs. He thought that the Dardanelles was the 'only extraneous operation worth trying'. But he had warned Asquith that troops might be required. *'From Lord Fisher downwards every naval officer in the Admiralty who is in the secret believes that the Navy cannot take the Dardanelles position without troops.'*[44] On the 17th he informed Balfour of the small War Council of the 16th which had taken 'decisions of the very first importance'. He was not in attendance (for once) and relied for his brief record on accounts given by Asquith, Lloyd George, and Fisher. This record, as communicated to Balfour, corresponded closely to that kept for future reference by Hankey. (It should be noted that Hankey's minutes were not circulated to members of the War Council or Cabinet. The Cabinet was given the gist of them orally by Asquith.) As far as Balfour was concerned, the salient facts were that the 29th Division, hitherto earmarked for France, was now to go to Lemnos (close to the Dardanelles) as soon as possible; and that, together with troops from Egypt, and some Marines, they were 'to be available in case of necessity to support the naval attack on the Dardanelles'.[45] However, no one seems to have suggested that the forthcoming naval bombardment should be delayed until a decision was reached on the kind of service to be required of the troops. It appears to have been universally assumed that no landing would be made till the Navy had forced the Dardanelles.

By 18 February Balfour was back in London. Churchill was then negotiating with Kitchener about employing troops at the Dardanelles. They were to land *after* the Navy had fought its way through to the Sea of Marmora. If the Turks did not withdraw from the Gallipoli Peninsula, the troops could be landed to defeat them (presumably in an unopposed landing); or they could occupy Constantinople if it was swept by revolution.[46] It will be seen that Balfour, like other members of the War Council, made a clear distinction between an opposed military landing and what he called 'the Bosphorous operation'. The decision to switch from the Bosporus plan to the opposed landings of 25 April—with all their bitter Australasian memories lingering to the present day—was taken without the War Council being called at all. As far as Balfour was concerned, the sequence of events was as follows:

[44] B.P. 49703, ff. 162–6.
[45] B.P. 49703, ff. 167–8, 17 Feb. 1915; Cab. 22/1/2, 16 Feb. 1915.
[46] Churchill to Kitchener, 18 Feb. 1915 (Gilbert, Companion Vol. iii, 518–19).

On 19 February the full War Council was convened. Haldane pointed out that it had not been settled how many troops would be sent to the Dardanelles any more than 'the precise purpose for which they were to be' used'. Churchill observed that, since the recent 'Russian defeat in the East', it had become 'desirable to ensure success in the Dardanelles'. Kitchener indicated that he might consequently be prepared to send the 29th Division to the Mediterranean. Haldane 'wanted to know what was the precise function' of the force, totalling some three divisions. Kitchener replied that 'a force of this size might be required to secure the passage of the Dardanelles after the fall of the forts.' Churchill confirmed that he 'did not ask for troops actually to be sent to the Dardanelles, but only that they should be within hail'. On the basis, therefore, of exploitation of a successful naval attack, it was decided to prepare transports to carry the Australian and New Zealand troops from Alexandria to Lemnos and to take the 29th Division to 'the Mediterranean, if required.' Balfour wanted a detailed study of the likely 'political effects of an occupation of the Gallipoli Peninsula combined with naval command of the Sea of Marmora'—thus implying his agreement with exploitation only. [47]

It was after the end of this meeting that the news came through that the naval bombardment had begun. Hankey has recorded in his memoirs the remarkable impact of this news on at least some of the members of the War Council. He indicates that, when they reassembled on 24 February, one speaker after another cast aside the assumption that, in case of failure, the naval attack could be broken off (and the troops used elsewhere). He lists the more or less passionate recorded statements of Churchill, Kitchener, and Grey to the effect that troops should be used to ensure the Navy's success, if necessary. He also gives Lloyd George credit for arguing that they 'were committed by this operation to some operation in the Near East, but not necessarily to a siege of the Dardanelles'. [48] Hankey's minutes show that Lloyd George was more specific than that. He asked 'whether, in the event of the naval attack failing (and it was something of an experiment), it was proposed that the Army should be used to undertake an operation in which the Navy had failed'. Churchill indicated that 'this was not the intention' but that troops might be used 'where a military force would just make the difference between failure and success'. Lloyd George said that if the Navy failed, they should be 'immediately ready to try something else'. Balfour then observed 'that, if the fleet failed in the Dardanelles, the Government would have a very serious decision to take'. Haldane was

[47]   Cab. 22/1/3.
[48]   Lord Hankey, *The Supreme Command 1914–1918*, London, 1961, 2 vols., i, 283.

equally cautious. There was no recorded comment from the 'experts', Admiral Fisher and General 'Sheep' Murray; but in order that Balfour's ensuing memorandum should not be misunderstood the following exchange towards the end of the meeting must be recorded:

THE PRIME MINISTER asked whether the question of opening the Bosphorous had been considered.

LORD KITCHENER said that it was easy by comparison with the Dardanelles. [49]

After the meeting, Balfour composed a paper entitled 'THE WAR'. This does not direct itself to the question whether or not troops should be used at the Dardanelles in the event of a naval failure. His assumption always is that (as the War Council had been assured, if with diminished confidence of late) the naval attack will succeed. In any case, it was for Kitchener to pronounce on the actual use to be made of the troops. Here are some extracts from Balfour's memorandum of 24 February:

I think it may help us to a sound decision on Friday if we bear clearly in mind that the forcing of the Dardanelles is the preliminary stage of *two* military operations . . . I will call them the Bosphorous operation and the Balkan operation.

By the Bosphorous operation I mean the control of the Sea of Marmora, the Bosphorous, and Constantinople. Were this carried out successfully, although it stood alone, we should paralyse Turkey; we should secure free communications with Russia, with all that this carries with it; we should have defeated German ambitions in the Near East; we should (I believe) have secured the neutrality of Bulgaria; and we should have shown to all the world what sea power means. These advantages are not easy to over-estimate. Yet I fully admit that they would be far surpassed if we could bring to a successful issue the second, or Balkan policy [advocated by Lloyd George] . . . It is unfortunately extremely difficult . . . to work out all the elements in the complicated problem which it presents . . . [The three small Balkan states] are obliged to incline to that side of the European struggle which they think is likely to win [and they] are largely swayed by the small local hopes and hatreds . . . [We are apt to forget] a very important point . . . The Roumanian, Bulgarian, and Greek armies are not only separately and collectively larger than any that the Allies, for a long time to come, can put into this theatre of operations, but they form very efficient fighting units . . .

The conclusions I draw are as follows:

We *must* send as many troops as may be required to make the Bosphorous operation, to which we are now committed, a success. But whether we should send more than this number depends upon the answer to two questions which I think we have not yet sufficiently discussed: (a) Do we want the Balkan States to join us at once? (b) Would sending 110,000 men induce them to join us?

---

[49]   Cab. 22/1/2, 24 Feb. 1915.

In so far as this meant sending out some 70,000 men in addition to what they were sending anyhow, he did not think 'that this would be regarded as a very important addition to the local armies'. However:

> We are all agreed that, whatever else is done, the Bosphorous operation must be carried through to a successful termination. This may involve a pitched battle with Turkish troops in the neighbourhood of Constantinople; and, so far as I could gather from our last discussion, we have no very precise information as to the number and quality of the Turkish troops with which, in such circumstances, we might have to deal. Evidently we must work with ample margins, for a check there might amount to disaster. [50]

The War Council met again two days later—on 26 February. By then, Balfour had received a memo from Churchill (dated 25 February and addressed also to Asquith and Lloyd George) which argued that, as the allied lines in the West were secure, 115,000 troops could be spared to attack the Gallipoli Peninsula if the Navy had not come through so as to command the Bulair Isthmus by 21 March. [51] Balfour wrote to Lloyd George a fortnight later saying that he thought the Admiralty plan of 'landing a large force on the Peninsula' was altogether absurd. [52] On 26 February Kitchener drew the War Council's attention to 'the serious position in Russia' and, though Churchill argued that the dispatch of the 29th Division might seal the capture of Constantinople in three weeks time, Kitchener would not be moved. 'He wanted to await two events, viz. (1) the clearing up of the situation in Russia [with its implications for the Western front], and (2) some signs of a probable result in the Dardanelles.' In the light of Churchill's memo of the 25th, Balfour now threw his weight behind Kitchener. He rehearsed the gains attainable by a 'purely naval operation'. Churchill responded that, in fact, supplies would not get through past Turkish guns to Russia and 'that no wheat could be obtained'. Hankey now broke silence twice without check from Asquith. He elaborated Churchill's arguments. It emerged that there was likely to be considerable Turkish resistance, even after the ships had knocked out the Dardanelles forts. Churchill did not reveal to the War Council the suggestion contained in his above-mentioned memo of the 25th. It must have seemed, at least to Haldane, Grey, and Crewe, that a naval success before use of troops was still assumed. However, it is significant that, when Kitchener repeated his refusal to send out the 29th Division till 'he felt quite secure about the

---

[50]   Cab. 42/1/44, 24 Feb. 1915.
[51]   Gilbert, Companion Vol. iii, 563–4.
[52]   B.P. 49692, ff. 222–31, 5 March 1915.

French position', he was again supported by Balfour. The latter stated that they 'were under an honourable obligation to keep' the British 'part of the line intact'. Grey also 'said he was most concerned about the position in the West'. Lloyd George wanted a large force in aid of his Balkan scheme, arguing that such action was needed before the Russians collapsed altogether. Asquith made no positive contribution, so Kitchener won the day. [53]

At the War Council of 3 March Churchill reported the continuing reduction of the outer forts at the Dardanelles. Otherwise, discussion was confined to subjects such as the future of Constantinople. [54] On the 10th, Kitchener announced that 'the situation was now sufficiently secure to justify the despatch of the 29th Division.' Balfour 'asked the strength of the Turkish forces'. Kitchener replied that 'there were supposed to be about 60,000 men in and about the Dardanelles, and possibly another 120,000 men for the defence of Constantinople'. Churchill concluded the discussion by saying that the Admiralty 'still believed that they could effect the passage of the Straits by naval means alone, but they were glad to know that military support was available, if required'. This hint that troops might be used to attack Gallipoli to open the way for the Navy elicited no recorded comment from a full meeting which, on this one occasion, included Bonar Law and Lansdowne among the twelve civilians present. They passed on to spend a great deal of time on 'Russia and Constantinople'. [55] As far as the attendance of Law and Lansdowne was concerned, Asquith thought their contribution slight and they, for their part, felt that further co-operation of this kind would weaken their hold on their party. [56] So Balfour remained on the War Council as a unique Conservative statesman, somewhat above the party battle. As it happened, he would be summoned to only two more meetings in the limited role of war counsellor.

After the War Council meeting of 10 March, which was held in the morning, Hankey conferred with Balfour. In the afternoon, he went back to the C.I.D. offices and looked up the pre-war minutes and memoranda relating to the morning's discussions. Hankey paid tribute to the strategic content of Balfour's report of February 1903 on Russia and Constantinople; but he had been unable to find anything about Alexandretta. [57]

---

[53] Cab. 22/1/2.
[54] Ibid.
[55] Ibid.
[56] Hazlehurst, pp. 230–1.
[57] B.P. 49703, f. 179, Hankey to B., 10 Feb. 1915; Cab. 4/1/1B, 'Report of the conclusion arrived at on the 11th February in reference to Russia and Constantinople', 14 Feb. 1903 (5 pp.).

The implication must be that the two men had not been talking much, if at all, about the use of troops at the Dardanelles.

By 16 March, however, Hankey had written a masterly memorandum focusing a clear light on the dangerous tendencies developing at the top level with regard to the Dardanelles. As expected by naval officers who knew the Straits, the Navy was being held up by Turkish mines and howitzers. Up till then, it had been agreed that troops were to be used only *after* the ships had silenced the forts. However, it now appeared that the Army might have to assault Gallipoli. Hankey emphasized that surprise, of great importance for such an enterprise, had not only been lost but replaced by alarm in Turkish quarters through deliberate British advertisement of the intention 'to force the Dardanelles at any cost'. Moreover, as history showed, combined operations were particularly hazardous and could only succeed on a basis of meticulous planning. He went on to supply a searching questionnaire, designed to render less likely the possibility of 'serious disaster'.[58] He showed the paper to the Prime Minister on the 17th. The latter seems to have indicated that it would be considered by the War Council on Friday, the 19th.[59]

The meeting of 19 March was to prove Balfour's final opportunity in the War Council to oppose the use of troops in a direct assault on Gallipoli. For once, he does not appear to have been primed by Hankey, and the latter's paper of the 16th received little attention.[60] Telegrams were read to the effect that heavy naval losses had been suffered in the attack on the Narrows on the 18th and that Sir Ian Hamilton (acting on far-reaching instructions from Kitchener) accepted that the Army now had to open the Straits for the Navy.

MR. McKENNA asked if the land forces would not be able to clear a passage.

MR. BALFOUR said he had heard Sir Ian Hamilton's telegrams with some misgivings
. . .

THE PRIME MINISTER asked if any general plan and scheme of disembarkation had been worked out. [This question evidently arose from Hankey's memorandum.]

LORD KITCHENER said that the question had been examined in the War Office, but that they had not sufficient information to form a detailed scheme of embarkation. This would be done by Sir Ian Hamilton and his Staff in concert with the Naval Commander-in-Chief.[61]

In effect, control over the ensuing military events had already been

[58] Roskill, *Hankey*, i, 163–4 has nearly all the text.
[59] Hankey, i, 292.
[60] Ibid., p. 293.
[61] Cab. 22/1/2, 19 Mar. 1915.

pre-empted by Kitchener. After the War Council of the 10th, he had decided to order a military attack if the Navy failed at the Narrows. The extreme weakness of the General Staff underlay Kitchener's wholly incompetent decision. Hankey did his best to substitute for an effective General Staff but, when Asquith failed to press home his criticisms, the Secretary could do nothing to prevent the disaster of 25 April.[62]

Within a few days of the War Council of the 19th, Balfour was agreeing with Hankey's original forerunner at the C.I.D., Lord Sydenham (G. S. Clarke), that 'a simultaneous land and sea attack on the Gallipoli Peninsula made earlier in the day would have had a completer success than we have yet attained.'[63]

As if to prove that a small War Council was as prone to blunder as a large one, Asquith on 6 April summoned Churchill and Kitchener, together with Hankey, to consider landing at the Dardanelles the troops being reorganized in Egypt. Hankey could not make any of the others recognize the grave difficulties involved. The meeting effectively endorsed the plan.[64]

On 19 March, Hankey had sought to recruit Lloyd George's support for a special committee to be appointed to go into the details of the Dardanelles attack. He wanted to keep Churchill and Kitchener away from it and to have just 'technical people' working under Balfour as chairman.[65] After the alarming meeting of 6 April, he plied Asquith with his worries, making only limited impact.[66] On the afternoon of the 8th at 4 Carlton Gardens he found Balfour 'fully agreed' on the hazards of a military assault at that stage. (Indeed, his awareness could be said to have dated back to 1892.)[67] Balfour dictated a letter to Churchill there and then.[68]

My dear Winston,
   In reference to our conversation of last night, I have looked up the account of the Gallipoli water supply [and find that the Turkish garrison is unlikely to run short.]
   As you know, I cannot help being very anxious about the fate of any military attempt upon the Peninsula. Nobody was so keen as myself upon forcing the Straits as long as there seemed a reasonable prospect of doing it by the fleet alone—even though the operation might cost a few antiquated battleships. But a military attack upon a position so inherently difficult, and so carefully prepared, is a different

[62] Hankey, i, 290–5. See John Gooch, *The Plans of War*, 1974, Ch. 10, for Kitchener and the General Staff in 1915.
[63] B.P. 49702, f. 301, B. to Syndenham, 23 March 1915.
[64] Hankey, i, 300; Cab. 22/1/2, 6 April 1915.
[65] Roskill, *Hankey*, i, 164.
[66] Gilbert, Companion Vol. iii, 775, Asquith to Venetia Stanley, 7 April 1915.
[67] See Ch. 5, pp. 64–5.
[68] Hankey, i, 301.

proposition; and, if it fails, we shall not only have to suffer considerably in men, and still more in prestige, but we may upset our whole diplomacy in the Near East, which, at the present moment, seems to promise so favourably . . .

Yours very sincerely,
Arthur James Balfour[69]

Replying the same day, Churchill asserted that the soldiers on the spot believed they could succeed. The naval and military attacks would proceed concurrently and success for one or the other would suffice.[70] As long as Churchill persisted with such views, Kitchener was the main determinant. Once he had, after 10 March, decided to abandon his opposition to any diversion of regular troops from the Western Front, the die was cast. From 25 April the surviving troops clung to ravaged footholds on the Gallipoli Peninsula. In terms of costly attacks on strongly defended positions, they might as well have been on the Western Front.

Apart from the Dardanelles, Balfour's concerns in April included the munitions question and the offensive staged the previous month at Neuve Chapelle. In March, Balfour had been working with Lloyd George when he was negotiating his famous 'Treasury Agreement' with the trade unions. This was aimed at relaxing union restraints on expanding production, especially in munitions; and in return the unions attained a new position of importance in the country. Early in April, Asquith at last reconstituted a cabinet munitions committee originally established in October 1914. Lloyd George was chairman with Balfour as the other principal member. The committee 'ought to have been appointed seven months ago', Balfour wrote to Bonar Law a few days before its public announcement.[71]

As for Neuve Chapelle, Balfour visited the front on or about 20 April and discussed this comparatively modest exemplar of future offensives with Field Marshal Sir John French. He wrote afterwards to his brother Gerald that

undoubtedly recent operations have, from many points of view, especially from the point of view of loss of life, been most unsatisfactory. Personally, I have never been able to see why French was so confident of being able to break the German line. We resisted their attempt to break *our* lines successfully against enormous odds . . .[72]

---

[69] B.P. 49694, ff. 105–7, 8 April 1915. The full text is also available in Gilbert, Companion Vol. iii, 779, and p. 781 has Fisher's excellent suggestion of 8 April (inspired by Hankey via Richmond) that British advertisement of the assault on Gallipoli should be used to produce complete surprise for a landing in Syria. He wanted the War Council to be specially convened.

[70] B.P. 49694, ff. 108–10.

[71] B.P. 49693, ff. 206–7, B. to Law, 3 April 1915; Hankey, i, 308–11.

[72] B.P. 49831, ff. 20–2, 31 May 1915.

Indeed, it was not only Balfour's intellect that was affronted by the policy of western offensives. Mrs Dugdale has recounted from her own recollections how, in the first days of the war, after a farewell meeting with his youthful nephew Oswald who was about to embark for France, Balfour 'gave way to an uncontrollable burst of tears'.[73] And as lately as early April, he had been writing to console Lady Desborough, one of his oldest friends, on the loss of her son Julian. Her reply leaves no room for doubt about the depth of Balfour's feelings.[74] Once he became First Lord of the Admiralty, Balfour would do his best to restrain the offensive policy in Flanders.

As the Liberal Government slid closer toward coalition with the Conservatives—who constituted, after all, the largest single party in the Commons—it was probable that Balfour would be asked to fill a high ministerial post. The range and quality of his mind had been reasserted at the War Council and in his memoranda. If Hankey (as already mentioned) would have placed him as chairman of something like the Chiefs of Staff Sub-Committee of later years to sort out the Dardanelles problem, others always realized that he was still well equipped to be Foreign Secretary. With the onset of the shells outcry and Fisher's final break with Churchill, the latter's own position as First Lord was threatened; and on 17 May he made the interesting suggestion that Balfour should replace Kitchener at the War Office. He wrote to Asquith that Lloyd George would not suit at the War Office but that, with Balfour there, the Welshman could do Munitions as well as his Chancellor's job.[75] Balfour was certainly in quite close touch with Churchill and the other leading governmental participants at the time; and it is likely that Churchill knew Balfour's feelings about Kitchener fairly well. A month earlier, on 16 April, Balfour had written to Lord Robert Cecil:

My dear Bob,

. . . I am in very low spirits about the way things are being done. I spent two hours with K. yesterday, whose conversation was at times incredible in its folly, and who was very angry with Lloyd George [about munitions, doubtless]. Then after Bonar Law's meeting I spent an hour with Haldane who begged me to do what I could (privately) to smooth down Von Donop [Master-General of the Ordnance], whose incapacity, in my opinion, is one of the chief causes of the present mess . . . After I left Haldane I spent three-quarters of an hour with Winston. Peacemakers may be

---

[73] Dugdale, ii, 122–3.
[74] WHI/166, 1 April 1915.
[75] Gilbert, Companion Vol. iii, 898.

'blessed' in the long run, but they certainly are not 'blessed' while they are making their efforts!

Yours affectionately,
A. J. B. [76]

The question arises, if Balfour had in fact gone to the War Office, what effect would this have had on offensive policy in the West? While there is no evidence from Balfour's career, either as Prime Minister or at the Admiralty, that he would have initiated any strengthening of General Staff organization, yet the conclusion must be that he would have respected professional advice where it was cogently presented. On the other hand, he would have reserved the right to veto proposals with which he seriously disagreed. His considered views on such matters are contained in a letter to Bonar Law of 10 September 1917 (by which time Lloyd George's small War Cabinet held full executive powers).

He referred to their conversation of the previous day 'about the proper relation between the Government and its military advisers'. The Cabinet, he wrote, was in a difficult position in having to take responsibility 'for all the acts of the Executive, including the operations of the Army and the Fleet. Actually [he continued], it would be disastrous if it attempted to control the details of naval and military proceedings.' He would not try to prescribe rules. 'But one or two things', he noted, 'have been borne in upon me during the war.'

In the first place, it seems very important not to try to make naval or military commanders carry out operations of which they really disapprove, though they may have given a formal assent to them. That was the fundamental error in the Dardanelles proceedings. It is not that the idea of the Dardanelles expedition was wrong . . . But, in the face of the real disapproval of Lord Kitchener and Lord Fisher, it was bound to end in disaster. The same vice robbed the Salonica expedition of any chance . . . of success . . . Half-hearted commanders never won a battle . . . If, therefore, the Cabinet finds that any proposed operation is one of which its military advisers do not thoroughly approve, I submit that it should either not be attempted, or else new military advisers should be secured who are in genuine agreement with the proposal.

Once an operation was begun, the commander should be given a free hand 'and every support'. Accordingly he had, of late, opposed taking guns for Italy away from Haig in Flanders.

The Cabinet was, for its part, free to 'veto proposals which it objects to, and require other proposals to be made to it. Nor', he concluded, 'is it

[76]   B.L. 51071, Cecil of Chelwood P.

debarred from suggesting operations or examining closely into advice given it by its experts.'[77]

This statement—together with his constant insistence on the overwhelming superiority of the Grand Fleet and, secondly, on the 'duty of checkmating the German advance in France and Flanders' (as stated in his 'Notes' of 1 February 1915)—summarizes his view of his role as First Lord of the Admiralty and a leading cabinet minister from 25 May 1915. The standard criticism of Balfour is that, in tandem with Sir Henry Jackson as First Sea Lord, he failed to provide enough drive and initiative. Certainly, these had never been Balfour's strong points. It is therefore tempting to speculate how a combination at the Admiralty of Balfour and Fisher would have worked out. Even if (as may well be doubted) Fisher had as First Sea Lord seriously proposed his Baltic 'scheme' to Balfour as First Lord, it is clear that the latter would have enlisted other professional opinions, such as Jellicoe's, to expose its hazards. In October 1916 Balfour wrote in a cabinet paper that such schemes would hardly be approved 'by any sailor with war experience'. What with the heavy German mining of the Baltic entrances and the proximity of their base at Kiel, an attempt to force a way through 'would be more costly than the naval attempt on the Dardanelles' without any 'prize comparable to Constantinople to reward our efforts if we succeeded'.[78] Hankey's subsequent comments on Fisher's undeveloped Baltic idea are very damaging. They may be found in a little-known memo written for Lloyd George on 31 March 1917:

. . . I do not think Lord Fisher's Baltic project, to which he alludes, was ever feasible. As outlined in these papers the project is extremely vague . . . My own opinion is that the whole plan was a chimera from the very beginning . . . If we have never been able to knock out from the sea Ostend and Zeebrugge, the defences of which have been wholly extemporised during the War, how could we ever have hoped to . . . penetrate through the narrow passages of the Skager-Rack, Cattegat, and the Great Belt, into the heavily mined seas of the Western Baltic? Moreover, the craft built to carry out this plan were not capable of accomplishing it. The famous monitors were . . . ramshackle and unseaworthy . . . The three famous 'mystery' ships [freak battle-cruisers] . . . turned out to draw too much water . . . Finally, no Admiral could be found to carry out the project [not even] Sir Lewis Bayly . . .[79]

In the light of such strictures from a comparatively sympathetic source the advantages to be gained by yoking Balfour with Fisher, rather than with the scientific, dismal, desk-bound Jackson, seem less than overwhelming.

[77] B.P. 49693, ff. 257–61, 10 Sept. 1917.
[78] Cab. 37/157/31, 'Report on Recent Naval Affairs', 14 Oct. 1916.
[79] Cab. 21/5, 'Baltic Project'.

Asquith, as late as 1916, admitted that Fisher was still 'a constructor, very fertile and ingenious'. But the types of vessel ordered by this remarkable old man (aged 74 by May 1915) had at times been bizarre. Too high a premium can surely be placed on restless activity. The fact that even the impetuous Beatty had adopted something very close to Jellicoe's cautious standpoint by January 1918 argues that patience was more relevant than 'hustle' (aptly attributed by Asquith to Fisher) when it came to strategy in the North Sea. As far as the U-boat problem was concerned, Fisher's approach did not differ from Balfour's. When placed by Balfour at the naval Board of Invention to organize the search for a detecting device (which *was* discovered before the end of the war)[80] he does not seem, any more than Balfour and his close advisers, to have thought in terms of convoy as an immediate palliative. If there was an imposing alternative to Jackson (who was known in the Admiralty to have opposed the Dardanelles project on thoroughly professional grounds but to have been overruled by Churchill) none of the subsequent commentators have suggested his identity—unless Jellicoe was, in May 1915, to be brought back from command of the Grand Fleet. Talent was scarce at the top. Fisher's new education scheme for young officers had only begun in 1903 and its early products were still junior Lieutenants in 1915.

On Monday, 17 May Bonar Law, having learned of Fisher's resignation, went to Lloyd George with a demand for a new Prime Minister: Balfour, Grey, or the Chancellor himself.[81] Lloyd George agreed to none of these suggestions but pressed Asquith to consent to a coalition. Asquith agreed. The Tories insisted that Churchill should leave the Admiralty and Haldane the Government. Churchill at first succumbed and suggested Balfour as his replacement, believing (correctly) that he would persist at the Dardanelles. As Lloyd George would subsequently remark, Balfour might be over-critical in reaching a decision, but he held that once a choice was made it should not be quickly abandoned.[82] That night, however, Churchill renewed his fight, suggesting Balfour for the War Office. By Wednesday the 19th Balfour had emerged as Churchill's probable replacement. Kitchener, of course, was still irremovable. Selborne wrote to Balfour recommending Fisher as the best available for First Sea Lord, little knowing that Fisher had been waving before a remonstrating Hankey the extraordinary demands which he sent later that day to the Prime Minister. (For instance, he wanted sole charge of naval operations and would not

[80] Mackay, pp. 506–9.
[81] Hazlehurst, p. 267.
[82] David Lloyd George, *War Memories*, London, 1933–6, 6 vols., ii, 1015.

serve under Balfour.) Fisher also wrote to Bonar Law, explaining that Balfour had 'been hypnotized by Winston over the Dardanelles', and had brought Churchill back into the Cabinet without portfolio, and that Churchill 'would be practically his adviser' instead of him, Fisher. Selborne heard of Asquith's outrage at Fisher's demands before the day's end and at once sent Balfour a card saying that he hoped Fisher would recant and that Balfour would still take him as First Sea Lord.[83] Balfour replied the next day:

My dear Willie,

Thanks very much for your two notes.

I do not the least know, as yet, what place Asquith desires me to occupy. I have told him that personally I would rather occupy *none*; but, after what Bonar Law said to me on Monday, this, I take it, is impossible. I saw Asquith on Tuesday evening, and wrote to him yesterday to say that the only administrative Office I thought I could usefully fill would be the Admiralty; but that I was prepared to join the new Government either with or without a portfolio, or in any of the non-administrative Offices, like the Duchy. This, indeed, is the course which I should prefer. I do not know what his decision will be.

I am afraid that Jacky is really a little mad. He has been using, I hear, the most violent language about me, whom I believe at one time he used to 'butter up to the skies'. I am not sure that even if Asquith consented to his remaining at the Admiralty [against which Asquith had now firmly set his face], he [Fisher] would consent to serve under me. There would be no use our attempting to work together unless he really was prepared to go cordially with me.

I am sorry you take so low a view of [Admiral of the Fleet Sir Arthur] Wilson. I am afraid from all I hear that he is a poor administrator. Do you think he would be a poor adviser on what is, after all, the most important matter during the war, namely *naval strategy*? I have heard very alarming accounts of his wild advice when we were on the verge with Germany in 1911!

I do not envy the new First Lord, and I hope it won't be me.

Yours affectionately,
Arthur James Balfour[84]

Selborne confirmed that he had heard 'from so many senior naval officers since the war began, including Fisher himself', that Wilson, 'always obstinate', had in his old age become 'a dangerous adviser'. Wilson would not admit that the submarine was 'a grave danger to all ships of war' and had, in his curious advisory role under Churchill, 'been constantly urging

[83] Mackay, pp. 500–3.
[84] Bodl., MS Selborne 1, 20 May 1915.

Jellicoe should be ordered to attack the forts of Heligoland with the Grand
Fleet'. This, thought Selborne, was 'stark staring madness'. [85]

So, in accordance with the Board's patent of 27 May, Balfour took
Admiral Sir Henry Jackson, F.R.S., the consistent opponent at the
Admiralty of naval attacks on fortresses wherever situated, to be his First
Sea Lord. Supported by the shrewd, hard-working Vice-Admiral Henry
Oliver who had been appointed Chief of the War Staff by Churchill the
previous November, Balfour and Jackson settled down to running the Navy
in conformity with the thoroughly sound, if unadventurous, policy established by Jellicoe in the early days of the War. The German fleet was to be
contained and trade protected. Naval officers invariably found Balfour
courteous, reasonable, quick in assimilation, and open to suggestion.
Oliver has left the following record:

> I liked Mr. Balfour. He had the sense to find out how the Admiralty machine
> worked before making changes. In the afternoons he would send for one of the
> Heads of Department and spend an hour or two questioning and learning all about
> the work of the Department. He lived at his house in Carlton Gardens . . . About
> once a week he, Balfour, would walk me over to his house and give me lunch and I
> got to know most of the Cabinet Ministers there. [86]

Perhaps the most substantial account, from direct personal knowledge, of
Balfour's term as First Lord was written by the respected Secretary of the
Admiralty at that time, Sir William Graham Greene. Here are some
extracts:

> Both in the Cabinet and the Admiralty his views were received with deference . . .
> at the Admiralty it was felt that if he personally did not favour any particular action
> or policy there was no need for further enquiry.
> [At the outset] the main question which confronted him and Sir Henry Jackson
> was that of the continuance of the operations [at the Dardanelles] . . . and it is
> probable that if a free choice had been possible he would have advised the
> abandonment of the Dardanelles operations. The country was, however, too far
> committed . . . [Moreover the] enormous strategic advantage which the Allies
> would derive from the fall of the Dardanelles Forts [still] appealed to him, and he
> gave full support to the consequential War plans . . . With regard to the administra-
> tion of the Admiralty . . . he mastered in a wonderful way the general organisation
> and details of official work as they came before the Board . . . In regard to demands
> made upon him, he was unsparing of himself in undertaking distant journeys to
> which his presence was essential. On at least four occasions he went to France in

[85] B.P. 49708, ff. 251–3, 20 May 1915.
[86] N.M.M., OLV/12, 'Recollections' of Adl. of the Fleet, Sir Henry Oliver, Vol. ii, p.
161.

order to consult French Ministers and Officers [with top-level British missions]; on another he travelled to the Far North in early winter to visit the Grand Fleet. Again, on a winter's day, he went with other Ministers to Hatfield Park to be present at the first practical trial of a new invention, the 'tank'.[87] [Though] his habit of reclining in an easy chair in his official room at the Admiralty gave him the appearance of debility or indolence [he was always ready to see officers.] To me, as Secretary of the Admiralty, he was accessible at all times, and never showed the slightest impatience or reluctance to discuss matters of business . . . Where, however, an incident seemed to him to involve unfair or ill-tempered conduct as between colleagues or superiors and subordinates, he was quickly aroused, and prompt to see that right ensued. In his presence all men seemed rather small and inferior, and this placed him as First Lord in an unrivalled position for settling differences of opinion or deciding important questions . . .[88]

No doubt Lloyd George had some justification for his retrospective view of Balfour as a 'dawdler', with the result that there was not enough collective thrust and inventiveness in technical matters, such as fitting the ships with director firing and the remedying of other defects revealed by the Battle of Jutland (31 May 1916).[89] While Balfour's appointment as First Lord brought to the Navy a restoration of confidence that professional opinion would prevail in operational matters, and therefore it was not to be expected that he would take much personal initiative in that field, it was always open to him to bring about the type of decentralization adopted by Sir Eric Geddes from September 1917.[90] By way of contrast, Selborne, the joint initiator of the C.I.D., showed natural interest in strengthening Hankey's co-ordinating function, soon after he entered the Asquith Coalition.[91] Balfour was capable of working out a reorganization of the Admiralty, but only if it was strongly pressed upon him. So how far did it matter that no such reorganization took place under Balfour and Jackson? Enhanced efficiency in the Admiralty's system of intelligence and communications might well, had it come soon enough, have produced a more convincing British success at Jutland and there might have been time for some further technical improvements in the Navy by the end of 1916. But whether all this would have brought the defeat of Germany much nearer is open to doubt. The main requirement was to avoid a disaster. It was the men

[87] This event took place on 2 Feb. 1916. Hankey, i, 496 continues: 'Balfour insisted on riding in a tank—just as years before, at an early demonstration of aeroplanes, I remembered him insisting on taking a flight.'

[88] N.M.M., GEE/13, 'Earl [of] Balfour as First Lord of the Admiralty', Feb. 1934.

[89] Arthur J. Marder, *From the Dreadnought to Scapa Flow*, London, 1961–70, 5 vols., ii, 298, 301; Stephen Roskill, *Admiral of the Fleet Earl Beatty*, London, pp. 191–3.

[90] Marder, ii, 300 and iv, 218–24.

[91] Roskill, *Hankey*, pp. 183–4.

of daring initiative and vivid imagination who were naturally prone to 'lose the war in an afternoon'. Balfour was not such a one. The story of his term as First Lord is hardly dramatic; but it will be seen that the sailors were sorry to see him go.

It was not until 1916 that Balfour started to come under serious criticism at the Admiralty. From May to December 1915 his standing as a minister was particularly high, as appears from the following (largely critical) notes made by Selborne about his cabinet colleagues in June 1916. Selborne resigned as Minister of Agriculture, with effect from 26 June, in protest at the Government's bid for Home Rule. He decided to write down his impressions of ministerial colleagues while they were still fresh in his mind. Having worked round the cabinet table at Downing Street from Asquith ('no ounce of drive in his composition, not a spark of initiative'), through Kitchener ('a strange mixture of streaks, genius and stupidity'), Churchill ('clever, but quite devoid of judgement'), and Lloyd George ('very clever, with vision, prevision, driving power and courage in wonderful combination [but] he would leave anyone in the lurch'), he came in due course to Balfour who

did his work at the Admiralty I believe quite admirably, but in Cabinet all the faults which he had shown as P.M. in the 1900 [Parliament] were accentuated. He yearned for decisions just as heartily as [Asquith] loathed them; yet he never did anything to obtain them. He seldom spoke (comparatively to his status, second in the Cabinet) and when he did it was critically and destructively and not constructively. He showed the same splendid staying power and absence of nerves as the P.M., but he had no more driving force than the P.M. He had the vision which the P.M. lacked, but it led to nothing. Philosophy is the worst possible training for politics. Arthur's personal charm was as great as ever; as loveable as ever. [92]

In so far as Selborne himself had been a leading 'Die-hard' in 1911 and a vehement advocate of an aggressive policy at Gallipoli in mid-1915,[93] while Balfour displayed what might be termed enlightened, or flexible, tenacity on both occasions, the latter's own gloss on Selborne's comments is implied in a note to Selborne of 29 November 1915. (Balfour had put forward the naval advantages of retaining a hold on Gallipoli but had been overborne on military grounds in the War Committee—the successor body to the War Council and the Dardanelles Committee.) Balfour wrote:

We cannot all make speeches in Cabinet; and I had already discussed the question

[92] Bodl., MS Selborne 80, dated simply '1916'.
[93] Hankey, i, 340–1.

of Gallipoli, first in a memorandum,[94] and secondly, at the War Committee. Asquith's remarks [at the Cabinet where evacuation was strongly opposed by Curzon and other non-members of the War Committee] very much represented my attitude on the facts then before me. I am sceptical myself about the catalogue of tragedies which are expected to follow in Egypt and the Far East; and they are at least as likely to follow upon an involuntary, as upon a voluntary retirement. This, however, is not true of Russia. This is an element in the question, but only one . . .[95]

The fact was that withdrawal from Gallipoli (to which Selborne was opposed) was linked with two other even more important issues: one was conscription (which was, of course, debated in the Cabinet, and was supported by Selborne, among others); and the other was the question of an offensive policy on the Western Front. It will be seen that for Balfour, and for Asquith, this was the really crucial issue and was to be settled in the War Committee of which Selborne was not a member.

Indeed, apart from his work at the Admiralty, Balfour's main effort as a minister went into the discussions and foreign missions arising, firstly, from the Dardanelles Committee (June–October 1915) and, secondly, the War Committee (November 1915–December 1916). As he wrote just after giving up his Admiralty post in 1916:

The Navy, especially in time of war, cannot and ought not to be regarded as a self-contained and separate entity. The part it plays depends upon its relations to other departments at home, and to allied Governments. The ordinary training of a sailor is an admirable one, but it is hardly suited to supply all the qualifications which such a situation requires . . .[96]

During 1916 his role in the War Committee was to an extent narrowed down to answering criticisms of Admiralty policy. But from June to December 1915 he had been much involved in the aforesaid issues of conscription and the Army's demand for further offensives on the Western Front. The two issues interlaced. As Hankey (himself an opponent of conscription) has explained, Balfour and the anti-conscriptionists adhered to a traditional British standpoint:

Not only had we to keep command of the sea—which no one disputed—but we were the principal banker, arsenal, manufacturer, and general purveyor to the

---

[94]   Cab. 37/137/36, 'Gallipoli', 19 Nov. 1915, 2 pp. 'Though I was not . . . in favour of its occupation, I venture . . . to give some reasons against leaving it now . . . To Russia the blow would be staggering . . .'. Retention tied down enemy troops. The Navy could more easily close the Dardanelles to enemy ships if Helles, at least, was still held. For reasons of prestige, and to avoid the risks of evacuation, he advised holding on.

[95]   Bodl., MS Selborne 1, 29 Nov. 1915.

[96]   B.P. 49715, f. 273, B. to Duke of Buccleuch, 8 Dec. 1916.

whole Alliance. The attempt to maintain an army on the continental scale would, in their opinion, be a fatal misapplication of our resources and bleed us to death, thereby depriving the Alliance of its greatest asset. [97]

In so far as conscription could produce more cannon-fodder than Kitchener's voluntary system, one might have expected Lloyd George to have been in the ranks of the anti-conscriptionists. In fact, he seems to have been governed by a nice blend of political instinct and objective judgement from his new (hardly traditional Liberal) viewpoint of the Ministry of Munitions, where his performance was to earn Balfour's ungrudging admiration. He was becoming isolated from the other Liberal ministers while being treated by Asquith as a rather troublesome cuckoo in the nest. [98] Typically, Asquith was happy to let Balfour state the anti-conscriptionist case in terms of cabinet memoranda. Kitchener, although he envisaged 70 divisions in France by 1916, still opposed compulsory military service in order to avoid premature losses before the year of supreme effort, 1917. Churchill supported Lloyd George and conscription. Otherwise, Liberal ministers opposed compulsion and Conservatives supported it. The cardinal argument in favour of it, which proved to have general backing in the country, was that there should be equality of sacrifice. But Lloyd George, for example, emphasized that only compulsion would produce the requisite numbers of troops for the various fronts and provide replacements for the large numbers of skilled men to be brought back to make munitions.

What with intense German pressure on the Russians in July and Joffre's demands for a joint Franco-British offensive in the West, there was little time available for Balfour to make his views prevail. But he was quickly off the mark with a two-page paper for the Cabinet dated 9 June 1915. This was addressed to the current question of compulsory registration. He pointed out that it was necessary to decide whether the proposed bill was to be seen 'merely as a step towards compulsory military service' or a basis for total industrial mobilization. He thought it was impossible to allot to each man

a task determined for him by some central or other authority. It is on this rock that, as most of us believe, Socialism would split, were it ever attempted; and that which would be impossible if we had time for quiet organisation is surely doubly impossible now.

He thought that some other means should be devised to meet the most pressing industrial need, namely for skilled men to make munitions. A bill to compel people to work in this field alone might well engender a sense of

[97]   Hankey, i, 425.
[98]   Peter Rowland, *Lloyd George*, London, 1975, p. 326.

grievance, refusal to obey in the name of personal liberty, and thus martyrs.[99]

A deeply matured paper followed some three weeks later on military strategy. It lacks a title but is dated 2 July. Its gist is as follows:

It is generally agreed [wrote Balfour] that this war has degenerated into one of attrition. On the Western frontier, at all events, great dramatic successes, which in one decisive moment shall put great armies out of action, can hardly be looked for.

In such circumstances the true measure of success is to be found in the casualty list. Operations in which the enemy suffer more than the Allies hasten the work of attrition; operations in which the Allies suffer more than the enemy delay the work of attrition . . .

These observations apply more particularly to operations in the West. Operations in the Eastern theatre of war are of the older pattern; and it is plainly one of the first duties of the Allies in the West to do all in their power to prevent troops being sent across Germany to crush the Russians . . . the operations in Gallipoli have undoubtedly relieved . . . the pressure on the Russians in the Caucasus . . .

He therefore advocated a policy of 'active defence'. 'Of course,' he continued, 'if the enemy refused to attack and were content to defend thinly-held lines, while despatching large forces to other theatres', the Allies would have to attack. But if it was true that the Germans intended to try to break through towards Paris or Calais, he thought the Allies should 'welcome such a policy'. Germany, hemmed in on three sides, might well be forced to persist with a war of attrition with the odds against her. At the present stage where British and Russian forces were still some way from their peak, it would be particularly counter-productive to indulge in costly offensives.[100]

Kitchener, however, was persuaded by news of Russian and Italian setbacks to co-operate with Joffre; and the result, on 25 September, was the commitment of Sir John French's army to the Battle of Loos. On the same day the War Office was strengthened when 'Sheep' Murray was replaced by Lieutenant-General Sir Archibald Murray as C.I.G.S. This marked the first inroad into Kitchener's powers and the beginning of the resurgence of the General Staff. These developments presaged an irresistible build-up of momentum behind the policy of British offensives in the West. Whether the plight of the Russians or of the French or of both necessitated a British offensive became a matter for the increasingly powerful General Staff rather than for the politicians to judge. Meanwhile, the British had lost some 60,000 in casualties during the Loos offensive. French casualties in

[99] Cab. 37/129/30, 9 June 1915.
[100] Cab. 37/144/4, 2 July 1915 (2 pp.).

Champagne and Artois totalled nearly 200,000. Already, by 30 September, Balfour was remarking in the Dardanelles Committee that he had put it to Sir John French that Allied casualties in the Loos offensive would exceed those of the Germans. French had demurred. It now seemed that the General was wrong. Lloyd George also expressed dissatisfaction.[101]

Meanwhile, in response to the Northcliffe press's campaign for conscription and Milner's manifesto of 20 August, Balfour produced a cabinet paper on the 22nd. He did not think that public opinion was ready for such a measure yet. (On this point, he proved, not altogether surprisingly, to be a fallible guide.) He wanted Kitchener to 'say on behalf of the Government that, for the present, universal military service is not needed'.[102] In the face of falling numbers of recruits, Kitchener did not go so far. Balfour came back again with a longer memorandum for the Cabinet dated 19 September. He rehearsed his previous arguments in favour of 'fleets, money and armies'—in that order—as the basis of war policy. He then restated the danger to national unity posed by compulsion, presenting the case thus:

> Two propositions, however, appear to me to be fairly clear. The first is that we shall never get the Irish to accept compulsion either in the House of Commons or in Ireland. The second is that in the ranks of organised labour, and perhaps outside them, there will be a great body of hostile opinion . . . Already the shadow of conscription has driven vast numbers of Irish labourers from employment in Britain, and has induced a great stream of emigration from Ireland to America . . . Nationalist Ireland, backed at this particular moment by the Irish vote in America, and by organised labour in Britain, would not be easy to deal with . . .

Finally, he said that during the past thirty years leading military authorities had assured him that soldiers could not be made in six months. Even if they might not be quite so sure about this now, what about the necessary 'generals, staff officers, the higher regimental officers, and artillerymen' needed for an army of 70 divisions?[103]

Asquith momentarily outmanoeuvred the conscriptionists by appointing Derby, a keen conscriptionist, as Director-General of Recruiting (5 October). Then Balfour came up with a further cabinet paper emphasizing the importance of Britain's maintaining her economic position and thus her credit-worthiness abroad. In particular, American loans could run out. 'I doubt', he wrote, 'whether a greater calamity could happen to Russia, France, and Italy than that Britain should cease to be able to purchase

---

[101]   Cab. 42/3/35, 30 Sept. 1915. Casualty figures come from John Terraine, *The Great War 1914–18*, London, (Arrow edn.), 1967, p. 119.

[102]   Cab. 37/133/7, 'National Service and the Nation', 22 Aug. 1915 (2 pp.).

[103]   Cab. 37/134/25, 'Efficiency in War and Compulsion', 19 Sept. 1915 (4 pp.).

abroad the food and munitions which she and they so urgently require.'[104] Bonar Law, as Conservative leader, was of course a key supporter of Lloyd George on the politically crucial question of conscription. It was perhaps significant for the eventual decline of Balfour's political standing that it was Bonar Law who hit back—if at Balfour's suggestion—with quite a lengthy paper, arguing that American prosperity and other suppliers' need of a market would result in the necessary credit being made available.[105]

All along, the conscriptionists had aimed at Kitchener's removal or demotion. There were also complaints about the size to which the 'War' Committee had been allowed to grow. Asquith's response, on 3 November, was to summon a new War Committee (replacing the Dardanelles Committee) consisting on this one occasion of only three members: Kitchener, Balfour, and himself—without Hankey.[106] In so far as Kitchener was then shunted off to inspect the position at the Dardanelles, Balfour's political standing had reached a height which he could not have anticipated since his retirement from leadership of his party. Now, however, the day of the General Staff was at hand.

There was a growing acceptance in high political and military circles that Sir William Robertson, hitherto Chief of Staff with the B.E.F., should go to the War Office as C.I.G.S. and that Sir Douglas Haig should replace Sir John French as C.-in-C. in Flanders. By 23 December Robertson had taken over on conditions that gave him virtual control over military strategy, leaving Kitchener as a figurehead. Robertson was henceforth responsible to the War Committee for strategy and had direct access to the Cabinet. As Lord Blake has written, one underlying political reality was that Bonar Law and Lloyd George had worsted Churchill (in May) and then Kitchener.[107] However, once the Army, in the person of Robertson, could argue its case powerfully, neither the politicians in general nor the Prime Minister in particular would be able to apply material checks. The professionals had superseded the amateurs. The outcome was the Battle of the Somme, 415,000 British casualties, and a trauma in the mind of a British generation.

On 23 December the War Committee experienced the impact of the new C.I.G.S. He insisted, against the arguments of Balfour (indicated above)[108] and others, that force must be concentrated on the Western Front and that therefore Gallipoli must be completely evacuated.[109] Although it transpired

---

[104] Cab. 37/135/18, 'Finance and the War', 17 Oct. 1915 (2 pp.).
[105] Cab. 37/135/30, 25 Oct. 1915.
[106] Hankey, ii, 441.
[107] Blake, p. 277.
[108] See his paper of 2 July quoted on p. 279.
[109] Gooch, pp. 328–9.

that the ground had effectively been cut from under Balfour's feet by the hobbling of Kitchener and the elevation of Robertson, the First Lord did not at once accept defeat. He continued with what should doubtless have been Asquith's fight.[110] Balfour's cabinet paper of 27 December surveyed the general conduct of the war with a view to moderating the Army's plan— amounting, as Hankey was to write the following May, to preparations for 'a regular orgy of slaughter'.[111] Here are some extracts from Balfour's argument:

The Cabinet have now decided [after much argument] to abandon our last position on the Gallipoli peninsula—a position which the Navy desired to keep, and the Generals on the spot were prepared to defend. [This decision must] be considered in connection with the general conduct of the war, and the views expressed in recent papers by the General Staff.[112]

The views of the General Staff are clear, simple, and definite. Victory, they think, is only to be won by an advance on the Western Front. Such an advance can, against modern trench fortifications, only be carried out successfully if the numbers of the assailants greatly exceed the numbers of the assailed. From this it follows that every fighting man who is not used to swell the Franco-British numbers on the Western front is a man withdrawn from the main theatre of operations, and is wasted on work which, however successful, cannot affect the ultimate issue of the war . . .

Now, I do not deny that there is some force in these arguments. When the British General Staff pointed out that the notion of saving Serbia by landing at Salonica in November was wholly illusory, they accurately gauged the military situation . . . Nevertheless, I venture to think that their general view . . . requires very careful consideration before it is adopted without qualification by the War Committee of the Cabinet.

In its origins this war is an Eastern war. Austria is fighting primarily because she desires the extension of her sway over the south-eastern Slavs and the control of Salonica. Germany is fighting primarily because she was determined to support Austria in this south-easterly movement, which was part of her own scheme for expanding her influence—commercial, political, and military—to Anatolia, to Persia, and ultimately to Egypt and India. Russia is fighting because she could not tolerate the Teutonisation of the south-eastern Slavs, and the Germanic exploitation of the Turk . . .

The Western view may be, and is, the broader; but the Eastern cannot be ignored . . . We did not take the Dardanelles by surprise when a surprise was possible . . . now, under the eyes of East and West, we avow ourselves defeated at Gallipoli . . . The Turks are to be permitted to bring large forces through Syria to Egypt . . .

---

[110]   See Roskill's assessment in *Hankey*, i, 266–7.
[111]   Ibid., p. 266.
[112]   See Cab. 24/1/G.33, 8 Nov. 1915, by Robertson, and 22/3/1, 16 Dec. 1915, by Murray (17 pp.), annexed to minutes of War Committee, 28 Dec. 1915.

This is probably inevitable, but we must not disguise from ourselves that it will damage our reputation. I hope, therefore, that we shall do what we can to counteract this result (a) by having a sufficient force in Egypt not merely to withstand the Turks but to smash them; and (b) by reconsidering our views about the Salonica expedition . . . it may be foolish to abandon an adventure which it was foolish to undertake . . . In any case its occupation compels Germany either to attack us or to admit that she is not master of the Balkans; and either alternative seems much to our advantage . . .

Therefore it was not clear to him that troops would, in every instance, be better employed in the West than in the East. From eastern possibilities he turned to examine the contention of the Westerners.

It is based upon the double argument that if we 'get through' on the West we can finish the war more or less on our own terms; and that, if we refuse to try and get through on the West, there is nothing left for us to do, and the war will drag on without limit.

I do not contest the force of either of these contentions; but they do not exhaust the subject. If success in a great frontal attack on the German fortified trenches means victory to the *Entente*, does not failure mean defeat? Can the Western Powers afford to fight on terms which may involve a far heavier loss of men for them than for their opponents? . . .

But, say the General Staff, why should failure be anticipated? The *Entente* will have a considerable superiority in numbers; they will have large supplies of guns and ammunition; and they will have learned the lessons which experience in trench warfare has taught them. All this may be granted. But it is probably not the attackers only who will have learnt something from a year and a half of trench warfare. There is no doubt whatever that the Germans are straining every nerve to make their line absolutely impregnable. All through this period of trench warfare they have been better off than the Allies in the mechanical instruments which secure success. We are gradually creeping up to them in the matter of shells and guns. But we have found no sufficient reply to the obstacles provided by successive lines of trenches, the unlimited use of barbed wire, and the machine gun . . .

Now I think that some members of the General Staff would admit that there was weight in these considerations. They know that the anticipations confidently expressed by the French and British Staffs in March and April, and again in August and September, have proved erroneous . . . But what are the possible alternatives? . . .

On this I may observe, in the first place, that if this be a difficulty for the *Entente*, it is not, so far as I can see, less of a difficulty for the Central Powers . . . surely the strain must be greater upon Germany and Austria than upon Russia, England, France, and Italy? Can the Central Powers afford, either from the material or the moral point of view, to drag on a defensive warfare, unrelieved by victory, through next summer and autumn?

Do not German theories of war, as well as German internal necessities, compel them, rightly or wrongly, to attempt the offensive? . . . When *they* have attempted and failed in an attack on the West; when *they* have lost in these operations three lives for every two that have been lost by the Allies; when *their* reserves have been reduced . . . *then* will be the time to attempt the general offensive on which the General Staff count for final victory.

They should therefore wait 'at least beyond the spring' before launching an offensive. The Germans could be expected to attack before the British attained their full equipment of guns and munitions in June. In brief, if in the coming months 'the Germans could be induced to waste their strength in attacking Salonica [reinforced from the West] and our Western front, so much the better for us'. [113]

It is curious that, in an excellent little chapter entitled 'The Beginning of the War of Attrition', Hankey never mentions Balfour by name. Yet his account of the 'misgiving' in the War Committee seems to have been largely reconstructed from Balfour's above-quoted memorandum—the 'formidable' character of which was admitted at the time by a dissenting Esher. [114] However, it is certainly true, as Hankey points out, that the firm recommendations emanating from the military conference held by allied military representatives at Chantilly from 6 to 8 December confronted the War Committee with a 'remarkable unanimity of military opinion'. It was there agreed that only by simultaneous offensives on the Western, Russian, and Italian fronts could a decision be obtained. [115]

Balfour's memorandum of the 27th was not printed in time for the War Committee meeting of 28 December 1915. In attendance as regular members were Asquith, Grey, Balfour, Jackson, Oliver, Lloyd George, Kitchener, and Robertson. Austen Chamberlain, with the Military Secretary of the India Office, was also there; and the fact that he was again called to a meeting on 13 January should be here remarked. The first item discussed on the 28th was 'The Future of Military Policy' and, as his paper had not been distributed, Balfour presented his case verbally. Kitchener declared for the General Staff plan. He thought that Britain should feel bound by Chantilly. Lloyd George, however, 'said he agreed with the First Lord. General Joffre had always favoured this idea of a great offensive on

[113]   The importance attached to this document is indicated by the fact that copies are to be found in at least three different sections of the archives: Cab. 37/139/55; Cab. 42/6, 27 Dec. 1915, annexed to War Committee mins. of 13 Jan. 1916; and Adm. 116/1437B, 27 Dec. 1915 (printed 31 Dec.).

[114]   Esher, iv, 4 (23 Jan. 1916). Esher thought that Britain should fit in with the offensive plans of her allies.

[115]   Hankey, ii, 466–70.

the West: he had always been confident, and he had always been wrong.'
But Bonar Law thought they should unite behind the General Staff. If they
did not, what plan would be adopted? Balfour held that they 'should try to
wear out the Germans by a series of offensive efforts', but the 'best place
for any attempt at penetration was on the East, and not on the West'.
Kitchener, followed powerfully by Robertson, pointed out the undeniable
fact that logistics favoured the West. Robertson 'thought that the chances
for an offensive on the West were much better than they had ever been, for
the Allies would have more men, more ammunition, more big guns'. (The
reference to big guns was, indeed, rather more prophetic than anyone
realized. They were used by both sides on an unprecedented scale during
1916 and seem to have equalized the enormous casualties of both sides,
tending also, however, to obliterate the presumed advantage of defensive
over offensive warfare.)[116]

Balfour saw that the best he could hope to achieve was to get the War
Committee to refuse to give Robertson unrestricted authority to prepare
for, and when ready to mount, an offensive in the spring. But Asquith's
attempt to produce an acceptable fudging of the issue was instantly accepted
by Robertson and consequently the relevant Conclusion 1 (ii) read: 'Every
effort is to be made to prepare for carrying out offensive operations next
spring in the main theatre of war in close co-operation with the Allies and in
the greatest possible strength.'[117] On that same day (28 December) Asquith
in Cabinet accepted a measure of compulsory service.[118] But the question of
a British offensive was not yet settled.

The First Lord's memorandum of 27 December and his challenge to the
Army at the War Committee on the 28th sparked off a sharp paper-war.
Robertson in a five-page memo written for the War Committee argued that
the next offensive would be of a different nature from that attempted
(against his advice in some respects) at Loos. This time reserves would be
adequate and effectively handled. Heavier French artillery would also be a
cardinal feature of the combined effort.[119] On 8 January Kitchener produced
a three-page riposte to various points raised in Balfour's memorandum. By
the 12th Balfour had already responded to the criticisms. On the same day,
in time for the War Committee meeting on 13 January, Balfour had
Kitchener's memo reprinted in a left-hand column on five successive sheets

---

[116] See Terraine, Chs. 9 and 11.
[117] Cab. 22/3/1, Minutes, 28 Dec. 1915.
[118] Hankey, ii, 471.
[119] Cab. 24/2/G.47, 'The Question of Offensive Operations in the Western Front', 5 Jan. 1916.

with his own replies in a column on the right. [120] Kitchener contested
Balfour's statement that Germany was fighting 'primarily' because of her
interest in a 'south-easterly movement'. Balfour escaped from this line of
criticism by saying that by ' "primary" I meant first in order of time'! But
he went on to demonstrate his mastery 'of every dialectical art' (to quote
Churchill on a later occasion) by making the valid point that, in the
perfectly possible event of a 'fairly satisfactory' peace in the West, they
might be left with 'a dangerous tradition of German superiority' in the East
if they allowed themselves 'to be worsted in Salonica, Egypt or Mesopotamia'. [121]

At the War Committee on 13 January, Asquith said that the question
before them 'hung on Conclusion 1(ii) of the previous meeting, which he
read'. Balfour insisted that the amendment therein embodied was inadequate: 'the Conclusion was still open to be read as implying that the
offensive was decided on. He considered it would be as well to make a note
that the alteration was intended to approve preparatory measures only.'
Asquith seems to have been, for once, at a loss to discover yet another
open-ended compromise. Hankey took his chance to intervene with a
suggested addition to the existing form of words and Balfour signified
acceptance. In the Conclusion of 13 January, it was noted that, 'to meet a
criticism by Mr. Balfour, it was agreed that Conclusion 1 Clause (2) of the
Minutes' of 28 December 1915 'should be amended to show that the War
Committee was not definitely committed to the plan of an offensive in the
West'; and the clause was to read: 'Every effort is to be made to prepare for
carrying out offensive operations next spring in the main theatre . . . in the
greatest possible strength, *although it must not be assumed that such
offensive operations are finally decided on.*' [122] Hankey, when compiling his
memoirs many years later, felt that Robertson had won his big point on
28 December 1915 by getting authority to set on foot his preparations for a
great offensive. [123] But Balfour's assertion of the War Committee's right of
veto certainly seemed more than an empty formula at the time. So seriously
did two cabinet ministers feel that (taking account doubtless of the long
delay over evacuating Gallipoli) the whole direction of the war was being
brought to a stop, they circulated protests to the War Committee.

Sir Edward Grey wrote on 14 January: 'The last meeting of the War
Committee has left me with serious apprehension that the division of

[120]   Cab. 37/140/15, 8 and 12 Jan. 1915.
[121]   Ibid.
[122]   Cab. 42/7/5, Minutes, 13 Jan. 1916.
[123]   Hankey, ii, 469.

opinion here is resulting in the paralysis of all strategy.' He was 'much impressed by the arguments against the offensive', but 'still more impressed by the fact that all military opinion is united in favour of it'. In a woolly, self-contradictory passage he forecast (*a*) that the Germans would 'be exhausted before another year is over' (thus supporting Balfour's argument); (*b*) that there would 'be a sort of general collapse' comprising the Allies as well; and he therefore felt (*c*) that there was 'nothing for it but to make every preparation for a great offensive in the West, combined with the best that we can get out of a Russian offensive in the East'. 'If', he continued, 'the decision remains in the state of suspense in which it was left at the last War Committee meeting, all the heart will be taken out of the Military Authorities.' He did not claim to be an expert strategist but, as Foreign Secretary, was anxious 'lest the difference of opinion between the Military Authorities—both French and British, in the War Office and in the field—on the one side, and some of the most important members of the Government on the other side, should end in paralysis of all plan and action'. [124]

Austen Chamberlain wrote a 'Note' on 'Military Policy' three days later. In this he repeated Grey's arguments, lending his support to all of them irrespective of their in-built elements of confusion. He urged, finally, that 'every effort should be made to prepare for a great offensive, at our own time if the choice is left to us, or at an earlier date if the operations of the Central Powers menace Petrograd or Moscow.' [125]

Whatever he may have thought of the quality of the guidance provided by Grey and Chamberlain, Balfour felt that he could not continue in all the circumstances to challenge the Army's reiterated assertion that the new offensive was to be different in nature from what had been seen before.

In a short paper for the Cabinet, dated 21 January, he said that since reading Grey's 'minute' of the 14th, he had had 'a long conversation with General Robertson'. They agreed that, while the British position in Salonica, Egypt, and Mesopotamia should be defended, it was only on the Western Front that an 'effective advance' could be made and that preparations must proceed. However, unless to 'extricate the Russians', no advance should be made until these preparations were complete. (Nor, indeed, did the British in fact advance until 1 July—of catastrophic memory.) The two men hoped that the Germans would 'attempt a great advance early in the year'. (The Germans did—at Verdun, with tremendous

[124] Cab. 42/7/8, 14 Jan. 1916, 2 pp. of typescript.
[125] Ibid., 17 Jan. 1916.

subsequent attrition on both sides.) The two agreed that there should be no irreversible commitment to a 'big offensive'. Balfour continued:

I told General Robertson that nothing had yet occurred to allay my deep misgivings as to the result of this forward policy; but that since a powerful diversion in the West might be rendered absolutely necessary in order to assist the Russians, it is clear that we must be ready to undertake it. I added that if I remained a member of the War Committee, I must retain the full liberty of objecting, when the time comes, to a general offensive, if undertaken for any other purpose than that of saving our Allies . . .[126]

Balfour wrote in a concluding Note of 25 January that he had discussed the matter with Kitchener. The latter stated that the current plan was 'of an essentially different character'.

He has no desire (if I understand him rightly) to repeat the Champagne experiment, and is keenly alive to the danger of any operations which would cause a heavier wastage among the French and British than among the German and Austrian troops opposed to them.

The idea was to develop 'operations of the type which are now being employed at the front, though on a much more formidable scale; as well as by other means to be devised by the Generals on the spot'. This would probably make the Germans retire to the Meuse, 'not because their front will have been broken by assault, but because the increasing shortage of men will make it impossible for them to keep up a sufficient reserve to hold their present defensive positions'. If the Russians could press forward in the East, the Central Powers might be brought 'to terms before the end of the year'. Balfour concluded:

I do not presume (need I say?) to offer an opinion upon the technical aspects of this plan of campaign; but I thought I was bound to mention it because its adoption would remove the last traces of those differences of opinion within the War Committee which Sir Edward Grey and Mr. Chamberlain regarded with natural and legitimate anxiety.[127]

Balfour had acted within the guidelines which he was to indicate in his letter to Bonar Law of 10 September 1917 (see pp. 170–1 above). The Cabinet, or in this case the War Committee, being the responsible body must be free to 'veto proposals which it objects to, and require other proposals to be made to it. Nor is it debarred from suggesting operations or

Cab. 37/141/17, 'The Present Military Position, and Opinions in the War Committee', 21 Jan. 1916.
[127] Cab. 42/7/12, 25 Jan. 1916, 2 pp. of typescript.

examining closely into advice given it by its experts.' However, in this case Robertson had not only just been appointed on his own terms but there was no acceptable substitute who disagreed with his views. The civilian ministers for their part could not agree on an alternative plan. Therefore, taking account of the diplomatic considerations to which Balfour was always sensitive (and with which he had been directly involved at Calais in October and December, and at Paris in November), he had no choice but to defer to the representations of Grey and Chamberlain. It is ironical that the outcome, namely the unprecedented British carnage on the Somme, should have been at the behest of two of the nicest, by common consent, of all the cabinet ministers of the day. Of course, as John Terraine has so effectively recounted, it was in any case the Germans who in February seized a fearsome initiative at Verdun, followed by the Austrian attack on Italy. After the Russians had advanced in June, it was hardly conceivable that the British, having built up their strength, would remain on the defensive. Again, as Terraine has argued, the Germans may have lost men in slightly greater number than their adversaries. But historians still question the necessity of British losses on such a scale—even if other nations did, as in past European wars, suffer more. Yet it must be admitted that if, in principle, Balfour's preference for an 'active defence' might have been co-ordinated with Britain's allies, it ran counter to the collective psychology of the Great War. Human nature being what it is, men of action rather than calmly rational men inevitably tended to prevail in the corridors of power.

Although Balfour had shown more fibre than Asquith in resisting military offensives, and thus by implication conscription, he was open to similar lines of criticism through failing to *appear* energetic. (Asquith was, of course, a very quick worker.) Balfour was in fact hardly less diligent as First Lord than he had been as Prime Minister. But he might doubtless have been prudent to have found a replacement for Jackson earlier than he did. There is here an echo of his failure to remove Neville Lyttleton from the General Staff in 1905. On the other hand, Balfour's loyalty to his professional advisers did little to diminish the regard in which he was personally held in the naval service.

The main themes and episodes of his career at the Admiralty in 1916 have been well, if a shade unsympathetically, covered by previous writers—notably in Arthur Marder's volumes and those of Stephen Roskill.

First came the totally unsuccessful challenge mounted by the ecstatically reunited Churchill (fresh home from the front) and an ageing but still voluble Jacky Fisher. [128] In the background was Jellicoe complaining about delays, especially in repair work and the construction of destroyers. By the time that Balfour came to make his statement to the Commons on the Navy Estimates (7 March 1916), there was also a press war in progress between pro-Fisher and anti-Fisher protagonists. Balfour asserted that naval construction had been on an unprecedented scale. Any deficiencies were due to the shortage of skilled labour. (As was well known in government circles the shortage had been caused by Kitchener in the first instance and, latterly, by Lloyd George as Minister of Munitions.) [129]

On the next day, 8 March, the Churchill – Fisher challenge was demolished. In the morning Lord Fisher, at the insistence of Lloyd George, was given his chance to impress the War Committee with his ability to produce what the Navy needed in the way of ships. Balfour kept him firmly impaled on the sharp stake represented by his freak battle-cruisers. He observed that 'if Lord Fisher recommended the construction of these ships for a specific purpose, he must have been satisfied as to the provision of other ships'—to which there came (understandably) no effective reply. As to the labour shortage, Fisher said that the Navy should get men 'just in the same way as Mr. Lloyd George had obtained his men for munitions work. Anyhow we should not let that class of men go away.' Balfour was unkind enough to observe 'that they mostly went in Lord Fisher's time, or at any rate in the early days of the War'. [130] Even Lloyd George (who still hankered after Fisher's driving power) admitted that he had not done well before the War Committee. [131]

Having dealt with Fisher in the morning, Balfour devoted attention to Churchill in the afternoon. The previous evening Churchill had delivered in the Commons a comprehensive attack on Balfour's regime at the Admiralty. For Churchill, it was apparently irrelevant that Balfour had behaved with such generous consideration to him and his family the previous May [see p. 249] (incidentally leading to the permanent estrangement of Balfour's henchman Sandars who could not stomach such

---

[128]   Gilbert, iii, 699–737 covers Churchill's side of the matter in detail.

[129]   Marder, *Dreadnought*, ii, 395–7. Marder goes so far as to dub 'fantastic' B.'s claim that there had never been 'the smallest difference of opinion between the Board of Admiralty and the Admirals in command'. But the Admiralty had completely accepted Jellicoe's strategic doctrine and did its best to meet all his seemingly endless demands. It was really *national* policy (e.g. munitions versus the Navy) that was in dispute.

[130]   Cab. 42/10/8, Minutes, 8 March 1916.

[131]   Marder, ii, 403–4.

kindness to the hated renegade). [132] Even if ten months might possibly be deemed a long time in politics, Churchill had committed a more costly tactical error in forgetting that he had, as recently as 15 November, informed the Commons of Fisher's unhelpfulness as a professional adviser. To the astonishment of the House, his big speech of 7 March 1916 culminated with a ringing call for Lord Fisher's restoration to the Admiralty! Balfour was wont to comment on his own poor memory for mundane detail. However, when he returned to the House of Commons in the afternoon of 8 March, it soon became evident he had not forgotten Churchill's peroration overnight. He had but to dwell with his accustomed lucidity and verbal resource on Churchill's surprising naval panacea to produce the latter's oft-quoted lame admission that Balfour was 'a master of parliamentary sword-play and of every dialectical art'!

A second theme of 1916 also afforded full scope to Balfour's dialectical prowess. This was the question of air forces. What were their functions, who should control their operations, and who should design and supply their equipment? These were questions which Balfour might have been expected to answer in a spirit of cool objectivity. Unfortunately, although he was prepared in the national interest to submerge his own per-sonality to a point where he could work amicably with almost anyone—for instance with Asquith at one extreme or with Lloyd George at another—there was just one individual of high standing who could be depended on to rouse him to a state of constant red alert. That person was George Nathaniel Curzon. There followed what Hankey afterwards described as 'an amazing dialectical duel, rapier versus bludgeon'. [133]

The outbreak of the War found the Royal Flying Corps at an early stage of its development. Its small forces were hard pressed to perform their basic function of supporting the B.E.F.; and during 1916 Haig and Trenchard were worried by the Germans' recovery of qualitative superiority in the air. [134] Consequently Balfour inherited a situation where the Royal Naval Air Service had undertaken roles which, in principle, should have been allocated to the R.F.C. The anti-aircraft defence of London was handed over to the War Office in February 1916 but the important question of long-distance (strategic) bombing was not conclusively settled. Having

[132] Sandars's revulsion can be traced in B.P. 49768 between ff. 152 and 164 (Mar. 1915—June 1916) and in Bodl. Sandars P., C.768, ff. 64–9 and 107, Short to Sandars, 3 June 1915 and 30 Nov. 1915.
[133] Hankey, ii, 551.
[134] David Lloyd George, *War Memoirs*, London, 1933–6, 6 vols.

started with the assumption that the Navy must have long-distance bombers, Balfour had by March conceded in principle that the R.F.C. should be responsible for attacks on Germany from bases in France. But he contended that the Admiralty should continue to build long-range aircraft to bomb enemy naval bases from the *coasts* of the United Kingdom or of the enemy. [135] When the R.F.C. was completely committed to tactical support during the battle of the Somme, the Admiralty actually went ahead with the establishment of a force of R.N.A.S. long-range bombers at Luxeuil in France until Haig wrote (1 November 1916) in protest to the War Office. [136]

The sparring between Balfour and Curzon was much concerned with control over the supply of aircraft and aeronautical equipment for the R.F.C. and R.N.A.S. Curzon had entered the Asquith coalition as Lord Privy Seal. Having no departmental duties, he had by January 1916 become Chairman of the important Shipping Control Board. In February he extended his sphere of interest by writing for the Prime Minister a memorandum arguing in favour of an Air Minister and an Air Department—leaving operational control with the Admiralty and the Army as before. [137] A committee to co-ordinate supply and design of *matériel* to the two air services was set up (by the War Committee) under Lord Derby but by April it had disbanded owing to the disagreements of the professional naval members with their military colleagues.

Curzon quite correctly refused to permit reversion to the status quo ante. In a second cabinet paper of 16 April he observed:

As regards the relations between the two branches of the service, so imperfect has been the co-ordination that, not merely are designs competed for and machines ordered, but operations have sometimes been undertaken, without any intercommunication. Each service still claims the right to conduct long-range offensive operations, and therefore to acquire high-power engines for this purpose.

As a solution he advocated a co-ordinating Air Minister of cabinet rank and quoted informed opinion in favour of amalgamation of all the air forces themselves into a single service. [138]

This latter, indeed, was the deceptively simple solution finally imposed (appropriate at least in the chosen date) on 1 April 1918. The result was that the Second World War found the strategic bombing role of the air forces

---

[135] Captain S. W. Roskill (ed.), *The Naval Air Service*, London (Navy Records Society) 1969, Vol. i, pp. 306, 333, 335–6, 420.
[136] Ibid., 272, 274, 405.
[137] Cab. 37/142/37, 'Air Service in the War', 14 Feb. 1916.
[138] Roskill, *Air Service*, pp. 270–1, 344–50.

enhanced and the maritime role (both in relation to fleets and anti-submarine work) comparatively neglected. Therefore, in so far as Balfour's rearguard action against Curzon led to the decision of 1918, he has been seen as an involuntary contributor to the imbalance of the inter-war years. But is this particular line of criticism the correct one? As has just been indicated, a ministerial authority was needed to allocate scarce resources on a rational basis between the strategic and maritime air forces. However controversial these aeronautical roles might have subsequently been, there can be no doubt about the continuing necessity of both of them. The best institutional answer was, surely, the establishment of a Ministry of Defence. Through unique personal interest and great diligence, Balfour had managed as Prime Minister to devise a broadly rational allocation of resources between Army and Navy through the medium of the C.I.D., and his work saw the country through until the outbreak of war in 1914. But the C.I.D., still seen by Hankey and Balfour in the 1920s as the best institutional machine, was to prove ineffective in the face of inter-service rivalry over aerial needs, a matter which enlisted deep-rooted instincts of departmental self-preservation. The existence of a third service did nothing to ease this problem.

On the more immediate level of Balfour versus Curzon, the latter had small grounds for personal dissatisfaction when he found himself appointed by the War Committee of 11 May 1916 as President of a new Air Board. In the light of the relations, noticed earlier, which had subsisted between Curzon and Balfour in 1905, and of Balfour's logical refusal to recommend him for an honour in deference to his achievements as Viceroy, the idea of personal revenge over Balfour had rarely been absent from Curzon's mind. Civilities, at least, were restored; but the memory of his various personal disappointments remained with him to the end. If Balfour was not the only demonic figure in Curzon's catalogue of personal grievances, he did loom large. For instance, when he was at last a Marquess and back in office as Foreign Secretary (and even a prospective Prime Minister), Curzon would devote time and energy, in the winter of 1921–2, to a 9,000-word memorandum on Balfour's ministerial career. Though intended as a devastating indictment, it is more notable for its comical effect, for instance:

The truth is that Balfour with his scintillating intellectual exterior had no depth of feeling, no profound convictions, and strange to say (in spite of his fascination of manner) no real affection. We all knew this, when the emergency came, he would drop or desert or sacrifice any one of us without a pang, as he did me in India, as he did George Wyndham over Ireland. Were any one of us to die suddenly he would

dine out that night with undisturbed complacency, and in the intervals of conversation or bridge, would be heard to murmur 'Poor old George'.[139]

However, though the presidency of the Air Board provided Curzon with
real possibilities for the diminution of Balfour, his formal powers were no
more than advisory. By the month of July, he was pushing for a degree of
financial control over air supplies and asserted the Air Board's 'general
responsibility'. Balfour minuted (25 July):

> I do not profess fully to understand the character and limits of the Air Board's
> duties, but I certainly cannot count among them any 'general responsibility for the
> policy and plans of the two Air Services'. It appears to me that the Navy at least must
> remain responsible for its own Air Service; and it cannot consent to regard itself as
> subject to any other Department in respect either of the organisation of its Air
> Service, the design of its air machines, or the use to which they are put . . .[140]

These attitudes were faithfully exhibited at meetings of the Air Board by the
two naval representatives (Rear-Admiral Tudor, Third Sea Lord and
Controller of the Navy, and Rear-Admiral C. L. Vaughan-Lee, Director of
Air Services, Admiralty). By October Curzon was furnished with adequate
material to deliver a satisfying onslaught on the Admiralty. In view of naval
dissent, he wrote his report (dated 23 October 1916) without reference to
the service members of the Air Board, but he derived support from the two
additional civilian members, one of whom was our old friend, of strong
views and controversialistic ability, Lord Sydenham. In what Stephen
Roskill has termed a 'slashing attack' on the Admiralty, the point was well
made that naval air organization should parallel that in the Army, both for
the Navy's own good and to simplify the work of the Air Board. Despite
Vaughan-Lee's above-quoted title, he did not have the same degree of
over-all responsibility for air services as that possessed by the chief military
representative on the Air Board (Lt.-General Sir David Henderson,
Director-General of Military Aeronautics). Curzon pointed to the need for
a solution of the strategic bombing issue; but the main thrust of the
document was directed towards naval refusal to co-operate with the Air
Board, and towards the Admiralty's failure to appoint (in effect) a Fifth Sea
Lord who would develop the naval air services in a more energetic and
far-sighted manner.[141]

---

[139] Quoted in Kenneth Rose, *Superior Person: a Portrait of Curzon and His Circle*,
London, 1969, pp. 380–1.

[140] Adm. 1/8464/187, min. (4).

[141] Roskill, *Air Service*, pp. 389–404.

Balfour's reply to the Air Board's report is dated 6 November and finds him in his best controversial form. Quotation must be restricted to the following sample:

For controversy I have little time and no inclination. But it would hardly be respectful either to the authors of the report or to our colleagues of the War Committee if I were to let it pass wholly without comment.

Of the Air Board's performances . . . I have little to say—and they have not much to say themselves.

To do the Air Board justice, however, they are much more interested in abusing the Admiralty than in praising themselves. I do not suppose that in the whole history of the country any Government Department has ever indulged so recklessly in the luxury of inter-departmental criticism. The temptation no doubt has often existed; but hitherto it has been more or less successfully resisted. In the case of the Air Board, however, the ardour of youth and the consciousness of superior abilities have completely broken through the ordinary barriers of official self-control . . .

Where Balfour attributes to Curzon 'consciousness of superior abilities', he alludes to the celebrated jungle, first printed in an Oxford broadsheet entitled 'The Masque of Balliol':

My name is George Nathaniel Curzon,
I am a most superior person,
My cheek is pink, my hair is sleek,
I dine at Blenheim once a week. [142]

Balfour went on to reject the Air Board's claim to become 'a great manufacturing and producing department' because, unlike the Ministry of Munitions, it wished also to 'constitute a standing committee of enquiry' into the way in which the Admiralty and War Office carried out 'their duties' with regard to aviation. [143]

Given the personal attitudes involved, together with the argumentative powers of the two contestants, there was no apparent reason why the duel should not be indefinitely continued. However, by 10 November Lloyd George (now War Secretary) was seriously contemplating resignation from the Government, partly on the grounds that the War Committee was over-congested with unsettled issues. [144] Although it was not the case, as he afterwards asserted, that 'the aeroplane' problem 'was always first in the list' after the military reports, it is true that, when the Air Board's Report was at last tackled by the War Committee on 27–28 November, it involved

[142] See Rose, *Curzon*, pp. 48–9, for the history of the jingle.
[143] Cab. 37/159/14, 'A Reply to the First Report of the Air Board', 6 Nov. 1916 (10 pp.).
[144] Hankey, ii, 557.

no less than three meetings on the two days. The first two meetings lasted for some three hours each. Although (as Lloyd George accurately recalled)[145] the important matter of the food supply was crowded out from consideration, no actual decision on the air problem was reached by the War Committee even then. But Hankey was at least able to draft a series of conclusions:

(1) The subject of immediate urgency is to supply aeroplanes in sufficient numbers and of the best possible types for the two services, but more particularly for the use of the British Expeditionary Force, whose present supremacy in the air is threatened . . .

(2) The object stated above can, in the opinion of the War Committee, best be achieved by handing over the supply and design of the aeroplanes, both for the Navy and the Army, to the Ministry of Munitions [now under Edwin Montagu] . . .

(3) The War Committee attach great importance to the maintenance of an Air Board . . . particularly for the purpose of allocating the aerial resources of the country between the Admiralty and War Office, wherever there is conflict or competition between them.

(4) . . . a fifth Sea Lord should be added to the Board of Admiralty [and] represent the Admiralty on the Air Board . . .

There follow more detailed guidelines for the proposed *modus operandi*.[146]

The War Committee reassembled at 6 p.m. on 28 November for what turned out to be its third to last meeting (the 142nd in 13 months). Balfour did *not* agree to allow design to go with supply as indicated in Conclusion (2) and final agreement was *not* reached.[147] Balfour fell ill on the 30th and did not attend the War Committee again.

By 22 December 1916, a new Prime Minister was presiding over a small War Cabinet with full executive powers. Their first meeting had been on the 9th. The meeting of the 22nd, which made a decision on the air question, was their fifteenth. The protests, along strict Balfourian lines, of a new First Lord (Carson) and a new First Sea Lord (Jellicoe) were overridden and the aforementioned draft conclusions adopted as drafted. No one had during 1916 come up with anything better than this imperfect remedy. No wartime Government seemed likely to find a better. If decisions in general were arguably no wiser under Lloyd George than under Asquith, they were at least reached quickly.

---

[145] Lloyd George, ii, 977–8.

[146] Cab. 42/26/2, War Committee: Draft Conclusions of Meetings held at 10 Downing Street, 27–28 Nov. 1916.

[147] Cab. 42/26/2, Minutes, 28 Nov. 1916, 2nd meeting.

Meanwhile, what else should be said of Balfour's tenure at the Admiralty in 1916? The Battle of Jutland took place during the evening and night of 31 May. Balfour, for once, was highly excited.[148] Oliver long afterwards remembered shunting him and his personal staff out of the chart room at the Admiralty after they had been there 'chatting all the afternoon and some of the evening'. He added: 'It was nice of him not to be offended'.[149] As for the notorious Jutland communiqué, Hamilton (the Second Sea Lord) wrote in his diary on 7 June:

On Saturday [3 June] I visited Rosyth . . . I found Beatty very well and cheerful but very angry with the Admiralty for their very stupid communiqué sent out on Friday evening which was really an apology for winning a victory. I subsequently on my return found that Masterton-Smith was the author of it, Jackson and Oliver having been too busy to attend to it properly and having told them to say anything they liked, as long as it was true.[150]

However, Graham Greene is adamant that Balfour, after a meeting 'with his chief Naval Advisers', drafted it himself 'and, after considerable discussion, decided that the losses sustained should be published without abridgement or any colourable explanation, so that there should be no charge, as had previously been made, that the Admiralty were suppressing any untoward circumstances'.[151] Of course, the relatively high British losses occasioned bitter disappointment; but it gradually became clear to everyone that the hold of the Grand Fleet on the North Sea had not been loosened and that the Admiralty had not been reluctant to tell the truth.

An episode unconnected with the Admiralty should be briefly mentioned here. This was the sequel to the Easter Rebellion in Dublin. Lloyd George, acting for the Government, agreed with Redmond and Carson a scheme for putting Home Rule into effect, with Ulster's six more-Protestant counties excluded till the end of the war. Lansdowne (Minister without Portfolio) soon came out against the plan and was backed by Walter Long (President of the Local Government Board) and Selborne (who resigned his office on the issue on 26 June). Balfour, however, saw the possibility of a viable settlement. In answer to his fellow Unionists, he argued in a cabinet paper of 24 June in favour of the agreement. Perhaps the key passage is:

Were Lloyd George's scheme carried through, the six Ulster counties would have permanently secured to them—by consent and without bloodshed—their place in

---

148 Hankey, ii, 491.
149 N.M.M., OLV/12, 'Recollections', ii, 175.
150 N.M.M., HTN/106.
151 N.M.M., GEE/13, 'Balfour', p. 4.

the United Kingdom. Will anybody assert that, if the settlement of their fate be deferred till peace is declared, terms equally good can be obtained without a dangerous struggle?

He continues with the following statement which shows that he was not (and perhaps never had been) more concerned about *social* order, as has sometimes been asserted, than about the rights, in particular, of loyal British Protestants. Here he seeks a solution by supporting Lloyd George and Bonar Law—not exactly members of the old aristocratic establishment!

I have always held that rather than submit to Nationalist rule Ulster would fight—and Ulster would be right. But I have never disguised from myself that this extreme measure would be so permanently damaging to the orderly constitution of a civilised country that the least of the evils which it would entail would be the sacrifice of life and property, by which alone its objects could be accomplished. Very strong, therefore, must be the arguments which would induce me to run the hazard of civil war, when we have offered us voluntarily all that successful civil war would give . . . [152]

On 7 July he supported Bonar Law on the subject at the Carlton Club; but Law realized that party feeling was against them. In so far as Law had drawn closer to Lloyd George but was sensitive to the danger of losing touch with his party, the way was being prepared for a new coalition, should discontent with Asquith mount. Meanwhile, soon before the Home Rule scheme was dropped late in July, Balfour was much depressed by what he judged to be the inevitability of Home Rule 'which had overtaken' (according to Lord Hugh Cecil) 'the political purpose of his life'. [153]

By the autumn of 1916, public feeling, affected by the Somme and absence of success for the Allies elsewhere, began to turn against the Government. Nor did the Admiralty, in particular, escape criticism. Sydenham, doubtless irritated by Balfour's fight against the Air Board, wrote letters to *The Times* attacking the defensive strategy now associated with the Admiralty and received a measure of journalistic and retired-naval support. Archibald Hurd replied with a reasoned rebuttal in the *Daily Telegraph*; and, of course, top naval opinion, while seeking a decisive battle on favourable terms, was in general agreement with the established strategy. Balfour pointed out the offensive aspect of the blockage strategy when he spoke at the Lord Mayor's banquet on 9 November. But

---

[152]   Cab. 37/150/17, 'Ulster and the Irish Crisis', 24 June 1916.
[153]   Blake, pp. 286–8; Sandars P., C.769, f. 181.

Northcliffe's *Daily Mail* specifically singled out the First Lord for alleged feeble conduct of naval affairs. [154]

The end of Balfour's regime at the Admiralty is linked with the growing U-boat menace and the question of Jackson. Balfour had, since 1904, been acutely aware of the threat presented by submarines to the predominant naval power and it was he who pointed out to Fisher, in May 1913, the implications for British commerce of the lately initiated German submarine force. If the sea surrounding Britain were, as Fisher had suggested, neutralized, 'we should not only [wrote Balfour] be useless allies to any friendly power on the Continent, but we should have the utmost difficulty in keeping ourselves alive.' [155] On 1 September 1915 he answered a query from Selborne about the submarine threat to the food supply. He wrote that even if 'Jellicoe has not, so far, been able to intercept *one* submarine of all those that go north about from Germany', yet 'the Germans are undoubtedly disappointed with the results of their campaign' and 'our own methods of anti-submarine warfare have not yet reached their full development.' However: 'If the submarines were to operate further from land, this would, of course [be] to our disadvantage.' [156] By the time that he presented his 'Report on Recent Naval Affairs' (14 October 1916) he saw the position thus:

Of all the problems which the Admiralty have to consider, no doubt the most formidable and the most embarrassing is that raised by submarine attack on merchant vessels. No conclusive answer has been discovered to this mode of warfare; perhaps no conclusive answer ever will be found. We must for the present be content with palliation . . .

He emphasized the success achieved in protecting the 'unceasing stream' of troops and munitions crossing the Channel. This, of course, did involve convoys, as did the transportation, equally safely, of 'great bodies of troops from the Dominions'. Statistics showed the great reduction in losses of merchant shipping to be gained by arming the merchantmen. [157]

No doubt, the above-quoted opening paragraph does indirectly reflect Jackson's exhaustion, pessimism, and lack of initiative. Yet Jackson's critics agree in condemning his successor, Admiral Jellicoe, for an even more determined resistance to the adoption of a general system of convoys. If it lay with Balfour to replace Jackson as First Sea Lord, it was hardly an

---

[154] Marder, *Dreadnought*, iii, 263–9.
[155] Mackay, pp. 303, 447.
[156] Bodl., MS Selborne 1, ff. 156–66.
[157] Cab. 37/157/31.

easy decision to take, in so far as Jellicoe was the only conceivable replacement at the time. The change was indeed precipitated by Jellicoe himself who, on 29 October, sent Balfour a memorandum arguing that the growing U-boat menace could, 'by the early summer of 1917', force the Allies to sue for peace. The first reason adduced for the deepening crisis was that anticipated in Balfour's letter to Selborne of September 1915, quoted above: the ability of larger German submarines to operate at longer range than hitherto.[158] Jellicoe recommended the formation of a committee to find means, 'not later than the spring of 1917', for defeating 'the most serious menace with which the Empire has ever been faced' and, in sharp contrast with his previous attitudes, was ready to contemplate diversion of destroyers from the Grand Fleet to an anti-submarine offensive in narrower waters around the Channel. He had sent a copy of his memorandum to Jackson; and two days later he communicated his warning direct to Asquith.

On 31 October 'Submarines' headed the War Committee's agenda. Asquith read Jellicoe's letter to the committee. Balfour then

said that Sir J. Jellicoe had also written to him and to the First Sea Lord. He thought that Sir J. Jellicoe had got the submarine menace on his nerves, and he was not surprised if that was so. It was so far satisfactory that we could hold up the submarines in closed waters; it had been made so disagreeable for them that they went further afield where it was impossible to use the same methods against them. He informed the Committee . . . of bomb [depth-charge] firing which was being tried. Admiral Sir J. Jellicoe was coming to London two days later, and he proposed that he might come before the Committee. For the first time since he had been in Command, Sir J. Jellicoe had suggested giving up some of his destroyers. They had produced 82 new destroyers which had all gone to him. Some of these would now be available to go elsewhere. It would be a very great relief to the Admiralty if they had some to dispose of.

SIR H. JACKSON thought that that was in consequence of his having written to Sir J. Jellicoe.

MR. BALFOUR continued that he could not see, and he thought Sir J. Jellicoe would not see any means of coping with this new menace . . .[159]

In the latter respect, Balfour proved substantially correct. Neither before attending the War Committee on 2 November nor after his arrival at the Admiralty did Jellicoe see that a general system of convoys would be the best palliative. Oliver, for his part, denies in his 'Recollections' that the

---

[158] A. Temple Patterson (ed.), *The Jellicoe Papers*, London (Navy Records Society), 1966–8, 2 vols., ii, 88–92.

[159] Cab. 42/22/13, Minutes, 31 October 1916.

Admiralty had been averse to convoys but says that they 'never had enough escorts to start regular Atlantic convoys'. He also recalls that such escorts as could be found were used for food convoys from Holland:

> Our Naval headache was the Dutch convoys protected by the Harwich force. It became a great strain on them. The merchant ships, many of them neutrals, were small and bad and slow and got strung out and difficult to protect and we lost several destroyers . . . I was always trying to get better merchant ships for it . . . [160]

His remarks about the shortage of escorts are certainly supported by the minutes of the War Committee for 24 November. These concern cross-Channel troop convoys and food convoys from Holland. In view of the desperate shortage of shipping, Lloyd George suggested (successfully in the outcome) that cross-Channel transports should be packed much more tightly with troops. Shipping would be saved (at a risk) and the (limited) destroyer escort proportionately strengthened. As for the Dutch convoys, Balfour's cousin Lord Robert Cecil (Minister for Blockade) emphasized their importance for the national food-supply: 'one convoy every six days was no good' and 'there must be one convoy every four days at least.' Oliver 'pointed out that for many months a convoy had come over three times a week' but subsequently destroyers had, of necessity, been diverted to the Dover Straits, 15 coming from the Humber and 12 from Harwich. Yet strong cover for the Dutch traffic was needed because 'the Germans had 130 destroyers and could sally forth at any time.' [161]

Remembering the limited capability until much later of surface vessels against submerged submarines, one can see that the standard objections to a general system of convoys would tend to seem insuperable *until it was clearly explained that convoys would cut losses even if they lacked escorts.* Hankey's well-known 'brainwave' of 11 February 1917[162] did at last make the point, though more by implication than by direct emphasis. Interestingly, the point had been cogently made by Captain Reginald Drax of the battle-cruiser *Lion* in a memo apparently sent to Rear-Admiral Pakenham (Beatty's successor in command of the Battle Cruiser Force) on 1 December.[163] But by 1 December Balfour was in bed suffering from influenza and had, though he did not know it, virtually come to the end of his term of office as First Lord. As in the case of Neville Lyttleton in 1905, he had been

[160] N.M.M., OLV/12, 'Recollections', ii, 171–2, 190.
[161] Cab. 42/25/8, Minutes, 24 Nov. 1916.
[162] Hankey, ii, 645–6.
[163] Churchill College, Drax P., 1/12 (submarines). Compulsory convoys are recommended—at first on a limited scale. 'Warships would be practically unnecessary.' Drax's draft is dated 16 Nov. 1916.

loath to scrap his professional adviser; but there is no reason to think, as far as anti-submarine measures were concerned, that he would have closed his mind to any new idea that had been lucidly presented to him. He was as open-minded as he was tenacious.

Meanwhile Jackson had responded to Jellicoe's move on the U-boat question (comprising a suggestion that an energetic Flag Officer should take charge of the matter) by offering on 6 November to give way to a new First Sea Lord with recent sea experience. Balfour did not want to replace him till the press agitation had died down.[164] However, he may well have been influenced by Grey who urged that Jellicoe 'with adequate power and scope' might be well worth trying. 'I know you are already considering it', he wrote, 'but I feel the situation to be so serious and critical.'[165] Certainly, when Asquith himself wrote in the same sense to Balfour on 20 November, there was little further delay. By the 29th, Jellicoe was installed in the post of First Sea Lord at the Admiralty.

In his letter of 20 November, Asquith wrote appreciatively of Jackson's 'very special attainments' and his 'great tenacity and staying power'. However, 'in view of the increasing seriousness of the submarine situation' and other undefined 'prospects hardly less grave', he thought that he should be 'replaced by the best naval expert' available, namely Jellicoe. He did not anticipate the awkward consequences which would shortly flow from his concluding paragraph:

I need scarcely add the assurance of my perfect confidence, which is shared by all our colleagues, in your supreme control in all that concerns the Navy. I regard it as one of our principal assets in the conduct of the war.[166]

There was one rather important ministerial colleague who would soon contest the validity of this assertion.

[164]   Marder, *Dreadnought*, iii, 282–3.
[165]   B.P. 49731, ff. 170–1, n.d.
[166]   B.P. 49692, ff. 175–7.

14

For England and Lloyd George

1916–1922

THE ascertainable facts concerning Asquith's supersession as Prime Minister by Lloyd George have been published in great quantity and detail.[1] As far as Balfour's role in the matter is concerned, the comments of Beaverbrook and Churchill tend to lodge in the reader's memory. They are so amusingly turned, so often quoted, and so persuasively cynical in their implication that their journalistic character tends to be ignored. Beaverbrook writes that when offered the Foreign Office in exchange for the Admiralty, Balfour 'jumped up instantly' and said: 'Well, you hold a pistol to my head—I must accept.'[2] For his part, Churchill comments: 'He passed from one Cabinet to the other, from the Prime Minister who was his champion to the Prime Minister who had been his most severe critic, like a powerful graceful cat walking delicately and unsoiled across a rather muddy street.'[3]

In fact, the documentary evidence published by Mrs Dugdale in 1936 is itself sufficient support for the view that, of all the leading participants in the 'Palace Revolution' (to quote Mr Jenkins's phrase) Balfour was least motivated by concern about his own political future. This is not to deny that, for all his wide interests, politics had been Balfour's greatest passion or to suggest that, once Britain went to war in 1914, he was anything less than a whole-hearted participant. But even at the height of his political revival in December 1915, when his niece and future biographer suggested that he (Balfour) could usefully supplant Asquith with the backing of the House and country, he replied that he hardly ever went to the House of Commons and felt instinctively that he could not lead it.[4] Yet throughout 1916 he remained absorbed, somewhat in prime-ministerial fashion, in all aspects of the conduct of the war.

[1] See esp. Dugdale, ii, 166–85 for Balfour's part; also Roy Jenkins, *Asquith*, London, 1964, pp. 416–41, and Roskill, *Hankey*, i, 320–6.
[2] *Politicians and the War*, vol. ii, London (Lane Publications), 1932, p. 300.
[3] *Great Contemporaries*, London (Fontana), 1959, p. 204.
[4] Dugdale, ii, 156–7, diary, 21 Dec. 1915.

Typical was his attitude at what proved to be his final War Committee meeting, held, as previously mentioned, at 6 p.m. on 28 November. Although his reserves of energy must have been somewhat drained by his struggle with Curzon and though he was geared to fight yet again for retention by the Admiralty of aircraft design, he instantly set aside his departmental worries in response to a warning aired at the outset by the Chancellor of the Exchequer. When McKenna explained that there were signs that American loans to Britain might be withheld, Balfour at once said 'that this was the most serious matter which had come up for consideration before the War Committee. It was infinitely more serious than the submarine menace.'[5] Again, in the field of foreign affairs, it was not Grey but Balfour who produced the most impressive cabinet paper on war aims to be written in 1914–1916, 'The Peace Settlement in Europe' (4 October 1916).[6] Although written at a discouraging time, the document is remarkable not only for its grasp of emergent reality but also for its governing assumption that allied victory was 'going to be complete'. The wisdom of this assumption remains to an extent controversial. But Balfour, though prone to balance inconclusively over problems of detail, imparted to both Asquith's and Lloyd George's governments a relentless consistency of underlying purpose which Lloyd George, in one of his graver moods, would fairly acknowledge:

During the War his unfailing courage steadied faltering spirits in hours of doubt and dread. There were times of weariness, many of depression, a few of genuine dismay during that terrible world conflict. When these occurred I have seen men who were reckoned by their public to be inflexible show signs of bending—but never Mr. Balfour.[7]

This indeed sums up Balfour's main positive wartime contribution. It also reflects his basic attitude during the cabinet crisis of early December 1916.

On Thursday, 30 November, he went to the meeting of Unionist ministers in Bonar Law's room at the House of Commons. It was proposed that a small committee to run the war, with Lloyd George as chairman and including Law, should be pressed on Asquith. However, there was considerable opposition to such a role for Lloyd George. That evening Balfour succumbed to influenza (which also felled Jellicoe soon after his arrival at the Admiralty on 29 November) and he was unable to discuss politics until

---

[5] Cab. 42/26/2, Minutes, 28 Nov. 1916.

[6] Cab. 37/157/7, printed 6 Oct. 1916, 6 pp. The text is given in full, and supplied with sub-headings, in Lloyd George, ii, 877–88 and in Dugdale, ii, 435–42. See also p. 327 below.

[7] Lloyd George, ii, 1014.

the evening of Sunday, 3 December. By the 4th, he knew that Asquith had apparently accepted a small War Council with Lloyd George as chairman but that there was a dispute about the other members. At some time during that day, Monday, the 4th, or possibly in the morning of Tuesday, the 5th, he realized that the dispute 'really centred about' *him*: 'L.G. wanted a change at the Admiralty, which was being resisted by the Prime Minister.'[8]

If Balfour saw the Prime Minister as less than perfect in his management of strategy and the government machine, he knew that Asquith still enjoyed considerable political support and held similar views to his own on many issues. He had, as has been seen, been recently reassured of Asquith's regard for him in his own role at the Admiralty. But he did not know that Lloyd George was that morning (the 5th) launching a direct challenge for the premiership or that, to some extent, Asquith was looking to him (Balfour) as a dependable counter-weight to Lloyd George. There is, however, little doubt that he felt surprised and hurt to hear that Lloyd George was demanding his removal from the Admiralty. Whether he knew by the 5th that Carson, the hammer of the Government in 1916, was his intended replacement seems doubtful. There was certainly no demand in the higher professional naval circles for Balfour's removal. His departure, when it became known, was regretted by Jellicoe and also by his successor as C.-in-C. of the Grand Fleet, David Beatty.[9] Before Jutland, George Ballard (Admiral of Patrols, East Coast) believed that the 'Service in general' had 'great confidence' in Balfour, especially when compared with the meddling Churchill; and after Jutland, Vice-Admiral Wemyss (then C.-in-C. East Indies and later Jellicoe's successor as First Sea Lord) found him 'delightful' to deal with.[10] Despite the oft-articulated distrust of such high-ranking officers for the politicians, the War ended with Balfour as an exceptional case. In Marder's words he alone was deemed to possess

[8]   B.P. 49692, ff. 179–215, 'Government Crisis December 1916: Memorandum by Mr. Balfour', 7 Dec. 1916. This memo (quoted extensively in Dugdale, ii, 168–81) is the main source. It was written to B's. dictation by Short who has pencilled on it: 'Not revised by Mr. B.'. This typifies B's lack of autobiographical interest and conflicts with any lingering idea that B. carefully covered up his personal ambition on this and other occasions. For a similar conclusion about the cabinet crisis of May 1915 see Hazlehurst, p. 257: 'The well-established fact is that Bonar Law and Lloyd George confronted Asquith. There was no pistol and no Balfour.'
[9]   Patterson, ii, 124; Roskill, *Admiral of the Fleet Earl Beatty*, London, 1980, p. 201.
[10]   WHI/75, Ballard to Mrs Robinson (copy) 18 Feb. 1916; Paul G. Halpern (ed.), *The Keyes Papers*, London (Navy Records Society), 1972–81, 3 vols., i, 365: Wemyss to Keyes, 17 July 1916.

'a sound grasp of naval strategy and the art of naval warfare'.[11] Bonar Law, also, while seeing that, for national and party-political reasons, he would probably have to force a show-down in support of Lloyd George, resisted on 1 December the latter's demand for Balfour's removal from the Admiralty; and it is probable that Balfour *did* know *this* by the morning of Tuesday, 5 December.[12]

Had Balfour been primarily interested in maintaining his own political position, he would surely have investigated the likelihood of Asquith and the Liberal ministers, among whom McKenna, Runciman, and Grey were presumably sympathetic to him, together with Bonar Law and the majority of Unionists, uniting on the principle of keeping him (Balfour) at the Admiralty and repulsing Lloyd George. Indeed, Lloyd George represented the political and social tendencies which Balfour himself had so tenaciously resisted throughout his pre-War career; and Balfour was himself uniquely experienced in the tactics of political survival. But he took no soundings. Instead, he reflected. Then he proceeded to make a sacrifice of his own position. By noon on Tuesday the 5th Masterton-Smith was on his way to Asquith with the following letter from Balfour:

My dear Asquith,

I have been mostly in bed since the political crisis became acute, and can collect no very complete idea of what is going on. But one thing seems clear: that there is to be a new War Council of which Lloyd George is to be the working Chairman, and that, according to his ideas, this Council would work more satisfactorily if the Admiralty were not represented by me. In these circumstances I cannot consent to retain my Office, and must ask you to accept my resignation.

I am well aware that you do not personally share Lloyd George's views in this connection. But I am quite clear that this new system should have a trial in the most favourable circumstances; and the mere fact that the new Chairman of the War Council *did* prefer, and, so far as I know, *still* prefers, a different arrangement is, to my mind, quite conclusive . . .

The fact that the first days of the reconstructed Administration find me more than half an invalid is an additional reason, if additional reason were required, for adopting the course on which, after much consideration, I have determined.

Yours very sincerely,
Arthur James Balfour.[13]

Balfour also sent a copy to Bonar Law. He wrote: 'My dear B-L, I have

[11]   Marder, v, 341–2.
[12]   B.L.P. 85/A/1, Law's memo of events dated 30 Dec. 1916. See also B.P. 497692, ff. 179–215.
[13]   B.P. 49692, ff. 185–6.

sent the enclosed letter to Asquith: it explains itself.'[14]

Asquith, however, obviously concluded that Balfour would take a different view once informed that he (Asquith) had, the previous evening, rejected Lloyd George's demand for a change at the Admiralty and had, in any case, queried Carson's qualifications to be a member of the War Committee. He therefore sent Balfour a copy of his comprehensive letter of the 4th to Lloyd George.[15] The letter also showed that Asquith was now empowered by the King to obtain the resignation of all ministers and reconstruct the Government as he wished.

By 4 p.m. Balfour had written in reply. He made it clear that he thought it better that Lloyd George should be given 'a free hand with the day-to-day work of the War Committee' as a worthwhile 'experiment' and repeated the argument that there was 'no use trying it except on terms which enable him to work under the conditions which, in his own opinion, promise the best results. We cannot, I think, go on in the old way.'[16]

In this letter Balfour recognized that Lloyd George enjoyed only the 'imperfect sympathy' of his prospective 'fellow-workers'; and he probably did not, at that stage, envisage Lloyd George's emergence as Prime Minister rather than as head of the proposed War Committee. Some three weeks later, at a family luncheon at Carlton Gardens, he remarked: 'Personally I am sorry Asquith is not still P.M.; that was what *I* wanted.'[17] What he did not know at 4 p.m. on the 5th was that Asquith, although reassured of the backing of nearly all the Liberal ministers, had just discovered that, if his new government did not include both Lloyd George, on his own terms, and Bonar Law, he would lack sufficient Unionist support. Having already rejected Lloyd George's terms, the Prime Minister himself therefore resigned.

In so far as Asquith had made his stand against Lloyd George's (arguably irresponsible) proposal to substitute Carson for Balfour at the Admiralty, Balfour's two letters of the 5th did contribute to Asquith's decision to resign. However, his decision was finally governed by the fact that Bonar Law, and eventually his Unionist colleagues, indicated that they preferred Lloyd George to Asquith as the effective leader of the administration.

The King now asked Bonar Law to form a government; and on the morning of Wednesday, 6 December—the decisive day—Bonar Law and a slightly uneasy Lloyd George were to be found hovering in Balfour's

[14] B.L.P. F/53/4/32, 5 Dec. 1916.
[15] B.P. 49692, ff. 189–92.
[16] Ibid., ff. 193–5, 5 Dec. 1916. There is also a copy in B.L.P. F/53/4/33.
[17] B.P. 49831, f. 250, Lady Betty Balfour to Lady Frances Balfour, 30 Dec. 1916.

bedroom. To Law, and especially to Lloyd George, Balfour's private feelings about his projected removal from the Admiralty were less than completely clear; but he was evidently an ideal man to negotiate Lloyd George's emergence as head of the War Committee, if his letters of the 5th to Asquith still represented his attitude. Indeed, Bonar Law had asked Asquith late on the 5th whether he would serve under Balfour—which, after brief consideration, he had deemed politically impracticable. [18]

The outcome was that Balfour sallied forth from his sick room, arriving at Buckingham Palace at 2.30 p.m.; and the King asked him to 'start the discussion' which began at 3. By then Asquith, Bonar Law, Lloyd George, and Henderson (the Labour leader) had assembled. According to Law, Balfour opened the discussion by 'strongly' suggesting that Asquith and Lloyd George should both serve under Law; and Law 'left the conference under the impression that Mr. Asquith would probably agree to it.' [19] Balfour seems to have been less sanguine. But in any event he wanted Law to accept the role which he had, till then, envisaged for Asquith—that of nominal Prime Minister and Leader of the House. But, once Asquith had declined to serve under him, Law wanted Lloyd George to have both the form and the substance of power. By that evening (the 6th) Lloyd George was Prime Minister. [20] As a first step Lloyd George asked Law to go at once to see Balfour and offer him the post of Foreign Secretary. Law's own account, which was later adjusted by Beaverbrook to produce the comical and belittling effect noted in the first paragraph of this chapter, conveys an entirely contrary effect. It was after half an hour's preliminary discussion that the offer was made. Balfour 'rose from his seat' rather than 'jumped up instantly'. He accepted 'without a moment's hesitation', it is true. But Law's account goes on to expunge the image of a Balfour grasping at office:

> Under all the circumstances I think that the part played by him was the biggest part played by anyone in the whole crisis. It was quite plain to me that he would have given anything, apart from his sense of duty, to be free from the responsibility of being a member of the Government. [21]

Having accepted the Foreign Office, for which he was obviously well qualified, Balfour tried to find out from Law why Lloyd George had wanted to get him out of the Admiralty. Law replied that he had better ask Lloyd George. But though the subject came up sometimes in family conversations, Balfour never did ask Lloyd George

[18]   Blake, p. 337.
[19]   B.L.P. 85/A/1, Law's memo of 30 Dec. 1916.
[20]   B.P. 49692, ff. 196–215.
[21]   B.L.P. 85/A/1, 30 dec. 1916; and see Blake, pp. 339–40.

directly. He doubtless realized that, if he had, he would not have received an unvarnished answer. In his memoirs Lloyd George, inevitably, rates Balfour an ideal man for the Foreign Office. [22] Elsewhere, he says that, in wartime, the First Lord of the Admiralty should

be a man of exhaustless industry and therefore of great physical energy and reserve. It was an office that called for unceasing attention to detail. It meant long hours, early and late. Mr. Balfour was obviously unsuitable for such a post. [23]

But was this view an adequate reason for the change? That Balfour was, in very important respects, suited to his Admiralty post has been argued above. More specifically, then, in what ways did Lloyd George see Sir Edward Carson as an improvement on Balfour at the material time? His memoirs are illuminating. He acknowledges that Bonar Law would probably not have moved against Asquith had it not been for Carson's destructive criticism of the Government. Carson had become an indispensable factor in making Lloyd George the national leader. [24] Elsewhere Lloyd George makes out that he never wanted to place such a poor administrator as Carson at the Admiralty but that he always saw his usefulness as a member of the War Cabinet without administrative duties. Unfortunately, he says, the Tories opposed his wishes. [25] However, Asquith's exchanges with Lloyd George, to which reference has been made, show that the latter from the beginning of the crisis insisted on Carson being both First Lord and a member of the new War Committee. Only thus, it seemed at the time, could Lloyd George ensure his ascent to power.

Hankey, who was privy to Lloyd George's manoeuvres from mid-November onwards, was naturally unable to discover why, for reasons of efficiency, he preferred Carson to Balfour. It was then assumed that, as long as Lloyd George retained his post at the War Office, the First Lord must also be on the War Committee. Hankey therefore concluded that Lloyd George was deliberately choosing a committee which he could easily dominate and that Balfour was 'too strong and too dialectically skilful to allow this'. Hankey felt that a War Committee composed of Bonar Law, Carson, and Henderson was 'really ridiculous'. Compared with Balfour, Henderson was quite lacking in relevant experience. As for Law and Carson, they were in Hankey's opinion 'really featherheads'. [26]

[22] Lloyd George, ii, 1017.
[23] Ibid., p. 1000.
[24] Ibid., pp. 1020–1.
[25] Ibid., pp. 1175–6.
[26] Hankey P., 1/1, Diary, 3 Dec. 1916.

In the interests, then, of a more decisive and radical conduct of the war, Balfour deliberately gave away his established personal position.[27] So it was partly in a moral sense that Bonar Law ascribed to him the 'biggest part' in the ministerial crisis. For in accepting the Foreign Office, despite his low physical state, he not only undertook duties scarcely less arduous than those of a First Lord. He also, through not being a member of the War Cabinet, accepted a material degree of exclusion from the conduct of the war. For example, Lloyd George chaired a Cabinet Committee on War Policy which, between 11 June and 11 October 1917, met on 21 occasions. Curzon, Milner, and Smuts were members, but not Balfour.[28] Moreover the direction of foreign policy itself lay essentially with the all-powerful War Cabinet although, due to the involvement of the Foreign Office in most developments, Balfour had access to the War Cabinet when he wished.

By the first meeting of the War Cabinet on 9 December, however, Carson had been excluded from its number at the behest of the Unionist leadership. Therefore, by the 10th, when he and Balfour took over at the Admiralty and Foreign Office (Balfour being still *in absentia* during convalescence) Carson found his right to attend the War Cabinet was on a purely departmental basis, like that of Derby at the War Office or Walter Long now at the Colonial Office. The War Cabinet originally consisted of Lloyd George, Curzon, and Milner, together with Henderson and, of course, Bonar Law.

Robert Vansittart, then (at 36) joint head of the contraband department at the Foreign Office, has remarked of his earlier chiefs:

Not all statesmen took so kindly to specialists [as did Lansdowne]. Edward Grey and Arthur Balfour were the easiest to work for once their confidence was given. Lloyd George often treated them harshly, and Curzon annexed their work as the Germans annexed Shakespeare.[29]

However, if his constitutional position, and thus the historical importance of his work, suffered some diminution after December 1916, Balfour still exerted a substantial influence at times. This may be seen to its best advantage in the War Cabinet's discussions arising in September 1917 from Kühlmann's peace feelers.

[27]   B.P. 49831, ff. 249–50, consists of two very interesting letters of 21 and 30 Dec. 1916 from Lady Betty Balfour to Lady Frances Balfour. The first has a report (by way of 'Vie'—presumably Lady Violet Cecil, later Viscountess Milner) about B.'s readiness to let Lloyd George be 'Dictator' if he wished. (See also Dugdale, ii, 170.) The second (quoted at length in Dugdale, ii, 170) shows how much B. had been impressed by Lloyd George's impact on the munitions problem and also on the army transport crisis in France during 1916.
[28]   Cab. 27/6. See also Hankey, ii, 670–86.
[29]   Lord Vansittart, *The Mist Procession*, London, 1958, p. 44.

In April the Allies had been fortified by the entry into the war of the United States, but there were heavy items on the debit side during 1917. Russia, generally regarded as crucial for the chances of a complete allied victory, was evidently near to final military collapse. France had suffered grievously from Nivelle's disastrous offensive earlier in the year and could bear little further military strain. Britain was but slowly extricating herself from the mortal threat of starvation by submarine blockade. Her army, having assumed a major role in France, was suffering heavily in the Passchendaele campaign (31 July to 12 November 1917). So in September the German government pursued, through its new Foreign Minister Baron von Kühlmann, the possibility of sowing dissension between Britain and her allies by the lure of a separate peace.

However, there was no significant demand in Britain for a compromise peace, short of a general German retirement and payment of reparations. At the War Cabinet on 24 September 1917 Balfour explained that the Germans appeared to be offering quite a lot to Britain, and also to France, Serbia, Italy, and Belgium, but nothing to Russia or Roumania. If Russia or Roumania heard that Britain was 'discussing peace on these lines, they would probably make a separate peace at once'. While he thought it essential to reply to Germany—for fear of German exploitation and British disunity if there was no British response—he proposed, as Hankey's minutes relate, 'to summon the ambassadors of France, Russia, the United States, Italy, and Japan' and tell them that Britain intended 'to hear what offer Germany was prepared to make'. However, Balfour soon became isolated in the ensuing discussion. Lloyd George, followed by others, did not wish to tell the Allies or the Americans for the moment. The Prime Minister was swayed by the feeling that Russia had let the Allies down and had foregone any claim on the latter. As far as he was concerned Germany could recoup in the east what she gave up in the west. However, it was agreed that he should at least inform Painlevé (then French premier) before any signal was made to the Germans.

Lloyd George was back from France by late on the 26th; and on 27 September the War Cabinet reassembled. The Prime Minister said that the French believed the German approach to be genuine. Painlevé feared that if Germany offered to give up Belgium and most of Alsace–Lorraine, the French would not wish to fight on. Lloyd George felt that the British people might take the same view. Carson, now out of the Admiralty and in the War Cabinet, agreed. Balfour 'expressed the view that, if the British people thought that Germany would be left stronger as a result of the peace, they would be ready to fight on'. Barnes, the new Labour member of the War

Cabinet, agreed with Balfour; but he added that the public would 'want to know what they were fighting for'. This allowed the Prime Minister to develop his line of thought. The French were very keen to make peace on reasonable terms. They were not attacking the Germans as they had promised; and they would not 'go on fighting for Russia, if the Russians would not fight for themselves'. Haig had told him that 'if Russia went out of the war, we could not inflict military defeat on Germany.' He thus clearly implied that Britain should, in conjunction with France, seek a negotiated peace.

Curzon, however, wondered whether the allied blockade would not still squeeze Germany. That country would need 'probably 6 or 8 months' to get significant supplies out of Russia. Balfour agreed with Lloyd George 'that it would be a most serious blow if Russia went out of the war' but thought that co-operation with France and the U.S.A. might 'still make Germany's economic position very difficult. He wished to emphasize that the danger of Russia going out would be enormously increased if it got about that we are prepared to make peace at her expense.' Barnes, responding to Lloyd George, thought that the Americans need not be consulted because, so far, their contribution had remained largely financial. Balfour 'pointed out that the U.S.A. was making a very great effort both in shipbuilding and in raising military forces'. In response to doubts aired by Carson about British military morale, Lloyd George said that the men at the front were now 'beginning to talk among themselves of what we were fighting for'. But meantime Curzon (as indicated) had been swinging round to Balfour's steady view. Smuts remained neutral. But when Milner veered towards Balfour and Barnes, only Lloyd George and Carson still inclined towards the hypothetical peace with Germany at Russia's expense. Balfour observed that his view on war aims had been developed in his paper 'The Peace Settlement in Europe'.[30] There, he had envisaged the Allies fighting until they were able 'to strip Germany of much of her non-German territory' (though he had hoped no attempt would be made 'to control or modify her internal policy'). The War Cabinet finally settled for Balfour's approach.[31]

In fact, the Germans did not want peace on the terms which they had seemed to offer Lloyd George and Painlevé. But it was Balfour who had

---

[30] This was written, as indicated above, in Oct. 1916—not 'two years ago', as B. is recorded to have said at the War Cabinet.

[31] Cab. 23/16, War Cabinet 238A & 239A, Minutes, 24 & 27 Sept. 1917. See also C. J. Lowe and M. L. Dockrill, *The Mirage of Power: British Foreign Policy 1902–22*, London, 1972, 3 vols., ii, 260–5.

already by 1916 thought out his position and was well qualified, as Lloyd George subsequently acknowledged, to keep the War Cabinet on a steady diplomatic course. (See p. 304 above for Lloyd George's acknowledgement.)

Among Balfour's special concerns—as implied by some of the exchanges in Cabinet just mentioned—were the maintenance of good relations with the United States and the encouragement of Russia. When the War Cabinet had met on 4 April 1917, the American declaration of war on Germany was expected. President Wilson's government would, it appeared, welcome a mission of British experts to inform them about how the U.S.A. could best help the common cause. 'The War Cabinet considered that it was of great importance that, in order to initiate the expert negotiations, someone of the highest status in this country, who was known to the American people, and who would have the *entrée* to all circles, should proceed to Washington.'[32] Apart from conveying the need for a big shipbuilding programme to beat the U-boat blockade, the need for standardization of guns, and also for supplies of wheat and steel, Balfour was to telegraph home his assessment of the American attitude to the Irish question. Having 'very sportingly', as Hankey thought, for a man of nearly 70 who hated sea voyages,[33] made the trans-Atlantic crossing, Balfour received on 26 April a telegram from his deputy at the Foreign Office, Lord Robert Cecil:

> The War Cabinet considered this morning the shipping situation which is most serious . . . We are proposing to start a system of convoy through dangerous waters but this system cannot possibly be put into form without more destroyers. Will you impress with great force upon the United States authorities the very urgent need for more destroyers being sent to assist us . . .[34]

By 4 May Balfour was communicating British thanks to the American Secretary of State both for the destroyers already sent and for the American government's 'generous intention' to supplement this force—such 'timely and prompt assistance' being 'invaluable'.[35] Otherwise, an impression of Balfour's successful mission is conveyed by the following account sent on 6 May from his personal secretary, Ian Malcolm, to Lord Robert Cecil:

> Much the most important thing is the Chief's health, and that is quite amazingly good . . . I won't let him have any engagement before 11 a.m. . . . and nothing is to interfere with his two hours late afternoon drives, which he takes alone, and so

---

[32] Cab. 23/2, W.C. 113, Mins., 4 Apr. 1917.
[33] Roskill, *Hankey*, i, 376.
[34] B.P. 49738, f. 54.
[35] F.O. 800/208. This volume contains many details of the mission.

cannot be molested by any of us . . . His speeches to deputations are quite A1—so (of course) are his conversations with Ministers, etc., and so, too, is his lawn tennis! . . .

The everlasting dinners and receptions and interviews have been something of a corvée to the Chief, but he has weathered them splendidly . . . The Irish have been persistent but not too troublesome . . . he has on each occasion scored a heavy personal success [with them, arguing that it was hardly fair to expect the U.K. government to force Ulstermen who insisted they were British into a Home Rulers' Ireland.] . . .

The Conferences between experts are going slowly but surely . . . The Reception at the House of Representatives yesterday was the climax of A.J.B.'s triumphs . . . a marvellous reception . . . [36]

But whereas the natural tendency of Anglo-American relations after April 1917 was favourable to Balfour's diplomacy, it was entirely another matter as far as his efforts to keep Russia in the war were concerned. Since the March Revolution, Kerensky's grip on his country had been constantly under threat. By September there was, as has been said, a despondency in the British War Cabinet. On 9 September Balfour was initiating an ultimatum to Kerenksy, presented on 9 October, whereby the allies would stop shipping supplies to Russia if General Korniloff's anti-Bolshevik remedies were not put speedily into effect. [37] But by 7 November Lenin and the Bolsheviks were in control at Petrograd and were prompt to move towards an armistice on the Russian front. This highly disturbing sequence of events formed an important part of the background against which the War Cabinet took their decision on what became known as the Balfour Declaration on Palestine.

It is for this document, in the form of a letter to Lord Rothschild dated 2 November 1917, that Balfour has been best remembered. In so far as the reasons for the Government's decision, together with Balfour's personal role and motivation, and the subsequent consequences of the Declaration have received much attention from a variety of commentators, it is not proposed to treat the matter at length here. [38] But an answer must be given to the question: how did it come about that a highly intelligent statesman, who was noted for his powers of criticism rather than for initiating radical or constructive schemes, and who was deeply informed on the conflicting national identities in Ireland, took a leading part in promoting a problem of nationalities in Palestine?

[36] B.P. 49738, f. 64. See F.O. 800/208 for B. and the Irish.
[37] Lowe and Dockrill, ii, 307, 400.
[38] See esp. Leonard Stein, *The Balfour Declaration*, London, 1961; and for Balfour's role, Dugdale, ii, Ch. 11, etc.

The answer is Voltairian in nature. If Balfour had not existed in 1917, steps would have been taken to invent his Declaration. Therefore, in so far as Balfour was the cabinet minister most sympathetic to Zionism, it need come as no surprise to find him advocating what Grey had wanted, in some fashion, under less compelling circumstances in March 1916. During 1917, Lloyd George saw the fall of Jerusalem to a victorious British army as the best procurable tonic for a public shocked by long casualty lists from the Western Front and threatened with starvation by U-boat. The Foreign Office, for its part, was convinced of the importance of winning over to the side of the Allies Jewish opinion in Germany, the United States, and especially Russia. In Russia the Jews had suffered more than elsewhere; and they were understandably well represented in Bolshevik ranks. Moreover, the Foreign Office picture was that all Russian Jews were Zionists and that German propaganda had been scoring easy victories amongst them. By 3 September, the War Cabinet found it necessary, despite the absence for recuperation of both Balfour and Lloyd George, to consider the pro-Zionist draft declaration which Balfour had held at the Foreign Office since August. Notwithstanding Edwin Montagu's opposition to the whole idea of a Jewish national home, the War Cabinet of four chaired by Bonar Law approved the request of Lord Robert Cecil (Balfour's deputy) that he be authorized to seek President Wilson's view on the proposed declaration. [39]

On 4 October, Balfour presented to the War Cabinet some of the aforementioned diplomatic reasons for issuing a sympathetic declaration to the Zionists. At this meeting, as at the decisive one on the 31st, the only member (or attender) to develop the likely Arab reaction was Curzon. But the crucial point is surely that none of the participants fully envisaged the future strength of Arab nationalism. Nor was it clear that Britain would carry political responsibility for Palestine after the war. Lloyd George seems, for strategic reasons, to have been bent on maintaining British control; but he did not find it necessary to make any contribution worthy of record at these two meetings. On 31 October the War Cabinet authorized:

The Secretary of State for Foreign Affairs to take a suitable opportunity of making the following declaration of sympathy with the Zionist aspirations:

'His Majesty's Government views with favour the establishment in Palestine of a national home for the Jewish people, and will use its best endeavours to facilitate the achievement of this object, it being clearly understood that nothing shall be done

---

[39] Cab. 21/58, 'The Zionist Movement', contains copies of relevant minutes and memoranda.

which may prejudice the civil and religious rights of existing non-Jewish com-
munities in Palestine, or the rights and political status enjoyed by Jews in any
other country.'[40]

Balfour duly embodied this declaration in his letter to Lord Rothschild
dated 2 November.

How, then, might so short-sighted and incomplete a view of the problem
have been avoided by the War Cabinet? It was pointed out by Lord Robert
Cecil at the meeting of 3 September 'that this was a question on which the
Foreign Office had been very strongly pressed for a long time past'. Before
it came up again at the War Cabinet on 4 October there was time for
memoranda to be written, notably by Curzon and Montagu, and a discussion took place on these papers after Balfour's pro-Zionist introductory
statement. But 'The Zionist Movement' was only one item out of twenty on
the agenda—No. 18, to be precise. When the decision was taken on
31 October, there was again some discussion—Curzon's objections focusing
on Palestine's poor economic resources rather than the likelihood of trouble
with the Arabs—but the item came last out of twelve on the agenda.
Therefore there can be no doubt about Balfour's prima-facie duty to
present the strength of the likely objections on the Arab side of the
question.[41] A clear analysis of the objections to any new departure could
normally be expected from him. Why, on this occasion, did his sympathy
with a cause result in submergence of his usual critical inclinations?

Balfour believed, and argued in his philosophical works, that his personal
God was the source of what was 'most assured in knowledge, all that is, or
seems, most beautiful in art or nature, and all that is, or seems, most noble
in morality'.[42] His religious philosophy governed his attitude to life and
politics. It informed his patriotism and sustained his devoted service during
the Great War. In so far as the doctrine of his own national churches
stemmed from the Old Testament, he was susceptible to the appeal of
Zionism. Even when confronted with the reality of Arab objections, which
arose as soon as the Declaration was propagated round the world, and faced
with the appeal of pro-Arab spokesmen to that principle of self-
determination generally accepted by the British Foreign Office, he would
reply in a speech at a Zionist rally of 1920:

Looking back on the history of the world, I say that the case of Jewry in all

[40]   Cab. 23/4, W.C. 261, 31 Oct. 1917.
[41]   Cab. 23/4, W.c. 227, 3 Sept.; W.C. 245, 4 Oct.; and W.C. 261, 31 Oct. 1917; also Cab.
21/58 (which includes the memoranda of Curzon and Montagu); and Lowe and Dockrill, ii,
227–33.
[42]   *Theism and Humanism*, pp. 18–19.

countries is absolutely exceptional, falls outside all the ordinary rules and maxims, cannot be contained in a formula or explained in a sentence. The deep underlying principle of self-determination really points to a Zionist policy. [43]

Secondly, Stein makes an apposite point where he refers to the possible role of 'sheer intellectual curiosity'. [44] Balfour's curiosity about the world of men, things, and ideas was inexhaustible. No wonder his intense religious interest was captured from the time of his first interview with the Zionist Chaim Weizmann in 1906 and was actively enlisted in the Zionist cause, despite powerful distractions, from the early months of the Great War.

Thirdly, there was the remarkable concentration of genius in the Jewish race. In 1917 Balfour waxed eloquent on the subject in a conversation with Harold Nicolson and described the Jews as 'the most gifted race that mankind has seen since the Greeks of the fifth century'. [45] Likewise, in the speech of 1920 already quoted, he answered the line of objection developed by Curzon before the Declaration in the following vein:

> Palestine, great as is the place which it occupies in the history of the world, is but a small and petty country looked at as a geographical unit . . . But what are the requisites of such development in Palestine as may accommodate an important section of the great race I am addressing? . . . One is skill, knowledge, perseverance, enterprise; the other is capital, and I am perfectly convinced that when you are talking of the Jews you will find no want of any one of these requisites . . . [46]

It may also be relevant to suggest that, by 1917, the traumas and urgent pressures of the War had developed in Balfour a new perception of the role of genius in world affairs. Whereas before the war he had been generally sceptical about the ability of governments to engineer fundamental improvements in the lot of mankind, after 1914 he moved towards a position where he could answer Lord Robert Cecil, whose distrust of Lloyd George's intuitive leadership had brought him to the verge of resignation, with a long rebuttal dated 12 September 1917—in the seed time of the Balfour Declaration:

> Is there any one of his colleagues in the present War Cabinet you would like to see in his place? Is there any member of the late Government you would like to see in his place? Do you believe there is in the House of Commons any genius on the back benches fit for the place? Do you think there is somewhere in the undistinguished mass of the general public some unknown genius to whom, if we could but find him,

[43] *Opinions and Argument*, p. 234 (speech at the Albert Hall, 12 July 1920).
[44] Stein, p. 157. See also Vansittart, p. 218.
[45] Stein, p. 157.
[46] *Opinions and Argument*, pp. 234–5.

we might entrust the most difficult, and the most important task with which British statesmanship has ever been confronted?[47]

Towards the end of his life Balfour observed that 'everything turns upon genius.'[48]

Certainly, in 1917, more of an experimental element can be detected in Balfour's approach to affairs of state than had appeared before his association with Lloyd George. Soon after Balfour had, in June 1917, told Weizmann and Lord Rothschild that they could let him have a draft Zionist declaration to put before the War Cabinet, Lloyd George consulted Balfour as to whether Montagu, whom he rated a moderate reformer, should be appointed to the key imperial post of Secretary for India. Balfour's response reveals a surprisingly open mind on this hallowed subject:

Montagu is very able: he knows a great deal about India; he would be very popular with the Indians. *Per contra* he would be disliked by the Anglo-Indians—partly because he is too much (in their opinion) of a 'reformer', partly because he is a Jew.

I should certainly not raise any objection to his appointment and I should be interested to see how the experiment succeeded.[49]

On 22 June 1922, in the House of Lords, Balfour eloquently defended what had by then become the troubled British Mandate in Palestine. The scheme, he said,

may fail: I do not deny that this is an adventure. Are we never to have adventures? Are we never to try new experiments? . . . Surely, it is in order that we may send a message to every land where the Jewish race has been scattered, a message which will tell them that Christendom is not oblivious of their faith, is not unmindful of the service they have rendered to the great religions of the world, and we desire to the best of our ability to give them the opportunity of developing, in peace and quietness under British rule, those great gifts . . .[50]

But as far as the course of the war was concerned, the Balfour Declaration of November 1917 had no discernible beneficial effect. In the country regarded as crucial, Russia, the Bolshevik coup followed within days of the Declaration's announcement; and it soon became evident that Trotsky and other Jewish activists were not by any means all Zionists. However, in

[47] B.P. 49738, ff. 147–52, Lord Robert Cecil to B., 12 Sept. and B.L. 51093, Cecil of Chelwood P., B. to Lord Robert Cecil, 12 Sept. 1917.

[48] Dugdale, ii, 401: notes of a conversation, Sept. 1929.

[49] F.O. 800/199, ff. 36–7, Lloyd George to B. and Lloyd George P., F/3/2/26, B. to Lloyd George, 16 July 1917.

[50] *Opinions and Argument*, p. 248.

dealing with Soviet Russia, Balfour showed no tendency to be rigidly governed by his anti-socialist views. In December 1917 he presented to the War Cabinet a well-argued case against a complete break with the Bolsheviks. [51] His view prevailed. The War Cabinet's policy, in a situation where Bolshevik control in Russia was far from complete—even after the Treaty of Brest-Litovsk in March 1918—was to support any forces or elements able and willing to oppose the German exploitation of Russia and to tie down German troops there. However, this policy of 'two Russias' lost its validity between July and September 1918. Against all British military expectation, the allied armies in the West, having weathered the great German offensive of March, moved forward to decisive success. Peace, on allied terms, prevailed from 11 November. In these circumstances the War Cabinet on 14 November, finally settled for the unfortunate compromise which led to the notorious Allied Intervention in Russia. What was Balfour's role?

From January 1919 he was tied down at the Paris Peace Conference and through most of the year he had comparatively little to do with the making of British policy towards Russia. However, as can be seen from Richard Ullman's account, Balfour's influence was to the fore at the crucial stage in November 1918 when a Russian policy was reviewed in the light of the German defeat. [52] The opportunity for a complete withdrawal of British troops, advocated by the C.I.G.S., Sir Henry Wilson, was missed. While Balfour, who had been ready to work with the deeply-loathed Bolsheviks as long as there was any chance of their resisting the Germans, sensibly deprecated 'an anti-Bolshevik crusade in Russia' along Churchillian lines, he articulated the feeling of the Conservative ministers that they should continue to support old anti-Bolshevik clients in Russia, using the British forces already there. This was the drift of the recommendations agreed at a conference of ministers and service experts held at the Foreign Office on 13 November 1918 under Balfour's chairmanship. One surprisingly bold line advocated by Balfour was that Britain should give military support to the newly emergent Baltic states (Estonia, Latvia, and Lithuania). However Milner—no longer in the War Cabinet but, as War Secretary, ready to fight for British imperial interests in unpromising southern areas like the Caucasus—opposed any military commitment to the Baltic states.

[51] Cab. 23/4, W.C. 296, 12 Dec. 1917 with B.'s 'Notes on the Present Russian Situation', G.T. 2932, printed as an appendix. Contrary to Lloyd George, v, 2573, the minutes show that B. did attend the meeting.
[52] Richard H. Ullman, *Britain and the Russian Civil War*, Vol. ii, London, 1968, pp. 11–18.

On the next day, 14 November, the War Cabinet met. In a lengthy statement Balfour presented the detailed recommendations of the previous day's conference. He said that he had tried to get the Scandinavian countries 'to assist in providing arms and in policing the Border States. They had, however, all refused, and, if anything was to be done, it would have to be done by the Allies.' Milner 'stated that under no circumstances could [Britain] send troops'. He got his way. Otherwise, the Prime Minister entirely agreed with Balfour 'as to the general line of policy to be pursued'. Towards the end of the discussion Lloyd George adumbrated the basis of his continuing coalition with the Conservatives by saying that

it was important that the public in England should realise more fully what Bolshevism meant in practice . . . Here we had a great, inflammable, industrial population, and it was very desirable that [it] should know how industrial workers had suffered equally with the rest of the population of Russia at the hands of the Bolsheviks.

His Conservative colleagues responded enthusiastically. Austen Chamberlain (Milner's replacement in the War Cabinet) was all for publicity and Balfour added that those worst treated by the Bolsheviks were 'people whom we should regard in this country as "blood-red Socialists"'. Bonar Law and Lord Robert Cecil wanted the press to be given full details of 'Bolshevik excesses'. It was left to the Foreign Office to arrange suitable publicity with Sir George Riddell and the press.[53]

During 1919 the cost to Britain of allied intervention was to prove heavy, in purely mathematical terms. Its impress on Anglo-Russian relations and on the sympathies of the British working class was, of course, also considerable. Not until November 1919 was Lloyd George in a position to call a halt.

However, in the month available between the 'coupon' election of 14 December and the opening of the Peace Conference in Paris, Balfour was able to deflate one potential bubble of British ambition in the Russian sphere. Curzon, in effect, had scored a substantial point against 'dear Arthur'[54] in March 1918 when he became chairman, by dint of his War Cabinet status, of the Eastern Committee. This was the only committee of

[53] Cab. 23/8, W.C. 502, 14 Nov. 1918, item 5 and the appendix, 'Minute of the Proceedings of a Conference held at the Foreign Office on November 13, 1918, at 3.30 p.m.'. Also Ullman, pp. 11–18.

[54] Curzon's letters to B. continue, in B.P. 49734, until Feb. 1923—for example (10 Dec. 1916): 'My dear Arthur, I suppose that in the role which I have (most reluctantly) to fill in the House of Lords, I shall have on many occasions to be the exponent of your Foreign Policy . . .' (f. 42).

the War Cabinet to trench specifically upon foreign affairs. On 2 December, in Balfour's absence, Curzon made out a case for a measure of British control in Transcaucasia, lately seen as being the German route to India as well as a source of oil supplies. On the 9th Balfour attended and crossed swords once again with 'dear George'. He said that if Britain were asked at the Peace Conference to accept a Caucasian mandate, it 'would be a most serious thing'. Would he, Curzon inquired, prefer the French to have it? 'I would not give it to the French', Balfour replied. 'I would exercise through the League of Nations a controlling influence.' 'How,' asked Curzon, 'would you prevent them from being crushed by Russia unless you had a military force?' Balfour replied: 'If Russia is in a position to crush them, why not? We should not go there to protect them from the Russians. It would be folly, from a purely military point of view, for us to try to keep a military force there.'

Sniping at Balfour's customary avoidance of the newspapers, Curzon said it was clear that the Caucasians could not stand on their own feet. He thought it inevitable that the Peace Conference would ask Britain to help them. Balfour said that in such an event Britain should temporize but be careful to make no promise.

Leaving that point, which is an international point, when we come to the point about the defence of India, I hope the General Staff will be a little careful about the demands they make upon us about India. Every time I come to a discussion—at intervals of, say, five years [1903–5, 1908, 1913–14, 1918]—I find there is a new sphere which we have got to guard, which is supposed to protect the gateways of India. Those gateways are getting further and further from India . . . Remember, before the war there was a great military Power in occupation of these places . . . which we could not hit, which we of all people were helpless against. They had it and we did not tremble . . .[55]

Balfour's substantial point that Britain would not try to defend Georgia or the other independent Caucasian states against Russia was upheld by Lloyd George at the Imperial War Cabinet on 12 December.[56] As for Curzon's desire that a Great Power should give the Caucasians 'a chance of standing on their own feet', Balfour, who was alarmed at the excessive responsibilities being canvassed by British imperialists, asked why the Caucasians should 'not be misgoverned?' Curzon replied ironically: 'That is the other

[55] Cab. 27/24, Eastern Committee, mins. of 42nd meeting, 9 Dec. 1918, pp. 11–12; Ullman, pp. 66–72.
[56] Ibid., pp. 75–6.

alternative—let them cut each other's throats.' Balfour at once responded: 'I am in favour of that.'[57]

As late as 9 December 1918 Curzon was deploring Balfour's wish to avoid defining British policy on such places as Georgia and Armenia. Said Curzon: 'I am trying to help you at the Peace Conference, Mr. Balfour, for you will be our chief representative there.'[58] Of course, Balfour did not occupy this role at Paris. From the time of his triumphant return by the electorate in December 1918 until the end of the coalition in October 1922, British foreign policy was dominated by Lloyd George. His own secretariat, the 'Garden Suburb', and the cabinet secretariat led by Hankey, reinforced his control over the War Cabinet (and, from November 1919, over the re-established Cabinet) and served his personal missions at the series of post-war international conferences beginning at Paris in 1919 and ending at Genoa in 1922.

Curzon, after succeeding Balfour at the Foreign Office, would greatly resent this subordination. In May 1919 FitzRoy noted: 'Arthur Balfour is too great, and philosophically too indifferent, to mind it.'[59] More impishly, Vansittart, who was a member of the large diplomatic contingent at Paris, records how Balfour 'enjoyed wondering what The Little Man—as he called his stocky Premier—would do next. He watched as if the Welshman were a dynamic insect under a microscope.' The same observer was a good tennis player who catered for Balfour's 'sedate passion' for the game; and according to him, Balfour's 'abandonment of golf for this temptress was his nearest approach to physical infidelity'. In sum, he notes: 'It was hopeless to avoid devotion to A.J.B., and I never tried.'[60]

Consistently with his past attitudes, Balfour had fully subscribed to the Government's approach to the German peace by seeking an Anglo-American accord rather than supporting French demands for a Rhine frontier. But by the autumn of 1919 President Wilson's loss of support at home entailed the collapse of this Anglo-American approach. France had been persuaded to accept moderation of her demands in return for an Anglo-American guarantee of her German frontier; but with American

---

[57] Eastern Committee, 9 Dec., pp. 13–14; and 43rd meeting, 16 Dec. 1918, p. 8 for B.'s fears about excessive British claims at the Peace Conference: 'The Colonial Office would like . . . as many colonies as they could get. We talk of huge protectorates all over the place . . . [The] War Office and the Treasury are mainly concerned. Where are they going to find the men or the money for these things? I do not know . . . and they seem to me to be the governing considerations.'

[58] Ibid., 9 Dec. 1918, p. 16.

[59] FitzRoy, p. 701 (diary, 2 May 1919).

[60] Vansittart, p. 218.

retreat the guarantee dissolved, leaving Britain and France on divergent
tacks.

However, although Balfour was unwell early in February,[61] he had
recovered by the time he was visited in the Rue Nitot by his brother Gerald
and Lady Betty at the end of the month. As Hankey records, in the absence
of the five national leaders Balfour did much during February to speed up
the work of the Conference. 'I had [he remarks] under-rated, not for the
first or last time in my life, Balfour's extraordinary aptitude for rising to the
occasion.'[62] Speed was, of course, important. An early German signature
on the peace treaty would ease the urgent British demobilization problem
and allow supplies to get through to the German population. Meanwhile,
Balfour had already helped, at the beginning of the Conference in January,
to settle the question of separate representation of the Dominions within the
British Empire Delegation. After the German Treaty had been signed at
Versailles on 28 June, Lloyd George and Wilson departed. Balfour
remained as leader of the British delegation. On 10 September the Austrian
Treaty was signed at St Germain.[63] In so far as Austria, after 1919, was felt
to be hardly viable as an independent entity, it is interesting to note, in
1983, that it has for some years now provided one of the models held up as
an example to the less successful British economy.

By 1919 Balfour had started to grow deaf. Lloyd George has described
how, when someone of indistinct utterance like Bonar Law started to speak
in the Cabinet, Balfour would at once get to his feet and stand beside the
speaker till he had finished.[64] Sir George Riddell, representing the main
English newspapers at the Paris Conference, noticed in May 1919 that
Balfour was suffering from this handicap (as had Lady Betty Balfour in
February) but notwithstanding he notes in his published diary: 'Mr. B. in
great form'.[65] It is true that by August Balfour was urgently craving a
holiday and wanting to hand over foreign affairs completely to Curzon,
who had been in charge of the Foreign Office while Balfour was in France.
But Balfour's continuing resilience is apparent from the fact that it was he
who chaired the committee arranging the composition of the King's

[61] WHI/277, Lady Betty Balfour to Alice Balfour, 28 Feb. 1919: 'His old internal trouble
(which I imagine means diarrhoea) and a sprained arm and broken tooth'.
[62] Hankey, *The Supreme Control at the Paris Peace Conference*, London, 1963, pp.
74–81.
[63] Dugdale, ii, 269–84.
[64] Lloyd George, ii, 1014.
[65] Lord Riddell, *Intimate Diary of the Peace Conference and After 1918–1923*, London,
1933, p. 84 (30 May 1919).

speech, soon after taking Curzon's place as Lord President of the Council on 23 October 1919. [66]

In his remaining years in the coalition government, he showed some continuing appreciation of what could be done to utilize the country's scientific talent for the benefit of the peacetime economy. On 24 November 1919 the Finance Committee of the Cabinet asked him to preside over a cabinet committee for the Co-Ordination of Scientific Research in Government Departments. As a result of the first meeting (16 December 1919) Balfour put pressure on the Treasury to determine salary scales for government scientists. Many had already left the service since the end of the war and, despite the worsening economic climate, the Lord President was eager for the Government to 'get the best men'. On 17 February 1921 two reports of sub-committees were adopted: one on agriculture and one on fisheries and agricultural science. [67] Balfour also interceded—unsuccessfully—with Lloyd George for the award of peerages to encourage science, nominating Sir Joseph Thomson, the eminent physicist, and Sir George Beilby, an industrial chemist who had been in government service during the war. Balfour noted: 'A great part of his life's work has been devoted to the application of science to industry.' Although Balfour's recommendation could hardly have been more appropriate to Britain's economic situation, neither Beilby nor Thomson were given peerages. [68]

After the Geddes Committee had been appointed in August 1921, Balfour perceived that the famous 'axe' was poised over two bodies under his aegis, namely the Department of Scientific and Industrial Research (established in 1915) and the Medical Research Council. He wrote to Eric Geddes, arguing that these bodies conferred direct financial benefit on the Treasury; also that if trade was bad and industry 'languishing', it was just the right time to 'improve our technical methods' and cited as an example 'the strenuous labours of Sir George Beilby in Fuel Research'. Beilby's services were, like those of other scientists, given gratuitously. [69]

In other ways, too, post-war development of his attitude to government can be traced. During the winter of 1919–20 when the economic boom had burst, Balfour received a letter from his old friend Lavinia Lyttleton, the wife of Bishop Talbot, wherein she complained about lavish spending in the

[66] Dugdale, ii, 288–94; Roskill, *Hankey*, ii, 132.
[67] Cab. 27/94.
[68] WHI/10, B. to Lloyd George, 16 Nov. 1920. See WHI/76 for B. to Alice Balfour, 26 Nov. 1924: 'Baldwin stayed a considerable time talking at large, but not upon anything that mattered, except perhaps the question of Honours for men of science.'
[69] WHI/19, B. to Sir Eric Geddes, 21 Oct. 1921.

West End which could provoke violent resentment in the East End of London. Balfour replied

> I believe I am right in the following statements:
>
> 1. The cost of necessaries is lower in this country than in any other, including America.
> 2. The wages of 'labour', speaking generally . . . have gone up more than the cost of necessaries . . .
> 3. . . . the well-to-do classes living (say) in Mayfair or Belgravia . . . are much poorer than they were; they are paying enormous Income Tax [at a standard rate of 6/− in the £ against 1/− in 1905 and 1/2d in 1914]; wages have immensely increased; rents and interest on ordinary securities have not . . .
> 4. The price of bread is being artificially kept down at the cost of the tax-payer. Building for the working classes is being encouraged at the cost of the ratepayer. We are the only country who, during the war, successfully rationed . . .
> 5. Coal is rationed, broadly speaking . . . Milk is a great difficulty, but the farmers are not making fortunes out of it; but one reason of its high cost is due to increase in the wages of those engaged in its production, and the increased freights due to the rises in the wages of railwaymen.

In terms which reflect his reasons for so strongly supporting continuance of the Lloyd George Coalition, he remarked that, 'before this iniquitous war . . . there was enough to go round. Now there is not enough to go round. Nothing will put this right but time, energy, good order, and industry.' In the wake of the wartime inflation he felt that 'the recipients of small fixed incomes' were 'greatly to be pitied'.[70]

While it is true that Balfour was at one with his Conservative colleagues in seeing the Coalition as the best political counter to socialism and to possible Bolshevist tendencies amongst the industrial working classes, he was prepared to go along with a programme of radical reforms on a scale that he would not have tolerated before 1914. When consulted by Bonar Law in October 1918 as to whether the Conservatives should continue to support Lloyd George in, and beyond, the coming election, Balfour had replied that he deprecated a reversion to 'ordinary party controversy'. He thought that, beyond victory, government should aim at 'Peace' and 'National Reconstruction' while 'drawing its strength from all sections of the community'.[71] In the light of the Labour Party's advance during 1919, the question of 'fusion' of Conservatives with Coalition Liberals had come to the fore; and Balfour's friend Herbert Fisher (still President of the Board of Education, with cabinet status confirmed since the October reorganization) wrote to

[70] WHI/26, 28 Feb. 1920.
[71] B.P. 49693, ff. 282−7, B. to Law, 11 Oct. 1918.

Balfour on 4 February 1920 enclosing extensive 'NOTES FOR A SPEECH'—that is, for a speech by Lloyd George. He set out the economic and international aims of the Coalition in Europe and listed its achievements in the areas of public education, the franchise, public health, and agriculture; its handling of demobilization and vast economic and labour problems; and the various facets of British life which it sought to preserve. He also listed dire possibilities which all Liberals and Conservatives wished to avoid: 'revolution; class war; the dissolution of the Empire; foreign commitments involving the maintenance of great armaments; the spread of materialism; the decline of industrial or commercial energy; the continued exasperation of the Irish against the English race'. [72] On 9 February Balfour sent his comments on Fisher's paper to Lloyd George. About the first six pages, comprising the material just mentioned, he had 'nothing to say, speaking generally, except praise'. But he thought that when Fisher then began to go into detail (on proportional representation, the extension of female suffrage, home rule for Scotland and Wales, and labour legislation) he was liable to cause too much dissension among supporters of the Coalition. Balfour continued:

> Consider, for example, such a phrase as this: 'The workers have no say in the management of the businesses they contribute to create.' I am an old and zealous advocate, both in public and in private, of co-operative production, and, where it is possible, of profit-sharing; but sentences like the one I have quoted will frighten every employer in the country, without, I think, conciliating a single wage-earner . . .

> Some general exposition of the trend of your policy is not only desirable but necessary . . . in substance, what the Coalition stands for is Reform versus Revolution. The danger they have got to avoid, if possible, is the familiar one, that those who are opposed to Revolution are so occupied with quarrelling with each other over less important matters that they fall an easy prey to revolutionaries—and only discover their mistake when it is too late to cure it. It is therefore essential that our friends should accustom themselves to work harmoniously together with a good deal of give and take, so that when our political organisation is threatened by the inevitable controversies over minor points, it shall be found strong enough to resist the strain. [73]

Lloyd George replied on 18 February. [74] He entirely agreed with Balfour, who is fairly rated by Maurice Cowling as still, at that stage, second in importance among Conservatives only to Bonar Law. As Mr Cowling

[72] WHI/1, H. A. L. Fisher to B., 4 Feb. 1920.
[73] Lloyd George P., F/3/5/1, B. to Lloyd George, 9 Feb. 1920 (copy in WHI/1).
[74] WHI/1, 18 Feb. 1920.

elsewhere implies, Balfour was also Lloyd George's strongest supporter amongst the Conservative leadership.[75] But it was the Coalition Liberal ministers who, in March, rejected 'fusion'; and with it, the chance to reconstruct British industrial, and even conceivably educational, policy along appropriate lines was thrown away. Instead, the country drifted along in the kind of anti-progressive haze symbolized by Baldwin.[76]

When, in October 1916, Balfour was writing his cabinet paper on 'The Peace Settlement in Europe', he saw the 'principal object of the War' as 'the attainment of a durable peace', firstly by limiting the resources of the Central Powers and secondly by applying, as far as practicable, 'the principle of nationality'. But he thought that Germany would remain 'more than a match for France alone'.

In that event [wrote Balfour] the entente is likely to be maintained. Germany may suffer a spiritual conversion; Russia may break up; France and Britain may be rendered powerless by labour troubles; universal bankruptcy may destroy universal armaments; international courts may secure international peace; the horrors of 1914, 1915, 1916, and 1917 may render the very thought of war disgusting to all mankind. On these subjects it is vain to speculate.[77]

By 1920, he found himself representing Britain on the Council of the League of Nations, although he knew only too well that the absence of the United States had reduced the potential for peace of that body, just as her change of heart had undermined the prospects of the peace settlement itself. However, much though he disliked the idea of having to spend several weeks each year at Geneva, he felt that the work was useful and he persisted with it beyond the term of the Coalition. Treasury objections to a permanent office in Geneva drew from him the comment:

Let me incidentally add that I do not mind being thwarted occasionally by departmental action. These incidents are inevitable. What I do object to is the dislike that certain Departments have to the whole idea and spirit of the League, and their obvious satisfaction in putting a spoke in the wheel. The French are much wiser. I believe they dislike the League as much as our official friends at home; but it is there, and they set themselves to work to use it for all it is worth.[78]

Balfour's manner of living up to these sentiments was described to Almeric FitzRoy by the Canadian representative at the League Assembly

---

[75] Maurice Cowling, *The Impact of Labour 1920–1924*, Cambridge, 1971, pp. 112 and 187.
[76] See Martin J. Wiener, *English Culture*, for comment on Baldwin.
[77] Cab. 37/157/7, 4 Oct. 1916. See p. 304 above.
[78] WHI/17, B. to Hankey, 18 Jan. 1921.

during the summer of 1921: 'Mr. Doherty had been immensely struck by the "consummate skill" with which [Balfour] handled several awkward situations and the moral earnestness time and experience had infused into his method of interpreting the League's mission.'[79] Even more striking is the impression recorded by Gilbert Murray who, from 1921 to 1923, acted as a delegate to the League:

AJB dominates the Assembly, easily and without effort. It is very curious, and has to be seen to be believed. It is partly mere charm and unassuming dignity, partly his great prestige, partly a real diplomatic power of making almost anyone do what he wants. It reminds me of what the autosuggestion people say, that any conflict or effort defeats itself. He makes no effort and is irresistible.

On another occasion Murray wrote from Geneva:

AJB makes himself loved by all his staff, and by everyone who has to do with him. They treat him as something frail and precious, eagerly saving him from fatigue and worry. All become sad if he looks ill or if he forgets his words, as he sometimes does. Indeed it will be an incalculable loss to the League if he dies or retires. He and [Herbert] Fisher are its only pillars, as far as I can see, inside the Government, and he carries far more weight than Fisher and has more independence and courage.[79a]

In October 1918 Balfour had urged that the mandate for Palestine should be awarded by the prospective League of Nations to the United States.[80] However, this proved as illusory as all the other hopes pinned on the Americans. By August 1919, Balfour was still hoping that some country other than Britain would accept the mandate, though he did not expect such relief.[81] By 1920 Britain was almost certain to get it. On 22 July 1921, Weizmann discussed the combustible situation in Palestine with Lloyd George, Churchill, and others at Balfour's London house. Both the Prime Minister and Balfour apparently assured Weizmann that they had always taken the Declaration to mean an eventual Jewish state.[82] However, it remains probable that Balfour, at least, had not been prepared, when in the official role of Foreign Secretary, to commit Britain to this objective.[83] While working, with limited expectations, for peace at the League of Nations, Balfour also contributed to the work of that familiar safeguard of

---

[79] FitzRoy, p. 762, diary, 10 Oct. 1921.
[79a] These quotations come from Duncan Wilson's life of Gilbert Murray—to be published in due course by Oxford University Press.
[80] Lowe and Dockrill, ii, 358.
[81] Stein, p. 618.
[82] Gilbert, Companion Vol. iv, 1559.
[83] Lowe and Dockrill, ii, 232.

national security, the C.I.D. It was Hankey who, as the pre-war Secretary of that body, took the initiative in pressing Lloyd George to reconvene it. He was anxious to pre-empt moves to create a Ministry of Defence in the wake of Churchill's appointment, in January 1919, as Secretary of State for War *and* Air. While Balfour, for one, was deeply impressed by the value of Hankey's wartime contribution,[84] it can hardly be said that the latter's prolonged opposition to a Ministry of Defence was in the country's best interests.[85]

On 29 July 1920, the 133rd meeting of the C.I.D. was held with the Prime Minister in the chair, and with seven other cabinet ministers together with five leading service-men in attendance. Balfour was the sole survivor from the team that had met on 23 February 1915 at the 132nd meeting, except, of course, for Hankey (who had become Sir Maurice Hankey in 1916 and was now flanked by three soldier-secretaries of descending rank). Balfour 'was of opinion that the pre-war machinery' would be 'the most suitable in the long run'. But he agreed with Walter Long (now First Lord) that 'the more the Naval and Military and Air Advisers discussed questions together the better.' This represented a move towards the establishment, from 1923, of the Chiefs of Staff Sub-Committee of the C.I.D. which was made collectively responsible for advising the Cabinet on defence policy. In so far as the advocates of a Ministry of Defence got nowhere, this Sub-Committee repaired some of the deficiency. Meanwhile it was decided to set up a Standing Sub-Committee of the C.I.D. to consider questions referred to it by the parent body, the first being the co-ordination of the fighting services.[86]

However, the Prime Minister did not find time for the Sub-Committee; and Balfour, though disqualified to an extent by his absences on League of Nations work, and his uncertain health, took the chair when the Sub-Committee at last met on 2 May 1921. Its membership was otherwise restricted to service ministers and chiefs. Despite further commitments abroad (at Geneva and Washington), Balfour chaired the Sub-Committee on most occasions; and, because of the rarity of meetings held by the parent body, the minutes of the Sub-Committee were subsequently reclassified as meetings of the C.I.D. Firstly, the possibility of developing a naval base at Singapore was examined.[87] On 16 June, this was approved in principle by the Cabinet. Then, after some inconclusive wrangling between the chiefs of

---

[84] Dugdale, ii, 242.
[85] See Roskill, *Hankey*, ii, 32, 110, 154, etc.
[86] Cab. 2/3.
[87] Cab. 2/3, 10 June 1921.

the three services, Balfour wrote 'a Paper for Cabinet use' (26 July 1921) on the role of the Air Force. Firstly, he recognized that 'home defence against air raids' was a function almost exclusively of the R.A.F. Secondly, however, influenced doubtless by the extent to which the air forces had been reduced since the war, he thought that 'attack on enemy harbours or inland towns' came into the sphere of inter-service 'co-operation'. Finally, where air forces played an 'auxiliary part', he held that they must come under the commanding General or Admiral.[88] Decisions along these lines were announced in the House of Commons on 16 March 1922, thus rebutting suggestions (to which Hankey had contributed) that the Air Ministry should be abolished.[89]

In the meantime, Balfour had rendered a notable diplomatic service appertaining to national defence. Having departed for Geneva in August, he was asked towards the end of September to lead the powerful British delegation at the Washington Conference on naval limitation. Lloyd George himself was preoccupied by his Irish negotiations. Miss Constance Bliss, who had taken over Short's secretarial duties in 1920, wrote to Alice Balfour that it was a pity Balfour had to go as he had had 'rather a strenuous time of it' at Geneva and was 'not looking so fit as when he first came'.[90] On 28 September Balfour had cabled to Curzon: 'I very much hope the P.M. will think better of it. Bonar is much more suited to the job and is at present one of the unemployed. Moreover he has not been an exile for two months as I have.'[91] However, this was to be another challenge to which, with Hankey at his elbow, he would triumphantly respond.

From Britain's viewpoint, the crucial object was to avoid a naval race with the United States. The Americans obviously had the capacity to put into effect the demands of their navalists, stimulated by the Great War, for a navy second to none. In so far as he had no precise instructions from the Cabinet, Balfour had much food for thought during the rather rough sea crossing to Quebec early in November. Having reached Washington on the 10th, Hankey reported to Lloyd George:

> Mr. Balfour . . . escaped sea-sickness by remaining in bed almost the whole time, which was very wise. He was also able to work very hard. He has consequently absorbed the mass of detail . . . involved in the Conference . . . Mr. Balfour felt it

[88]   Cab. 5/4, C.I.D. Paper 149C, 'The Part of the Air Force of the Future in Imperial Defence', 26 July 1921.

[89]   Cab. 16/47, 'Summary' prepared for the Salisbury Committee, 9 Mar. 1923, para. 7; Roskill, *Hankey*, ii, 107.

[90]   WHI/76, Miss Bliss to Alice B., 29 Sept. 1921.

[91]   Ibid.

most important that you should know how his mind is working as you may be coming out yourself . . .'[92]

Balfour's own dispatch to the Prime Minister of 11 November shows clearly enough that, even if the Americans were to reveal their crucial and indispensable willingness to accept naval parity with the British, there was still plenty of room for failure at the Conference:

From the discussions which took place at the Cabinet before my departure I formed the clear impression that the ultimate aim . . . is to secure the largest possible limitation of armaments consistent with the safety of the British Empire. It is clear however . . . that [British] adherence to the [Japanese] Alliance in its present form will be very unpopular in the United States of America, and will render the conclusion of a satisfactory and enduring arrangement for the limitation of armaments extremely difficult to negotiate.

Therefore, he proposed a 'Tripartite Arrangement', without military commitments, but including the United States. Thus the British would be able to end the Anglo-Japanese Alliance 'without hurting the feelings' of their ally and yet would be able to revive the alliance at once if Japan were again threatened by Russia or Germany.[93]

The initiative was, in the event, firmly held by the Americans who would not accept a treaty with the Japanese as close as that suggested by Balfour. He apparently believed that the loose four-power arrangement adopted (which included France) did not involve a greater risk of Japanese hostility towards Britain. In 1927 he commented that 'there never was any question that the dropping of the Alliance with Japan involved any change of Anglo-Japanese relations.'[94] Howbeit, he greatly assisted, by his charm, tact, and skill, the achievement of Britain's main original object—in so far as naval parity with the U.S.A. was agreed in terms of capital ships and aircraft carriers. Hankey's admiration for him reached its highest point. On 5 December, he wrote to his understudy Thomas Jones: 'A.J.B. is the pivot of this show. If anything goes wrong with him I *must* have the P.M. . . . A.J.B. has achieved a very great position—he is such a gentleman, so different from the crowd, and so very adroit. A really great figure.'[95]

Riddell bears out Hankey's account of Balfour being at the top of his form in Washington and captures his sense of being a family man. In response to

[92] Cab. 63/34, 11 Nov. 1921.
[93] Cab. 21/218, ff. 117–18, 'Washington Conference'.
[94] Cab. 27/355, Naval Programme Committee, 22 Nov. 1927.
[95] Roskill, *Hankey*, ii, 238–58; Thomas Jones, *Whitehall Diary*, London, 1969, 2 vols., i, 182. See also Roskill, *Naval Policy Between the Wars*, Vol. i, London, 1968, Ch. 8 and Lowe and Dockrill, ii, 298–303.

a remark of Hankey's about satisfactions reserved for 'happy parents', Balfour replied: "I don't quite agree. I have twelve nephews and nieces who have made my house their home, and can honestly say that so far as one can see no man ever had greater satisfaction out of his own family than I have had out of my nephews and nieces". He said this with real affection.'[96]

When Balfour returned to London in mid-February, he was quite embarrassed by the plaudits. He was met at Waterloo station by the Prime Minister and the Cabinet, and attracted public attention in the streets as he had not done since the 1890s. He had managed to evade a peerage in October 1919;[97] but on 14 February 1922 King George V wrote to him in his own hand in such warm, congratulatory terms that further refusal seemed almost impossible.[98] Balfour confided in his friend of long standing, Edward Talbot, that he was in 'a terrible perplexity' over 'changing a name I have borne for nearly 74 years'. But he no longer counted himself 'as a political combatant in the firing line', it was difficult to refuse a King who 'in the goodness of his heart, and in the enthusiasm of the moment, has written to me that he *has* conferred upon me (so he puts it) an Earldom and the Garter'. Bishop Talbot replied: 'Dearest A.J., . . . I think we both (L. and I) cast our vote *for*.'[99] But it is clear that this solution was not altogether welcome in Balfour's domestic circle. A month later, while he was recuperating at Cannes, his sister Alice, on whom he had depended for many years for the running of his household, confided that she had pondered the 'very tiresome subject' of the peerage (which Balfour had finally accepted in March).[100] She had thought of a way of his 'retaining the name Balfour' and yet avoiding the appellation Earl Balfour. There were two places in Fife called Balfour. One belonged to a relative.[101] So, after polite exchanges of letters with cousins, her brother duly became 'Earl *of* Balfour'.[102]

Such was Balfour's renown on his return from Washington that, in the shaky condition of the Coalition, there was even speculation in Conservative circles as to whether he would form a government.[103] Lloyd George, on 12 February, awaited Balfour's imminent return with interest. If he wanted

[96] Riddell, p. 337, 12 Nov. 1921.
[97] WHI/21, B. to Stamfordham, 24 Oct. 1919.
[98] WHI/10.
[99] WHI/26, B. to Talbot, 18 Feb.; Talbot to B., 20 Feb. 1922.
[100] Lloyd George P., F/3/5/18, B. to Lloyd George, Paris, 16 March 1922.
[101] WHI/231, 21 Mar. 1922.
[102] WHI/231, Alice Balfour to B., 21 Mar.; B. to Ruth Balfour (daughter of Gerald and married to another Balfour), 29 May 1922.
[103] FitzRoy, p. 774, 18 Feb.; Sandars P., C.770, S. to Stamfordham (draft), [Mar. 1922].

to be Prime Minister, he (Lloyd George) would support him. [104] Such an outcome was far from Balfour's thoughts but he was fully prepared to continue to support Lloyd George in his increasingly untenable role.

During Balfour's three months' absence the Conservatives had tired of standing aside in favour of Coalition Liberals in the constituencies. Although the Irish Treaty was Lloyd George's greatest political *tour de force*, it was inevitably resented by many Unionists. During the Irish conscription crisis of 1918, Balfour had again reluctantly agreed to Home Rule 'as a war measure'. [105] After the war, however, he seems to have consistently advocated a tough line in dealing with Sinn Fein. At the time of De Valera's visit to London in July 1921, Lloyd George said that he intended to have Balfour alone with him during the subsequent negotiations, precisely because he was the most irreconcilable of the British ministers. [106]

As has been seen, Balfour was chosen late in September to go to Washington and was therefore not one of the team selected by the Cabinet on 6 October for the main Irish negotiations. However, it should be noted that earlier, after a cabinet committee had considered drafts by Smuts and Sir James Craig of the prospective speech by the King at the opening of Stormont, it was decided (16 June 1921) to ask Balfour to prepare a fresh draft. It thus came about that, by way of the famous speech delivered by the King in Belfast on 22 June, Balfour played a part in opening the way towards a settlement. [107] Although the King's speech, following Balfour's draft, did not hint at Dominion status in the direct manner suggested by Smuts, it rallied British opinion to the idea of a settlement and prepared the exhausted Sinn Fein leaders for the intimation of Dominion status delivered to them by Smuts on 6 July. [108] Balfour had always, in the last resort, preferred independent status for Dublin to Home Rule; and, shortly before leaving for Geneva, he had collaborated with Lloyd George and Austen Chamberlain (now leading the Unionists during the short-lived retirement of Bonar Law) in drafting the 'Proposals of the British Government for an Irish Settlement' dated 20 July 1921. These offered 'the status of a

---

[104]   Riddell, p. 356.

[105]   Cab. 23/6, W.C. 392, 16 April 1918.

[106]   WHI/19, B. to Austen Chamberlain, 14 Aug. 1920; Jones, i, 163 (13 July 1921); Gilbert, *Winston S. Churchill*, vol. iv, London, 1975, p. 666.

[107]   Cab. 27/107, 'Conclusions of a Meeting at 10, Downing Street, London, S.W. on Friday, 17th June, 1921, at 6.45 p.m.'. The draft speech, 'as approved for submission to the King' and dated 10 June, constitutes an Appendix. The opening paragraph was supplied by Sir Edward Grigg. See also Thomas Jones, ii, 162–3.

[108]   Jones, i, 162–3 (précis).

Dominion with all the powers and privileges set forth'. Amongst the provisos, however, the exclusion of Northern Ireland was specific.[109] So when on 6 December, a message was sent to Balfour in Washington that the July proposals had in essence been accepted, he lost no time in returning his congratulations to the Prime Minister. Of course, the news of the settlement was also seen by Balfour as helpful to his naval negotiations with the Americans. But he confessed to his sister Alice: 'I cannot help feeling a little uneasy about Ulster—I trust without good reason.'[110] Soon before leaving for Washington, he had sent Lloyd George dictated notes of a conversation they had held the previous night: 'We are all agreed that we cannot and ought not to coerce Ulster.' But, he added, he had always thought that an Ulster of four counties would have been better than the six, with their 'Home Rule majority' areas.[111]

Before departing for his holiday at Cannes in mid-March, Balfour responded to appeals from Austen Chamberlain and others to make it clear to Conservatives that he still supported Lloyd George and his policies. Sir Edward Grigg (an ardent member of the Prime Minister's secretariat) wrote that Conservatives particularly wished to know what Balfour felt about the Irish bill.[112] Replying to Grigg, Balfour affirmed: 'If a "lead" from me is really what people want they shall certainly have it on Tuesday [7 March] when I speak in the City.' He ended: 'Ireland, as usual, seems to me the real point of danger; but we must hope for the best.'[113] He duly made his speech at the City Carlton on the 7th; and Austen Chamberlain apparently considered asking Sir George Younger, an important focus of resistance to continuance of the Coalition, to treat Balfour's address as a statement of official Conservative policy. But he decided against.[114]

On the day after his speech, Balfour attended a cabinet meeting. Pressures had grown for restoring an independent naval air service and Austen Chamberlain wanted immediate adoption of the conclusions of Balfour's abovementioned C.I.D. paper of 26 July 1921. Balfour said that

the question was one of appalling difficulty, mainly because conditions in regard to air matters were changing every day. His views had changed in consequence of his experiences at Washington. He learned there that millions of pounds were to be

---

[109] Cab. 23/26, Cab. min. and the 'Proposals' in an appendix, 20 July 1921.

[110] Cab. 63/34, Hankey to Lloyd George, 9 Dec. 1921; Thomas Jones, i, 183; WHI/76, B. to Alice Balfour, 9 Dec. 1921.

[111] Lloyd George P., F/3/5/17, B. to Lloyd George, 2 Nov. 1921.

[112] A.C.P., AC 33/1/42, A. Chamberlain to Sir George Younger (draft) 8 Mar. 1922; Cowling, pp. 157–8; WHI/1, Grigg to B., 3 Mar. 1922.

[113] Ibid., 4 Mar. 1922.

[114] A.C. 33/1/42, 8 Mar., above—endorsed 'Not accepted. AC'.

spent by the navies of the Powers on special vessels to carry aircraft and operate with the fleet. In a future naval war aircraft would be a vital and essential element in all fleet actions . . . the Admiralty must have command of the part of the air service that works with the fleet.

However, after Chamberlain had pointed out 'that it was not the Admiralty but the Air Force who had first discovered the value of aircraft in naval operations', Lloyd George thought that Balfour's previous conclusions in favour of a single air service might well stand. A further meeting on the 15th embodied them in the parliamentary statement of the 16th which upheld a separate Air Ministry. It was decided that a sub-committee should investigate 'Air Force co-operation with the Navy'.[115]

However, it was not only the dispute between the services about control of the air forces that led to the consolidation of the Air Ministry. Air Marshal Sir Hugh Trenchard had, through depletion of his service, experienced sharp vicissitudes since the end of the war. It was doubtless due to him that Balfour had informed the C.I.D.'s Standing Committee on 14 October 1921, soon before leaving for Washington, that 'he had just learned that the French were overwhelmingly superior to us in regard to air power. They had at present forty-seven independent air squadrons, whereas we had only three. He viewed the situation with profound alarm.'[116] The result was the appointment of a special sub-committee to report on what was, for some months, called 'The Continental Air Menace'. On 14 March 1922 (just prior to his post-Washington trip to Cannes) 'Sir Arthur Balfour'—as he was called till May, owing to the preremptory award of the Garter—chaired a meeting of the Standing Sub-Committee to vet the information to be given to the League of Nations for the forthcoming disarmament negotiations.[117] The Standing Sub-Committee next met on 24 May, this time under the chairmanship of 'The Right Hon. the Earl of Balfour, K.G., O.M.'. Otherwise the principal attenders were Lord Lee of Fareham (First Lord), Admiral of the Fleet Earl Beatty (First Sea Lord and Chief of the Naval Staff), General the Earl of Cavan (C.I.G.S.), Captain F. E. Guest (Secretary of State for Air), and Air Chief Marshal Sir Hugh Trenchard (Chief of the Air Staff). The report of the special sub-committee on the 'Continental Air Menace' was now available. It cited the opinion of the Air Staff that the 'establishment of the Air Force at home should be increased in order to enable an offensive organisation to be built up' and that 'a zone of defence' should be

[115] Cab. 23/29, 8 and 15 Mar. 1922.
[116] Cab. 21/218. The number of aircraft in a squadron was 12.
[117] Cab. 2/3, 21st meeting (156th of C.I.D.), 14 Mar. 1922.

established. While implying that the reality of the French threat was disputable, it said that it was up to the Government to weigh the risk. If it was seen to be 'sufficiently serious', the necessary money should be found. [118] Leading his committee's discussion of the report, Balfour at once pointed to the wide divergence, in this case, between a diplomatic and a strategical assessment. 'Viewed from a purely strategic point of view, the aerial danger was most grave. If the Air Staff were correct in their forecast, it would be possible for an enemy to strike a blow which would render this country almost impotent.' Even allowing that 'French public opinion' was 'never likely to approve' of such an attack, it should be put to the Prime Minister and Chancellor of the Exchequer 'at a special meeting' of the C.I.D. that Britain should be able to retaliate against Paris to safeguard London from 'destruction'. Trenchard pointed out that the French had a big industrial lead as a result of government expenditure and they could, incidentally, call on the service of conscripted mechanics at cheap rates. Finally, 'Lord Balfour consented to prepare a note giving briefly the substance of the foregoing discussion, for submission to the Prime Minister, with a view to its consideration by the Committee of Imperial Defence.' [119]

Balfour's 'Note' (dated 29 May) duly brought Lloyd George and Sir Robert Horne to a full C.I.D. meeting on 5 July; and on 2 August the C.I.D. concluded that the Air Ministry's scheme for 501 aircraft ready to defend the U.K. should be adopted. [120] This decision had limited effect because, by October, Bonar Law was in power at the head of a purely Conservative administration. But in so far as a passage in Balfour's 'Note' was reprinted for the Salisbury Committee set up by Law in 1923, it will be quoted here:

If we had to depend solely on anti-aircraft guns and other land defences, the French air force at their present strength, or, to be precise, at the strength they would possess after a rapid mobilisation, would enable them to drop on London a continuous torrent of high explosives at the rate of 75 tons a day for an indefinite period. When it is remembered that in the worst German raid only 3 tons were dropped on London, and that every raid was separated from its successor by a considerable interval of time, the overwhelming seriousness of the situation thus revealed must be obvious to all. Day after day, and night after night, the capital of the Empire would be subject to an unremitting bombardment of a kind which no city effectively acting as the military, naval and administrative centre of a country engaged in a life and death struggle, has ever had to endure. The War Office and the Admiralty would be paralysed by the destruction of the material instruments which

[118]   Cab. 16/47, C.I.D. 106A, in 'Summary of Inquiries'.
[119]   Cab. 2/3, 24 May 1923.
[120]   Ibid., 2 August 1922.

are necessary for the conduct of their business. Lines of communication would be cut, and London would be uninhabitable—probably in fact, certainly in the opinion of those who now dwell there.

I say nothing about the arsenals, dockyards and defended harbours, nor about the shipping crowded in the Port of London, for the details of the picture I have just outlined are easily filled in.

This passage was used by the Salisbury Committee of the C.I.D. in support of its argument for a home defence force of some 600 aircraft. [121] All such references to France were excised from the published report (1924); but they played a material part in the emergence of the R.A.F. as a major service with its own *raison d'être*. In this regard, some other passages emanating from Balfour on this occasion are worth recording. Near the beginning of his 'Note' he wrote: 'The only country which can seriously menace us is France. A war with France would be a world calamity which seems almost unthinkable; but where national security is concerned even the unthinkable must be faced . . .'. And further on he asked: 'Have we any adequate methods of parrying a blow so sudden and so deadly? I cannot think so. The proper reply to aerial attack is aerial defence and aerial counter-attack; and our relatively insignificant air force is incapable of either.' So here we have a clear assertion of the deterrent role of a strategic bomber force. This underlying reason for an expanded R.A.F. does not emerge even in the unpublished report of the Salisbury Committee; but it was surely one of the main motives for expansion. (Trenchard, of course, had for some years been impressed by the potential of the bomber.) As Balfour went on to remark, one possible line of action was to 'trust to the impossibility' of war between the two Allies. Unfortunately, 'the impossible might after all occur'; or French statesmen might, more plausibly, take diplomatic advantage of their aerial superiority. 'The second way,' he continued, 'is to expand our air force at home until it is equal to defending England and retaliating on France.' [122]

If Balfour's 'Note' on the 'Continental Air Menace' was a positive contribution to the evolution of the R.A.F., the summer of 1922 saw the composition of another 'Balfour Note', this time on international war debts. In June and July the issue was intensively discussed in the Cabinet. In order to persuade the United States to cancel Britain's American debt, it was agreed to publish a dispatch, addressed to France and other Allies indebted

---

[121] Cab. 16/46, Report of Salisbury Sub-Committee of the C.I.D., 10 Nov. 1923, pp. 14–15.

[122] Cab. 3/3, C.I.D. 108A, 'Continental Air Menace: Note by Lord Balfour on the Report of the Sub-Committee on Continental Air Menace', 29 May 1922, 2 pp.

to Britain, suggesting a general liquidation. It happened that Balfour, as in the summer of 1920, was then standing in for Curzon at the Foreign Office. The Cabinet could happily confide to him the task of drafting so intricate and sensitive a document. [123]

On 30 July R. H. Brand (later Baron Brand), who had corresponded with Balfour on Britain's financial problems during the War and was currently one of the experts advising the German government on the stabilization of the Mark, wrote from Cliveden to Balfour warning him against what he correctly understood to be the Cabinet's policy; namely to propose that inter-allied war debts be cancelled but to indicate that, if the United States (as main creditor) did not agree, Britain would wrest from her former allies enough to pay off her own American debt. Brand approved the impeccable logic of this proposal but (having been Deputy Chairman of the British Mission in Washington, 1917–1918) thought that American opinion was not ready to receive this enlightened advice. [124] On 1 August, the date of the dispatch's publication, Balfour replied from Carlton Gardens:

My dear Brand,

You are in error in supposing that all this affair of inter-allied debts is in my hands. The policy . . . has been decided upon in the Cabinet after very long and anxious discussion . . .

The whole argument of the admittedly high authorities who dislike the policy of the despatch rests on the view that a true picture of the inter-allied situation will be resented by American public opinion, and that to incur such resentment at this moment is highly inexpedient. I am not likely to under-rate the value of this argument, for nobody living estimates more highly than I do the value of good relations among the English-speaking peoples. But though I admit the danger, and am prepared to run it, I personally entertain some hopes that it is exaggerated. I have always held that the best opinion in America is a generous one, and if I am right it is likely to be influenced by a proper presentation of the facts. I do not believe that these facts are known to the world at large, not even perhaps to our own people—certainly not to the people of the United States. I think they should be known to everybody. If after that the nations of the world—be they debtors or be they creditors—refuse to follow our lead [which involved giving up the British share of German reparations as part of the all-round liquidation], it cannot be helped. We shall have done our best, and shall have nothing with which to reproach ourselves.

Yours sincerely,
Balfour [125]

As far as American reaction was concerned, Brand's pessimism was unhappily justified. However, in 1929, Austen Chamberlain, who had opposed the policy represented by the dispatch in 1922,[126] wrote to the ailing Balfour: 'In my considered opinion the Balfour Note has been, ever since you penned it, the foundation alike of the financial and political rehabilitation of Europe.'[127]

Balfour was not in London during the Chanak crisis owing to his commitments in Geneva. But, in view of his remarkable support for Lloyd George up to, and even beyond, the fateful party meeting at the Carlton Club in October, a first-hand impression of Balfour's relations with Lloyd George during the final year of the Coalition Cabinet is of interest. Arthur Griffith-Boscawen recalls that at cabinet meetings the 'painstaking and clear-headed' Austen Chamberlain sat on the Prime Minister's left.

Then came Arthur Balfour, by all regarded as the elder statesman of the party, who rarely spoke, but whose words when he did carried immense weight. Lloyd George was always greatly impressed by his opinions, and it was obvious that there was a strong mutual understanding and respect between the two men. [128]

At Geneva, Balfour was much involved in an attempt, ultimately successful, to organize through the League the restoration of Austria's national credit. In late September he wrote to Hankey (who had kept him up-to-date with British policy in the Near Eastern crisis):

Your letters and telegrams have been most helpful and interesting . . . I greatly admire and highly approve of the Prime Minister's statement of policy . . .

I am taking comparatively little public part in the work either of the Assembly or of its Commissions, having for the most part been absorbed either in arranging with my colleagues from Great Britain and the Empire the policies to be pursued, or else occupied with the heavy work of the Council of the League . . .

The great Austrian experiment has caused me endless trouble, as they made me Chairman of the Sub-Committee of the Council which is doing all the work. I really believe that if the Italians can get their Government to pay we may do something to extricate Austria from the bog in which she is almost smothered . . . [129]

When Balfour returned to London in mid-October, he found Austen Chamberlain under pressure to seek a replacement for Lloyd George as leader of the Coalition. Indeed, there were many signs of Conservative impatience with the Coalition as such. Balfour evidently accepted the

[126]   Cab. 23/30, 25 July 1922.
[127]   WHI/11, A. Chamberlain to B., 17 Apr. 1929.
[128]   Sir Arthur Griffith-Boscawen, *Memories*, London, 1925, pp. 230–1.
[129]   WHI/2, B. to Hankey, 29 Sept. 1922.

Cabinet's decision of 10 October to hold an early election though, when
Churchill had sought his opinion in mid-September, he had written back
from Geneva that he would advocate staying in office for another nine
months if any important measures were in view. [130]

As Maurice Cowling has explained, Austen Chamberlain might not have
tried to whip the party into line at the Carlton Club on 19 October if he had
realized the strength acquired by the various anti-Coalition forces in the
preceding few days. [131] However, Balfour's name, and perhaps a little more,
can be added to Cowling's account of a dinner at Churchill's house on the
15th at which the decision to call the Carlton Club meeting was taken.
Balfour wrote on the 16th to his sister Alice:

> Politics are a great nuisance, and are always interfering with the best laid plans . . .
> We had a small dinner at Winston's last night. The decision arrived at was to have a
> Party meeting . . . on Thursday [the 19th] to debate the present condition of the
> Party, especially in relation to the Coalition. It will not be a pleasant meeting,
> though a necessary one; and for many reasons I must be there, the more so as the
> plan was suggested by myself. Nothing was suggested about an Election; but it is
> fairly clear to me that whatever happens at the meeting an immediate Election is
> inevitable . . . whether we are in or out after the Election I still hope to deliver my
> first Gifford Lecture on some day in the week beginning November 13th . . . I only
> wish the lectures were finished; but in this matter I have been very unlucky! [132]

In order to exclude certain elements particularly hostile to Lloyd
George's continuance as coalition leader, the meeting at the Carlton Club
on 19 October was restricted to sitting Conservative MPs and ministers
who, like Balfour, were peers. After Baldwin and others had shown cause
for dispensing with Lloyd George, the re-emergent Bonar Law made the
decisive speech in favour of ending the Coalition. Balfour supported
Chamberlain's argument, delivered at the outset, that the present coalition
was preferable to a coalition of socialists and Asquithians; but he was at
once opposed by Leslie Wilson, the Chief Conservative Whip. The incensed Chamberlain then brought the issue to a vote. Those voting for an
independent Tory leader at the coming election numbered 188. Those
against numbered 88.

Lloyd George tendered his resignation that afternoon and the King asked
Bonar Law to form a government. Law wanted time to consult his
adherents. Meanwhile, Balfour and the other leading Unionist coalitionists
forgathered in Chamberlain's house and drew up a statement of their

[130] WHI/19, 14 B. to Churchill, 14 Sept. 1922.
[131] Cowling, pp. 198–209.
[132] WHI/231, B. to Alice Balfour, 16 Oct. 1922.

position for the press. [133] The typed draft, on notepaper headed 11 Downing Street and bearing the signatures of Austen Chamberlain, Birkenhead, Balfour, Horne, Worthington-Evans, Lee of Fareham, Crawford-Balcarres, and four others, is amended at several points by a Balfourian pen—just like the drafts of dictated letters, kept as copies, which form so full and valuable a feature of his collected correspondence. Seeing that this declaration of continuing adherence to Lloyd George therefore expresses, at least to a material extent, what may be taken as Balfour's view of 'the little man' and his achievements, some passages may be cited: 'The Prime Minister in our judgement rendered incalculable service to this country during the War. With high courage and resource . . .'. After the war, he faced problems 'hardly less grave'.

Trade disputes on an alarming scale, revolutionary activities, chronic unemployment, financial stringency, and recurrent European crises have presented a series of problems the like of which has never before confronted a British Government. During the whole of this period most of us have shared the anxieties and labour of the Prime Minister; and we desire to record our unanimous view that his resource, energy and patriotism have been as strongly exhibited during the period as during the War itself.

To a statement that Lloyd George's prestige helped the Conservatives at the 1918 election, Balfour added in his own hand: 'We made the fullest use of it.' The signatories ended by declaring that, in view of the foregoing considerations, they could not now carry a message of rejection to the Prime Minister. Instead they called for a united stand against 'legislative proposals disruptive of the economic and financial system' of the country. [134]

But, having recruited the turncoat Curzon, Bonar Law became Prime Minister on 23 October. For Balfour, and for the country, the exciting days were at an end.

---

[133] Cowling, pp. 209–14, 252; Jones, i, 211–12 (19 Oct. 1922).
[134] A.C.P., 33/2/93.

15

Parting Shots

1922–1930

ON 21 October 1922 Balfour wrote in characteristic vein to Lady Wemyss (formerly Elcho) about the ending of the Coalition:

I gather the newspapers gave a full account of our proceedings at the Carlton Club, and published a statement signed by the Unionist members of the out-going government. Bonar, poor man, is trying to make a Government, and no doubt will find plenty of material, though what its quality will be is perhaps more doubtful . . .

I am sorry for Austen, who I think has been ill-used. But so far as I am concerned, I feel more free from care than I have been since the last week in July 1914. I really hope now to make some progress with my Giffy Gaffs [i.e. Gifford Lectures]. If all goes well, I may start for Whittingehame on Friday or Saturday, and remain there, I trust undisturbed, until after Christmas. What a blessing that I took a Peerage! . . .

The 'little man' seems in the highest spirits . . .[1]

Balfour, like other coalitionists, rather expected the November election to leave no party with a decisive majority.[2] However, three-cornered fights, with the 'progressive' vote split between Labour and the disunited Liberals, left Bonar Law with control over the House of Commons. In these circumstances, Balfour was at last able to give his second course of Gifford Lectures at Glasgow and they were published as *Theism and Thought* the following year (1923). The religious theme was reaffirmed but there was no fundamental philosophical development beyond what he had produced before the War. At the end of the day, it was politics or, to be more precise, statecraft that proved to be Balfour's abiding passion.

By December, he had agreed to help Law by going to the Council of the League of Nations in January. The problem was how to get the French out of the Ruhr; but the Powers could not agree to act. From the inception of the League, its secretary-general had been Sir Eric Drummond who had served during 1917–1918 as Balfour's private secretary at the Foreign Office—including the Washington mission of 1917. Early in February Drummond

---

[1] WHI/229.
[2] WHI/19, B. to Churchill, 14 Sept. 1922; also Cowling, p. 220.

intimated to Law via Hankey that Balfour would be willing to join the ministry for a year; and on 27 February Balfour himself wrote from Carlton Gardens to the Prime Minister that the chief British representative should, as he had explained to Law the previous December, be a member of the Cabinet. This strong hint produced no unambiguous offer from Law; and Balfour did not return to Geneva.[3] It seems reasonable to conclude that Balfour would have accepted restoration to his former post of Lord President, with a view to continuing to the end of the Government's term—perhaps for five years, his health permitting. Indeed, between the fall of Lloyd George in October 1922 and Baldwin's electoral triumph in October 1924, Balfour, despite his age and his peerage, was still often mentioned in political circles among the various possible Prime Ministers.[4]

After Bonar Law's final retirement with throat cancer on 20 May 1923, Balfour advised the King through Stamfordham to prefer Baldwin to Curzon. Although he then had no great opinion of Baldwin's abilities as compared with Curzon's, he thought it inopportune to appoint as Prime Minister a member of the House of Lords.[5] This advice apparently confirmed the King's inclination;[6] so when Balfour returned to his hotel at Sheringham in Norfolk and was beset by questions from his friends, he was qualified to deal with the inquiry: 'And will dear George be chosen?' The answer was: 'No, dear George will not.'[7] Although Balfour publicly supported him as Prime Minister, Baldwin waited until Curzon's death in April 1925 before bringing his pre-war leader back into the Cabinet in the now-familiar role of Lord President. Baldwin was only too well aware of his own limited political stature, to say nothing of intellect, compared with Balfour's; and, in his early months as Conservative leader (from May 1923), he limited Balfour to attendance at a shadow cabinet in February 1924. However, twelve months later, Baldwin had returned as Prime Minister after Labour's spell in office during 1924. He was well in the saddle with Churchill back in the party fold as Chancellor of the Exchequer and Austen Chamberlain as Foreign Secretary. Now that Balfour was that much older and deafer he could be seen, even by Baldwin, in the light of a harmless adornment.[8]

---

[3] WHI/19, B.'s 'Memorandum of a conversation with Mr. Bonar Law at Whittingehame', 22 Dec. 1922; B. to Law, 27 Feb.; Law to B., 1 Mar.; B. to Law, 2 Mar.; Law to B., 2 Mar. 1923; Jones, i, 228; Roskill, *Hankey*, ii, 328.

[4] Cowling, pp. 193, 220, 232–4, 338, 386–7; Jones, i, 297.

[5] WHI/1, memo 'Dictated by A.J.B. to Miss Bliss May 22nd 1923 at 4 Carlton Gardens', 22 May 1923.

[6] Ibid., Stamfordham to B., 25 May 1923.

[7] Winston S. Churchill, p. 234.

[8] Cowling, pp. 267, 294, 337–8, 341, 383; Jones, i, 303.

If debating was for Balfour largely a thing of the past, what side of political life held most attraction for him by 1923 or 1925? His unique knowledge and peerless lucidity in the sphere of defence policy had long been recognized on a cross-party basis; and he readily accepted his appointment on 9 March 1923 to the C.I.D.'s 'Sub-Committee of National and Imperial Defence' headed by his cousin, Lord Salisbury.

At stake was the continued existence of two entities in which Balfour had a deep interest, namely the C.I.D. itself and the R.A.F. In the prevailing atmosphere of strict economy, there was parliamentary concern about overlapping expenditure, together with continuing calls for a Ministry of Defence. A Ministry would avoid some of the problems presented by air forces designed for work with the Navy, for work with the Army, and for an independent role.

Retrospectively, it can be said that the timing of the Salisbury inquiry was unfortunate. Even though the R.A.F. was beginning to recover from its post-war decimation, the prospect that the training and administration of the Fleet Air Arm would be handed back to the Navy seemed at the time equivalent to a death sentence for a separate air service. Yet, by the early 1930s, such a body as the Salisbury committee would inevitably have accepted the R.A.F.'s home defence and bombing roles as sufficient justification for that service's separate continuance. The Navy could thus have recovered full control of its air arm without mortal damage to the R.A.F. But in 1923 an unhappy compromise was an almost inevitable outcome. Indeed, the R.A.F. did remain substantially responsible for naval air services; and it was not until July 1937 that Inskip recommended complete transfer to the Navy. Meanwhile, in the Navy, the theory and development of air power undoubtedly suffered, and it was impossible to repair all the damage before the outbreak of war in 1939.[9]

As for the suggested Ministry of Defence, the need for this was becoming more obvious by the 1930s. Its earlier establishment might have avoided the underdevelopment of the Fleet Air Arm, within the limits imposed by government economy. In the opinion of the high civil servant of those years, Edward Bridges, the establishment of a Ministry of Defence in good time before 1939 would have made 'a vast difference' to defensive preparation.[10]

Balfour attended the first and second meetings of Lord Salisbury's Committee (15 and 20 March 1923). At the first he was named as chairman

---

[9] See Geoffrey Till, *Air Power and the Royal Navy 1914–1945*, London, 1979, and Roskill, *Naval Policy between the Wars*, London, 1968–76, 2 vols.

[10] Roskill, *Hankey*, ii, 146.

of 'a special Subcommittee' on 'Relations between the Navy and Air Force'. The other members of the 'Balfour' Committee were Viscount Peel (Secretary for India and pro-Navy) and Lord Weir (Air Secretary during the last six months of the War and strongly in favour of the R.A.F.'s continuing over-all control). Out of the twelve meetings held by his committee, Balfour was able to preside over only five. These included the first three which were held on successive days, namely 20 to 22 March. Procedure was decided and evidence was heard from the main contestants, Beatty and Trenchard. Then Balfour succumbed to phlebitis and missed four meetings between 10 and 20 April. He reappeared on 8 May and heard Admiral Sir John de Robeck, and other naval officers. By 20 May he had arrived with a party of close friends at Sheringham but was still suffering from his ailment. Nevertheless, as mentioned above, he then went back to London to advise on the premiership and 'dear George'. After returning to Sheringham he was laid up for some weeks.

Having missed two more meetings, Balfour conducted a crucial one on Sunday, 15 July, from his bed at the hotel. Peel and Weir reported on their visit of the 13th to an R.A.F. airfield and training establishment at Gosport and to the aircraft carriers *Argus* and *Eagle* at Portsmouth. Their favourable account of the inter-service relations subsisting there caused Balfour to revise his own pro-Navy draft report. This decision was reached after the meeting had lasted for three hours. Hankey, as Secretary to both committees, had plied Balfour with arguments in favour of a compromise (pro-R.A.F. in its general tendency) in order to avoid deadlock on the main committee. Moreover, Balfour himself certainly wished to ensure the R.A.F.'s survival.[11] By 20 July, Weir was prepared to sign the 'ingenious document' now produced by Balfour.[12] On the 26th Hankey reported that the main committee had 'passed a Resolution in favour' of it—over the objections of Amery, the First Lord of the Admiralty.[13]

Meanwhile, Balfour's further direct contribution to the work of the main committee had been limited to meetings held on 10 and 16 May. On the 10th Trenchard was giving evidence for the sixth and last time. Balfour's exchanges with Sir Hugh about the psychological factors making for 'unstable equilibrium' in aerial rivalry between Britain and, in this case, France led Balfour to state that he had 'gradually been driven to' the awesome conclusion

---

[11] See Cab. 16/48 for the proceedings of B.'s committee and WHI/8 for his extensive correspondence with Hankey, 6 Apr. 1923–18 Jan. 1924.

[12] Cab. 16/48, p. 258.

[13] WHI/10.

that nothing, not the League of Nations or anything else, is going to give us peace, but the certainty of every civilised man, woman and child that everybody will be destroyed if there is war; everybody and everything. I think, perhaps, if the energies of our Research Departments in all countries are carried on with sufficient ability, that that might be arrived at.

Then, in answer to an apparently unruffled Sir Samuel Hoare (Secretary for Air), he agreed that he would like a 'one-power standard' based upon 'numerical equality'.[14] As for the other main issue, discussed by the main committee in his prolonged absence, the victory of the C.I.D. over the idea of a Ministry of Defence meant that in November he could sign the report without tribulation.[15]

Although Balfour had assumed that an irreducible modicum of human rationality would, after the three-sided election of December 1923, lead to the exclusion from office of Labour by an anti-socialist alliance, the actual attempts of Ramsay MacDonald to govern, while dependent on Liberal support, seem to have reassured Balfour. In July 1924 MacDonald utilized the flexibility offered by the C.I.D. when he consulted four ex-premiers—Balfour, Baldwin, Asquith, and Lloyd George—at a full C.I.D. meeting on the question of a Channel Tunnel. Beatty effectively rehearsed the agreed objections to the project of the newly-established Chiefs of Staff Sub-Committee and clinched his argument by saying 'that Lord Balfour had summed up the whole situation in his Memorandum [of 1920], in which he stated that "So long as the ocean remains our friend, do not let us deliberately destroy its power to help us."' Balfour said that he had hesitated about the advantages of a Tunnel during the War, but had since 'reverted with undiminished strength' to his former adverse opinions.[16]

With his deep-rooted fear of Lloyd George and a new coalition of the 'first class brains' Baldwin, as mentioned, held back from offering Balfour a post when forming his Cabinet in November 1924—despite Balfour's lack of personal ambition, his evidently failing health, his 76 years, and despite his own recent electoral triumph. However, he did risk putting Balfour back on the C.I.D.[17] 'If I am to do any political work at all this exactly suits me', wrote Balfour to his sister Alice. Baldwin (he wrote) paid him a call and said that the C.I.D. had 'to deal with the very tiresome and embarrassing problem of the Disarmament Protocol'. Balfour was happy to undertake the task of demolition at the C.I.D. He did not 'much like' this

[14] Cab. 16/46, 10 May 1923, p. 11.
[15] Ibid., C.I.D., Sub-Committee of National and Imperial Defence, Report, 10 Nov. 1923.
[16] Cab. 2/4, 1 July 1924.
[17] Jones, i, 302–3 (4 and 8 Nov. 1924).

optimistic proposal for disarmament and the peaceful settlement of international disputes, lately promoted by MacDonald at Geneva. [18]

On 13 February 1925 the C.I.D. met with as many as seventeen members
present. In the Prime Minister's absence the chair was dignified by 'The
Most Hon. the Marquess Curzon of Kedleston, K.G., G.C.S.I., G.C.I.E.,
Lord President of the Council'; and in the course of the magisterial opening
statement to be expected from him on such an occasion, he observed that
Balfour had stated, in a draft dispatch:

in a manner of which he alone is capable the principal objections advanced by
himself and by others, and indeed by the Committee, to the main provisions of the
Protocol. In substance his draft is a rejection of the Protocol, formulating the
objections to it in the most general terms in a manner incapable, as it seems to me, of
exciting prejudice, and carrying with it the weight both of philosophic reasoning
and of logical expression.

In the record, this handsome seal of approval is followed by no less than
twenty pages of minuted discussion. This ended, somewhat as it began, with
the conclusion:

That the Secretary of State for Foreign Affairs [Austen Chamberlain] should be
requested to prepare for consideration by the Committee . . . a draft dispatch . . .
which might be, in the main, based on the draft dispatch of Lord Balfour, contained
in C.I.D. Paper No. 581-B . . .

A second item on the meeting's agenda was influenced by Balfour. This
concerned preparation of a 'draft instrument' to meet France's (understand-
able) craving for a guarantee against a German resurgence. Here, the
conclusion tended towards the multi-power guarantee embodied later that
year in the Treaty of Locarno, the terms of which induced an unfortunate,
rigid defensiveness in French military thinking—ultimately embodied in
the Maginot Line.

Balfour, in the light of the French 'Air Menace' and the occupation of the
Ruhr, admitted to not feeling a 'fair judge' of the needs of the French
because he was 'so cross' with them. 'They are so dreadfully afraid of being
swallowed up by the tiger, but yet they spend their time poking it.' [19]

The Government subscribed to the Treaty of Locarno in October 1925.
Balfour, at this time of Austen Chamberlain's consequent renown,
meditated on the subject of treaties in general:

Why did nations patiently go on making treaties with each other all through the

[18] WHI/76, B. to Alice B., 26 Nov. 1924.
[19] Cab. 2/4, 194th meeting of C.I.D., 13 Feb. 1925.

centuries, seeing that to all appearance they broke them without the least scruple? The answer can only be that a world in which many treaties were broken and some were kept was better than a world in which no treaties existed at all. [20]

Balfour's actual response to the death, on 20 March 1925, of George Nathaniel Curzon does not seem to be on record. However, on returning in April from his visit to Palestine and Syria (featuring Jewish acclaim in Jerusalem—still to be seen on film—and Arab fury in Damascus), [21] Balfour, on 27 April, took over Curzon's ministerial post and also chaired the C.I.D. through much of the year. He again presided at an important meeting on 10 June 1926. The establishment of the Imperial Defence College was approved, the joint responsibilities of the Chiefs of Staff further defined, and a memorandum by Hankey envisaging a debate in the Lords on a Ministry of Defence was considered. Churchill thought that if the Estimates of the three services were, as proposed, henceforward presented jointly, natural evolution might well lead to a Ministry of Defence in five or six years. 'Lord Balfour expressed the view'—faithfully recorded by an approving Hankey—'that it was not possible to foresee what ultimate developments would take place, but, at the present time, the creation of a single Minister was inexpedient and the work would be quite beyond the capacity of any one individual'. Churchill responded by giving the committee a vivid preview of the arrangements he would, indeed, adopt as Prime Minister and Minister of Defence in the Second World War; but no fundamental change was agreed at that meeting. [22]

Balfour was still quite active during 1927. At a C.I.D. meeting on 25 February he neatly illustrated the way in which his clear, methodical thinking in defence matters imparted consistency to his views on defence policy. His way of contributing to a discussion about international control of chemical warfare was to read a telegram which he had sent to Lloyd George from the Washington Naval Conference of 1921–2 because the Americans then wanted to discuss the subject. If it was still relevant in 1927, it likewise seems so in the revolutionized context of the 1980s:

(1) That no international ruling can prevent plant being erected for purposes of peaceful industry which could be used almost without change for manufacture of poison gas.

[20] WHI/17, B. to Hankey, 19 Oct. 1925.
[21] Dugdale, ii, 364–70.
[22] Cab. 2/4, 214th meeting of C.I.D., 10 June 1926. For Hankey's key role (1926–8) in opposing a Ministry of Defence see Roskill, *Hankey*, ii, 419–20; and for his industrious enlistment of B.'s support during 1927 see WHI/17.

(2) That nothing can stop the discovery of new gases.

(3) That no country can allow its safety to be wholly dependent on faithful observance by other States of rules to which they are pledged.

(4) That we shall, therefore, have to take precisely the same precautionary measures whether Conference condemns gas warfare or whether it does not. [23]

Later in 1927, Balfour attended all five meetings, held between 10 November and 12 December, of the Naval Programme Committee. This was set up under Lord Birkenhead by a cabinet decision of 28 August and in 1928 became a Standing Sub-Committee of the C.I.D. The meetings of 1927 arbitrated between the economizing Chancellor of the Exchequer (Churchill!) and the Admiralty on the question of the cruiser-building programme. Balfour agreed with the cuts suggested by the chairman both on diplomatic and on technical grounds. The Americans, he argued, were matching all new British cruisers, and the Japanese in turn reacted to the Americans. This 'absurd' sequence should be discouraged. If the Japanese ever attacked the British Empire, they (the Japanese) would know that 'public opinion in America would be on the side of this country.' On the naval side, constant technical change made it undesirable to fix building programmes as much as ten years ahead. [24] The cuts were duly made.

After a severe set-back to his health in March 1928, Balfour returned to the C.I.D. on 5 July. Unavailingly he condemned as 'dangerous' and 'wholly impracticable' Churchill's notorious innovation of the constantly self-renewing 'Ten Year Rule' which assumed no major war within that period, but bound government departments to ask for a C.I.D. review if they thought that circumstances had changed. [25]

At his final appearance, on 15 July 1928, at the Committee where he had made so outstanding a contribution since 1902, Balfour said that the money available 'might be far better spent in providing for an anti-aircraft programme than an increase in cruiser building'. [26] Had he survived the Japanese onslaught on the *Prince of Wales* and *Repulse* on 10 December 1941, Admiral Sir Tom Phillips would doubtless have endorsed Balfour's view. In the later stages of the Pacific War American battleships, heavily armed against aircraft, proved more than a match for the latter.

---

[23]   Cab. 2/5, 221st meeting of C.I.D., 25 Feb. 1927.

[24]   Cab. 27/355, Naval Programme Committee of the Cabinet, 4th meeting, 1 Dec. 1927.

[25]   Cab. 2/5, 236th meeting of C.I.D., 5 July 1928.

[26]   Cab. 2/5, 237th meeting of C.I.D., 10 July 1928. B. also attended a Sub-Committee on Belligerent Rights on 27 July 1928 (Cab. 16/79).

But defence was by no means Balfour's only sphere of activity. From his re-appointment as Lord President on 27 April 1925, Balfour took a continuing interest in the two departments for which he was responsible, namely the Department of Scientific and Industrial Research and the Medical Research Council. He also pursued with enthusiasm an idea originated in 1918 by Haldane, and approved in principle by MacDonald's Government in 1924, that a committee like the C.I.D. should collate information available in government departments for use by the Cabinet when discussing economic and scientific issues. [27] On 26 May 1925 he wrote a memorandum entitled 'Foresight and Co-ordination in Economic Enquiry'. He recommended that the 'new Advisory Committee' should be linked up with the Committee of Imperial Defence in a kind of dual Department under the general superintendence of the Cabinet Secretary' (Hankey). Thus clerical staffs would be kept to a minimum and it would be clear that 'the new organisation' would 'follow in the footsteps of the old'. He recognized that it was going to be more difficult 'to ask the right questions in the right order' in the proposed 'Committee of Civil Development' and 'to provide the special machinery for finding the right answers' than it had been in the case of the C.I.D. [28]

The potentiality of this body, as indicated by Balfour's original choice of the word 'Development', was considerable. One major ingredient in the long comparative decline of the British economy has surely been the lack of a body better designed to reshape and modernize industry than the disputatious ministries set up by Harold Wilson in the 1960s. It has been said of the more successful machinery represented in France after 1946 by the Commissariat du Plan that it

(1) 'produced compelling facts and figures about the French economy and its prospects which everybody felt obliged to absorb'; (2) 'it used strong incentives or penalties to persuade industries into desirable courses without recourse to statutory compulsion'; (3) 'it worked its way through the economy sector by sector, choosing to tackle four or five areas at a time and not moving on to others until its studies and reports on these had been completed. [29]

Balfour's organization anticipated the Commissariat in being less of an overt challenge to the Treasury and other established departments than Wilson's Ministry of Economic Affairs. Through its association with the

---

[27] S. S. Wilson, *The Cabinet Office to 1945*, London (H.M.S.O. for P.R.O.), 1975, p. 83.
[28] Cab. 24/173; Jones, i, 317–19.
[29] P. Calvocoressi, *The British Experience 1945–75*, London (Penguin), 1979, p. 71.

C.I.D. it also implied a non-party basis for long-term planning. But, of course, it lacked the powers of the Commissariat.

In the event, Balfour accepted for his body the title of 'Committee of Civil Research'. That is, though definitely concerned with the moderniz-ation of industry, he settled for item (1) above of the *modus operandi* adopted by the Commissariat and something of item (3). But that he even suggested the term 'Development' testifies to the extent of his intellectual response to the post-war world. In an address of 1926, he pointed speci-fically to Britain's comparative weakness in applying science to industry. [30] Even if it was anyhow characteristic of him to be interested in research rather than *dirigisme* yet the Committee represented a remarkable develop-ment in the thinking of a man who had played down the role of government for so many years before the Great War and was now aged 77. While it was in no more than an advisory role, the C.C.R.—with a Cabinet minister (sometimes Baldwin himself) in the chair—undertook fourteen major inquiries in the four years left to the Government, including Overseas Loans (a success), Iron and Steel Safeguarding, Electrical Development, Coal Industry and Unemployment, Safeguarding and Unemployment Policy, and Partnership in Profit-sharing. [31] Balfour chaired most of the meetings held in 1925. On 10 November, with Baldwin presiding, the steel industry was under discussion. A combine along German lines was sug-gested. Balfour asked what would happen in a slump?

> The Government would say: 'This is a most serious thing; here is the whole of the steel industry, our basic industry [an evaluation which, incidentally, Balfour queried in the light of developments] apparently going to smash?' You would be on the very edge of carrying out the socialistic idea of the Government managing the great industries of the country . . .

Balfour's last attendance at the main Committee was on 11 July 1927 when unemployment in the mining industry was discussed. [32]

The Committee virtually died away with Balfour's illness in the spring of 1928, though it was revived by MacDonald in the form of the Economic Advisory Council in January 1930. The Labour premier hoped to find an answer to the general problem of unemployment. Meanwhile, the work of numerous technical sub-committees went on. Balfour had chaired two of these in 1926: on Quinine, and on Indian Railways (where the members, all

---

[30] *Opinions and Argument*, p. 164 (23 July 1926).
[31] Keith Middlemas in Jones, ii, pp. x–xii; Roskill, *Hankey*, ii, 391–2.
[32] Cab. 58/1, 10 Nov. 1925; 11 July 1927.

ministers, hoped that the Indian Government would undertake a pro-gramme of construction and create a demand for British steel). [33]

In so far as the C.C.R. was associated with the C.I.D., and the latter body was always valued by Balfour as providing a forum for co-operation between Britain and the increasingly independent Dominions, he was uniquely fitted to play a leading role at the critical Imperial Conference of 1926. Baldwin was not thus qualified. In the face of threats of imperial disintegration, he apparently sought refuge in silence. Soon after the Conference opened on 19 October, Balfour was imported into the key role of chairman of the Committee on Inter-Imperial Relations. Amery, as Colonial Secretary, on the one hand, and the potentially rebellious Hertzog of South Africa on the other, provided much of the content of the celebrated 'Balfour definition' of the relationship between Great Britain and the Dominions. But Balfour, so fully abreast of the various Dominion attitudes and so free from die-hard attitudes, once again, as at Washington, rose splendidly to the occasion—not least as a draftsman. While Australia and New Zealand were reassured still to find themselves 'within the British Empire' though 'equal in status' with the United Kingdom and with one another, Hertzog was so pleased to know that South Africa was 'freely associated' as a member of the 'British Commonwealth of Nations' that he was afterwards even prepared to co-operate in the work of the C.I.D. Like most of Balfour's state papers, the 'definition' imparted clarity to the situation. But above all, as Hankey rightly discerned, it changed 'men's hearts'; and as Hankey's biographer observes, Britain came to know the value of such care for the Dominions' aspirations when, in 1940 to 1942, she stood otherwise alone. [34]

On 25 July 1928, his eightieth birthday, Balfour was presented at the Palace of Westminster with a well-chosen tribute from the members of both Houses—a Rolls Royce. He had loved motor cars since the turn of the century. Mrs Dugdale noticed how Balfour addressed the earlier part of his speech of thanks 'almost personally to Mr. Lloyd George'.

Late in January 1929 he moved from Whittingehame to his brother Gerald's home in Surrey—a final move, as it proved. Baldwin remained constantly solicitous and refused to let Balfour resign. When the Government ultimately left office in May, Balfour was received by the King at Bognor. The following day, he found himself immobilized by phlebitis; and thenceforward he was confined to his bed.

[33] Wilson, pp. 83–4, 195–6; Cab. 58/100, Indian Railways Sub-Committee, 11 March 1926.

[34] Judd, pp. 327–39; Dugdale, ii, 374–85; Roskill, *Hankey*, ii, 349, 427–33; Jones, ii, 63.

Soon after receiving a visit of deep emotional significance from Weizmann, Balfour, with members of his family about him, died rather suddenly, early in the morning of 19 March 1930, at the age of 81.

16

Overview and Estimate

IT is not commonly recognized that Balfour held cabinet rank for longer than Winston Churchill, or Lord Liverpool, or Gladstone, or Lord Palmerston, or the younger Pitt. The number of years served on that level by the statesmen mentioned are: Balfour 27, Churchill 26, Liverpool 25, Gladstone 24, Palmerston 23, and Pitt 22. This count alone testifies to Balfour's calibre as a statesman. The unique character of his career is further emphasized by the fact that none of the others listed, having ended their prime-ministerial careers, came back, as it were, from the political dead to hold other high ministerial posts. Balfour not only came back. He held these subsequent offices for a total of more than eleven years.

He entered Parliament in the 1870s uncertain whether politics justified the consequent loss of time available for games, conversation, music, and, in particular, philosophical inquiry. But so great was his curiosity about the world of men and affairs that politics gradually supervened as his greatest passion. This slow development was crucially aided and stimulated by his uncle, Lord Salisbury. Always keen to excel at games, Balfour likewise worked at the art of debating in the House of Commons and showed increasing promise by the mid-1880s. After useful ministerial experience at the Local Government Board and the Scottish Office, he entered the Cabinet in November 1886. Though always lacking in ambition to climb the ministerial ladder, he responded triumphantly to the challenge of a turbulent Ireland between 1887 and 1891.

At one with his uncle on the absolute need to re-establish law and order in Ireland, he was also ready to adapt to the permanent change brought about by Gladstone's Irish Land Act of 1881 and, in due course, to assist the Irish economy by government measures of a type which he deprecated in a developed economy such as that of mainland Britain. His success, especially in achieving his first objective, came as an unexpected but extremely welcome surprise from the Conservative viewpoint. In retrospect, it may be seen as materially assisted by Parnell's withdrawal, in the later 1880s, from the forefront of the land battle. Without Parnell's whole-hearted leadership, the Plan of Campaign (1886–1890) could not attain the irresistible momentum of the earlier Land League.

So great was Balfour's suddenly acquired renown that he found himself pressed, in 1891, into the dual role of Conservative leader in the Commons and leader of the whole House. Never by nature attuned to electioneering or speaking from the platform, he found the inexorable duties now imposed upon him in the Commons well-nigh unendurable. He had revelled in the cut and thrust of Irish debates and had developed as a parliamentarian and tactician. But he had never aspired to the inexhaustible patience required of a Leader of the House of Commons. Yet painfully, despite backslidings, he schooled himself to bear the burden. Party loyalty and native tenacity combined with an inbred sense of duty to keep him at his post. To his party he was ever true. Only a national emergency might, in his eyes, suffice to justify collaboration with the party-political enemy.

As First Lord of the Treasury and Conservative leader in the Commons, he continued to seek the conciliation of Ireland and to confer material benefit on that country. Faced with another challenge, which he found increasingly tiresome, in the form of state education, he rose to his parliamentary zenith in passing the Education Act of 1902.

In that same year he had, on 12 July, become Prime Minister by dint of his Irish record, his close links with Salisbury, and his manifest courage, charm, resource, intellect, and high debating skill. Behind the scenes he had steadied the Government in face of the ominous reverses suffered during the South African War. However, he had no definite plan for national reorganization and was slow to adopt suggestions for repairing national deficiencies.

By the beginning of Balfour's premiership, the country was beginning to turn against Unionism; but he was not inclined to seek electoral support by offering constructive programmes. He did not dissent from his supporters' wish to keep taxation low. Earlier, he had bestowed enlightened (if ineffectual) attention on governmental machinery for the more efficient control of defence policy but, exhausted by the burden of the Education Bill,[1] he was slower than he might otherwise have been to respond, in the wake of the Boer War, to demands for the better co-ordination of defence. However, after initial hesitations, he fully met these demands. He used the C.I.D. to investigate the defensive needs of the United Kingdom and the Empire, especially India, and in consequence was able to reduce overlapping expenditure on the two fighting services. The services became better

[1] See Lady Rayleigh's Diary, 12 July 1902.

prepared for their respective roles. Moreover, partly through his personal flair for strategy and partly by gearing the C.I.D. to cabinet discussion of foreign and defence problems as they arose, Balfour succeeded in imparting a new consistency and coherence to both aspects of policy. If he was reluctant to accept the emergence of a German rather than a Russian menace, he nevertheless ensured that his system could be swiftly reorientated if necessary. His work in this field represents his main constructive achievement as Prime Minister.

In that connection, it is doubtless worth repeating here that the prospect of new Japanese negotiations early in 1905 allowed him to investigate with eagerness what seemed an opportunity to bring Britain into closer alliance with the United States.[2] But this objective remained substantially out of reach. However, an enduring *entente* with France had been achieved by then.

Meanwhile, Chamberlain's declaration for Tariff Reform in May 1903 seemed almost certain to split the party and bring it to electoral defeat. Partly out of deference to Chamberlain as a great protagonist of Unionism and Empire—causes in which Balfour himself whole-heartedly believed— he veered somewhat to Chamberlain's side in the controversy. Balfour had, for his part, been long inclined towards greater flexibility in the regulation of British trade, allowing freedom to retaliate against the protectionist powers with a view to subsequent negotiation. Hoping that even Chamberlain's supporters would, given time, recognize the grave electoral disadvantage of a system entailing food taxes, he persisted with his own doctrine of 'retaliation' as a less damaging basis for party unity. Finally, towards the end of 1905, the exasperated Chamberlain forced him to resign from office. Although Balfour went to the country with a record looking respectable in more distant perspective, his party was overwhelmed by a confluence of unfavourable factors—not least its own manifest and continuing disunity.

In introducing a series of biographical essays on modern British Prime Ministers,[3] the late J. P. Mackintosh has remarked that interest resides in the way that these leaders dealt with (1) the Whitehall machine, (2) their own party in the Commons and in the country, and (3) Parliament as a whole. How does Balfour's performance appear from such a standpoint?

As has been seen, Balfour relied to a greater extent than his primeministerial predecessors on his private secretary, John Satterfield Sandars

---

[2] On this item, see Monger, pp. 180–1.

[3] *British Prime Ministers in the Twentieth Century*, London, 1977. The essay on Balfour is contributed by Peter Fraser.

(rewarded for his efforts with P.C. and C.V.O.), for carrying on the work of his office. Writing in 1917, Sandars comments as follows:

> On a memorable day, the policy of Tariff Reform had split the party from top to bottom, and ruined leadership and political organisation alike . . . [Sir Alexander Hood as Chief Whip] loyally took orders, and carried them out. He never professed to understand the philosophical dexterity of his Chief or to fathom the economic subtleties of his policy . . . In whispered confidences Hood would say: 'My complaint is that the Chief thinks his party are as clever as he is . . . I cannot get him into touch with our men.' The truth was that Mr. Balfour was overwhelmed with the claims of the House of Commons. Owing to the weakness of his colleagues in debate he had to assume responsibility for every critical issue in Parliament, and he had no time to master the business of party management. Lord Salisbury, on the other hand, when the House of Lords rose after its half-hour's work, would slowly wend his way to the Central Office and there would sit in long intercourse with his Chief Agent, studying the reports from the constituencies, and cynically discussing the merits and demerits of aspirants for honours or promotions.[4]

Indeed, it was on Sandars that much of the last-mentioned kind of work tended to fall. As he remarks elsewhere, Balfour 'found official appointments a bore, and promotions a vexation'.[5] But Balfour should probably be acquitted of an excessive tendency to prefer old friends and relatives for all ministerial vacancies. For instance, despite his disillusionment with Balfour (as already related) from 1915 onwards, Sandars nevertheless subsequently insists—in an essay in which he praises Milner above Balfour—that Balfour had no great wish to appoint his long-cherished familiar Alfred Lyttleton to the Colonial Office in 1903. Balfour 'pleaded hard' with Milner to accept; and it 'was Milner who suggested A. Lyttleton for the vacant post'.[6] Balfour had yet again to make do with the slender talent on offer.

In 1922, when further disillusioned by Balfour's acceptance of a peerage, Sandars nevertheless recalled the somewhat old-fashioned, aristocratic, but unsullied image presented by Balfour as Prime Minister,

> at times the despair of his Whip, who loved him, and a riddle to his party agent, who admired him. In truth he was not of the party pattern, for he could never learn the *patois* of the Patronage Secretary, nor understand the temper and disposition of the Lobby.

He maintained a calm detachment and 'suffered without complaint the petty

---

[4] *Studies of Yesterday by 'A Privy Councillor'*, London, 1928, pp. 166–7.
[5] Ibid., p. 180.
[6] J.C.P. 18/16/30, 'Alfred Milner'.

cabals, the narrow views and stupid prejudices of many of his professed adherents'. In sum:

Upon his surrender of office in December 1905, the succession passed to a different type of social value with another standard of life and manners. Leadership of the House no longer reflects the refined critical faculty, the temperate philosophy, the ease of dialectical mastery, and the polished serenity of mind and bearing upon which the storms of embittered personal attacks beat in vain. [7]

In such respects, then, Balfour seems even more of a patrician than his uncle the Third Marquess of Salisbury.

But, of course, there was another side to Balfour. This is well exemplified in his supplementary career after 1911; but even before 1905 he can be seen as 'modern' in terms of Mackintosh's three criteria. Behind the scenes, his work for defence had implications beyond the rationalization of current policy. The machinery developed at the C.I.D. can in retrospect be seen as the first step in the evolution of a secretariat for the Cabinet itself, together with that provision of agenda and records of conclusions required in the interests of greater efficiency. Likewise, the C.I.D. machinery marks the initial stage of that strengthening of the office of Prime Minister which has been a feature of British political development in the twentieth century.

Secondly, as implied earlier, Balfour brought about a decisive change in the relations between the executive and Parliament. Shortly before his inevitable succession as Prime Minister, Balfour established new rules of procedure in the House of Commons to render more complete and permanent the similar reform that he had, with fair success, attempted in the previous parliament. In consequence the executive permanently obtained control over the allocation of parliamentary time. As a contribution to the modernization of the government machine, it must be compared favourably with the establishment of the C.I.D.

Thirdly, the Education Act of 1902, even if it implied an inadequate modernization of social and economic attitudes, did undoubtedly bring about a structural change of fundamental value and importance. In such ways, Balfour as Prime Minister may be seen as the most modern forerunner of Lloyd George.

However, any over-all estimate of Balfour as Prime Minister must doubtless be influenced by the writer's evaluation of his handling—in the Cabinet, in the party, and the country—of the Tariff Reform crisis. A feature of subsequent commentaries on this subject is the variety of tactical solutions enjoined on Balfour beyond the grave. Despite the not incon-

[7] *Studies of Yesterday*, pp. 180–1.

siderable advantages of hindsight, Balfour's critics seem unable to reach agreement on where he made his crucial mistake. It seems to this writer significant that Mr Alan Sykes, after his particularly thorough investigation of Tariff Reform in British politics, is disinclined to prescribe the best answer to the Prime Minister's tactical problems—setting aside the theoretical possibility of a Balfourian constructive programme which might have changed the whole political context.

Otherwise, it should once more be observed that, however completely Balfour dominated his Cabinet after the multiple resignations of 1903, he was much less assured of such control on his first appointment as Prime Minister. Joseph Chamberlain, with his thrusting strength of personality and general stature as a politician, had to be regarded more as a partner in government than as a subordinate. With his sharply contrasting style, he was Balfour's superior in parliamentary impact and in an altogether higher class as a platform speaker. Secondly, there was the Duke of Devonshire. In 1902 he was still the accredited leader of the Liberal Unionist Party and, with his considerable personal standing, was another key figure in the potentially unstable coalition bequeathed to Balfour by his uncle. However, once both Chamberlain and Devonshire had resigned from the Cabinet in 1903, Balfour was left unchallenged by his remaining ministers as to the best line to follow on Tariff Reform.

Balfour may perhaps have erred in under-estimating the strength and persistence of the passions attaching to Tariff Reform on the one hand and to Cobdenism on the other—the one impractical in political terms and the second, in its pure form, outdated by foreign protectionism. But it was not illogical, in this situation, to play for time. Balfour certainly understood that only a revival in full force of the Irish Question, which was, after all, the crucial nexus of the Unionist Coalition, was likely to recapture Unionist passions and cause them to blend in blessed harmony. It remains true even so that he failed to persuade either the Unionist rank-and-file or the electorate more generally that his doctrine of 'retaliation' offered a reasonable way of shelving a futile and damaging controversy. Being ill qualified, through refined temperament and a lack of the common touch, to succeed in this educative task, he tended to withdraw from it and seek solace on the golf course at North Berwick. Whatever the merits of this very Balfourian solution, it must doubtless be admitted that it denotes his limitations as a political leader in twentieth-century Britain, despite all his abilities.

The peculiarly intellectual flavour attaching to Balfour's premiership is well illustrated by a memorandum he composed in April 1904 on the question of a government grant to the British Academy, of which he had been a fellow since its inception in 1901(and for which, in the light of his modified post-war attitudes, he would as President of the body obtain a grant from the Labour Government of 1924). In 1904, he was not disposed to dissent from the Treasury view 'that no money' could, 'in existing circumstances, be given to the British Academy'. However, despite urgent calls on prime-ministerial time, he could not resist explaining to the civil servants concerned that the grounds of their opposition to the Academy's plea were mistaken. He develops his theme as follows:

The fundamental error, however, of the Memorandum appears to me to lie in this: it seems to be taken for granted that an Academy dealing with a whole group of subjects is not required, because those subjects are already dealt with by a variety of more specialized Societies. This is, I think, a superficial view of the case. If it constitutes an objection to the Academy, it is an objection at least equally valid against the Royal Society [of which Balfour had been a fellow since 1888]. There is, so far as I know, no important branch of scientific study which has not at least one Society—in some cases more than one Society—specially devoted to its furtherance. The Mathematical, Chemical, Geographical, Botanical, Astronomical, Entomological, and Physical Societies will at once occur to everyone . . .

An attempt is made in the Memorandum to show that the Royal Society is more worthy than the Academy of Treasury support because 'the objects which science has in view are practical'. I suggest that, in the main the Royal Society (as we know it) is occupied with the discovery of the laws of nature, not with their utilitarian application.

The idea of seeking advice from the Academy on literary matters with which the Government may be concerned is treated in the Memorandum as an absurdity. With this I cannot wholly agree. It is true, no doubt, that British Governments do not greatly concern themselves with these matters, and I am quite ready to believe that the Treasury, as at present constituted, is thoroughly competent to make a comparison of the relative importance of such undertakings as the publication of Leibnitz's works and the support of an Archaeological School at Rome—to take two of the instances mentioned in the Memorandum. But these conditions may not be eternal . . .

Personally, I have always been doubtful whether the Academy will be able, even with the lapse of time, to conquer a position at all resembling that now actually held by the Royal Society. But that, if it should happen, it would be a great national advantage, I have no doubt at all, and I should therefore like to see it given all due encouragement. In the meanwhile, however, it seems to me clear that if we have any money to expend upon Science and Learning, it is more required by such Institutions as the National Physical Laboratory even than by the Academy.

I therefore concur in the refusal which it is proposed to give to their request.

A. J. B. [8]

---

[8]   B.P. 49856, ff. 81–4, 'Memorandum by the Prime Minister in regard to the Question of a Grant to the British Academy', 17 Apr. 1904.

Two days after dictating this memorandum, Balfour was hastily apologizing to the King, in a letter which he failed to date, for the recent absence of prime-ministerial communication to the Crown. He explained that he had 'been working under circumstances of unusual pressure'.[9]

King Edward does not, through concern for foreign and defence policy, seem to have wished to see his friend Campbell-Bannerman replace Balfour as Prime Minister. However, he did at times feel that he was being suavely patronized by Balfour; and there can be no doubt that Balfour, for his part, did not hold the King's intellectual ability in very high regard. Yet no one can read the correspondence cited above about the appointment of a new War Secretary in 1903, or of an education minister at that time,[10] without being impressed by the King's sound instincts in such far from negligible matters. Nevertheless, Balfour can only be seen as correctly interpreting the modern constitution in denying the King's right to see cabinet or C.I.D. papers before the relevant meeting. In February 1904, while still recuperating from influenza, he dictated the following note dispatched from Brighton to Sandars:

> The King cannot be allowed to see 'confidential' Cabinet papers *as of right*. Any decision of the Cabinet, and the reasons for it, he has, of course, a right to see. But the policy while it is being matured, and the Cabinet memoranda relating to it must obviously be regarded as 'confidential'.
>
> Do not put the matter thus to Knollys exactly in this way! But it is impossible for us to yield in a matter of this kind. You might so inform Arnold-Forster.[11]

But the most striking and sustained demonstration of Balfour's firm over-all control of his administration is undoubtedly to be found in the spheres of foreign and defence policy. These he welded into a unity. Sandars corresponded in 1928 with Lord Newton about his forthcoming life of Lansdowne and he commented on the Marquess's '1917 escapade'—when he laid himself open to opprobrium by publicly querying allied war aims—in the following terms: 'Personally I cannot think how Ld. L. screwed himself up to do it. In office [as Foreign Secretary under Balfour] he would hardly send off a despatch of minor significance without getting approval.'[12]

---

[9] Cab. 41/29, n.d. This cabinet letter can, however, be dated 19 Apr. 1904 by the copy in Sandars P., C.716.

[10] On this, see Sandars P., C.715, 4 Oct. 1903, where the King suggests that Londonderry might become Lord President and leave Sir William Anson to take charge of education.

[11] B.P. 49762, ff. 92–3, B. to Sandars, 27 Feb. 1904.

[12] Sandars P., C.771, ff. 70–2, holo. draft of Sandars to Newton, n.d., but answered by Newton on 5 Dec. 1928 (f. 76).

Yet under Campbell-Bannerman and, to an extent, under Asquith, Sir Edward Grey at the Foreign Office was something of a law unto himself, while defence policy, through lack of firm prime ministerial control, did not possess the coherence and the degree of linkage with foreign policy which Balfour had maintained. Nor did Lloyd George in his post-war Government, match Balfour's over-all control in those areas. While foreign policy was subjected to excessive prime ministerial domination, defence policy tended to be hived off.

In sum, then, Balfour's record as Prime Minister, remembering once more the culmination of his constructive policy in Ireland, seems in the light of his severe parliamentary difficulties to constitute a very respectable achievement.

After the general election of January 1906, when he even lost his own Manchester seat, Balfour was faced with a much diminished party in the House of Commons. As anticipated, this consisted largely of members sympathetic to Tariff Reform; but Balfour was saved from having to surrender much of his declared position on that subject by Chamberlain's sudden physical incapacitation. As Leader of the Opposition, Balfour by degrees re-established much, if not all, of his former parliamentary standing and made electoral headway by controversial use of the Upper House to hamper the legislative projects of the Liberal Government. Even if Lloyd George's 1909 budget allowed Balfour at length to reunite his party on a basis of anti-socialism, that same budget enabled the Liberals to inflict severe strategic reverses on the Unionists. Although he had presided over a material electoral recovery and had finally adopted a Tariff-Reforming stance, Balfour could not make the electoral pendulum swing beyond a certain point. He was twice defeated, albeit quite narrowly, in the two general elections of 1910. These defeats implied a curtailment of Unionist power by way of a Parliament Bill which, in its turn, threatened the likely success of an Irish Home Rule Bill. Meanwhile, through offering in December 1910 to submit Tariff Reform to a referendum as a means of escape from his electoral strait-jacket, Balfour had greatly offended many Chamberlainite Tariff Reformers. When Balfour recommended that, to save the remnants of Unionist power in the Lords, the Parliament Bill should be allowed to pass, a large minority of the shadow cabinet refused to follow his lead. In consequence of this and reports of widespread dissatisfaction in the party, Balfour finally resigned the Unionist leadership in November 1911. He knew that the introduction of a Home Rule bill in 1912 would give him a good chance of recovering his hold on the party, but felt that he could not contemplate a subsequent return to office followed, perhaps, by a recurrence of disunity.

It must also be repeated that his natural distaste for aspects of party leadership was an unspecified influence on his decision. In addition to what has already been said, it is of interest to find Sandars later recalling, in his unpublished memoir of Milner, how Balfour confided to him apparently in 1909 or 1910 that 'he had quite determined that under no circumstances whatever would he accept the responsibility of forming an Administration. His reasons for this', Sandars continued, 'were of a purely personal character, and limited to the conditions of the time at which he spoke.'[13] But the impression of disinclination is much more pervasive than this. For example, the most intimate picture of Balfour on his succession to his uncle as Prime Minister and Conservative leader, supplied by his sister Lady Rayleigh,[14] shows him as looking 'very worn and tired'. It conveys no hint of enthusiasm on her brother's part. Nor does he seem to have evinced more gratification on his ascent, a decade earlier, to the leadership of the Conservatives in the House of Commons. Without at least a minimal natural drive for personal power, a sense of duty alone, however deeply rooted, might well be expected to run out of steam at times. Only a simpler man less prone to boredom and less contemptuous of common clay could have continued indefinitely on such a basis.

Once the Great War had begun, Balfour's counsel on high policy was sought by the Asquith Government. After serving on the War Council, he was brought into Asquith's Coalition as First Lord of the Admiralty. In this post he performed to the Navy's satisfaction and followed sound strategic policies. He tried to forestall excessive casualties on the Western Front and exercised a valuable steadying influence on the general conduct of the war. This influence was again appreciated after Lloyd George had replaced Asquith in the leading role—Balfour having evinced an outstanding spirit of unselfish patriotism in helping to resolve the ministerial crisis of December 1916. Balfour then proved to be, as expected, an able Foreign Secretary who was particularly happy in his dealings with the United States. However, he also shared importantly in the collective misjudgements leading to a British Mandate in Palestine and to the Allied intervention in Russia.

[13] J.C.P. 18/16/30.
[14] Diary entry of 12 July 1902 about a visit to B. at 10 Downing Street the previous day.

After the Great War, he displayed continuing ministerial usefulness, particularly in diplomatic and imperial roles. The Washington Conference of 1921–2 was one high point for Balfour and the Imperial Conference of 1926 was another. On an international level he had attained a position of exceptional distinction. He showed his grasp of changing economic and governmental circumstances by his drafting of the Balfour Note on war debts in 1922 and by establishing, as Lord President under Baldwin, the Committee of Civil Research. To the end, in 1929, of his prolonged career of service in Baldwin's Cabinet, he remained a uniquely sophisticated and clear-thinking minister in the sphere of defence policy.

In thus surveying his record, reference has also inescapably been made to Balfour's personal characteristics. However, some further comment on them seems apposite by way of completing an estimate of the man as distinct from his work.

Being so essentially detached and intellectual, rather than instinctive and ambitious, in his approach to politics, Balfour also acquired a reputation for indecisiveness—although, as noticed, this did not apply to the application of his fundamental principles. Both Lloyd George and Hankey, as eye-witnesses, recount an incident involving Clemenceau and Balfour at a Supreme War Council held in June 1918 at Versailles which they think typical of Balfour. A material question had been delegated to a meeting of Foreign Ministers with Balfour in the chair. In due course Balfour reported the outcome of the discussion. His speech lasted twenty minutes and comprised a nicely balanced account of the arguments deployed on both sides of the question. A moment's silence ensued. Clemenceau inquired whether that was all. Balfour confirmed that it was. With predictable and rising irritation, the 'Tiger' wanted to know whether Balfour was for or against? Balfour evidently saw his function as discharged by clarification of the pros and cons. However, pressed by Clemenceau, he declared himself against.[15]

There was indeed a negative tendency allied with Balfour's deep conservatism—both traits being, however, more obvious before the Great War than after it. But even in his prime-ministerial days his declared mistrust of constructive legislation always had a positive side, an ability to respond constructively to the inescapable need to act. This is well captured by Austen Chamberlain when he writes:

Indeed to me the most remarkable thing about Balfour is that with a mind so critical, so little inclined to expect great results from any accomplishment within the

---

[15] Lloyd George, ii, 1015; Roskill, i, 559 (Hankey's Diary, 3 June 1918).

power of man, he did take so passionate an interest in mundane affairs . . . Though he constantly reminded us that Parliament could achieve little, and that the best that could be hoped from legislation, even his own, was that it would do no harm and might even do a little good, he fought his battles with a passion that I have seen elsewhere only in men of far more positive and sanguine temperament. [16]

While Balfour's conservatism was associated with an apparent lack of drive and a marked reluctance to initiate, his positive attributes as a statesman were of course considerable. Among these were unceasing curiosity, lucidity, logic, consistency, and an extreme quickness of apprehension. Despite his languid exterior, he was really a very hard-working minister—certainly during the period 1887 to 1905 and also through most of the years 1915 to 1922.

Among politicians, Balfour lacked the ability of a Gladstone or a Joseph Chamberlain to inspire; but his courage, integrity, charm, and wit commanded much admiration and a good deal of affection. His air of philosophic detachment was derived, at least in part, from a deep-seated religious sensibility. While it limited his appeal as a leader, it contributed to the dignity and distinction which especially marked his later career. Much the same may be said of his openness of mind and the wide range of his cultural and intellectual interests. If his lack of ambition cannot be dissociated from his resignation of 1911—or from that of 1916—yet tenacity and resilience were hallmarks of his long career. He did not relinquish a task unless he believed that duty pointed in that direction.

[16] *Down the Years*, p. 218.

List of Sources

NOTE. See also the Preface and the List of Abbreviations above.

A. UNPUBLISHED PAPERS

Birmingham University Library

Joseph Chamberlain Papers
Sir Austen Chamberlain Papers

Bodleian Library

J. S. Sandars Papers
Selborne Papers

British Library

H. O. Arnold-Forster Papers
Balfour Papers (These comprise Add. MSS 49683–49962, amounting to 280 bound volumes or bundles, and include copies of a large number of Balfour's out-letters.)
Cecil of Chelwood Papers

Churchill College, Cambridge

Esher Papers
Fisher Papers
Hankey Papers

Hatfield House

Papers of the Third Marquess of Salisbury

House of Lords Record Office

Bonar Law Papers
Lloyd George Papers

National Library of Scotland

Haldane Papers

National Maritime Museum

Papers of Sir William Graham Greene
Papers of Sir Henry Oliver

Public Record Office

Cabinet Papers (including the Papers of the C.I.D. and those of the War Council, together with its successor bodies of 1915–16, and also those of the Cabinet Office, 1916–29. See H.M.S.O. Handbooks Nos. 4, 6, 9, 10, 11, and 17 for lists and descriptions of these materials.)

Papers of the Education Department (Ed. 24).

Papers of the Foreign Office (especially F.O. 800/1215–146 for Lansdowne and F.O. 800/199–217 for Balfour).

Scottish Record Office

A. J. Balfour Papers (i.e. the Whittingehame MSS, seen at the Scottish Record Office by arrangement).

Terling Place, Essex

Diary of Evelyn, Lady Rayleigh

B. PUBLISHED WORKS

Alderson, Bernard, *Arthur James Balfour*, London, 1903.

Allen, B. M., *Life of Sir Robert Morant: a Great Public Servant*, London, 1938.

Amery, Julian: *see* Garvin.

Amery, L. S., *My Political Life*, London, 1953–5, 3 vols.

Ashby, E. and Anderson, M., *Portrait of Haldane at Work on Education*, London, 1974.

Balfour, Arthur James, *Chapters of Autobiography*, London, 1930.

———, *The Currency Question: an Address*, London, 1893.

———, *A Defence of Philosophic Doubt*, London, 1879.

———, *Economic Notes on Insular Free Trade*, London, 1903.

———, *Essays and Addresses*, Edinburgh, 1893.

———, *Essays Speculative and Political*, London, 1920.

———, *The Foundations of Belief*, London, 8th rev. edn., 1901. First pub. 1895.

———, *Opinions and Argument*, London, 1927.

———, *Theism and Humanism*, London, 1915. Based on Gifford Lectures.

———, *Theism and Thought*, London, 1923. Based on further Gifford Lectures.

Balfour, Lady Frances, *Ne Obliviscaris*, London, 1930, 2 vols.

Barnett, Correlli D., *The Collapse of British Power*, London, 1972.

Beach, Lady Victoria Hicks, *Life of Sir Michael Hicks Beach*, London, 1932, 2 vols.

Beaverbrook, Lord, *Politicians and the War*, Vol. ii, London, 1932.

Beckett, Ian F. W. and Gooch, John (eds.), *Politicians and Defence*, Manchester, 1981.

Blake, Robert, *The Unknown Prime Minister: the Life and Times of Andrew Bonar Law 1858–1923*, London, 1955.

Blewett, Neal, *The Peers, the Parties, and the People: the General Elections of 1910*, London, 1972.

Blunt, Wilfred Scawen, *The Land War in Ireland*, London, 1912.

——, *My Diaries 1888–1914*, London, 1919–20, 2 vols.

Boyle, Andrew, *Trenchard*, London, 1963.

Brodrick, William St. John Fremantle: *see* Midleton.

Butler, David (ed.), *Coalitions in British Politics*, London, 1978.

Calvocoressi, Peter, *The British Experience 1945–75*, London (Penguin), 1979.

Carter, Mark Bonham (ed.), *The Autobiography of Margot Asquith*, London, 1962.

Cecil, Lady Gwendolen, *The Life of Robert Marquess of Salisbury*, London, 1921–31, 4 vols.

Chamberlain, Sir Austen, *Down the Years*, London, 1935.

——, *Politics from Inside*, London, 1936.

Churchill, Randolph S., *Winston S. Churchill*, Companion Vol. ii, London, 1969 (and *see* Gilbert below).

Churchill, Winston S., *Great Contemporaries*, London (Fontana), 1959.

Cowling, Maurice, *The Impact of Labour 1920–1924*, Cambridge, 1971.

Curtis, L. P., Jr., *Coercion and Conciliation in Ireland 1880–1892*, Princeton, 1963.

D'Ombrain, Nicholas, *War Machinery and High Policy 1902–1914*, Oxford, 1973.

Dugdale, Blanche E. C., *Arthur James Balfour, First Earl of Balfour*, London, 1936, 2 vols.

Eaglesham, Eric, *The Foundations of Twentieth Century Education in England*, London, 1967.

——, *From School Board to Local Authority*, London, 1956.

——, 'Planning the Education Bill of 1902', *British Journal of Educational Studies*, ix (Nov. 1960).

Egremont, Max, *Balfour*, London, 1980.

——, *The Cousins*, London, 1977.

Ensor, R. C. K., *England 1870–1914*, Oxford, 1936.

Esher, Viscount, *Journals and Letters of Reginald, Viscount Esher* (ed. M. V. Brett and Oliver, Viscount Esher), London, 1934–8, 4 vols.

Feuchtwanger, E. J., *Gladstone*, London, 1975.

FitzRoy, Sir Almeric, *Memoirs*, London, 4th edn., 1925.

Fraser, Peter, 'Arthur James Balfour': *see* Mackintosh below.

——, *Joseph Chamberlain: Radicalism and Empire 1868–1914*, London, 1966.

——, *Lord Esher*, London, 1973.

Garvin, J. L. and Amery, Julian, *The Life of Joseph Chamberlain*, London, 1932–69, 6 vols.

Gilbert, Martin, *Winston S. Churchill*, Vols. iii–v and Companion Vols. iii–iv, London, 1971–6.

Gollin, A. M., *Balfour's Burden: Arthur Balfour and Imperial Preference*, London, 1965.

——, *The Observer and J. L. Garvin 1908–1914*, London, 1960.

____, *Proconsul in Politics: a Study of Lord Milner*, London, 1964.

Gooch, G. P., *The Life of Lord Courtney*, London, 1920.

Gooch, John, *The Plans of War: the General Staff c. 1900–1916*, London, 1974.

____, 'Sir George Clarke's Career at the C.I.D., 1904–7', *Historical Journal*, xviii (1975).

Gordon, Peter, *The Victorian School Manager*, London, 1974.

Grenville, J. A. S., *Lord Salisbury and Foreign Policy*, London, 1964.

Griffith-Boscawen, A. S. T., *Memories*, London, 1925.

Haldane, R. B., *An Autobiography*, London, 1929.

Halévy, Elie, *Imperialism and the Rise of Labour 1895–1905* (*History of the English People*, Vol. v), London (Benn), 1961.

Halpern, Paul (ed.), *The Keyes Papers*, London (Navy Records Society), 1972–81, 3 vols.

Hankey, Lord, *The Supreme Command 1914–1918*, London, 1961, 2 vols.

____, *The Supreme Control at the Paris Peace Conference 1919*, London, 1963.

Hazlehurst, Cameron, *Politicians at War July 1914 to May 1915*, London, 1971.

Hewins, W. A. S., *Apologia of an Imperialist*, London, 1929, 2 vols.

Hodgkinson, Ruth, *The Origins of the National Health Service 1834–1871*, London, 1967.

Holland, Bernard, *Life of Spencer Compton, 8th Duke of Devonshire*, London, 1911, 2 vols.

Howard, Michael, *The Continental Commitment*, London, 1972.

Hyde, H. Montgomery, *Baldwin: the Unexpected Prime Minister*, London, 1973.

Jay, Richard, *Joseph Chamberlain: a Political Study*, Oxford, 1981.

Jenkins, Roy, *Asquith*, London, 1964.

____, *Mr. Balfour's Poodle*, London, 1968.

____, *Sir Charles Dilke*, London (Fontana), 1968.

Jones, Thomas, *Whitehall Diary*, London, 1969, 2 vols.

Judd, Denis, *Balfour and the British Empire*, London, 1918.

____, *Radical Joe: a Life of Joseph Chamberlain*, London, 1977.

Kedourie, Elie, *In the Anglo-Arab Labyrinth 1914–39*, Cambridge, 1976.

Kekewich, Sir George W., *The Education Department and After*, London, 1920.

Kennedy, Paul M., 'The development of German naval operations plans against England 1896–1914', *English Historical Review*, lxxxix (1974).

____, *The Rise of the Anglo-German Antagonism 1860–1914*, London, 1980 (with a fine bibliography).

Koss, Stephen, *Asquith*, London, 1976.

Lloyd George, David, *War Memoirs*, London, 1933–6, 6 vols.

Lowe, C. J. and Dockrill, M. L., *The Mirage of Power: British Foreign Policy 1902–22*, London, 1972, 3 vols.

Lowndes, G. A. N., *The Silent Social Revolution 1895–1965*, London, 3rd edn., 1969.

Lucy, H. W., *A Diary of Two Parliaments*, London, 1886, 2 vols.

____, *A Diary of the Salisbury Parliament 1886–1892*, London, 1892.

_____, *A Diary of the Home Rule Parliament 1892–95*, London, 1896.

_____, *A Diary of the Unionist Parliament 1895–1900*, London, 1901.

_____, *A Diary of the Balfourian Parliament 1900–1905*, London, 1906.

_____, *Peeps at Parliament*, London, 1903.

_____, *Later Peeps at Parliament*, London, 1905.

Lyons, F. S. L., *Charles Stewart Parnell*, London (Fontana), 1978.

_____, *Ireland Since the Famine*, London (Fontana), 1973.

Lyttleton, Alfred, 'Mr. Balfour as Leader', *Nineteenth Century and After*, lxx (Dec. 1911).

Mackail, J. W. and Wyndham, Guy, *Life and Letters of George Wyndham*, London, 1925, 2 vols.

Mackay, Ruddock F., *Fisher of Kilverstone*, Oxford, 1974.

Mackintosh, John P. (ed.), *British Prime Ministers in the Twentieth Century*, London, 1977.

Malcolm, Sir Ian, *Lord Balfour: a Memory*, London, 1930.

Mallet, Bernard, *British Budgets 1887–1913*, London, 1913.

Mansergh, Nicholas, *The Irish Question 1840–1921*, London, 3rd edn., 1975.

Marder, Arthur J., *The Anatomy of British Sea Power 1880–1905*, Hamden, Conn., repr., 1964.

_____, *Fear God and Dread Nought: Admiral Fisher's Correspondence*, London, 1952–9, 3 vols.

_____, *From the Dreadnought to Scapa Flow: the Royal Navy in the Fisher Era, 1904–19*, London, 1961–70, 5 vols.

Marsh, Peter, *The Discipline of Popular Government: Lord Salisbury's Domestic Statecraft 1881–1902*, Sussex, 1978.

Masterman, Lucy, *C. F. G. Masterman: a Biography*, London, 1939.

Masterman, Lucy (ed.), *Mary Gladstone (Mrs. Drew): Her Diaries and Letters*, London, 1930.

Mathias, Peter, *The First Industrial Nation*, Oxford, 1969.

Midleton, Earl of, *Records and Reactions 1856–1939*, London, 1939.

Midleton, Earl of, *et al.*, *The Post Victorians*, London, 1933.

Milner, Viscountess, *My Picture Gallery 1886–1901*, London, 1951.

Monger, G. W., *The End of Isolation: British Foreign Policy 1900–1907*, London, 1963.

Munson, J. E. B., 'The Unionist Coalition and Education 1895–1902', *Historical Journal*, xx (1977).

Murray, Bruce K., *The People's Budget 1909–10: Lloyd George and Liberal Politics*, Oxford, 1980.

Newton, Lord, *Lord Lansdowne*, London, 1929.

Nicolson, Harold, *King George the Fifth: His Life and Reign*, London, 1952.

Nish, Ian H., *The Anglo-Japanese Alliance 1894–1907*, London, 1966.

O'Day, Alan (ed.), *The Edwardian Age 1900–1914*, London, 1979.

Ogg, David, *Herbert Fisher*, London, 1947.

Patterson, A. Temple (ed.), *The Jellicoe Papers*, London (Navy Records Society),

1966–8, 2 vols.

Pelling, Henry, *Popular Politics and Society in Late Victorian Britain*, London, 2nd edn., 1979.

Petrie, Sir Charles, *Life and Letters of the Rt. Hon. Sir Austen Chamberlain*, London, 1939, 2 vols.

____, *The Powers Behind the Prime Ministers*, London, 1958.

Ponsonby, Sir Frederick, *Recollections of Three Reigns*, London, 1951.

Porter, A. N., *The Origins of the South African War*, Manchester, 1980.

Ramsden, John, *The Age of Balfour and Baldwin*, London, 1978.

Read, Donald, *England 1868–1914*, London, 1979.

Reader, W. J. *Architect of Air Power: the Life of the First Viscount Weir 1877–1959*, London, 1968.

Rempel, Richard A., *Unionists Divided: Arthur Balfour, Joseph Chamberlain and the Unionist Free Traders*, Newton Abbot, 1972.

Riddell, Lord, *Intimate Diary of the Peace Conference and After 1918–1923*, London, 1933.

Robbins, Keith, *Sir Edward Grey*, London, 1971.

Rose, Kenneth, *The Later Cecils*, London, 1975.

____, *Superior Person: a Portrait of Curzon*, London, 1969.

Rose, Michael E., *The Relief of Poverty 1834–1914*, London, 1972.

Roskill, Stephen W., *Admiral of the Fleet Earl Beatty*, London, 1980.

____, *Documents Relating to the Naval Air Service*, Vol. i (1908–18), London (Navy Records Society), 1969.

____, *Hankey: Man of Secrets*, London, 1970–4, 3 vols.

____, *Naval Policy Between the Wars*, London, 1968–76, 2 vols.

Rowland, Peter, *The Last Liberal Governments: the Promised Land 1905–10*, London, 1968.

____, *Lloyd George*, London, 1975.

Russell, A. K., *Liberal Landslide: the General Election of 1906*, Newton Abbot, 1973.

Sandars, John S., *Studies of Yesterday by a 'Privy Councillor'*, London, 1928.

Satre, Lowell J., 'St. John Brodrick and Army Reform 1901–3', *Journal of British Studies*, xv (1976).

Searle, G. R., *The Quest for National Efficiency*, Oxford, 1971.

Short, W. M. (ed.), *Arthur James Balfour as Philosopher and Thinker*, London, 1912.

Sidgwick, Ethel, *Mrs. Henry Sidgwick*, London, 1938.

Simon, Brian, *Education and the Labour Movement 1870–1920*, London, 1965.

Spinner, Thomas J., Jr., *George Joachim Goschen*, Cambridge, 1973.

Stein, Leonard, *The Balfour Declaration*, London, 1961.

Steiner, Zara S., *Britain and the Origins of the First World War*, London, 1971.

Sutherland, Gillian (ed.), *Education in Britain*, Shannon, 1977.

Sykes, Alan, *Tariff Reform in British Politics 1903–1913*, Oxford, 1979.

Taylor, A. J. P., *Beaverbrook*, London (Penguin), 1972.

Taylor, Robert, *Lord Salisbury*, London, 1975.

Templewood, Viscount, *Empire of the Air: the Advent 1922–1929*, London, 1957.

Terraine, John, *The Great War 1914–18*, London (Arrow), 1967.

Till, Geoffrey, *Air Power and the Royal Navy 1914–1945*, London, 1979.

Ullman, Richard, H., *Anglo-Soviet Relations 1917–21*, Princeton, 1961–82, 3 vols.

Vansittart, Lord, *The Mist Procession*, London, 1958.

Webb, Beatrice, *Our Partnership*, London, 1948.

Wiener, Martin, *English Culture and the Decline of the Industrial Spirit 1850–1980*, Cambridge, 1981.

Williamson, Samuel R., Jr., *The Politics of Grand Strategy*, Harvard, Mass., 1969.

Wilson, S. S., *The Cabinet Office to 1945*, London (H.M.S.O.: P.R.O. Handbook No. 17), 1975.

Young, Kenneth, *Arthur James Balfour*, London, 1963.

Zebel, Sydney H., *Balfour: a Political Biography*, Cambridge, 1973.

Index

For officers, the highest rank attained is given here, if readily available. Where titles were conferred on a person after the date of initial reference, they are shown in brackets.